MIND, VALUE, AND REALITY

MIND, VALUE, AND REALITY

• • •

John McDowell

HARVARD UNIVERSITY PRESS
Cambridge, Massachusetts
and London, England

Copyright © 1998 by the President and Fellows of Harvard College
All rights reserved
Printed in the United States of America
Second printing, 2002

Library of Congress Cataloging-in-Publication Data
McDowell, John Henry.
Mind, value, and reality / John McDowell.
p.   cm.
Includes bibliographical references and index.
ISBN 0-674-57613-6 (hardcover : alk. paper)
ISBN 0-674-00713-1
1. Philosophy. 2. Wittgenstein, Ludwig, 1889-1951. I. Title.
B29.M426   1998
100—dc21   97-38090

CONTENTS

PREFACE   vii

I
GREEK ETHICS

1. The Role of *Eudaimonia* in Aristotle's Ethics   3
2. Some Issues in Aristotle's Moral Psychology   23
3. Virtue and Reason   50

II
REASON, VALUE, AND REALITY

4. Are Moral Requirements Hypothetical Imperatives?   77
5. Might There Be External Reasons?   95
6. Aesthetic Value, Objectivity, and the Fabric of the World   112
7. Values and Secondary Qualities   131
8. Projection and Truth in Ethics   151
9. Two Sorts of Naturalism   167
10. Non-Cognitivism and Rule-Following   198

III
ISSUES IN WITTGENSTEIN

11. Wittgenstein on Following a Rule   221
12. Meaning and Intentionality in Wittgenstein's Later Philosophy   263
13. One Strand in the Private Language Argument   279
14. Intentionality and Interiority in Wittgenstein   297

IV
MIND AND SELF

15. Functionalism and Anomalous Monism   325
16. The Content of Perceptual Experience   341
17. Reductionism and the First Person   359

BIBLIOGRAPHY   385

CREDITS   393

INDEX   397

Preface

In this volume, I have collected versions of some of the papers I have written over the last two decades or so.

There is some repetition from one essay to another. The most notable case is the way Essay 10 essentially repeats an exploitation of Wittgenstein from Essay 3. I have left this kind of thing unaltered, so that each essay can in principle stand on its own, at least as much as when it first appeared. No doubt there is not only repetition, but also some inconsistency—although I find it gratifying, on rereading these papers, to see how single-minded I seem to have managed to be over the years.

Of course I would not write precisely these essays if I sat down to write on these topics today. But I have resolutely resisted any temptation to make alterations of substance; it would have been improper to turn the papers into shifting targets. I have, however, made stylistic changes at points where how I originally said something, even if not what I said, struck me as especially unbearable. Of course that is not to say that I am content with how things are said here.

I have divided the essays into four groups, although the dividing lines are not sharp.

The first group concerns how to interpret some central contentions of Socratic, Platonic, and especially Aristotelian ethics. My main aim in these papers is to counteract a way in which, as I see it, modern prejudices about rationality tend to distort our understanding of Greek ethics. When a Greek thinker says something to the effect that a life of virtue is a life in accordance with reason, modern commentators tend to suppose he must mean that such a life can be recommended as worth going in for, with the recommendation not needing to appeal to habituated propensities to be attracted towards, and recoil from, actions of different kinds—the features of a person's make-up that figure, for instance, in Aristotle's discussion of virtue of character. This reflects a dualism between reason and the more evidently "natural" aspects of character. I think it leads commentators to miss a possibility of profiting from Greek ethical reflection: a possibility of appreciating, as best we can from our different vantage point, what it might have been like to think about character, reason, and conduct in an intellectual climate that was not shaped by the pressure towards such dualisms. Our intellectual climate is irreversibly so shaped, but the strands in Greek ethics I consider, read as I urge, help to bring out that it is possible, even for us, to resist the pressure.

The papers in the second group are less directly anchored in readings of ancient texts, though they are animated by what I take to be the spirit of ethical reflection in the Socratic tradition. Their focus is partly on moral psychology, in particular on how to think about the role of reason in action that flows from ethical character. By way of a natural connection between reason and objectivity, in an unambitious sense involving no more than the idea of getting things right, that general theme acquires a metaphysical aspect, again in an unambitious sense. Some of these essays can thus be taken to defend a version of what has been called "moral realism". But that label would risk obscuring the fact that what I urge is more negative than positive; my stance in these essays is better described as "anti-anti-realism" than as "realism". What I urge is that anti-realist positions such as emotivism and its sophisticated descendants, all the way down to Simon Blackburn's projectivist quasi-realism, are responses to a misconception of the significance of the obvious fact that ethical, and more generally evaluative, thinking is not science. This misconception is cognate with the dualisms that tend to deform our understanding of, say, Aristotle's conviction that a person of good ethical character has the right answer to the question how one should live.

Already in the first group of essays, and again in the second, there are places where I exploit ideas from Wittgenstein about reason in action. The papers in the third group offer direct readings of Wittgenstein. Essay 11, among other things, aims to entitle me to appeal to Wittgenstein on rule-following in the way I do in Essays 3 and 10. The other essays in this group deal with the implications of Wittgenstein's work for how we should think about how speech and thought are directed at reality, and for how we should think about the idea of an inner life.

By now we are in the midst of the philosophy of mind, and the papers in the fourth group deal with some topics that fall under that head: the character of the mental in general, and of perceptual experience in particular; and the implications, for reflection about personal identity and thereby on the nature of persons, of our first-personal angle on our own lives and the continuity they display.

I have cited works by author's name and title alone, reserving details of publication to the Bibliography at the end of the volume.

PART I

GREEK ETHICS

ESSAY 1

The Role of *Eudaimonia* in Aristotle's Ethics

1. In book 1 of the *Nicomachean Ethics,* Aristotle evidently endorses the thesis that *eudaimonia* is the chief good, the end for all that we do. Following Anthony Kenny, we can distinguish at least two possible interpretations of that thesis: either as claiming that *eudaimonia* is that for whose sake all action is undertaken (an indicative thesis), or as claiming that *eudaimonia* is that for whose sake all action ought to be undertaken (a gerundive thesis).[1] Kenny is reluctant to attribute any doctrine of the former kind to Aristotle. But on the face of it an indicative thesis is what Aristotle appears to accept. At 1102a2–3, he says ". . . it is for the sake of this [sc. *eudaimonia*] that we all do all that we do"; and there seems to be no prospect of taking this to express a gerundive thesis.[2] And the general drift of book 1 points in the same direction. At 1094a18–22, Aristotle says: "if, then, there is some end of the things we do, which we desire for its own sake (everything else being desired for the sake of this), . . . clearly this must be the good and the chief good." Whether or not we suppose that the second "if" clause, which I have omitted, is

---

1. Anthony Kenny, "Aristotle on Happiness". Kenny further distinguishes two versions of the indicative thesis (logical truth and empirical observation); and he is concerned with a scope ambiguity in the thesis that everyone has a single end (see §2 below).
2. *Pace,* apparently, Kenny's added footnote, p. 28. I quote (as throughout) from the translation of Sir David Ross, *The Nicomachean Ethics of Aristotle;* but I shall sometimes substitute a transliteration for Ross's "happiness", in order not to prejudice the sense of *"eudaimonia".* Citations and references are from the *Nicomachean Ethics* unless otherwise specified.

meant as an argument for the truth of the first,[3] what I have quoted appears to say that if the indicative thesis about a single end of action is true, then the single end whose existence it asserts is the chief good; and it is hard to resist the impression that *eudaimonia* figures in the later chapters of book 1 as verifying the antecedent of that conditional: first at 1095a17–20, on the strength of general consensus, and then at 1097a25–b21, on the strength of its satisfying the two conditions, finality and self-sufficiency, that Aristotle argues the chief good must satisfy.

2. Suppose someone says that everyone has a single end he pursues in all his actions. We might ask: does he mean (i) that there is some end of action common to everyone? or (ii) that everyone has his own end, but one that may differ from his neighbour's?

1095a17–28 indicates that Aristotle's answer would be "Both". Which answer is appropriate depends on the level of specificity with which ends are formulated. People have divergent views about what *eudaimonia* amounts to in substantive detail: if we formulate a person's end at a level of specificity at which such divergences appear, then *ex hypothesi* we cannot find *that* end shared by all ((ii) above). But a thesis on the lines of (i) can be true nevertheless, in virtue of the availability of the term *"eudaimonia"* itself as a specification of the common end whose existence such a thesis asserts.

Aristotle himself has a specific view about what kind of life constitutes *eudaimonia*.[4] He certainly does not hold that everyone aims to lead *that* kind of life. But this yields no argument against attributing to him a thesis like (i). It would be a mistake—a missing of the nonextensionality of specifications of aim or purpose—to think one could argue on these lines: *eudaimonia* is in fact such-and-such a kind of life; there are people who do not have that kind of life as

---

3. See, e.g., Kenny, p. 26; on the other side, see §VI of J. L. Ackrill, "Aristotle on *Eudaimonia*".

4. Or perhaps two specific views: an intellectualist view, and a different view that more easily accommodates the excellences of character discussed in books 2–5. My concern is with the role of Aristotle's notion of *eudaimonia* and not with the content of his conception of it, so I shall not discuss this well-known problem of interpretation; for discussion and references see, e.g., John M. Cooper, *Reason and Human Good in Aristotle*. I shall proceed throughout as if Aristotle were single-minded about what *eudaimonia* amounts to.

their aim; therefore there are people who do not have *eudaimonia* as their aim.

If it is the availability of the specification *"eudaimonia"* that permits the unification of substantively divergent ends in life, the question arises whether the unification is merely verbal. I shall revert to that question in due course (§§7 ff.).

3. Kenny's reluctance to attribute an indicative thesis to Aristotle deserves sympathy. Even if we bracket the question whether any interesting unification of divergent ends in life is effected by the specification *"eudaimonia"*, there is still room for suspicion of the claim that any one person has, in any interesting sense, a single end in all his actions. If "actions" means something like "voluntary or purposive doings", there is surely no plausible interpretation of the notion of *eudaimonia* that would make it true that all of anyone's actions are undertaken for the sake of what he conceives *eudaimonia* to be. Worse: that is conceded by Aristotle himself, when he recognizes the occurrence of incontinence. When someone acts incontinently in pursuit of a pleasure, he differs from an intemperate person—who would also pursue the pleasure—in that pursuit of the pleasure would conform to the intemperate person's conception of the sort of life a human being should lead (hence, his conception of *eudaimonia*); whereas for the incontinent person that is precisely not so. The incontinent person has a different conception of what it is to do well (i.e., of *eudaimonia*), but allows himself to pursue a goal whose pursuit in the circumstances he knows to be incompatible with what, in those circumstances, doing well would be.[5] So his action, though voluntary, is not undertaken for the sake of (his conception of) *eudaimonia*.

4. But we can eliminate this counterexample, and so preserve the possibility of ascribing an indicative thesis to Aristotle, as book 1 seems to require (§1 above), without accusing him of inconsistency. What is needed—and independently justifiable—is to equip Aristotle

---

5. Compare Kenny, pp. 27-8, presumably on the strength of, e.g., 1146b22-4. Kenny seems to me to be clearly right about this, *pace* (by implication) Cooper, p. 16. (On 1097b1-5, on which Cooper partly relies, see §5 below.)

with a concept of *action* under which not just any voluntary or purposive doing falls.

The chief good is the end of the things we do (*telos tōn praktōn*: 1094a18–19, 1097a22–23); and in the explicit statement of 1102a2–3, quoted in §1 above, the verb is *"prattein"*. Now we know in any case that *"prattein"* and its cognates have a quasi-technical restricted use at some points in Aristotle. At 1139a19–20 and at *Eudemian Ethics* 1222b18–21, *praxis* ("action") is restricted to man and denied to other animals. Voluntary behavior, however, is allowed to other animals by 1111b7–10. That passage suggests that we should connect the field of application of the restricted use of *"prattein"* and its cognates with the field of application of the notion of *prohairesis* (standardly translated "choice"), since *prohairesis* is similarly denied to non-human animals (and also to children). As for *prohairesis*, one might have thought, from 1113a9–12, that just any deliberative desire to do something would count for Aristotle as a *prohairesis*. But that does not square with the fact that, while denying that someone who acts incontinently acts on a *prohairesis* (e.g. 1111b13–15), he recognizes that an incontinent act can issue from deliberation (1142b18–20). The best resolution is to suppose that a *prohairesis* is a deliberative desire to do something with a view to doing well (*eupraxia*: see 1139a31–b5).[6] "Doing well" (*"eu prattein"*) is by common consent a synonym for "having *eudaimonia*" (1095a19–20). So, given the conjecture that *praxeis*—actions in the restricted sense—are doings that issue from *prohairesis*, we have it guaranteed, by the implicit explanation of the restricted use, that all praxeis are undertaken for the sake of *eudaimonia* (i.e., *eupraxia*).

We might reach the same conclusion, without the detour through *prohairesis*, from 1140b6–7: ". . . while making has an end other than itself, action *(praxis)* cannot; for good action *(eupraxia)* itself is its end." This passage forces a further refinement into our picture. Aristotle here appeals to his distinction (e.g., 1094a3–5) between two sorts of application of the notion of an end, or of expressions like "for the sake of", according to whether or not that for whose sake something is done is distinct from that which is done for its

---

6. See G. E. M. Anscombe, "Thought and Action in Aristotle". "Deliberative desires" are desires the reasons for which can be reconstructed in the form of a deliberation, not necessarily desires actually arrived at by deliberation; see Cooper, pp. 5–10.

sake. In the terminology that commentators have adopted from Greenwood, this is the distinction between *productive* means (where the end is distinct) and *constituent* means (where the end is not distinct).[7] Now in order to respect the distinction between *praxis* and making, we have to recognize that, even if undertaken for the sake of *eudaimonia*, a bit of behaviour need not thereby be shown to be a *praxis*. To count as a *praxis* it must be undertaken as a *constituent* means to *eudaimonia* (that is, the agent's reason must be expressible on these lines: "Doing this is what, here and now, doing well is"), as opposed to a *productive* means (with the agent's reason expressible on these lines: "Doing well is doing such-and-such, and I cannot get into a position in which I can do such-and-such except by doing this").[8]

5. Kenny does consider (p. 28) the possibility of getting round the problem posed by incontinence (§3 above) in something like the way I have suggested: he contemplates the suggestion that since the incontinent person does not act on a *prohairesis* ("choice"), one might ascribe to Aristotle the thesis that whatever is *chosen* is chosen for the sake of *eudaimonia*. Kenny rejects this suggestion on the basis of 1097b1–5: "for this [sc. *eudaimonia*] we choose always for itself and never for the sake of something else, but honour, pleasure, reason, and every virtue we choose indeed for themselves (for if nothing resulted from them we should still choose each of them), but we choose them also for the sake of *eudaimonia*, judging that by means of them we shall have *eudaimonia*." But this is inconclusive.

According to Kenny, it is clear that Aristotle "means not that on some particular occasion honour and pleasure are chosen both for their own sakes and for the sake of [*eudaimonia*], but that on some occasions they are chosen for their own sakes, and on other occasions for the sake of [*eudaimonia*]". This is open to dispute. Presumably Kenny's idea is this: the parenthesis shows that choosing those things for themselves is not choosing them as means to anything else; hence it can be true both that we choose them for themselves and that we choose them for the sake of (as means to) *eudaimonia*, only

---

7. L. H. G. Greenwood, *Aristotle: Nicomachean Ethics Book VI*, pp. 46–7.
8. See Anscombe, pp. 149–50.

if the occasions of these choosings are different. However, the terminology of the parenthesis (note "resulted") suggests the possibility of a different construal, according to which what it shows is that choosing those things for themselves is not choosing them as *productive* means to anything else. With that construal of the parenthesis, the language of the passage is compatible with the idea that choosing those things for themselves, so far from excluding their being chosen, on the same occasions, for the sake of *eudaimonia*, actually *is* choosing them as constituent means to *eudaimonia*.[9]

However, although the language of the passage permits this interpretation, I am doubtful whether the substance does. Virtue and reason are surely not constituent means to *eudaimonia* (though they may be productive means); nor is it obvious that that is the right view of the relation of pleasure and honour to *eudaimonia*. Such a view has its plausibility in the context of a conception of *eudaimonia* as an aggregate of independently recognizable goods, and I shall be questioning (§§12–14 below) whether that conception is Aristotle's.

Suppose, then, that Kenny is right about the meaning of the passage: that, according to it, there are, or could be, choosings of, say, pleasure in the belief that the behaviour motivated thereby will neither constitute nor produce *eudaimonia*—hence, choosings of pleasure otherwise than for the sake of *eudaimonia*. Even so, my suggestion is not refuted. The verb translated "choose" in this passage is not *"prohaireisthai"*, which, with its cognate noun, has the quasi-technical use discussed in §4, but *"haireisthai"*, which can mean (what *"prohaireisthai"* in Aristotle's quasi-technical use does not mean, and what he must sometimes have needed a word for) simply "prefer", or "choose" in an ordinary sense. In that case the concession that in the sense appropriate to this passage, there can be choosings of pleasure otherwise than for the sake of *eudaimonia* need involve no more than the familiar point about incontinence (§3 above); or a similar point about pursuit of pleasure, not contrary to one's conception of *eudaimonia*, as in incontinence, but engaged in by those (e.g., children or non-human animals) who do not pursue *eudaimonia* at all. Such points pose no threat to the thesis that all be-

---

9. See Ackrill, §V. Cooper's idea, at p. 16, is a different one: that honour etc. are chosen for themselves and *also* for the sake of *eudaimonia*.

haviour that issues from *prohairesis* is undertaken for the sake of *eudaimonia*.[10]

6. At *Eudemian Ethics* 1214b6–12, Aristotle says: ". . . everybody able to live according to his own *prohairesis* should set before him some object for noble living to aim at—on which he will keep his eyes fixed in all his *praxeis* (since clearly it is a mark of much folly not to have one's life regulated with regard to some End). . . ."[11] Kenny remarks (p. 29): "The fact that this is made as a recommendation shows that what is recommended is not something that is already the case in the behaviour of all men."

Curiously enough, the "should" that occurs in the Loeb translation I have quoted[12] corresponds to nothing in the text translated (although some manuscripts do have *"dein"*). One might argue that even if the text contains no "should", it needs in any case to be understood, because the parenthesis is evidently meant to back up a recommendation.[13] But it is not obvious that the parenthesis cannot be understood differently, as a sort of gloss on the restriction "able to live according to his own *prohairesis*". In that case, with the Loeb text, the passage yields an indicative thesis about those to whom the restriction applies (sc. all but the very foolish).

In any case, once the character of the indicative thesis that I am ascribing to Aristotle is clear, it does not ultimately matter if this passage has to be read as making a recommendation. The recommendation is that those able to act on *prohairesis* should do so, that is, should form a conception of *eudaimonia* and act for its sake; that this is made as a recommendation does not presuppose that a piece of behaviour may both issue from *prohairesis* and not be undertaken for the sake of *eudaimonia*.

---

10. The other objects of choice mentioned would require different treatment. A great deal more would need to be said in a full account of this difficult passage; all I have aimed to do is to show that Kenny's use of it is not conclusive.
11. Translation (with substituted transliterations) from H. Rackham, ed. and trans., *Aristotle: The Athenian Constitution; The Eudemian Ethics; On Virtues and Vices*.
12. And in the Oxford translation quoted by Kenny.
13. Compare Cooper, p. 94.

7. Suppose Aristotle does wish to maintain that *praxeis* are (by definition) bits of behaviour undertaken as constituent means to *eudaimonia*. What would be the point of such a thesis?

If we can find something more than merely verbal unification of divergent ends in life effected by the specification *"eudaimonia"*, then "undertaken as constituent means to *eudaimonia*" marks out, in spite of the divergences, a distinctive sort of reason an agent can have for behaving as he does. In that case the point of the thesis can be to introduce us, by way of our grasp of that distinctive sort of reason, to a restricted class of bits of behaviour that, because undertaken for that sort of reason, are of special interest in ethics. I suggest that we can indeed grasp such a distinctive sort of reason: it is the sort of reason for which someone acts when he does what he does because that seems to him to be what a human being, circumstanced as he is, should do. The ethical interest of such behaviour is that the behaviour, with its reasons, is indicative of the agent's character.[14]

8. It is important not to be misled about the kind of classification of reasons I have in mind. One possible classification of reasons is by general features of their content, into such categories as moral, aesthetic, or prudential. But that is not the kind of classification I have in mind.

To say that someone should do something is to say that he has reason to do it. Since reasons fall under categories of the sort I have just mentioned, it might seem to follow that uses of "should" fall under categories likewise. On this view, when "should" is used in characterizing the distinctive sort of reason that is involved in acting with a view to *eudaimonia,* what is involved would have to be one such specific kind of "should", say a moral or prudential "should". But that is not how I intend the suggestion.

Consider a dispute on the following lines. One party (X) says that a human being should exercise certain virtues, including, say, justice

---

14. Perhaps in a sense of "character" stipulatively determined by this thesis itself; but that would not make the thesis any less worth considering. It is because they are undertaken for the distinctive sort of reason involved in *prohairesis* (see §6) that bits of behaviour belong in the restricted class of *praxeis;* that explains why Aristotle says (1111b5-6) that *prohairesis* is more indicative of character than *praxeis* are.

and charity. The other party (Y) says: "Nonsense! That's a wishy-washy ideal, suitable only for contemptible weaklings. A real man looks out for himself; he certainly doesn't practise charity, or justice as you conceive it." Now when X applies his view to specific circumstances, he will produce reasons that, according to him, people so circumstanced have for acting as he says they should; and the reasons will belong to one of the categories into which reasons fall. As his position has been described, the reasons will, at least in some cases, be moral ones. Y's reasons will be of a different category: namely, reasons of selfish interest. If we can nevertheless understand the exchange as a genuine dispute, with the recognizable topic "How should a human being behave?", then we cannot take the "should" in the question to have a sense that permits it to be backed only by one of the favoured categories of reason. And surely we can so understand the exchange.

9. I have been using the word "moral" for a certain category of reasons to which a person may or may not think he should conform his life: a category of reasons on a level with, and distinguished by their content from, say, aesthetic reasons, so that if someone argues that human beings should not act in a certain way because it would be, say, inelegant, we might describe him as adducing not a moral but an aesthetic reason.[15] Some philosophers may want to object, in the interest of a use of "moral" according to which the reasons to which someone thinks a human being should conform his life are, *eo ipso*, the reasons he counts as moral. Thus, in the case I have just mentioned, the person is described, according to this view about the use of "moral", as thinking that the avoidance of inelegance is morally required; and similarly Y, in §8, thinks looking out for oneself is morally called for. This is to insist that the "should" that fixes the topic of such disputes as the one I described in §8 is a moral "should".

It is a terminological question whether we should use "moral" in this way. The terminological proposal does not conflict with the substance of my suggestion: namely, that we can make sense of a

---

15. I have deliberately left open the question what general features of their content mark out reasons as moral reasons in this sense.

"should" (it does not matter whether we describe it as a moral "should") that, since it intelligibly locates disputes of the sort I described in §8, is not proprietary to any one specific mode of appraisal—in the sense in which, on this terminological proposal, moral appraisal is no longer a specific mode of appraisal.

Some will be tempted by a different way of insisting that the "should" in question does, contrary to my suggestion, belong to a specific category: namely, the thesis that ultimately it stands revealed as a certain sort of prudential "should". This is not merely a terminological proposal. I shall postpone discussion of it until I have related the suggestion to Aristotle's text.

10. At 1097b22–1098a20, Aristotle exploits the thesis that the *ergon* of man consists in rational activity, and the conceptual connections between the notions of *ergon*, excellence, and activity, in order to reach the conclusion that *eudaimonia*, the good for man, is rational activity in accordance with excellence. This passage is commonly taken as a (purported) argument for Aristotle's own substantive view about with *eudaimonia* is. But it can be read in such a way that the conclusion is (so far) neutral, as between Aristotle's own substantive view and, say, a view of *eudaimonia* corresponding to the position of Y in the dispute I described in §8. With such a reading, the point of the passage can be, not to justify Aristotle's own substantive view, but rather to help the reader to comprehend the distinctive kind of reason that, according to the suggestion of §7, the concept of *eudaimonia* serves to delimit.

What is the *ergon* of a kind of thing? Kenny (p. 27) objects to "function", and proposes the translation "characteristic activity". If that phrase is understood merely statistically, the required connection with the notion of excellence is not plausible. To underwrite that connection, we had better understand the *ergon* of an F as something like: what it is the business of an F to do.[16] This paraphrase leaves it open that, for different substitutions for "F", different sorts of consideration may be appropriate in justifying a candidate specification of the *ergon* of an F. For a range of cases it will be

---

16. Note the normative force that has to be attributed to "work", in Cooper's rendering "definitive work" (p. 145).

a matter of extracting, from an account of what it is to be an F, a specification of something that is indeed appropriately spoken of as the function of F's; but the concept of an *ergon* does not require the argument to take that shape in all cases.

Now disputes of the sort I described in §8 could evidently be conducted as disputes about what it is the business of a human being to do. Equally, they could be conducted as disputes about what human excellence is.[17] The thesis that man's *ergon* consists in rational activity obviously excludes what might otherwise have been a conceivable view of *eudaimonia*, namely, a life of unreflective gratification of appetite; in the spirit of the *ergon* argument, we might say that that embodies no recognizable conception of a distinctively human kind of excellence. But no other likely candidate is clearly excluded by the eliminative argument for that thesis (1097b33–1098a7).[18] Aside from its exclusion of the brutish life, then, the *ergon* argument can be understood neutrally. Its upshot is not to identify *eudaimonia* with one of the disputed candidates, namely, Aristotle's own, but to bring out how the issue between the candidates can be seen as an issue between competing views about which specific properties of a person are human excellences; and the route to the conclusion brings out how the issue can be seen as an issue between competing views about what it is the business of a human being to do.

11. It will be protested that I have got this far only by ignoring that aspect of the sense of *"eudaimonia"* that makes the standard translation, "happiness", not completely inept. That aspect ensures that the term is correctly applied only to the life that is maximally attractive or desirable.

Thus if disputes about how a human being should live, like the one I considered in §8, are disputes about what *eudaimonia* is, then,

---

17. This is sometimes obscured because of the way "excellence", and still more "virtue", have been commandeered by those whose substantive view is a moral one, in the narrow sense. But obviously Y's position, in §8, could be intelligibly expressed by saying "Genuine human excellence is the intelligence and strength needed to further one's own selfish ends".

18. *Pace* those who suppose that the *ergon* argument, as it stands, is meant to prove that *eudaimonia* is, as in book 10, to be equated with a life of "contemplation"; see, e.g., Cooper, pp. 99–100. Against that view, see Ackrill, §VII (and note the end of Cooper's n. 10, pp. 100–1).

according to the protest, that ensures that the "should" in the competing theses must claim its justification from considerations about the attractiveness or desirability, to a person wondering how to arrange his life, of the competing lives. Hence it is, after all, a "should" of a specific category, namely, a kind of prudential "should". (Of course the prudence in question need not be wholly self-centred.)

Again: even if the words "*Eudaimonia* is rational activity in accordance with excellence" can be accepted by all parties in substantive disputes about what *eudaimonia* is, still Aristotle thinks there is a correct position, namely, his own, on the topic of substantive dispute. According to the protest, now, even if the *ergon* argument does not actually constitute Aristotle's justification of his own position on the substantive issue, nevertheless, because it is *eudaimonia* that he identifies with rational activity in accordance with excellence, he is committed to the availability of a certain sort of justification for his own view about what rational activity in accordance with excellence is, namely, a kind of prudential justification: it must be possible to demonstrate, to a person who is wondering what sort of life to lead, that Aristotle's own recipe marks out the kind of life that is in fact most desirable for a human being.

If someone supposes that Aristotle undertakes this commitment, he will naturally suspect that there is more to the *ergon* argument than §10 allowed. A natural speculation will be that the argument is meant to bring the investigation of human nature to bear on the specification of the good life, by way of the thesis that a specification of the *ergon* of F's is derivable from an account of the nature of F's. With this speculation, the *ergon* argument is conceived as a promissory note for something much more elaborate, in which the claim that Aristotle's own recipe marks out the most desirable life for a human being would be grounded in some prior doctrine about human nature.

12. This protest begins with something indisputable: the concept of *eudaimonia* is in some sense a prudential concept. When Aristotle says that activity in accordance with excellence is *eudaimonia,* what he says can be paraphrased as the claim that two prima facie different interpretations of phrases like "doing well" coincide in their ex-

tension: doing well (sc. in accordance with excellence: living as a good man would) is doing well (sc. as one would wish: living in one's best interest). But we need to ask which way round this equation is to be understood.

If, as in the protest, the prudential nature of the concept of *eudaimonia* is taken to show that that concept yields something like a decision procedure for disputes like the one I described in §8, then we have to suppose that we are meant to make our way into the equation at the right-hand side. The requisite idea of the most desirable life must involve canons of desirability acceptable to all parties in the disputes, and intelligible, in advance of adopting one of the disputed theses, to someone wondering what sort of life he should lead. Such prior and independent canons of desirability would presumably need to be constructed somehow out of the content of desires any human being can be expected to have: thus, desires conceived as manifestations of a fairly stable and universal human nature, susceptible of investigation independently of adopting one of the disputed theses about *eudaimonia*.[19]

If someone demands that the exercise of moral excellences must be shown to make up a life that is maximally desirable, and his canons of desirability are of that independent sort, then he risks being accused of missing the point of moral thought; that the demand is a mistake is a well-known doctrine of H. A. Prichard.[20] Commentators who take Aristotle's equation this way round sometimes acquit him of this charge by alleging that his conception of the left-hand side of the equation is shaped precisely so as to make the equation come out true. Thus: Aristotle's admiration for what he regards as human excellence is not moral admiration, in the (it is alleged) peculiarly modern sense that makes Prichard's thesis plausible; what it is to be an excellence, in the sense in which that notion figures on the left-hand side of Aristotle's equation, is to be explained precisely in terms of the role played by states of character in enabling their possessors to secure for themselves maximally desirable lives.[21]

---

19. Compare, e.g., Cooper, pp. 120–1.
20. "Does Moral Philosophy Rest on a Mistake?".
21. See Kathleen V. Wilkes, "The Good Man and the Good for Man in Aristotle's Ethics"; also Cooper, pp. 125 and ff. (and, for a remark about the modernity of the concept of morality, p. 77, n. 104). This view of the appropriate concept of excellence pervades Terence Irwin's account of Socratic and Platonic ethics, in *Plato's Moral Theory*.

But this seems unsatisfactory. Certainly Aristotle's list of excellences of character includes states that it is difficult to believe anyone could find morally admirable; since he sees no noteworthy difference of kind among those excellences, it is plausible to conclude that he lacks our concept of moral appraisal as a distinctive mode of appraisal, to be contrasted, say, with aesthetic appraisal. But from the thesis that he lacks the conceptual equipment required to see it this way, it does not follow that, in the case of those of the excellences he recognizes that we can make sense of someone's morally admiring, his admiration for them cannot be classified by us as moral admiration; and if it can, then in respect of those excellences Prichard's objection tells against the equation, on the present interpretation, to exactly the extent to which it would have told if "excellence" on the left-hand side had been explicitly announced as a moral term. Moreover, if Prichard's thesis is plausible about the specifically moral dimension of thought, then it seems equally plausible about the not specifically moral (perhaps undifferentiatedly moral-cum-aesthetic) kind of appraisal apparently effected by the concept that unifies Aristotle's admiration for his excellences of character, namely, the concept of the fine or noble (*to kalon:* see, e.g., 1115b11–13; 1120a23–24; 1122b6–7). The attempt to disarm Prichard's objection on the score of anachronism is, to say the least, not unproblematic.[22]

13. However, the equation can also be understood the other way round. If our way into it is meant to be at the left-hand side, then the point is this: if someone really embraces a specific conception of human excellence, however grounded, then that will of itself equip him to understand special employments of the typical notions of "prudential" reasoning—the notions of benefit, advantage, harm,

---

22. Wilkes combines this attempt with the claim that Aristotle's thesis, as she interprets it, is "exciting and intellectually satisfying" (p. 571). But if, for better or worse, we are stuck with a notion of morality about which Prichard's doctrine is true (as I believe we are), the thesis cannot be intellectually satisfying to *us*. Wilkes's enthusiasm is unjustified unless Prichard is wrong about *our* notion of morality; and if he is (which she does nothing to show), then she did not need to make so much of the claim that Aristotle lacks that notion.

loss, and so forth—according to which (for instance) no payoff from flouting a requirement of excellence, however desirable by the sorts of canons that I considered in §12, can count as a genuine advantage; and, conversely, no sacrifice necessitated by the life of excellence, however desirable what one misses may be by those sorts of canons, can count as a genuine loss.[23]

Consider, for example, a specific conception of excellence that includes some form of temperance. The exercise of temperance will on occasion require sacrificing the opportunity of some otherwise attractive gratification of appetite. According to the way of employing the prudential notions that is appropriate to the position I considered in §12, that means that to live the life of excellence will be, on such an occasion, to incur a loss; and Aristotle's equation, on the interpretation I considered in §12, could be maintained in the face of such occasions only by claiming that acting temperately would involve a gain (in terms of the independent standards of gain and loss appropriate to the position of §12) sufficient to outweigh that loss. In suitably described cases any such claim would be implausible to the point of being fantastic. On the different interpretation of the equation that I am considering now, the thesis is not that the missed chance of pleasure is an admitted loss, compensated for, however, by a counterbalancing gain; but, rather, that in the circumstances (viz., circumstances in which the missed pleasure would involve flouting a requirement of excellence) missing the pleasure is no loss at all.

How this derivative employment of the "prudential" notions comes about can be explained as follows. To embrace a specific conception of *eudaimonia* is to see the relevant reasons for acting, on occasions when they coexist with considerations that on their own would be reasons for acting otherwise, as, not overriding, but silencing those other considerations—as bringing it about that, in the circumstances, they are not reasons at all. Now for any way of employing the notion of a reason, we can make sense of a derivative way of employing the "prudential" notions, controlled by such formal interdefinitions as that a benefit is what one has reason to pursue and a harm is what one has reason to avoid. In the case considered in the

---

23. See D. Z. Phillips, "Does it Pay to be Good?"; and D. Z. Phillips and H. O. Mounce, "On Morality's Having a Point".

last paragraph, even though the attractiveness of the missed pleasure would have been a reason to pursue it if one could have done so without flouting a requirement of excellence, nevertheless in the circumstances that reason is silenced. And if one misses something that one had no reason to pursue, that is no loss.[24]

There seems to be no obstacle to allowing this derivative employment of the "prudential" concepts to occur side by side with a more ordinary employment—except that there is a risk of confusing them. If we take seriously Aristotle's contention that a person's *eudaimonia* is his own doing, not conferred by fate or other people,[25] but also try to make room for his common-sense inclination to say (e.g. 1099a31–68) that external goods make a life more satisfactory, we are in any case required to distinguish, on his behalf, two measures of desirability or satisfactoriness: one according to which a life of exercises of excellence, being—as *eudaimonia* is—self-sufficient (1097b6–21), can contain no ground for regret in spite of great ill fortune;[26] and one according to which such a life would have been better if the fates had been kinder. The derivative employment of the "prudential" notions yields the former measure; and the strains in Aristotle's treatment of the relation between *eudaimonia* and external goods can be plausibly explained in terms of an intelligible tendency to slide between the derivative employment and a more ordinary conception of prudence.

With the equation understood this way round, it is because a cer-

---

24. I exploit the idea of silencing, in order to interpret Aristotle's distinction between virtue and continence, in Essay 4 below. The idea will seem unintelligible if one finds the following assumption plausible: if a certain general consideration (e.g., that something would be pleasant) is ever a reason for acting in a certain way, then it can be rational to act otherwise, on an occasion on which that consideration is known to obtain, only if the agent has weighed that reason against a reason for acting otherwise and found it outweighed. But we should not simply assume that the philosophical framework that makes that assumption plausible is shared by Aristotle; see §14 below.

25. See Cooper, pp. 123–4, and the Aristotelian texts he cites there.

26. Compare 1100b33–1101a8. Commentators who interpret the passage about self-sufficiency in terms of W. F. R. Hardie's notion of an inclusive, as opposed to dominant, end (see "The Final Good in Aristotle's *Ethics*") tend not to notice, or sufficiently emphasize, the constraints that Aristotle's doctrine that *eudaimonia* is one's own doing places on the interpretation of the claim that it is "that which when isolated makes life desirable and lacking in nothing" (1097b14–16). Kenny's construal (p. 31) has more to be said for it than Ackrill (§V) allows; though I do not think the upshot is felicitously expressed in terms of the notion of a dominant end either.

tain life is a life of exercises of human excellence, or, equivalently, because it is a life of doing what it is the business of a human being to do, that that life is in the relevant sense the most satisfying life possible for its subject, circumstanced at each point as he is. How one might argue that this or that is what it is the business of a human being to do is left open. It does not have to be by showing that a life of such doings maximizes the satisfaction of some set of "normal" or "natural" desires, whose role in the argument would need to be justified by a prior theory of human nature.

We may still find an intelligible place, in the different position I am considering, for some such idea as this: the life of exercises of excellence is the life that most fully actualizes the potentialities that constitute human nature. But the point will be that the thesis—justified in the appropriate way, whatever that is—that this or that is what it is the business of a human being to do can be reformulated, with an intelligibly "value-loaded" use of "human nature", as the thesis that this or that is most in keeping with human nature; not that the justification of the thesis about the business of a human being is to be found in an independent, "value-free" investigation of human nature.

Such an explicit mention of human nature would be a sort of rhetorical flourish, added to a conclusion already complete without it. It is arguable, however, that human nature itself is more importantly involved in disputes like the one I described in §8. The suggestion would be that it is our common human nature that limits what we can find intelligible in the way of theses about how human beings should conduct their lives, and underlies such possibilities as there are of resolving such disputes, or at least of stably adopting one of the competing positions for oneself in a reflective way (aware that there are others). I do not intend to discuss these very difficult issues here. What I want to emphasize is that if, according to the position I have considered in this section, human nature is involved in this sort of way, then what it has is what David Wiggins calls "a causal and enabling role"; not the "unconvincing speaking part" that it would need to be credited with in the position I considered in §12.[27]

27. See "Truth, Invention, and the Meaning of Life", p. 134. I have borrowed Wiggins's phrase; but when he accuses "Aristotelian Eudaemonism" of assigning human nature an "unconvincing speaking part", he does not have in mind the interpretation of Aris-

14. The price of supposing that Aristotle's equation is to be understood as in §13 rather than as in §12 would be to deprive him of what, in §12, looked like a sketch of a decision procedure for disputes like the one I described in §8, and hence a programme for a justification for his own substantive view of *eudaimonia*. But how high a price is that?

It is not obvious that Aristotle has any pedagogic purposes that require him to sketch a decision procedure for disputes like the one I described in §8; for he carefully stipulates (1095b4–6) that he is not addressing people like the antimoralist Y.

It would be rash to suggest that there are no difficulties about making the position of §13 cohere with everything Aristotle wrote.[28] But I believe the main reason why commentators tend to take for granted the interpretation I considered in §12, in spite of the philosophical difficulties it involves, is not textual but philosophical. A position on the lines of §12 strikes them as so obviously what Aristotle needs that charity demands ascribing it to him; or they assume a philosophical framework within which the possibility of a position like that of §13 is not so much as visible.[29]

---

totle that I consider in §12. (If Wiggins were interpreting Aristotle on those lines, then I would be about to suggest, in §14 below, that he is reading Aristotle in the distorting framework of a Humean view about practical reason. But the rest of his lecture makes it obvious that Wiggins is not liable to such a temptation.) What Wiggins has in mind is a position in which, while the investigation of human nature is not conceived as prior to the specification of *eudaimonia*, claims about human nature are nevertheless thought capable of exerting some leverage in justifying candidate specifications. For my part, I would be inclined to view such a position (which I believe might meet with Aristotle's approval) as a response to the following fact (which is insufficiently recognized in the penultimate paragraph of §13): the concept of human nature constitutes a natural focus for the rhetoric with which one might naturally try to recommend a particular conception of *eudaimonia*. (There is very nearly an example of this in my gloss, in §10 above, on Aristotle's exclusion of the brutish life.) If crediting this sort of speaking part to human nature is combined with a clear recognition that there is no question of an appeal to truths that can be established independently of disputation about *eudaimonia* (that the leverage is not Archimedean), the position strikes me as innocuous. The speaking part need not be unconvincing; that depends on the quality of the rhetoric.

28. In particular, something needs to be said (but not here) about the "first principles" or "starting points" of 1095a30–b13.

29. Cooper (p. 120) briefly considers something like the leading idea of that position, but he dismisses it as "trivial". (Similarly, discussing Plato, Irwin, *Plato's Moral Theory*, pp. 9–10.) This complaint seems to issue from the philosophical framework I am about to describe.

Such a framework would be one within which it seems obvious that if disputes like the one I described in §8 are to be recognizable as genuine disputes, then it must be possible in principle to resolve them by means of the sort of external decision procedure, independent of any one of the disputed theses, that the position of §12 envisages. Now that might be represented as an application of a quite general claim, to the effect that where there is a real question, there is a method for answering it. In that case discussion would need to focus on the question whether what truth there is in the general claim really does justify, in the case of disputes like the one I described in §8, the demand for an external decision procedure. But the philosophical framework I have in mind purports to justify that demand directly, by way of the Humean thesis that a genuine reason for acting owes its rational cogency ultimately to the fact that the action for which it is a reason will satisfy an unmotivated desire—a desire that the agent just has, without having any reason for it.[30] Given that thesis, an account of practical rationality—of the reasons to which we should conform our lives—cannot but be on the lines of the position of §12: that is, in terms of the maximizing of some bundle of goods recognizable as such from outside any of the disputed positions about excellence. And the idea that there is an objective topic for disputes about how a human being should live must needs be anchored, as in the position of §12, in a conception of human nature as a subject for prior investigation.

Prima facie conflicts arise in the application of an individual's conception of excellence, and this may seem similarly to necessitate a view of rationality as involving the maximizing of independently recognizable goods. For if there is no externally applicable method of resolution, does not the conception of excellence collapse, in virtue of the conflicts, into a mere random heap of intuitions?[31] The same philosophical framework is operative here. A possibility not being contemplated—rendered invisible by the subjectivism about reasons for acting that the Humean thesis seems to entail—is this. A coherent conception of excellence locates its possessor in what is, for him at

---

30. David Hume, *A Treatise of Human Nature* 2.3.3. (Of course Hume does not express the thesis in terms of reasons for acting.) The distinction between motivated and unmotivated desires is drawn in chap. 5 of Thomas Nagel, *The Possibility of Altruism*.
31. See Cooper, pp. 95–6 (similarly Irwin, pp. 264–5).

least, a world of particular facts, which are often difficult to make out. Faced with a prima facie conflict, one has to determine how things really are, in the relevant corner of the world that one's conception of excellence makes more or less dimly present to one. What makes it the case that the conception of excellence is a unity, in so far as it is one, is not that prima facie conflicts are resolved by asking what will maximize some independently recognizable goods but that the results of those efforts at discernment tend to hang together, in the way that particular facts hang together to constitute a world.[32]

This is not the place to mount an attack on the Humean thesis about reasons. But whatever one's attitude to that thesis, one ought to be able to see that it would be a pity if commentators allowed their acceptance of it to blind them to this possibility: Aristotle may simply not be moving within the framework it characterizes. Of course such blindness will seem more deplorable to those who would like to regard Aristotle as an ally in their opposition to the Humean cast of thought.

32. The Humean thesis about reasons, suggesting as it does a quasi-hydraulic model of their cogency, underlies the assumption that I mentioned in n. 24 above.

ESSAY 2

Some Issues in Aristotle's Moral Psychology[1]

1. Action that displays the ethical character of its agent does so by virtue of the purposiveness that is operative in it. (See *Nicomachean Ethics*—henceforth *NE*—1111b5–6.)

The category of purposive behaviour, behaviour that can be explained by giving its end, extends to brutes as well as human beings. But human beings are special among animals in having a capacity for articulable thought. Purposive behaviour in brutes is an immediate response to an opportunity for gratification of non-rational motivational impulses; its explanation draws only on those impulses and unconceptualized perception. The peculiarly human capacity for thought allows for purposiveness without that immediacy; thought can mediate gaps between project and execution. Thought that bridges such gaps is what Aristotle calls *"bouleusis"* ("deliberation"): see *NE* 3.3.

Deliberation as Aristotle discusses it seems to be a process of thinking engaged in before acting, in terms of which we could understand the action that ensues. But we can sometimes make sense of human behaviour in an importantly similar way, even though the agent did not actually deliberate. The form of deliberation is a form into which we can cast an explanation by reasons, and such an explanation can be appropriate for actions that did not issue from

---

1. This paper is a descendant of a talk I gave to a National Endowment for the Humanities summer school on Aristotle in 1988; I am grateful to participants for helpful responses. Some of the material appears, in a slightly different form, in my paper, "Comments on T. H. Irwin's 'Some Rational Aspects of Incontinence'".

prior deliberation. And it is the nature of an agent's reasons, whether explicitly thought through or not, that reveal his ethical character. It seems best to give Aristotle a pinch of salt on this: to take it, for instance, that when he suggests choice *(prohairesis)* is the upshot of prior deliberation (*NE* 1112a15), his point is really that the conceptual structure that is characteristic of deliberation figures in the proper explanation of the relevant actions, whether or not prior deliberation takes place.[2]

2. The most straightforwardly intelligible application for the idea of a gap between end and behaviour, to be bridged by deliberative thought, is to cases in which the end sought is *instrumentally* remote from the agent's immediate behavioural possibilities. In such a case, there is no problem about what it would be for the end to have been achieved (for instance, for the agent to possess a winter covering). But the end as posited does not select from among the things the agent can do here and now, so the motivating power of the end gets no grip, so far, on the agent's behavioural predicament. Deliberation overcomes this kind of remoteness of the end from the predicament by finding a *means,* which it is within the agent's present power to realize; perhaps step-wise, by finding intermediate means so as to bring the project successively closer to something the agent can simply set about doing.

If behaviour-directed thought is to be recognizable as thought at all, an exercise of the intellect, there must be room for the notion of getting things right. With instrumental deliberation, this requirement is comparatively easy to satisfy. This kind of deliberation is not called on to establish that the posited end is worthy of pursuit; we can take that as given from outside the deliberation itself. (See *NE* 1112b11–16.) Assuming the end, we can satisfyingly base the notion of deliberative correctness on the notion of reliable efficacy.[3] (Not "reduce to", because there are other desiderata that bear on the decision what to do: see *NE* 1112b16–17. But efficacy must be central.) This does not require us to countenance an excellence in thought

---

2. See John M. Cooper, *Reason and Human Good in Aristotle,* pp. 5–10.
3. Notice that the fact that the goal is achieved does not suffice for deliberation to have been well done; success may be due to luck. It has to be that the achievement of the goal could reasonably be expected.

that is in any real sense distinctively practical; the ideal for this kind of deliberation is to apply, in the pursuit of given ends, knowledge that is in itself theoretical, about what can be relied on to bring about what.

3. But this is only part of the story about how behaviour can manifest the distinctively human kind of purposiveness.

When behaviour is intelligible in terms of an instrumentally deliberative structure, the end in view is external to what is done; it will be brought about by what is done, if all goes well. But one of Aristotle's conditions for action to manifest ethical character (virtue in particular, if the character is as it should be) is that the action undertaken be chosen for its own sake (see *NE* 1105a31–2 for the case of virtue). If choice here retains its usual link with deliberation, there must be a non-instrumental kind of deliberative structure.

It can seem difficult to fit this requirement into Aristotle's scheme. He says of choice *(prohairesis)*, as of deliberation, that it fixes on means to ends (as the most familiar translation has it): *NE* 1111b26–7, 1112b11–12. How can something chosen as a means be chosen for its own sake?[4]

But this difficulty is only a creature of the translation. Aristotle's Greek distinguishes ends from "things towards" ends; and "towards" *("pros")* expresses just what is expressed elsewhere by "for the sake of" or "with a view to" (*"hina"* or *"heneka"*). Now in the very first chapter of *NE* (1094a3–5), Aristotle has equipped himself with the point that what some activity is undertaken for the sake of can be either something separate from the activity, a product, or the activity itself.[5] Some commentators have made heavy weather of the idea of an activity as its own end, but the basic point is straightforward. Answering the question "For the sake of what?" makes sense

---

4. "Means" is the translation of Sir David Ross, *The Nicomachean Ethics of Aristotle*.

5. This distinction is related to the distinction between production *(poiēsis)* and action (in a strict sense: *praxis*), for which see *NE* 1140b6–7, 1139b1–4. But the distinctions do not seem to be exactly the same: it seems plausible that an activity can be undertaken for its own sake (e.g., for the fun of it) without being undertaken for the sake of doing well *(eupraxia)*, which seems to be the mark of *praxis*. "For the sake of doing well" restricts us to reasons for acting that draw on a conception of human excellence; this is the point of the "function" argument in *EN* 1.7. (See Essay 1 above; for a contrasting view, see Troels Engberg-Pedersen, *Aristotle's Theory of Moral Insight*.)

of behaviour by revealing how it strikes the agent as worth undertaking; and an intrinsic characterization of an activity, not in terms of an external product, can reveal the worthwhileness the agent sees in it.

The choices that display character are choices for the sake of doing well (*eu prattein,* which according to *NE* 1095a18–20 is platitudinously equivalent to *eudaimonein:* that is the verb corresponding to the noun *"eudaimonia",* standardly translated "happiness"). These choices reveal character because they display in practice the agent's conception of how a human being should conduct his life. The fact that these choices are for the sake of doing well ensures that they conform to the general claim about choice, that what is chosen is chosen "towards" an end. But in these cases an agent's choosing his action for the sake of doing well is his choosing it as a *case* of doing well. If he is right, what he does (say facing the enemy at just this juncture of the battle) is what doing well, here and now, is; doing well is not something external to what he does, to be brought about by it.[6] And this secures conformity to the other claim, that actions that reveal character are chosen for their own sake: they are chosen under intrinsic specifications that reveal them as worth engaging in, in the specific way signalled by "doing well".

4. This brings into view a different application for the idea of a gap that thought can bridge between end and action. Now the situation is not, as before, that it is clear what it would be for the end to have been attained, but deliberation is required to select a means of bringing that about. The initial remoteness of end from action is now, as we can put it, *specificatory:* to say that the end is doing well singles out nothing the agent can here and now undertake, because the question is what doing well here and now would be.

What shape does thought directed at this sort of question take? And what is the content, here, of the idea of getting things right?

Many commentators respond to such questions by equipping Aristotle with a kind of practical thinking that applies rules to cases.[7]

---

6. Or "promoted" by it; Irwin's substitute for the Ross rendering, in his translation of *NE,* does not fit the bill. See my "Comments on T. H. Irwin, 'Some Rational Aspects of Incontinence'", pp. 90–1.

7. The *locus classicus* for this idea is probably D. J. Allan, "The Practical Syllogism".

The idea is that a conception of doing well (the virtuous person's correct conception among others) can be spelled out as a set of rules of conduct, presumably in some such form as this: "In such-and-such conditions, one should do such-and-such (doing such-and-such is what doing well is)." The answer to our first question is: this kind of practical thinking is applying such rules when one recognizes that the specified conditions obtain.

If we had a set of rules of this kind, there would be no problem about what it would be to apply them correctly, as it were by their own lights; that would be a matter of deduction. So if there is anything interesting about the second question, it directs us to the question what it is for the rules to be the right ones; and this picture encourages the idea, to which we shall return, that the practical intellect must determine the content of the correct conception of living well.[8]

5. There are two connected difficulties about this "rule"-"case" picture, as an account of the non-instrumental kind of deliberative structure that Aristotle must have in mind.

First, to have the required deductive powers, the rules would need to be formulable in universal terms, with all conditions made explicit. But Aristotle repeatedly insists, surely with great plausibility, that we should not look for this kind of universal truth in ethics. (See, for instance, NE 1094b11–27, 1109b12–23; there are many similar passages.)[9]

Second, this reading cannot make sense of Aristotle's claim that practical wisdom *(phronēsis)*, the intellectual excellence operative in

---

My remarks at the end of §3 already commit me to allowing room for the notion of a case or instance: I said that the virtuous person chooses an action as a case of doing well. But the idea of "rule"-"case" practical thinking goes beyond that: it is meant to yield an answer to the question *how* the choice locates its object.

8. See Allan, "Aristotle's Account of the Origin of Moral Principles".

9. Aristotle does seem (reasonably enough) to envisage universal prohibitions on, for instance, adultery or murder (see NE 1107a9–12). The point is, as he makes clear, that badness is part of the very idea of such actions. If we formulated universal rules in such terms, the sort of specificatory problem that "rule"-"case" thinking is supposed to address would show up, on occasion, in the form of questions about the applicability of the key terms in the rules. In any case, it is hardly plausible that a conception of how a human being should live could be fully captured in terms of these universal prohibitions.

behaviour that manifests good character, is a perceptual capacity. (See *NE* 1142a23–30, 1143a5-b5.) In the "rule"-"case" picture, the most obvious role for perception is to contribute awareness that certain conditions, which are in fact the conditions specified in a rule, are satisfied.[10] That kind of awareness is presumably available to anyone. It is hard to see why perception, so understood, should seem distinctive of someone whose practical intellect is as it should be. On this picture, the proper state of the practical intellect should consist, rather, in having the right universal principles.[11]

We need a non-instrumental kind of deliberative structure in order to make sense of action that puts into practice an agent's conception of doing well, which is correct if his character is virtuous. Aristotle's scepticism about universal ethical truth implies that the content of the conception a virtuous person acts out cannot be formulated, in such a way that its application can be expressed in the "rule"-"case" form.[12] And the appeal to a notion of perception makes perfect sense as, precisely, a response to that impossibility.

The picture we need (applied to the case of virtue in particular) is on these lines.[13] Having the right conception of the end is, at least, a state of one's motivational propensities. It involves having a number of concerns: that is, motivational susceptibilities, for instance to op-

---

10. This is the role credited to perception on Aristotle's behalf by Irwin, "Some Rational Aspects of Incontinence"; see especially p. 65.

11. Cooper, *Reason and Human Good in Aristotle*, pp. 39–45, offers a different reading of Aristotle's appeal to perception, which seems unsatisfactory in a similar way. Cooper suggests Aristotle is alluding (in 1143a5-b5) to the capacity to recognize kinds of objects (and so forth) that is necessary if one is to be able to put into practice a course of action hit on by prior deliberation, and (in 1142a23–30) to the capacity to tell that deliberation has been taken as far as it needs to be, that is, to an action-specification that the agent can immediately put into practice. That the action-specification arrived at specifies the *right* action, from among those that are feasible here and now, is taken care of by the deliberation's being done correctly, which Cooper evidently conceives as a separate matter. But affirming the perceptual character of the capacity in question, as Aristotle does at *NE* 1142a23–30, seems more naturally taken as a way of claiming that the capacity yields right answers (compare 1109b23), not just that it recognizes when a procedure that is anyway such as to yield right answers has been taken far enough.

12. Of course Aristotle himself undertakes what is, in one sense, a formulation of the content of the conception of doing well he himself endorses, when he gives his character sketches of the possessors of the various virtues in books 3 to 5 of *NE*. But one could not extract rules, such as the "rule"-"case" picture requires, from those passages.

13. What follows is, in its essentials, the account offered by David Wiggins, "Deliberation and Practical Reason".

portunities to help others. Now it may be that more than one such concern is potentially appealed to by features of a situation one finds oneself in. One response to this is to credit Aristotle with "ordering principles", whose effect is to rank the concerns in urgency, perhaps relatively to features of situations.[14] But this is just a version of the "rule"-"case" picture; it flies in the face of Aristotle's scepticism about the codifiability of virtuous action. In Aristotle's picture, a correct conception of how one should live does not yield a *method* for determining which concern one should act on. Nevertheless, one rather than another of the potentially practically relevant features of the situation would strike a virtuous person, and rightly so, as salient, as what matters about the situation. If there were "ordering principles", they would yield an argument that what appeals to one rather than another of the concerns is what matters about the situation. In the absence of such an argument, it comes naturally to say "You have to see it", with the perceptual concept marking a point at which discursive justifications have run out (compare NE 1143b1).

We can capture this picture in terms of the "practical syllogism".[15] What is yielded by the perceptual capacity Aristotle appeals to? Not awareness of the truth of the minor premise (which is presumably afforded by ordinary cognitive capacities), but its selection from among other features of the situation *as* minor premise: as what matters about the situation. The *De Motu Animalium* (701a9 ff.) distinguishes premises of the good and premises of the possible. In those terms, the premise of the good in the cases we are considering is the content of the correct conception of doing well (compare NE 1144a31–3). If someone gets things right in the kind of practical thought we are considering, what happens is that one feature of the situation rather than another (say, that a friend is in trouble rather than that one has a professional obligation to be elsewhere) comes to serve as premise of the possible, that is, as pointing to something that can be done to gratify the orectic or desiderative state whose

---

14. See, for instance, Cooper, *Reason and Human Good in Aristotle*, p. 97.
15. I use this phrase as orthodox commentators do, to label a structure, parallel in some respects to the structure of a certain sort of theoretical argument, that can be used to characterize cases of deliberation or practical reasoning, or the deliberative shape in which an agent's reasons for action can be organized even if no deliberative process entered into the generation of his action. For an unorthodox account of the notion, see Cooper, *Reason and Human Good in Aristotle*, pp. 24–46.

content is the premise of the good.[16] We have here a recognizable version of the structure indicated by the terms "premise of the good" and "premise of the possible". We can make sense of a piece of behaviour, in this case in a way that involves understanding the fact that the agent identifies behaving in that way as what doing well amounts to in the circumstances in which he finds himself, in terms of the interaction between, on the one side, an orectic state and, on the other, a doxastic state that registers the feasibility of a specific gratification of the orectic state.

6. We can see the orectic state and the doxastic state as interlocking elements in a mechanism, like the ball and socket of a joint. But the capacity that determines which of the potentially motivating features of the situation is to serve as premise of the possible cannot be separated from the orectic state whose content constitutes the premise of the good. Having the right end is not a mere aggregate of concerns; it requires the capacity to know which should be acted on when. If that capacity cannot be identified with acceptance of a set of rules, there is really nothing for it to be except the capacity to get things right occasion by occasion: that is, the perceptual capacity that determines which feature of the situation should engage a standing concern. So the premise of the good, and the selection of the right feature of the situation to serve as premise of the possible, correspond to a single fact about the agent, which we can view indifferently as an orectic state or as a cognitive capacity. This explains how Aristotle can equate practical wisdom both with the perceptual capacity (*NE* 1142a23–30) and with a true conception of the end (*NE* 1142b33). It is not just that he credits each of these to the practically wise person, as if they might be independent attributes of him; he says of each that it is what practical wisdom is.

This double aspect of practical wisdom, as correctness of motivational orientation and as cognitive capacity, is something Aristotle risks obscuring in passages like *NE* 1144a7–9, where he says that "virtue makes the goal right, practical wisdom the things with a view to the goal". (There are similar remarks at 1144a20–2 and

---

16. I presuppose the reading of the passage from the *De Motu Animalium* given by Wiggins, "Deliberation and Practical Reason".

1145a3–6.) This claim might seem to represent having the right goal, which is, presumably, having one's desiderative element (one's *orektikon*) as it should be, as one thing, and practical wisdom as quite another; as if practical wisdom, the intellectual excellence operative in virtuous behaviour, serves merely as handmaiden to a separate motivational propensity, which exerts its influence from outside the intellect.

There is an exegetical tradition, not nowadays widely in favour, that reads these passages on such lines. On this interpretation, Aristotle's view is quasi-Humean: the relevant intellectual excellence is the slave, not indeed of the passions, but at any rate of a non-intellectual motivational directedness.[17]

Much modern discussion has been shaped by a recoil from this quasi-Humean interpretation. The recoil is surely right, but we need to be careful about where it places us. One common result is taking Aristotle to hold that it must be the intellect that determines the content of the virtuous person's correct conception of the end. This requires that we discount, with more or less embarrassment, passages such as the one I have just cited (*NE* 1144a7–9), or that we read them, with more or less strain, in such a way as to soften the contrast they seem to draw between the roles of practical wisdom and virtue.[18]

But we can avoid the quasi-Humean reading while taking *NE* 1144a7–9 fully at its word. The point of the contrast is this: what determines the content of a virtuous person's correct conception of the end is not an exercise of the practical intellect, but rather the moulding of his motivational propensities in upbringing, which is described in book 2 of *NE* as instilling virtue of character. This need not be a quasi-Humean thought, because there is no reason why a

---

17. On the usual reading, *NE* 1142b33 says that practical wisdom is a true conception of the end; that would be inconsistent with representing the proper motivational orientation as simply separate from anything intellectual. The quasi-Humean interpretation gives the relative pronoun, in "of which practical wisdom is a true conception", a different antecedent, making the passage identify practical wisdom with a true conception not of the end but of what is conducive towards it.

18. See, for example, Irwin, "First Principles in Aristotle's Ethics", p. 268. Irwin suggests that "virtue's grasp of the goal" is itself dictated by a prior exercise of practical wisdom. This ignores the clear implication, from the contrastive structure of 1144a7–9, that what makes the goal the right one is virtue *as opposed to* practical wisdom.

state whose content is so determined cannot be an intellectual excellence. The claim is that it is not practical wisdom that *makes it the case* that the goal is the right one. This leaves intact the thesis that *having* the right goal, being, as it is, inseparable from the ability to know what is to be done occasion by occasion, is what practical wisdom is. (Recall the double aspect of practical wisdom.) Having the right motivational orientation can be something other than a product of argument (or intellectual intuition), without any implication that it is extra-intellectual, something that directs the practical application of the intellect from outside.

7. Commentators sometimes suggest that if we take such a passage as *NE* 1144a7–9 at face value, we restrict the practical intellect to a merely instrumental role. But that is simply wrong. The claim is that the content of a virtuous person's correct conception of the end is determined by upbringing, not by an exercise of the intellect; this makes no difference to the fact that a virtuous person confronts practical questions of the form "What does doing well here and now amount to?" The deliberation such a question calls for is precisely not instrumental deliberation; instrumental deliberation looks for how to bring about an end where what counts as its having been brought about is not part of the problem.

We should distinguish two possible kinds of practical thought, both of which can be seen as responding to questions of that specificatory type. One kind would confer determinate general content on an end hitherto adopted only under a quite indeterminate specification like "doing well"; this kind of deliberation would work towards a blueprint for the sort of life a human being should lead, perhaps by reflectively identifying components of a good life and working out principles for their combination. The other would be aimed not at *forming* a general conception of the end, but at *putting one into practice* in specific circumstances. If the content of a general conception of the end cannot be formulated in rules, applying it to particular predicaments is not a straightforward matter. No doubt we cannot always sharply distinguish between shaping part of the general content of a conception of the end and discerning what an already held conception of the end requires of one in a given predicament.

But that is not to say that we should always gravitate to the former description.

The second of these conceptions of specificatory practical thought is enough to make room for a non-instrumental kind of practical thinking. Commentators have almost universally found in Aristotle a concern with the first; but I do not believe this has any textual basis, and I think it reflects saddling Aristotle with alien, and dubious, philosophical aspirations.[19]

We should discount the possibly confusing effects of using the expression "determinate end" for the kind of end whose pursuit calls for instrumental deliberation.[20] The point of the expression is that instrumental deliberation does not have to address the question what it would be for the end to have been achieved. That contrasts with deliberation needed to determine what it would be to achieve the end. Now this description fits occasions for the second kind of specificatory deliberation that I distinguished above, no less than occasions for the first. But the corresponding label, "indeterminate end", tends to restrict attention to the first: to cases where what still needs to be determined is the general content of the end, so that deliberation is towards a general blueprint for a life rather than towards a specification of what to do here and now.

8. There is a philosophical motivation for the style of reading I am disputing, in which what determines the content of a virtuous person's conception of the end is an exercise of the intellect.

The thought is this. If the shape of one's conception of the end is the upshot of upbringing, as opposed to an exercise of one's intellectual powers, then one's having one rather than another conception

---

19. This is why, in discussing the two sorts of application for phrases like "for the sake of", I did not follow the usual practice of distinguishing instrumental from constituent means (derived from L. H. G. Greenwood, *Aristotle: Nicomachean Ethics Book VI*, pp. 46–7). That terminology does not discriminate between thought that concludes, say, that satisfactory social relations are a component of the good life, and thought that concludes, say, that facing the enemy is what doing well is here and now. It is the latter, not the former, that exemplifies the "for the sake of" relation I believe we need to consider; the constituents of doing well, in the relevant sense, are not components in a general blueprint for a life but particular actions. But when commentators talk of constituent means they almost always have in mind the former rather than the latter.

20. I believe this use derives from Irwin, *Plato's Moral Theory*.

of the end is (merely) a non-rationally moulded state of one's desiderative make-up. One such state is rationally speaking on a level with another. So this way—the thought goes—we lose what Aristotle obviously wants to have, the idea that just one conception of the end is the correct one. According to this line of thought, that requires that one could establish by argument that the conception is correct. And, on pain of falling back into reliance on a mere non-rationally moulded motivational and valuational propensity, the argument's persuasiveness would have to be independent of the specific propensities to value this and despise that that are inculcated in a proper upbringing (by Aristotle's lights). The validating argument would have to be, in an obvious sense, from outside the initially merely inherited ethical outlook that it would validate.[21]

I suggested that commentators who accept the "rule"-"case" picture do not take seriously enough Aristotle's scepticism about universal truth in ethics. This line of thought may underlie the tendency to miss the full force of that scepticism. If there is to be an external certification that a given conception of the end is the right one, we must be able to formulate the content of the conception in such a way that the certification can get a grip on it. The content of the conception must be able to figure as the conclusion of a discursive argument, whose cogency can be clear in abstraction from any particular series of practical predicaments. Only a set of rules, with all relativity to situations made explicit in universal terms, could serve the purpose.[22]

---

21. Irwin, in *Plato's Moral Theory* (see, e.g., pp. 9, 159, 175), attributes the idea of an external standard for the rationality of virtue not to Plato (or Aristotle) but to Socrates, whom he takes (wrongly in my view, but that is another story) to have represented virtuous actions as instrumental means to an end that everyone pursues. For Irwin's Plato, the standard by which virtue is revealed to be rational is not external to the distinctive valuations of a virtuous person; being persuaded into acceptance of the standard is the same thing as being persuaded into virtue. And Irwin's account of Aristotle's view on this matter is similar. The distinction Irwin draws here is certainly important. For Irwin's Socrates, the rationality of virtue is reducible to something extra-ethical, and for Irwin's Plato and Aristotle this is not so. The fact remains, however, that Irwin conceives persuading someone into accepting the standard as proceeding step-wise, in such a way that each step is revealed as rationally required according to standards of rationality already endorsed before the step is taken (for Plato, see pp. 167–72). This is precisely a picture of validation from outside; that it is non-reductive makes no difference to that.

22. Even commentators who appreciate Aristotle's hostility to the idea that the truth about how to live can be captured once and for all in a set of rules tend to suggest that we can meet Aristotle's point by thinking in terms of "broad principles", to be applied with

9. An external validation of the correctness of a specific ethic would be enormously significant. If Aristotle really thought he could give such a thing, one would expect him to highlight it. In fact one looks for it in vain. At *NE* 1095b4–6 he implies that he is not even going to address questions of validation. And wherever someone who believes in this kind of external validation might expect Aristotle to appeal to it, in saying what determines the rightness of right action, or the propriety of proper deliberation, or whatever, he disappoints such expectations; rather than giving a criterion that works from outside the ethic that he takes for granted, he says that such things are as the virtuous person determines them. (See, e.g., *NE* 1107a1–2, 1139a29–31, 1144a34.)

To many commentators the argument from the "function" *(ergon)* of a human being in *NE* 1.7, reprised in 2.6, suggests that Aristotle envisages an external validation for his ethic, starting from the facts about human nature. But proponents of all sorts of non-Aristotelian conceptions of doing well could accept the conceptual connections that the *ergon* argument exploits, between "function", excellence, and doing well. Such people would dispute a view of the human "function", and hence of human nature, that made Aristotle's own list of virtues come out correct. They would not thereby be disputing anything in the "function" argument.[23]

In fact there are only two substantive points on which Aristotle suggests that facts about human nature constrain the truth about a good human life, in a way that might be supposed to be independent of inculcated propensities to value this and despise that. First, a good human life must be an active life of that which has *logos* (*NE* 1098a3–4); this excludes, for instance, the ideal of uncontrolled gratification of appetite with which Socrates saddles Callicles, in Plato's *Gorgias*. Second, human beings are naturally social (*NE* 1097b11, 1169b18–19); this excludes a solitary life. Obviously these two points fall a long way short of purporting to afford a validation of

---

discretion. (See, e.g., Cooper, *Reason and Human Good in Aristotle*, pp. 134–5.) The idea here is that discretion mediates between something general, suitable to be validated from outside, and the detail of real life. I believe this underplays how important situation-specific discernment is for Aristotle, in the interest of keeping in the picture a suitable conclusion for the supposed external validation.

23. See Essay 1 above.

Aristotle's ethic in full. But it is the whole substance of his ethic, not just these two somewhat structural features of it, that he wants to represent as objectively correct.

10. The reading I am considering is shaped by the thought that, as far as objective correctness goes, one non-rationally moulded state of one's desiderative make-up (one's *orektikon*) is on a par with another, unless the conception of the good that is embodied in one of them can be certified as true from outside. But why should we suppose Aristotle would accept that? It is common ground that, in his view, at most one of two different conceptions of the end could involve the desiderative element's being as it should be. Suppose he were pressed about the valuation implicit in that "should". Why not suppose he would say something like this: "Only by living in accordance with the correct conception of the end can we fill our lives with actions that are noble *(kalon)*"? That would exactly not be offering to ground his valuational scheme from outside. It would be appealing to the habits of valuation that are inculcated in the kind of upbringing he is confident his audience has had (*NE* 1095b4–6).

This may make it seem that Aristotle's moral psychology rests on an unreflective contentment with the mores of his audience. And such an accusation would probably not be completely unfair. However, there are passages that do not fit this picture, but place Aristotle rather in a line of descent from Socrates' commendation of the examined life. Consider, for instance, the distinction between having "the that", which is where properly brought up people begin, and having "the because", at *NE* 1095b6–7.[24] Working towards a comprehending acceptance of a scheme of values (having "the because" as well as "the that") would be a matter of reflection. The essential thing for my present purposes is that this reflection need not be conceived as stepping outside the standpoint constituted by an inherited mode of thought, so as to supply it (if all goes well) with an external validation. There is an alternative, which seems fully in keeping with Aristotle's conception of philosophical method: a conception of reflection for which the appropriate image (at least for us: see below) is Neurath's, of the mariner repairing his ship while afloat.

---

24. See M. F. Burnyeat, "Aristotle on Learning to be Good".

There is a temptation to think that Neurathian, or internal, reflection could only be second best. This belongs with the tendency to be disappointed when Aristotle rests within the circle of his own ethic, letting the virtuous person be the measure of (say) how one should act. Here the philosophical basis for the kind of reading of Aristotle that I am deploring comes to the surface; and we can begin to see, at least in outline, how it falsifies him. Neurathian reflection on an inherited scheme of values takes place at a standpoint within that scheme; the scheme can be altered piecemeal, but not suspended in its entirety, with a view to rebuilding from the ground up. The disappointment results from the idea that one could not achieve a justified conviction of objective correctness, in thought about anything, from within something as historically contingent as a conceptual scheme; what is required is to break out of a specific cultural inheritance into undistorted contact with the real. Now this idea is distinctively modern. I do not mean that it has happened to occur to people only in modern times, but that it is not really even intelligible except as a response to modern currents of thought. Loss of confidence in internal reflection just as such requires an awareness, not shared by all ages, of the historical contingency of actual modes of thought.[25] And the consoling counterpart idea, that of a mode of contact with the real in which we transcend our historicity, can seem to be available only by way of a philosophical misconception of the achievements of modern science, a misconception that is itself in turn partly motivated by that modern loss of confidence.[26]

In saying this, I do not mean to suggest we can patronize Aristotle for insensitivity to a good question about ethical objectivity, one that we have more recently learned to ask. It is only in that modern philosophical framework that the question looks like a good one. We ought to be suspicious of our tendency to suppose genuine objectivity would require something more than Neurathian reflection. One of the benefits of studying a great philosopher from an alien age is

---

25. Ancient ethical scepticism, vividly represented in, e.g., Plato's *Gorgias*, was not like this.
26. Insisting that scientific modes of thought are products of history too is often represented as disparaging them. But it looks like that only in the context of a conception of what it would be to give science its due that is shaped by the questionable philosophy I am describing.

that it can help us to see that we do not have to swim with the currents of our own time.

It would be anachronistic to suggest the Neurathian image might fit Aristotle's own conception of reflection towards "the because". The image is apt for explicitly rejecting the hankering after an external standpoint; the image has its resonance only in the context of felt pressures towards losing confidence in internal reflection as such. My claim is that Aristotle is healthily innocent of all that. The point of the image for us is to express a philosophically knowing stance that is as close as we, with our irrevocably lost innocence, can come to Aristotle's outlook.[27]

11. Aristotle organizes his discussion of the human virtues by distinguishing virtues of character (courage, temperance, and so forth) from intellectual virtues (see NE 1103a3–18). The intellectual virtues include excellences in behaviour-directed thought, notably practical wisdom, and this sets up a link between the two sorts of virtue: practical wisdom is an intellectual excellence displayed in those actions that manifest virtues of character strictly so called (see NE 1144b1–17).

I have been discussing a reading of Aristotle that recoils as far as possible from the quasi-Humean reading. In the quasi-Humean reading, the intellectual excellence exercised in actions that display virtue of character is subservient to an extra-intellectual motivational orientation. In the polar opposite that I have been discussing, there is still a relation of subservience, but in an opposite direction. On this view, it is an exercise of the intellect that determines a fully virtuous person's motivational orientation. The "virtues of character" whose

---

27. Contrast Irwin, *Aristotle's First Principles*. Irwin represents Aristotle as a "metaphysical" (as opposed to "internal") realist. I think this is damagingly anachronistic. Wanting one's realism "metaphysical" as opposed to "internal" is a confused response to distinctively modern intellectual pressures. I have been acknowledging that there is anachronism in reading Aristotle as an "internal" (or Neurathian) realist, but this anachronism is not symmetrical, because the point of labelling one's realism "internal" is to *reject* a modern philosophical confusion. "Internal" realism is the nearest we can get to an outlook that (to its advantage) would not so much as understand the temptation towards "metaphysical" realism. (These remarks exemplify how issues in the history of philosophy are inextricably bound up with issues in philosophy; the history looks different to Irwin and to me because the philosophy does.)

origin in habituation Aristotle describes in *NE* book 2 are non-intellectual motivational propensities whose ultimate role in the psychological organization of a fully virtuous agent is to make him receptive to the independent dictates of the practical intellect. In *NE* 6.13 it turns out that those states are not virtues of character in the strict sense. A virtue of character strictly so called is a harmonious composite of intellectual and non-intellectual elements; the non-intellectual element ensures the agent's obedience to requirements set by pursuit of an end whose content is autonomously fixed by the intellectual element.[28]

I have urged that we do not need to choose between these polar opposites. Aristotle does not attribute dominance in the genesis of virtuous behaviour either to the practical intellect, conceived as operating autonomously, or to a wholly non-intellectual desiderative state. In fact the wholly extra-intellectual motivational propensity that both these extreme readings find in the initial discussion of virtue of character, as the product of habituation, is an abstraction; it fits nothing Aristotle seems to be concerned with. Correspondingly, he does not picture the practical intellect as operating independently of moulded motivational propensities.

Already in *NE* book 2, in which the stress is on states that result from upbringing, he insists that the actions that manifest virtue of character must be *chosen* (1105a31–2). By way of the link between choice and deliberation, this imports the specially human capacity for discursive thought. It is already implicit, even at this early stage in the exposition, that virtue of character requires an intellectual excellence. We travesty Aristotle's picture of habituation into virtue of character if we suppose the products of habituation are motivational propensities that are independent of conceptual thought, like a trained animal's behavioural dispositions. On the contrary, the topic of book 2 is surely initiation into a conceptual space, by way of being taught to admire and delight in actions in the right way. The space is the one we move in as we read the subsequent character sketches of possessors of the particular virtues; it is organized by the concepts of the noble and the disgraceful (see, e.g., *NE*

---

28. For an especially clear exposition of an account on these lines, see Cooper, "Some Remarks on Aristotle's Moral Psychology".

1120a23–4).[29] Possessing "the that", those who have undergone this initiation are already beyond uncomprehending habit; they are already some distance into the realm of the relevant intellectual excellence. They have a conceptual attainment that, just as such, primes them for the reflection that would be required for the transition to "the because". And the transition need not involve new conceptual substance injected from outside. Reflection towards "the because" can be Neurathian; it needs no material besides the substance of the conceptual space that a subject already inhabits, in a partially comprehending way, in consequence of upbringing.

On this reading, it is not that practical wisdom issues orders, whose content it determines by its own independent operations, to motivational propensities that have been separately moulded to obedience. A virtue of character, strictly so called, involves a harmony of intellect and motivation that is more intimate than that. Practical wisdom *is* the properly moulded state of the motivational propensities, in a reflectively adjusted form; the sense in which it is a state of the intellect does not interfere with its also being a state of the desiderative element.[30]

12. Aristotle frames his treatment of the virtues within a discussion of "the good and the chief good" (*NE* 1094a22). He appeals to common consent in favour of identifying the good with "happiness" *(eudaimonia)*, which in turn is equated with living well and doing well (1095a14–20). The first part of *NE* 1.7 spells out the content and basis of this common consent: the identification of the good with *eudaimonia* is justified on the ground that *eudaimonia* meets some quasi-formal requirements involved in the idea of the good

---

29. See Burnyeat, "Aristotle on Learning to be Good".
30. Cooper, "Some Remarks on Aristotle's Moral Psychology", deliberately refrains from offering a justification from the texts for his different reading of Aristotle. The case would have to rest largely on *NE* 1.13. I think we should be careful not to overread that passage; its purpose is to introduce an architectonic structure for expository purposes, and the subsequent development itself shows that we should not take the structure too rigidly. Cooper's main justification comes from a view about how Aristotle fits into the evolution of Greek moral psychology, from Socrates to the Stoics. I cannot discuss the whole sweep of Greek ethics in this paper. I can only say, dogmatically, that I think Cooper's account is badly mistaken, and I suspect the main culprit is a misreading of Stoicism, reflected back into the earlier thinkers.

(1097a25-b21), and the argument from the "function" of man confirms the equation of *eudaimonia* with acting well, with "well" spelled out as "in accordance with virtue" (1097b22-1098a20).

This connection between virtue and *eudaimonia* is often thought to mark the point at which the supposed external validation of Aristotle's ethic gets its grip. The concept of *eudaimonia* is supposed to locate a kind of reflection whose upshot would be a blueprint for a life, capable of being recognized as determining what it is rational to do even from a standpoint outside the valuations that result from being brought up into a particular ethical outlook. The connection of virtue with *eudaimonia* would then serve to establish, from outside those valuations, that Aristotle's own list of virtues is correct, in the sense that a life of activity in accordance with them will meet independent standards for being worth going in for.

This view of the role of *eudaimonia* in Aristotle's thinking reflects the philosophical expectations that I have been urging are alien to Aristotle. Unsurprisingly, I think it distorts his intentions. In any case, it should be of interest to consider an alternative reading, whose possibility is obscured by the assumption that Aristotle aims at an external validation.

According to the alternative, the point of the concept of *eudaimonia* is not to suggest a general determination of what can be practically rational, on the basis of some idea like that of an optimal combination of items that can be seen to be elements in a good human life anyway, independently of any particular ethic. We need not credit Aristotle with such a monolithic, if comprehensive, conception of reasons for acting in general. In any case reasons for acting in general need be no concern of his when he discusses *eudaimonia*. The concept of *eudaimonia* marks out, rather, just one dimension of practical worthwhileness. Practical worthwhileness in general is multi-dimensional, and the considerations that occupy different dimensions are not necessarily commensurable with one another.[31] The significance of the fact that *eudaimonia* is equated with *the* good is not that all possible reasons for acting (all goods, in one obvious sense: see *NE* 1094a1-3) are embraced under *eudaimonia*, but that worthwhileness along the dimension marked out by the concept of

---

31. See Burnyeat, "Aristotle on Learning to be Good", pp. 86-7, and p. 91, n. 29.

eudaimonia is worthwhileness *par excellence*. The relevant dimension is worthwhileness consisting in reasons for acting that depend on a conception of human virtue (that is the point of the "function" argument). If one's conception of human virtue is the right one (by Aristotle's lights), that will show in one's valuing the right actions as noble; and the value of nobility will be what organizes one's conception of the eudaimonic dimension of practical worthwhileness. It is not that nobility as Aristotle understands it is certified as an authentic value on the basis that a life of noble actions can be seen to meet independent standards for being worth going in for; it is rather that someone who has learned to delight in noble actions has thereby come to see those actions as pre-eminently worth going in for, just because they are noble.[32]

I think the main obstacle to a reading on these lines is the philosophical disappointment I have already discussed. But I shall mention some texts that may seem to raise problems for it.

NE 1097b6–20 says *eudaimonia* is self-sufficient, in the sense that it "on its own makes life pursuit-worthy and lacking in nothing"; this is its conformity to one of the quasi-formal requirements I mentioned for being the good. The passage goes on to say that *eudaimonia* is "most pursuit-worthy not counted in with others; if it were so counted, clearly it would be more pursuit-worthy with the addition of the smallest of goods". To many commentators, this seems to represent *eudaimonia* as embracing anything whose presence would in any way make a life more desirable. But such a reading will not cohere with the fact that Aristotle is unwilling to count gifts of chance, which surely do make a life more desirable, as contributing to *eudaimonia* (see *Politics* 1323b24–9; compare *Eudemian Ethics* 1215a12–19, *NE* 1099b18–25).[33] To make the passage about the self-sufficiency of *eudaimonia* cohere with that, we must anyway take it that not just any desirability is relevant to the claim that *eudaimonia* leaves nothing to be desired. *Eudaimonia* can leave nothing to be desired in the relevant sense, even though it can be true of a life exemplifying *eudaimonia* that the fates could have been kinder. This structural requirement is met if we take it that the dimension

---

32. See Essay 1 above.

33. These citations are from Cooper, *Reason and Human Good in Aristotle*, pp. 123–4; see his discussion there.

along which *eudaimonia* leaves nothing to be desired is the one I have extracted from the "function" argument, that of considerations whose appeal depends on a conception of virtue.[34] As for the rejection of "counting in with others", I think the point is the one I have tried to capture in terms of worthwhileness *par excellence*. The relevant dimension of worthwhileness is such that, if a consideration that belongs to it bears on a practical predicament, anyone who has learned to appreciate such considerations will see that nothing else matters for the question what shape his life should take here and now, even if the upshot is a life that is less desirable along other dimensions. If the upshot is a life that is more desirable along other dimensions, that is a kind of bonus, irrelevant to the self-sufficiency of *eudaimonia*.[35]

NE 1102a2–3 says "it is for the sake of this [*eudaimonia*] that we all do everything else that we do". But Aristotle does not think all purposive behaviour, even of the distinctively intellect-involving human kind, is aimed at *eudaimonia*. This is clear from the case of the calculating incontinent person, who uses his intelligence in purposive behaviour that precisely flies in the face of his conception of *eudaimonia*. (See *NE* 1142b18–20, 1146b22–4.) We had better read 1102a2–3 so as not to contradict that. One way to do so is by finding in it a special, quasi-technical use of words for "doing" (*"praxis", "prattein")*, to be understood precisely in terms of a conceptual link to *eudaimonia*.[36] Read like this, the passage does not represent *eudaimonia* as embracing reasons for acting quite generally.

From *NE* 1098a18–20, it is clear that Aristotle conceives *eudaimonia* as, primarily, an attribute of a whole life. This can encourage the idea that the point an agent sees in an action undertaken for the

---

34. On this view, the relevant dimension of desirability comes clear only after this passage, in the "function" argument itself. This is unsurprising in view of the way Aristotle approaches his favoured framework through dialectical exploitation of common and philosophical ideas. When he claims a correspondence with common sense, we may need the whole development for a full comprehension of what that means.

35. It will be clear that I am not reading Aristotle's conception of the end as inclusive, in the sense of W. F. R. Hardie, "The Final Good in Aristotle's *Ethics*". (But I do not think I am reading it as dominant—Hardie's alternative—either.)

36. Equivalently (on the strength of *NE* 1095a19–20), *eupraxia* (the word is an abstract noun corresponding to the verb phrase "doing well"): for *eupraxia* as the end of *praxis*, see *NE* 1139b1–4, 1140b6–7). There is more discussion of this in Essay 1 above.

sake of *eudaimonia* must be derivative from the independent attractiveness of a life lived according to a certain blueprint.[37] But this idea is anyway hard to make cohere with the thesis that character-revealing action (which reveals character precisely by revealing, because undertaken so as to act out, its agent's conception of doing well) is undertaken for its own sake. That seems to rule out taking the point of such action for the agent to lie outside itself, in the independent attractiveness of a life into which, if all goes well, it will fit. Suppose all does not go well, and one's life does not achieve the projected shape; does that mean that this particular action, say one of standing one's ground in battle, did not after all have the point it seemed to have?[38] Surely not. Of course this does not rule out the possibility that if one's life as a whole goes badly enough, in respect of modes of desirability that are intelligible independently of the worthwhileness of virtuous behaviour, one can lose one's grip on the distinctive point of virtuous behaviour; see perhaps *NE* 1099b2–6.

The links exploited in the "function" argument suggest a different way to take the idea that seeing a particular action as doing well is seeing it under the aspect of a whole human life. Doing well is acting in accordance with virtue, and the question what the human virtues are belongs in the context of reflection on what shape a human life should take. If such reflection is Neurathian, the "should" here need not take us outside the ethical. And this allows us to respect Aristotle's claim that the concept of doing well is in the first instance the concept of a way of life, while holding that when one sees an action as a case of doing well, the point one sees in it need not be independent of the delight one's upbringing has taught one to take in noble actions just as such.[39]

---

37. This may account for Irwin's use of "promote"; see n. 6 above. The primacy of the whole life can render invisible the possibility that when one acts on a particular occasion for the sake of doing well, what one does can *be* (not promote) that for the sake of which one does it.

38. Irwin, *Plato's Moral Theory*, p. 262, responds to this sort of problem by simply separating "for its own sake" from "for the sake of happiness": "Aristotle's virtuous man ... recognizes that part of the life which secures happiness will be virtuous action for its own sake, without caring about happiness." But for Aristotle virtuous action, undertaken for its own sake, is what "happiness" is; he would surely find this separation of concerns ("without caring about happiness") unintelligible. (The translation "happiness" seems seriously damaging here.)

39. Cooper, *Reason and Human Good in Aristotle*, pp. 124–5, sees that *eudaimonia* must *be* (a life of) virtuous action for its own sake, not something "secured by" such ac-

13. We can take the central books of *NE* to spell out a conception of doing well as living in accordance with virtue, comprehensively understood. Book 10 introduces a conception of the highest *eudaimonia* as living in accordance with the highest virtue, the virtue of what is best in human beings (1177a12–13); this is a contemplative life. Such a life engages that in us in respect of which we come closest to the divine. From this point of view, the life of ordinary virtue of character that has seemed to be Aristotle's main topic so far, although it is distinctively human in so far as it involves the intellectual excellence of practical wisdom, can be depreciated as *merely* human; and we have it in us to be more than merely human. With hindsight, we can perhaps find this "intellectualistic" conception of the highest *eudaimonia* alluded to already in the conclusion of the "function" argument; having identified *eudaimonia* with activity in accordance with virtue, Aristotle goes on to say "and if there are several virtues, in accordance with the best and most perfect" (*NE* 1098a17–18).

If we suppose a conception of *eudaimonia* is meant to embrace all potential reasons for acting, and yield a procedure for resolving conflicts between them, this singling out of contemplation is extraordinarily difficult to swallow. We have to take it that all other activity is to be evaluated in terms of conduciveness to contemplation, which makes the picture of book 10 contradict the earlier suggestion that the actions required by the ordinary virtues of character are worth

---

tion (if all goes well). He keeps a role for the idea of an orderly combination of elements independently recognizable to be worth pursuing, not, as in Irwin, as what *eudaimonia* is, but as serving in a confirmation that what Aristotle takes to be virtues are indeed states worth cultivating: virtuous activity for its own sake is what *eudaimonia* is, and it is worth becoming the kind of person who lives like that because such a life is likeliest to be satisfactory by independent standards. This avoids Irwin's idea that going in for virtuous action for its own sake can be simply separated from "caring about" *eudaimonia*, but the supposed external recommendation for cultivating the virtues still strikes me as foreign to Aristotle. And the position seems vulnerable to a version of a standard problem for any indirect consequentialism. Suppose one knows the story about why the virtues are worth cultivating, and knows that the independently recognizable satisfactoriness of life that figures in that story will probably not be achieved by a virtuous action one has in prospect (say because the action in question is facing the enemy in battle, and one will probably be killed or maimed). How can this not tend to undermine one's virtuous motivation? We have no such problems if we simply stop looking for external authentication for virtuous motivation. The only relevant satisfaction is the satisfaction one has learned to take in noble actions as such.

going in for in their own right; alternatively we have to suppose that book 10 presents not just a novel conception of *eudaimonia,* but a novel concept of it.[40] But if we exorcize the idea that a conception of *eudaimonia* is a general conception of practical rationality, we can take the introduction of the contemplative life in our stride. We can see how Aristotle might want to single out, as the highest worthwhileness of the distinctively eudaimonic sort (that is, worthwhileness depending on a conception of virtue), the worthwhileness of exercises of our highest excellence. His identification of what that is does in a way disparage the worthwhileness of acts of ordinary civic ("merely human") virtue. But the worthwhileness of civic virtue can still be genuine (though second-grade), and intrinsic, not derivative from a higher end to which its acts are supposedly conducive. Without needing to explain away the treatment of *eudaimonia* in book 10, as an expression of an inconsistent alternative view, we can avoid letting it disrupt our appreciation of the main body of *NE*, which we naturally find more congenial.

14. No discussion of Aristotle's moral psychology could be complete without mentioning his interest in "incontinence" *(akrasia)*. I cannot give a full treatment here, but the general outlines of an interpretation are implicit in what I have already said.

Practical wisdom is a capacity to discern which of the potentially action-inviting features of a situation is the one that should be allowed to engage with one of the standing concerns of a virtuous person, so as to induce an action. Consider a situation that calls for the most striking sort of exercise of temperance—abstaining from an available but excessive bodily pleasure. That the pleasure is available is a fact about the situation, at the disposal of a temperate person no less than anyone else. Such facts can engage a motivational susceptibility that is one of the standing concerns of a virtuous person. (Too little interest in the pleasures of appetite is a defect of character: see *NE* 3.11.) But on this occasion what matters about the situation, as the practically wise person correctly sees it, is not the opportunity

---

40. There is no sign anywhere in Aristotle of the idea that conduciveness to contemplation is supposed to yield a criterion for the worthwhileness of other activity. On *Eudemian Ethics* 1249a21–b23, which comes closer to this than anything else, see Cooper, *Reason and Human Good in Aristotle*, pp. 135–43.

for pleasure but, say, the fact that this would be his fifth doughnut at one sitting. The practically wise person registers, but counts as irrelevant to the question what to do, an instance of a kind of consideration (that pleasure is available) that does bear on that question in other circumstances. His counting it as irrelevant shows in his being unmoved by it, by contrast with the merely continent person (the *enkratēs*), who has to overcome temptation in order to get himself to do the right thing (see *NE* 1151b34–1152a3).

This makes it obvious why Aristotle should have a problem over the possibility of incontinence (at any rate the variety distinguished at *NE* 1150b19–22 as weakness). As we intuitively picture him, a weak person's practical thinking matches that of a practically wise person (he knows what he should do), but he succumbs to temptation and acts differently. But a practically wise person sees the potential temptations in temperance-requiring predicaments as practically irrelevant, and this conception of their status prevents them from actually tempting him. (If they actually tempted him, his best prospect would be continence.) There cannot be both a perfect match with the practical thinking of a fully virtuous person and a felt temptation to do otherwise. (It does not matter whether the felt temptation is acted on or not; continence poses the same conceptual difficulty.)

If we discount simply denying the existence of weakness, the shape of a resolution for this difficulty is virtually dictated by the shape of the difficulty. The match with the practical thinking of a practically wise person has to be imperfect. In the operation of full-fledged practical wisdom, the agent singles out just the right one of the potentially action-inviting features of a predicament, in such a way that all his motivational energy is concentrated into the concern to which that feature appeals. He has no errant impulses that might threaten to lead him astray, so that he would be at best continent even if he managed not to be sidetracked. The closest we can get to this, while allowing errant impulses to arise, is a flawed approximation to the special perceptual capacity that is practical wisdom—something capable of yielding a similar selection of what matters about the situation, but without the singleness of motivational focus on that feature of the situation that practical wisdom would achieve. I believe we can find an idea on these lines in *NE* 7.3.

It is important to realize that Aristotle's problem about incontinence is a problem about acting otherwise than, as one (in a way) realizes, doing well requires. *Eudaimonia* is, as I have insisted, just one dimension of practical worthwhileness, although those who appreciate it take it, rightly, to be pre-eminent over others; it is not a balance in which all potential reasons for acting are somehow combined. This means that Aristotle's difficulty over incontinence does not reflect an unwarranted expectation that practical exercises of intelligence *in general* should progress inexorably into action, so that there would be no room for breakdowns and no need for executive virtues to ensure that one sticks to one's decisions. (Such a general expectation is often attributed to Socrates, wrongly in my view.) Aristotle has specific reasons for supposing that a properly focused application to a situation of a correct conception of doing well, in particular, must issue in action; that idea, which dictates his attitude to incontinence, reflects no general dogma of the efficacy of the intellect.[41]

In full-fledged practical wisdom the correct conception of doing well, with the understanding that the worthwhileness that it embraces is pre-eminent, is so ingrained into one's motivational make-up that when an action is singled out as doing well, any attractions that alternatives might have are seen as having no bearing on the question what to do. An incontinent or continent person has a flawed approximation to practical wisdom. He has, in a way, a correct conception of doing well, and applies that conception to particular predicaments; but he reveals that his resemblance to a possessor of full-fledged practical wisdom is only partial, by the fact that he is swayed by the attractions of alternatives to what he (in a way) knows to be doing well. It helps to make this idea of a flawed approximation to practical wisdom intelligible if we take continence

---

41. These remarks are directed against the way Wiggins, in "Weakness of Will, Commensurability, and the Objects of Deliberation and Desire", deplores what Aristotle says about incontinence as excessively "Socratic". Wiggins's account of what Aristotle should have said instead relates to the progression of thought in general into action. As far as I can see, nothing in Aristotle prevents him from taking Wiggins's view of that topic, consistently with being as "Socratic" as he is about the efficacy of practical wisdom in particular. (Wiggins also suggests that the view I am urging requires a cognitive or perceptual difference between a continent person and an incontinent person, but that is a misunderstanding. The perceptual difference I envisage is between a virtuous person on the one side and, indifferently, a continent or incontinent person on the other. This leaves it open what determines whether someone who is tempted away from the course of virtue, thereby showing that he does not fully share a virtuous person's view of his situation, acts on the temptation or not.)

and incontinence to characterize people who are on their way to acquiring virtue. There are genuine attractions in some courses of action that virtue requires us to renounce, and the renunciation is not compensated in kind by the course of virtue.[42] So it is only to be expected that there should be stages of moral development at which an appreciation, of sorts, of virtue's requirements, and even of their status as pre-eminent, does not yet have its full motivational realization, the capacity to be unmoved by competing attractions.

Apart from the intrinsic interest of the conceptual puzzle about its possibility, then, we can attribute to incontinence a more systematic significance in Aristotle's exposition of his moral psychology: by reflecting on the nature of the flaw in incontinence (or continence), we can be helped to understand what these states fall short of, the intimate integration of conceptual thought and moulded inclination that makes up full-fledged virtue of character as Aristotle pictures it.[43]

42. See Wiggins, "Weakness of Will, Incommensurability, and the Objects of Deliberation and Desire".
43. See Burnyeat, "Aristotle on Learning to be Good".

ESSAY 3

Virtue and Reason

1. Presumably the point of, say, inculcating a moral outlook lies in a concern with how people live. It may seem that the very idea of a moral outlook makes room for, and requires, the existence of moral theory, conceived as a discipline that seeks to formulate acceptable principles of conduct. It is then natural to think of ethics as a branch of philosophy related to moral theory, so conceived, rather as the philosophy of science is related to science. On this view, the primary topic of ethics is the concept of right conduct, and the nature and justification of principles of behaviour. If there is a place for an interest in the concept of virtue, it is a secondary place. Virtue is a disposition (perhaps of a specially rational and self-conscious kind) to behave rightly; the nature of virtue is explained, as it were, from the outside in.

My aim is to sketch the outlines of a different view, to be found in the philosophical tradition that flowers in Aristotle's ethics. According to this different view, although the point of engaging in ethical reflection still lies in the interest of the question "How should one live?",[1] that question is necessarily approached via the notion of a virtuous person. A conception of right conduct is grasped, as it were, from the inside out.

2. I shall begin with some considerations that make it attractive to say, with Socrates, that virtue is knowledge.

---

[1] Aristotle, *Nicomachean Ethics*, e.g. 1103b26–31; compare Plato, *Republic*, 352d5–6.

What is it for someone to possess a virtue? "Knowledge" implies that he gets things right; if we are to go any distance towards finding plausibility in the Socratic thesis, it is necessary to start with examples whose status as virtues, and hence as states of character whose possessor arrives at right answers to a certain range of questions about how to behave, is not likely to be queried. I shall use the example of kindness; anyone who disputes its claim to be a virtue should substitute a better example of his own. (The objectivity that "knowledge" implies will recur later.)

A kind person can be relied on to behave kindly when that is what the situation requires. Moreover, his reliably kind behaviour is not the outcome of a blind, non-rational habit or instinct, like the courageous behaviour—so called only by courtesy—of a lioness defending her cubs.[2] Rather, that the situation requires a certain sort of behaviour is (one way of formulating) his reason for behaving in that way, on each of the relevant occasions. So it must be something of which, on each of the relevant occasions, he is aware. A kind person has a reliable sensitivity to a certain sort of requirement that situations impose on behaviour. The deliverances of a reliable sensitivity are cases of knowledge; and there are idioms according to which the sensitivity itself can appropriately be described as knowledge: a kind person knows what it is like to be confronted with a requirement of kindness. The sensitivity is, we might say, a sort of perceptual capacity.[3]

(Of course a kind person need not himself classify the behaviour he sees to be called for, on one of the relevant occasions, as kind. He need not be articulate enough to possess concepts of the particular virtues; and even if he does, the concepts need not enter his reasons for the actions that manifest those particular virtues. It is enough if he thinks of what he does, when—as we put it—he shows himself to be kind, under some such description as "the thing to do". The description need not differ from that under which he thinks of other actions of his, which we regard as manifesting different virtues; the division into actions that manifest kindness and actions that manifest other virtues can be imposed, not by the agent himself, but by a possibly more articulate, and more theoretically oriented, observer.)

---

2. Compare *Nicomachean Ethics* 6.13, on the distinction between "natural virtue" and "virtue strictly so called".

3. I shall consider non-cognitivist objections to this sort of talk later.

The considerations I have adduced so far suggest that the knowledge constituted by the reliable sensitivity is a necessary condition for possession of the virtue. But they do not show that the knowledge is, as in the Socratic thesis, to be identified with the virtue. A preliminary case for the identification might go as follows. On each of the relevant occasions, the requirement imposed by the situation, and detected by the agent's sensitivity to such requirements, must exhaust his reason for acting as he does. It would disqualify an action from counting as a manifestation of kindness if its agent needed some extraneous incentive to comply with the requirement—say, the rewards of a good reputation. So the deliverances of his sensitivity constitute, one by one, complete explanations of the actions that manifest the virtue. Hence, since the sensitivity fully accounts for its deliverances, the sensitivity fully accounts for the actions. But the concept of the virtue is the concept of a state whose possession accounts for the actions that manifest it. Since that explanatory role is filled by the sensitivity, the sensitivity turns out to be what the virtue is.[4]

That is a preliminary case for the identification of particular virtues with, as it were, specialized sensitivities to requirements. *Mutatis mutandis*, a similar argument applies to virtue in general. Indeed, in the context of another Socratic thesis, that of the unity of virtue, virtue in general is what the argument for identification with knowledge really concerns; the specialized sensitivities that are to be equated with particular virtues, according to the argument I have considered so far, are actually not available one by one for a series of separate identifications.

What makes this plausible is the attractive idea that a virtue issues in nothing but right conduct. Suppose the relevant range of behav-

---

4. There is a gap here. Even if it is conceded that the virtuous person has no further *reason* for what he does than the deliverance of his sensitivity, still, it may be said, two people can have the same reason for acting in a certain way even though only one of them acts in that way. There must then be some further explanation of the difference between them: if not that the one who acts has some further reason, then perhaps that the one who does not is in some state, standing or temporary, that undermines the efficacy of reasons, or perhaps of reasons of the particular kind in question, in producing action. This suggests that if we are to think of virtue as guaranteeing action, virtue must consist not in the sensitivity alone but in the sensitivity together with freedom from such obstructive states. These issues will recur in §3 below.

iour, in the case of kindness, is marked out by the notion of proper attentiveness to others' feelings. Now sometimes acting in such a way as to indulge someone's feelings is not acting rightly: the morally important fact about the situation is not that A will be upset by a projected action (though he will), but, say, that B has a right—a consideration of a sort sensitivity to which might be thought of as constituting fairness. In such a case, a straightforward propensity to be gentle to others' feelings would not lead to right conduct. If a genuine virtue is to produce nothing but right conduct, a simple propensity to be gentle cannot be identified with the virtue of kindness. Possession of the virtue must involve not only sensitivity to facts about others' feelings as reasons for acting in certain ways, but also sensitivity to facts about rights as reasons for acting in certain ways; and when circumstances of both sorts obtain, and a circumstance of the second sort is the one that should be acted on, a possessor of the virtue of kindness must be able to tell that that is so.[5] So we cannot disentangle genuine possession of kindness from the sensitivity that constitutes fairness. And since there are obviously no limits on the possibilities for compresence, in the same situation, of circumstances of the sorts proper sensitivities to which constitute all the virtues, the argument can be generalized: no one virtue can be fully possessed except by a possessor of all of them, that is, a possessor of virtue in general. Thus the particular virtues are not a batch of independent sensitivities. Rather, we use the concepts of the particular virtues to mark similarities and dissimilarities among the manifestations of a single sensitivity, which is what virtue, in general, is: an ability to recognize requirements that situations impose on one's behaviour. It is a single complex sensitivity of this sort that we are aiming to instil when we aim to inculcate a moral outlook.

3. There is an apparent obstacle to the identification of virtue with knowledge. The argument for the identification requires that the deliverances of the sensitivity—the particular pieces of knowledge with

---

5. I do not mean to suggest that there is always a way of acting satisfactorily (as opposed to making the best of a bad job); nor that there is always one right answer to the question what one should do. But when there is a right answer, a virtuous person should be able to tell what it is.

which it equips its possessor—should fully explain the actions that manifest virtue. But it is plausible that appropriate action need not be elicited by a consideration apprehended as a reason—even a conclusive reason—for acting in a certain way. That may seem to open the following possibility: a person's perception of a situation may precisely match what a virtuous person's perception of it would be, although he does not act as the virtuous person would. But if a perception that corresponds to the virtuous person's does not call forth a virtuous action from this non-virtuous person, then the virtuous person's matching perception—the deliverance of his sensitivity—cannot, after all, fully account for the virtuous action that it does elicit from him. Whatever is missing, in the case of the person who does not act virtuously, must be present as an extra component, over and above the deliverance of the sensitivity, in a complete specification of the reason why the virtuous person acts as he does.[6] This destroys the identification of virtue with the sensitivity. According to this line of argument, the sensitivity can be at most an ingredient in a composite state, which is what virtue really is.

If we are to retain the identification of virtue with knowledge, then, by contraposition, we are committed to denying that a virtuous person's perception of a situation can be precisely matched in someone who, in that situation, acts otherwise than virtuously. Socrates seems to have supposed that the only way to embrace this commitment is in terms of ignorance, so that, paradoxically, failure to act as a virtuous person would cannot be voluntary, at least under that description. But there is a less extreme possibility, sketched by Aristotle.[7] This is to allow that someone who fails to act virtuously may, in a way, perceive what a virtuous person would, so that his failure to do the right thing is not inadvertent; but to insist that his failure occurs only because his appreciation of what he perceives is clouded, or unfocused, by the impact of a desire to do otherwise. This preserves the identification of virtue with a sensitivity; contrary to the counter-argument, nothing over and above the unclouded deliverances of the sensitivity is needed to explain the actions that manifest virtue. It is not that some extra explanatory factor, over and above

---

6. If we distinguish the reason why he acts from his reason for acting, this is the objection of n. 4 above.
7. *Nicomachean Ethics* 7.3.

the deliverances of the sensitivity, conspires with them to elicit action from the virtuous person, but rather that the other person's failure to act in that way is accounted for by a defectiveness in the approximations to those deliverances that he has.

It would be a mistake to protest that one can fail to act on a reason, and even on a reason judged by oneself to be better than any reason one has for acting otherwise, without there needing to be any clouding or distortion in one's appreciation of the reason one flouts.[8] That is true; but to suppose it constitutes an objection to Aristotle is to fail to understand the special nature of the conception of virtue that generates Aristotle's interest in incontinence.

One way to bring out the special nature of the conception is to note that, for Aristotle, continence is distinct from virtue, and just as problematic as incontinence. If someone needs to overcome an inclination to act otherwise, in getting himself to act as, say, temperance or courage demand, then he shows not virtue but (mere) continence. Suppose we take it that a virtuous person's judgement as to what he should do is arrived at by weighing, on the one side, some reason for acting in a way that will in fact manifest, say, courage, and, on the other side, a reason for doing something else (say a risk to life and limb, as a reason for running away), and deciding that on balance the former reason is the better. In that case, the distinction between virtue and continence will seem unintelligible. If the virtuous person allows himself to weigh the present danger, as a reason for running away, why should we not picture the weighing as his allowing himself to feel an inclination to run away, of a strength proportional to the weight he allows to the reason? So long as he keeps the strength of his inclinations in line with the weight he assigns to the reasons, his actions will conform to his judgement as to where, on balance, the better reason lies; what more can we require for virtue? (Perhaps that the genuinely courageous person simply does not care about his own survival? But Aristotle is rightly anxious to avert this misconception.)[9] The distinction becomes intelligible if we stop assuming that the virtuous person's judgement is a result of balancing reasons for and against. The view of a situation that he arrives at by exercising his sensitivity is one in which some aspect of the situation is seen

---

8. Compare Donald Davidson, "How is Weakness of Will Possible?"
9. *Nicomachean Ethics* 3.9.

as constituting a reason for acting in some way; this reason is apprehended, not as outweighing or overriding any reasons for acting in other ways, which would otherwise be constituted by other aspects of the situation (the present danger, say), but as silencing them. Here and now the risk to life and limb is not seen as any reason for removing himself. Aristotle's problem about incontinence is not "How can one weigh considerations in favour of actions X and Y, decide that on balance the better reasons are in favour of X, but nevertheless perform Y?" (a question that, no doubt, does not require the idea of clouded judgement for its answer); but rather (a problem equally about continence) "How can one have a view of a situation in which considerations that would otherwise appeal to one's will are silenced, but nevertheless allow those considerations to make themselves heard by one's will?"—a question that clearly is answerable, if at all, only by supposing that the incontinent or continent person does not fully share the virtuous person's perception of the situation.[10]

A more pressing objection is one directed against the special conception of virtue itself: in particular, my use of cognitive notions in characterizing it. According to this objection, it must be a misuse of the notion of perception to suppose that an unclouded perception might suffice, on its own, to constitute a reason for acting in a certain way. An exercise of a genuinely cognitive capacity can yield at most part of a reason for acting; something appetitive is needed as well. To talk of virtue—a propensity to act in certain ways for certain reasons—as consisting in a sensitivity, a perceptual capacity, is to amalgamate the required appetitive component into the putative sensitivity. But all that is achieved thereby is a projection of human purposes into the world. (Here it becomes apparent how the objection touches on the issue of objectivity.) How one's will is disposed

---

10. On this view, genuine deliverances of the sensitivity involved in virtue would necessitate action. It is not that action requires not only a deliverance of the sensitivity but also, say, freedom from possibly obstructive factors, for instance distracting desires. An obstructive factor would not interfere with the efficacy of a deliverance of the sensitivity, but rather preclude genuine achievement of that view of the situation. This fills the gap that I mentioned in n. 4 above. (My discussion of incontinence here is meant to do no more than suggest that the identification of virtue with knowledge should not be dismissed out of hand, on the ground that it poses a problem about incontinence. I say a little more in §§9 and 10 of Essay 4 below. But a great deal more would be needed in a full treatment.)

is a fact about oneself; whereas a genuinely cognitive faculty discloses to one how the world is independently of oneself, and in particular independently of one's will. Cognition and volition are distinct: the world—the proper sphere of cognitive capacities—is in itself an object of purely theoretical contemplation, capable of moving one to action only in conjunction with an extra factor—a state of will—contributed by oneself. I shall return to this objection.

4. Presented with an identification of virtue with knowledge, it is natural to ask for a formulation of the knowledge that virtue is. We tend to assume that the knowledge must have a stateable propositional content (perhaps not capable of immediate expression by the knower). Then the virtuous person's reliably right judgements as to what he should do, occasion by occasion, can be explained in terms of interaction between this universal knowledge and some appropriate piece of particular knowledge about the situation at hand; and the explanation can take the form of a "practical syllogism", with the content of the universal knowledge, or some suitable part of it, as major premise, the relevant particular knowledge as minor premise, and the judgement about what is to be done as deductive conclusion.

This picture is congenial to the objection that I mentioned at the end of §3. According to this picture, the problematic concept of a requirement figures only in the major premise, and the conclusion, of the syllogism that reconstructs the virtuous person's reason for acting. Knowledge of the major premise, the objector might say, is none other than the disposition of the will that is required, according to the objection, as a further component in the relevant reasons for acting, and hence as a further component in virtue, over and above any strictly cognitive state. (We call it "knowledge" to endorse it, not to indicate that it is genuinely cognitive.) What a virtuous person really perceives is only what is stated in the minor premise of the syllogism: that is, a straightforward fact about the situation at hand, which—as the objection requires—would be incapable of eliciting action on its own.

This picture fits only if the virtuous person's views about how, in general, one should behave are susceptible of codification, in principles apt for serving as major premises in syllogisms of the sort envisaged. But to an unprejudiced eye it should seem quite implausible that any reasonably adult moral outlook admits of any such codification. As Aristotle consistently says, the best generalizations about how one should behave hold only for the most part.[11] If one attempted to reduce one's conception of what virtue requires to a set of rules, then, however subtle and thoughtful one was in drawing up the code, cases would inevitably turn up in which a mechanical application of the rules would strike one as wrong—and not necessarily because one had changed one's mind; rather, one's mind on the matter was not susceptible of capture in any universal formula.[12]

A deep-rooted prejudice about rationality blocks ready acceptance of this. A moral outlook is a specific determination of one's practical rationality: it shapes one's views about what reasons one has for acting. Rationality requires consistency; a specific conception of rationality in a particular area imposes a specific form on the abstract requirement of consistency—a specific view of what counts as going on doing the same thing here. The prejudice is the idea that acting in the light of a specific conception of rationality must be explicable in terms of being guided by a formulable universal principle. This prejudice comes under radical attack in Wittgenstein's discussion, in *Philosophical Investigations,* of the concept of following a rule.

Consider an exercise of rationality in which there *is* a formulable rule, of which each successive action can be regarded as an application, appropriate in the circumstances arrived at: say (Wittgenstein's example) extending a series of numbers. We tend to picture understanding the instruction "Add 2"—command of the rule for extending the series 2,4,6,8, . . .—as a psychological mechanism that, aside from lapses of attention and so forth, churns out the appropriate behaviour with the sort of reliability that a physical mechanism, say a piece of clockwork, might have. If someone is extending the series correctly, and one takes his behaviour to be compliance with the understood instruction, then, according to this picture, one has postulated such a psychological mechanism, underlying his behaviour, by an inference analogous to that whereby one might hypothesize a physical structure underlying the observable motions of some inanimate object. But this picture is profoundly suspect.

---

11. See, e.g., *Nicomachean Ethics* 1.3.
12. See *Nicomachean Ethics* 5.10, especially 1137b19–24.

What manifests the pictured state of understanding? Suppose the person says, when asked what he is doing, "Look, I'm adding 2 each time". This apparent manifestation of understanding (or any other) will have been accompanied, at any point, by at most a finite fragment of the potentially infinite range of behaviour that we want to say the rule dictates. Thus the evidence for the presence of the pictured state is always compatible with supposing that, on some future occasion for its exercise, the behaviour elicited by the occasion will diverge from what we would count as correct. Wittgenstein dramatizes this with the example of the person who continues the series, after 1000, with 1004, 1008, ...[13] If a possibility of the 1004, 1008, . . . type were to be realized (and we could not bring the person to concede that he had simply made a mistake), that would show that the behaviour hitherto was not guided by the psychological conformation that we were picturing as guiding it. The pictured state, then, always transcends the grounds on which it is allegedly postulated.

There may be an inclination to protest: "This is merely inductive scepticism about other minds. After all, one knows in one's own case that one's behaviour will not come adrift like that." But this misses the point of the argument.

First, if what it is for one's behaviour to come adrift is for it suddenly to seem that everyone else is out of step, then clearly the argument bears on one's own case just as much as on the case of others. (Imagine that the person who goes on with 1004, 1008, . . . had said, in advance, "I know in my own case that my behaviour will not come adrift".)

Second, it is a mistake to interpret the argument as making a sceptical point: that one does not know, in the case of another person (or in one's own case either, once we have made the first correction), that the behaviour will not come adrift. The argument is not meant to suggest that we should be in a state of constant trepidation lest possibilities of the 1004, 1008, . . . type be realized.[14] We are confident that they will not: the argument aims, not at all to undermine

---

13. *Philosophical Investigations* §185.
14. Nor even that we really *understand* the supposition that such a thing might happen. See Barry Stroud, "Wittgenstein and Logical Necessity".

this confidence, but to change our conception of its ground and nature. We tend to picture our transition to this confident expectation, from such grounds as we have, as being mediated by the postulated psychological mechanism. But we can no more find the putatively mediating state manifested in the grounds for our expectation than we can find manifested there the very future occurrences we expect. Postulating the mediating state is an idle intervening step; it does nothing to underwrite the confidence of the expectation.

(The content of the expectation is not purely behavioural. We might have a good scientific argument, mediated by postulation of a physiological mechanism, for not expecting any particular train of behaviour, of the 1004, 1008, . . . type, that we might contemplate. Here postulating the mediating physiological state would not be an idle intervening step. But the parallel is misleading. We can bring this out by considering a variant of Wittgenstein's example, in which, on reaching 1000, the person goes on as we expect, with 1002, 1004, . . . , but with a sense of dissociation from what he is doing. What he does no longer strikes him as going on in the same way; it feels as if a sheer habit has usurped his reason in controlling his behaviour. We confidently expect that this sort of thing will not happen; once again, postulating a psychological mechanism does nothing to underwrite this confidence.)

What *is* the ground and nature of our confidence? About the competent use of words, Stanley Cavell writes:

> We learn and teach words in certain contexts, and then we are expected, and expect others, to be able to project them into further contexts. Nothing insures that this projection will take place (in particular, not the grasping of universals nor the grasping of books of rules), just as nothing insures that we will make, and understand, the same projections. That on the whole we do is a matter of our sharing routes of interest and feeling, modes of response, senses of humor and of significance and of fulfilment, of what is outrageous, of what is similar to what else, what a rebuke, what forgiveness, of when an utterance is an assertion, when an appeal, when an explanation—all the whirl of organism Wittgenstein calls "forms of life." Human speech and activity, sanity and community, rest upon nothing more, but nothing less, than this. It is a vision as simple as it is difficult, and as difficult as it is (and because it is) terrifying.[15]

---

15. *Must We Mean What We Say?*, p. 52.

The terror of which Cavell speaks at the end of this marvellous passage is a sort of vertigo, induced by the thought that there is nothing but shared forms of life to keep us, as it were, on the rails. We are inclined to think that is an insufficient foundation for a conviction that when we, say, extend a number series, we really are, at each stage, doing the same thing as before. In this mood, it seems to us that what Cavell describes cannot be a shared conceptual framework within which something is, given the circumstances, objectively the correct move;[16] it looks, rather, like a congruence of subjectivities, with the congruence not grounded as it would need to be to amount to an objectivity. So we feel we have lost the objectivity of (in our case) mathematics (and similarly in other cases). We recoil from this vertigo into the idea that we are kept on the rails by our grasp of rules. This idea has a pair of twin components: first, the idea (as above) that grasp of the rules is a psychological mechanism that (apart from mechanical failure, which is how we picture mistakes and so forth) guarantees that we stay in the straight and narrow; and, second, the idea that the rails—what we engage our mental wheels with when we come to grasp the rules—are objectively there, in a way that transcends the "mere" sharing of forms of life (hence, for instance, platonism about numbers). This composite idea is not the perception of a truth, but a consoling myth, elicited from us by our inability to endure the vertigo.

Of course, this casts no doubt on the fact that we can put explanations of particular moves, in the extending of a number series, in a syllogistic form: universal knowledge of how to extend the series interacts with particular knowledge of where one is in it, to produce a non-accidentally correct judgement as to what the next number is. In this case we can formulate the explanation so as to confer on the judgement explained the compellingness possessed by the conclusion of a proof. What is wrong is to take that fact to indicate that the explanation lays bare the inexorable workings of a machine: something whose operations, with our understanding of them, would not depend on the deliverances, in particular cases, of (for instance, and

---

16. Locating the desired objectivity *within* the conceptual framework is intended to leave open, here, the possibility of querying whether the conceptual framework itself is objectively the right one. If someone wants to reject the question whether this rather than that moral outlook is objectively correct, he will still want it to be an objective matter whether one has, say, succeeded in inculcating a particular moral outlook in someone else; so he will still be susceptible to the vertigo I am describing.

centrally) that shared sense of what is similar to what else that Cavell mentions. The truth is that it is only because of our own involvement in our "whirl of organism" that we can understand the words we produce as conferring that special compellingness on the judgement explained.

Now it is only this misconception of the deductive paradigm that leads us to suppose that the operations of any specific conception of rationality in a particular area—any specific conception of what counts as doing the same thing—must be deductively explicable; that is, that there must be a formulable universal principle suited to serve as major premise in syllogistic explanations of the sort I considered above.

Consider, for instance, a concept whose application gives rise to hard cases, in this sense: there are disagreements that resist resolution by argument, as to whether or not the concept applies. Convinced that one is in the right on a hard case, one will find oneself saying, as one's arguments tail off without securing assent, "You simply aren't seeing it", or "But don't you see?" In such cases the prejudice takes the form of a dilemma. One horn is that the inconclusiveness of one's arguments stems merely from an inability, in principle remediable, to articulate what one knows. It is possible, in principle, to spell out a universal formula that specifies the conditions under which the concept, in the use of it that one has mastered, is correctly applied. That would elevate one's argument to deductiveness. (If one's opponent refused to accept the deductive argument's major premise, that would show that he had not mastered the same use of the concept, so that there would be, after all, no substantive disagreement.) If this assimilation to the deductive paradigm is not possible, then—this is the other horn of the dilemma—one's conviction that one is genuinely making a correct application of a concept (genuinely going on in the same way as before) must be an illusion. The case is revealed as one that calls, not for finding (seeing) the right answer to a question about how things are, but (perhaps) for a creative decision as to what to say.[17] Thus: either the case is not really a hard case, since sufficient ingenuity in the construction of ar-

---

17. Why not abandon the whole practice as fraudulent? In some cases something may need to be said: for instance by a judge, in a lawsuit. Against the view that in legal hard cases judges are free to *make* the law, see Ronald Dworkin, "Hard Cases".

guments will resolve it; or, if its hardness is ineliminable, that shows that the issue cannot, after all, be one about whether an application of a concept is correct.

In a hard case, the issue turns on that appreciation of the particular instance whose absence is deplored, in "You simply aren't seeing it", or that is unsuccessfully appealed to, in "But don't you see?" The dilemma reflects the view that a putative judgement that is grounded in nothing firmer than that cannot really be going on in the same way as before. This is an avoidance of vertigo. The thought is: there is not enough there to constitute the rails on which a genuine series of consistent applications of a concept must run. But in fact it is an illusion to suppose that the first horn of the dilemma yields a way of preserving from risk of vertigo the conviction that we are dealing with genuine concept-application. The illusion is the misconception of the deductive paradigm: the idea that deductive explicability characterizes an exercise of reason in which it is, as it were, automatically compelling, without dependence on our partially shared "whirl of organism". The dilemma registers a refusal to accept that when the dependence that induces vertigo is out in the open, in the appeal to appreciation, we can genuinely be going on in the same way; but the paradigm of a genuine case, that with which the rejected case is unfavourably compared, has the same dependence, only less obviously.[18]

Contemplating the dependence should not induce vertigo at all. We cannot be whole-heartedly engaged in the relevant parts of the "whirl of organism", and at the same time achieve the detachment necessary in order to query whether our unreflective view of what we are doing is illusory. The cure for the vertigo, then, is to give up the idea that philosophical thought, about the sorts of practice in question, should be undertaken at some external standpoint, outside our immersion in our familiar forms of life.[19] If this cure works where explanations of exercises of rationality conform to the deductive paradigm, it should be no less efficacious where we explicitly appeal to

---

18. In the rejected case, the dependence is out in the open in an especially perturbing form, in that the occasional failure of the appeal to appreciation brings out how the "whirl of organism" is only partly shared; whereas there are no hard cases in mathematics. This is indeed a significant fact about mathematics. But its significance is not that mathematics is immune from the dependence.

19. I am not suggesting that effecting this cure is a simple matter.

appreciation of the particular instance in inviting acceptance of our judgments. And its efficacy in cases of the second kind is direct. Only the illusion that the deductive cases are immune can make it seem that, in order to effect the cure in cases of the second kind, we must first eliminate explicit dependence on appreciation, by assimilating them, as the prejudice requires, to the deductive paradigm.

If we make the assimilation, we adopt a position in which it is especially clear that our picture of a psychological mechanism, underlying a series of exercises of rationality, is a picture of something that transcends the grounds on which it is ascribed to anyone. In the cases in question, no one can express the envisaged universal formula. This transcendence poses difficulties about the acquisition of the pictured state. We are inclined to be impressed by the sparseness of the teaching that leaves someone capable of autonomously going on in the same way. All that happens is that the pupil is told, or shown, what to do in a few instances, with some surrounding talk about why that is the thing to do; the surrounding talk, *ex hypothesi* given that we are dealing with a case of the second kind, falls short of including actual enunciation of a universal principle, mechanical application of which would constitute correct behaviour in the practice in question. Yet pupils do acquire a capacity to go on, without further advice, to novel instances. Impressed by the sparseness of the teaching, we find this remarkable. But assimilation to the deductive paradigm leaves it no less remarkable. The assimilation replaces the question "How is it that the pupil, given that sparse instruction, goes on to new instances in the right way?" with the question "How is it that the pupil, given that sparse instruction, divines from it a universal formula with the right deductive powers?" The second question is, if anything, less tractable. Addressing the first, we can say: it is a fact (no doubt a remarkable fact) that, against a background of common human nature and shared forms of life, one's sensitivities to kinds of similarities between situations can be altered and enriched by just this sort of instruction. This attributes no guesswork to the learner; whereas no amount of appealing to common human nature and shared forms of life will free the second question from its presupposition—inevitably imported by assimilation to the deductive—that the learner is required to make a leap of divination.[20]

20. See Wittgenstein, *Philosophical Investigations*, e.g. §210.

It is not to be supposed that the appreciation of the particular instance that is explicitly appealed to in the second kind of case is a straightforward or easy attainment on the part of those who have it; that either, on casual contemplation of an instance, one sees it in the right light, or else one does not, and is then unreachable by argument. First, "Don't you see?" can often be supplemented with words aimed at persuasion. A skilfully presented characterization of an instance will sometimes bring someone to see it as one wants; or one can adduce general considerations, for instance about the point of the concept a particular application of which is in dispute. Given that the case is one of the second kind, any such arguments will fall short of rationally necessitating acceptance of their conclusion in the way a proof does.[21] But it is only the prejudice I am attacking that makes this seem to cast doubt on their status as arguments: that is, appeals to reason. Second, if effort can induce the needed appreciation in someone else, it can also take effort to acquire it oneself. Admitting the dependence on appreciation does not imply that, if someone has the sort of specific determination of rationality we are considering, the right way to handle a given situation will always be clear to him on unreflective inspection of it.

5. If we resist the prejudice, and respect Aristotle's belief that a view of how one should live is not codifiable, what happens to our explanations of a virtuous person's reliably right judgements as to what he should do on particular occasions? Aristotle's notion of the practical syllogism is obviously meant to apply here; we need to consider how.

The explanations, so far treated as explanations of judgements about what to do, are equally explanations of actions. The point of analogy that motivates the quasi-logical label "practical syllogism" is this. If something might serve as an argument for a theoretical conclusion, then it can equally figure in an account of someone's reasons for believing that conclusion, with the premises of the argument giving the content of the psychological states—beliefs, in the theoretical case—that we cite in the reason-giving explanation. Now actions too are explained by reasons; that is, by citing psychological states in the

---

21. If general considerations recommend a universal formula, it will employ terms that themselves give rise to hard cases.

light of which we can see how acting in the way explained would have struck the agent as in some way rational. The idea of a practical syllogism is the idea of an argument-like schema for explanations of actions, with the "premises", as in the theoretical case, giving the content of the psychological states cited in the explanation.[22]

David Wiggins has given this account of the general shape of a practical syllogism:

> The first or major premise mentions something that can be the subject of desire, *orexis,* transmissible to some practical conclusion (i.e., a desire convertible via some available minor premise into action). The second premise details a circumstance pertaining to the feasibility, in the particular situation to which the syllogism is applied, of what must be done if the claim of the major premise is to be heeded.[23]

This schema fits most straightforwardly when reasons are (in a broad sense) technical: the major premise specifies a determinate goal, and the minor premise marks out some action as a means to it.[24]

The role played by the major premise, in these straightforward applications of the schema, is to give the content of an orectic psychological state: something we might conceive as providing the motivating energy for the actions explained. Aristotle's idea seems to be that what fills an analogous role in the explanation of virtuous actions is the virtuous person's conception of the sort of life a human being

---

22. I distinguish practical reason from practical reasoning. From *Nicomachean Ethics* 1105a28–33, with 1111a15–16, it might seem that virtuous action, in Aristotle's view, must be the outcome of reasoning. But this doctrine is both incredible in itself and inconsistent with 1117a17–22. So I construe Aristotle's discussion of deliberation as aimed at the reconstruction of reasons for action not necessarily thought out in advance; where they were not thought out in advance, the concept of deliberation applies in an "as if" style. See John M. Cooper, *Reason and Human Good in Aristotle,* pp. 5–10. (It will be apparent that what I say about Aristotle's views on practical reason runs counter to Cooper's interpretation at many points. I am less concerned here with what Aristotle actually thought than with certain philosophical issues; so I have not encumbered this paper with scholarly controversy.)

23. David Wiggins, "Deliberation and Practical Reason", p. 227. The passage I have quoted is an explanation of Aristotle, *De Motu Animalium* 701a9 and ff. My debt to Wiggins's paper will be apparent.

24. There is an inclination to insist on the only, or the best, means. But this is the outcome of a suspect desire to have instances of the schema that *prove* that the action explained is the thing to do.

should lead.²⁵ If that conception were codifiable in universal principles, the explanations would take the deductive shape that is insisted on by the prejudice I discussed in §4. But the thesis of uncodifiability means that the envisaged major premise, in a virtue syllogism, cannot be definitively written down.²⁶ Any attempt to capture it in words will recapitulate the character of the teaching whereby it might be instilled: generalizations will be approximate at best, and examples will need to be taken with the sort of "and so on" that appeals to the co-operation of a hearer who has cottoned on.²⁷

If someone guides his life by a certain conception of how to live, then he acts, on particular occasions, so as to fulfil suitable concerns.²⁸ A concern can mesh with a noticed fact about a situation, so as to account for an action: as, for instance, a concern for the welfare of one's friends, together with awareness that a friend is in trouble and open to being comforted, can explain missing a pleasant party in order to talk to the friend. On a suitable occasion, that pair of psychological states might constitute the core of a satisfying explanation of an action that is in fact virtuous. Nothing more need be mentioned for the action to have been given a completely intelligible motivation. In Aristotle's view, the orectic state cited in an explanation of a virtuous action is the agent's entire conception of how to live, rather than just whatever concern it happened to be; and this may now seem mysterious. But the core explanation, as so far envisaged, lacks any indication that the action explained conformed to the agent's conception of how to live. The core explanation would apply equally to a case of helping one's friend because one thought it was, in the circumstances, the thing to do, and to a case of helping one's friend in spite of thinking it was not, in the circumstances, the thing to do.

---

25. *Nicomachean Ethics* 1144a31-3.
26. This is distinct from the claim that a person may at any stage be prone to change his mind. Wiggins appears at some points to run the two claims together, no doubt because he is concerned with practical reason generally, and not, as I am, with the expression in action of a specific conception of how to live. The line between realizing that an antecedent conception of how to live requires something one had not previously seen it to require, on the one hand, and modifying one's conception of how to live, on the other, is not a sharp one. But I do not want to exploit cases that are most happily described in the second way.
27. Compare Wittgenstein, *Philosophical Investigations* §208.
28. I borrow this excellent term from Wiggins.

A conception of how one should live is not simply an unorganized collection of propensities to act, on this or that occasion, in pursuit of this or that concern. Sometimes there are several concerns, fulfilment of any one of which might, on a suitable occasion, constitute acting as a certain conception of how to live would dictate, and each of which, on the occasion at hand, is capable of engaging with a known fact about the situation and issuing in action. Acting in the light of a conception of how to live requires selecting and acting on the right concern. (Compare the end of §1, on the unity of virtue.) So if an action whose motivation is spelled out in our core explanation is a manifestation of virtue, more must be true of its agent than just that on this occasion he acted with that motivation. The core explanation must at least be seen against the background of the agent's conception of how to live; and if the situation is one of those on which any of several concerns might impinge, the conception of how to live must be capable of actually entering our understanding of the action, explaining why it was this concern rather than any other that was drawn into operation.

How does it enter? If the conception of how to live involved a ranking of concerns, or perhaps a set of rankings each relativized to some type of situation, the explanation of why one concern was operative rather than another would be straightforward. But uncodifiability rules out laying down such general rankings in advance of all the predicaments with which life may confront one.

What I have described as selecting the right concern might equally be described in terms of the minor premise of the core explanation. If there is more than one concern that might impinge on the situation, there is more than one fact about the situation that the agent might, say, dwell on, in such a way as to summon an appropriate concern into operation. It is by virtue of his seeing this particular fact rather than that one as the salient fact about the situation that he is moved to act by this concern rather than that one.[29] This perception of saliences is the shape taken here by the appreciation of particular cases that I discussed in §4: something to which the uncodifiability of an exercise of rationality sometimes compels explicit appeal when we aim to represent actions as instances of it. A conception of how

---

29. This use of "salient" follows Wiggins.

to live shows itself, when more than one concern might issue in action, in one's seeing, or being able to be brought to see, one fact rather than another as salient. And our understanding of such a conception enters into our understanding of actions—the supplementation that the core explanation needs—by enabling us to share, or at least comprehend, the agent's perception of saliences.[30]

It is not wrong to think of the virtuous person's judgements about what to do, or his actions, as explicable by interaction between knowledge of how to live and particular knowledge about the situation at hand. (Compare the beginning of §4.) But the thought needs a more subtle construal than the deductive paradigm allows. With the core explanations and their supplementations, I have in effect been treating the complete explanations as coming in two stages. It is at the first stage—hitherto the supplementation—that knowledge of how to live interacts with particular knowledge: knowledge, namely, of all the particular facts capable of engaging with concerns whose fulfilment would, on occasion, be virtuous. This interaction yields, in a way that is essentially dependent on appreciation of the particular case, a view of the situation with one such fact, as it were, in the foreground. Seen as salient, that fact serves, at the second stage, as minor premise in a core explanation.[31]

6. We can go back now to the non-cognitivist objection that I outlined at the end of §3. Awareness that one's friend is in trouble and open to being comforted—the psychological state whose content is the minor premise of our core explanation—can perhaps, for the sake of argument, be conceded to be the sort of thing that the objection insists cognitive states must be: something capable of eliciting action only in conjunction with a non-cognitive state, namely, in our

---

30. On the importance of appreciation of the particular case, see *Nicomachean Ethics* 1142a23–30, 143a25–b5. See Wiggins's discussion of these passages. (For the point of "at least comprehend", see n. 33 below.)

31. That the interaction, at the first stage, is with *all* the potentially reason-yielding facts about the situation allows us to register that, in the case of, say, courage, the gravity of the risk, in comparison to the importance of the end to be achieved by facing it, makes a difference to whether virtue really does require facing it; even though at the second stage, if the risk is not seen as salient, it is seen as no reason at all for running away. I am indebted here to Wiggins.

example, a concern for one's friends.[32] But if someone takes that fact to be the salient fact about the situation, he is in a psychological state that is essentially practical. The relevant notion of salience cannot be understood except in terms of seeing something as a reason for acting that silences all others (compare §3). So classifying that state as a cognitive state is just the sort of thing that the objection attacks.

The most natural way to press the objection is to insist on purifying the content of what is genuinely known down to something that is, in itself, motivationally inert (namely, given the concession above, that one's friend is in trouble and open to being comforted); and then to represent the "perception" of a salience as an amalgam of the purified awareness with an additional appetitive state. But what appetitive state? Concern for one's friends yields only the core explanation, not the explanation in which the "perception" of salience was to figure. Perhaps the conception of how to live? That is certainly an orectic state. But, given the thesis of uncodifiability, it is not intelligible independently of just such appreciation of particular situations as is involved in the present "perception" of a salience; so it is not suitable to serve as an element into which, together with some genuine awareness, the "perception" could be regarded as analysable. (This non-cognitivist strategy is reflected in assimilation to the deductive paradigm: that the assimilation is congenial to the non-cognitivist objection was noted early in §4. The failure of the strategy is reflected in the failure of the assimilation, given the thesis of uncodifiability.)

If we feel the vertigo that I discussed in §4, it is out of distaste for the idea that a manifestation of reason might be recognizable as such only from within the practice whose status is in question. We are inclined to think there ought to be a neutral external standpoint from which the rationality of any genuine exercise of reason could be demonstrated. Now we might understand the objection to be demanding a non-cognitive extra that would be analogous to hunger: an appetitive state whose possession by anyone is intelligible in its own right, not itself open to assessment as rational or irrational, but conferring an obvious rationality, recognizable from outside, on be-

---

32. Actually this is open to question, because of special properties of the notion of a friend.

haviour engaged in with a view to its gratification. In that case it is clear how the objection expresses the craving for a kind of rationality independently demonstrable as such. However, it is highly implausible that all the concerns that motivate virtuous actions are intelligible, one by one, independently of appreciating a virtuous person's distinctive way of seeing situations. And even if they were, the various particular concerns figure only in the core explanations. We do not fully understand a virtuous person's actions—we do not see the consistency in them—unless we can supplement the core explanations with a grasp of his conception of how to live. And though this is to credit him with an orectic state, it is not to credit him with an externally intelligible over-arching desire; for we cannot understand the content of the orectic state from the envisaged external standpoint. It is, rather, to comprehend, essentially from within, the virtuous person's distinctive way of viewing particular situations.[33]

The rationality of virtue, then, is not demonstrable from an external standpoint. But to suppose that it ought to be is only a version of the prejudice that I discussed in §4. It is only an illusion that our paradigm of reason, deductive argument, has its rationality discernible from a standpoint that is not necessarily located within the practice itself.

7. Although perceptions of saliences resist decomposition into "pure" awareness together with appetitive states, there is an inclination to insist, nevertheless, that they cannot be genuinely cognitive states. We can be got into a cast of mind in which—as it seems to us—we have these problematic perceptions, only because we can be

---

33. The qualification "essentially" is to allow for the possibility that one might appreciate what it is like to be inside a way of thinking without actually being inside it, on the basis of a sufficient affinity between it and a way of thinking of one's own. These considerations about externally intelligible desires bear on Philippa Foot's thesis, in "Morality as a System of Hypothetical Imperatives", that morality should be construed, or recast, in terms of hypothetical imperatives, on pain of being fraudulent. Her negative arguments seem to me to be analogous to an exposé of the emptiness of platonism, as affording a foundation for mathematical practice external to the practice itself. In the mathematical case it is not a correct response to look for another external guarantee of the rationality of the practice, but that seems to me to be just what Mrs Foot's positive suggestion amounts to in the case of morality. (If the desires are not externally intelligible, the label "hypothetical imperatives" loses its point.) See, further, Essay 4 below.

brought to care about certain things; hence, ultimately, only because of certain antecedent facts about our emotional and appetitive make-up. This can seem to justify a more subtle non-cognitivism: one that abandons the claim that the problematic perceptions can be analysed into cognitive and appetitive components, but insists that, because of the anthropocentricity of the conceptual apparatus involved, they are not judgements, true or false, as to how things are in an independent reality; and that is what cognitive states are.[34]

I cannot tackle this subtle non-cognitivism properly now. I suspect that its origin is a philistine scientism, probably based on the misleading idea that the right of scientific method to rational acceptance is discernible from a more objective standpoint than that from which we seem to perceive the saliences. A scientistic conception of reality is eminently open to dispute. When we ask the metaphysical question whether reality is what science can find out about, we cannot, without begging the question, restrict the materials for an answer to those that science can countenance. Let the question be an empirical question, by all means; but the empirical data that would be collected by a careful and sensitive moral phenomenology—no doubt not a scientific enterprise—are handled quite unsatisfyingly by non-cognitivism.[35]

It would be a mistake to object that stress on appreciation of the particular, and the absence of a decision procedure, encourages everyone to pontificate about particular cases. In fact resistance to non-cognitivism, about the perception of saliences, recommends humility. If we resist non-cognitivism, we can equate the conceptual equipment that forms the framework of anything recognizable as a moral outlook with a capacity to be impressed by certain aspects of reality. But ethical reality is immensely difficult to see clearly. (Compare the end of §4.) If we are aware of how, for instance, selfish fantasy distorts our vision, we shall not be inclined to be confident that we have got things right.[36]

It seems plausible that Plato's ethical Forms are, in part, at least, a response to uncodifiability: if one cannot formulate what someone

---

34. On anthropocentricity, see David Wiggins, "Truth, Invention, and the Meaning of Life".

35. See Wiggins, "Truth, Invention, and the Meaning of Life"; and Iris Murdoch, *The Sovereignty of Good*.

36. Compare Iris Murdoch, *The Sovereignty of Good*. I am indebted here to Mark Platts.

has come to know when he cottons on to a practice, say one of concept-application, it is natural to say that he has seen something. Now in the passage that I quoted in §4, Cavell mentions two ways of avoiding vertigo: "the grasping of universals" as well as what I have been concerned with so far, "the grasping of books of rules". But though Plato's Forms are a myth, they are not a consolation, a mere avoidance of vertigo; vision of them is portrayed as too difficult an attainment for that to be so. The remoteness of the Form of the Good is a metaphorical version of the thesis that value is not in the world, utterly distinct from the dreary literal version that has obsessed recent moral philosophy. The point of the metaphor is the colossal difficulty of attaining a capacity to cope clear-sightedly with the ethical reality that *is* part of our world. Unlike other philosophical responses to uncodifiability, this one may actually work towards moral improvement; negatively, by inducing humility, and positively, by an inspiring effect akin to that of a religious conversion.[37]

8. If the question "How should one live?" could be given a direct answer in universal terms, the concept of virtue would have only a secondary place in moral philosophy. But the thesis of uncodifiability excludes a head-on approach to the question whose urgency gives ethics its interest. Occasion by occasion, one knows what to do, if one does, not by applying universal principles but by being a certain kind of person: one who sees situations in a certain distinctive way. And there is no dislodging, from the central position they occupy in the ethical reflection of Plato and Aristotle, questions about the nature and (hardly discussed in this paper) the acquisition of virtue.

It is sometimes complained that Aristotle does not attempt to outline a decision procedure for questions about how to behave. But we have good reason to be suspicious of the assumption that there must be something to be found along the route he does not follow.[38] And there is plenty for us to do in the area of philosophy of mind where his different approach locates ethics.

---

37. This view of Plato is beautifully elaborated by Iris Murdoch.

38. The idea, for instance, that something like utilitarianism must be right looks like a double avoidance of vertigo: first, in the thought that there must be a decision procedure; and second, in the reduction of practical rationality, at least in its moral application, to the pursuit of neutrally intelligible desires.

PART II

REASON, VALUE, AND REALITY

ESSAY 4

Are Moral Requirements Hypothetical Imperatives?

1. In "Morality as a System of Hypothetical Imperatives", Philippa Foot argues against the Kantian doctrine, and prevailing orthodoxy, that the requirements of morality are categorical imperatives. She notes that there is a distinction between a use of "should" in which a "should" statement needs withdrawing if the action in question cannot be shown to be ancillary to the agent's desires or interests, and one in which that is not so; and that moral uses of "should" are of the latter sort. She argues, however, that this latter use of "should" does not mark a categorical imperative in the sense intended in the orthodox doctrine; for it is found equally in expressions of the requirements of etiquette. Defenders of the orthodoxy, she assumes, would deny that the requirements of etiquette are categorical imperatives, and would ground the denial on the thesis that it is possible, without irrationality, to question whether one has reason to conform to them. On this assumption, the orthodoxy amounts to the claim that such questioning is not possible with morality. But Mrs Foot insists that the claim is false: there is no irrationality in questioning whether one has reason to act as morality is alleged to require. On this construal of the orthodoxy, then, a categorical imperative is something that must, on pain of irrationality, be recognized as a reason for acting; and Mrs Foot's thesis is that moral requirements are not categorical imperatives in that sense. She concludes that the requirements of morality exert a rational influence on the will only hypothetically; their influence is conditional on the presence of desires that are lacked by those who question whether they have reason to conform.

I want to agree that one need not manifest irrationality in failing to see that one has reason to act as morality requires, but I want to query whether it follows that moral requirements are only hypothetical imperatives.

2. The terminology calls for some preliminary comment. As Mrs Foot notes, Kant's concern was not with imperatives on a strict grammatical construal of the classification. She concentrates on judgements expressible with the words "should" or "ought"; but I prefer to shift attention away from explicitly prescriptive or normative language altogether.

It seems plausible that if one accepts that one should do something, one accepts that one has a reason to do it. But the reason is not expressed by the "should" statement itself. The reason must involve some appropriate specific consideration that could in principle be cited in support of the "should" statement. Thus, if one does something because one thinks one should, then unless the thought that one should is merely accepted on authority, a more illuminating account of one's reason will be available, citing the appropriate specific consideration that one takes to justify the view that one should act in that way. A formulation of the specific consideration will at least include a mention of what one takes to be relevant features of the circumstances in which the action is to be performed.

Now the fundamental difference that I think Kant was aiming at is one between different ways in which conceptions of circumstances influence the will; that is, between different ways in which they function in the explanation of behaviour in terms of the agent's reasons. To a virtuous person, certain actions are presented as practically necessary—as Kant might have put it—by his view of certain situations in which he finds himself. The question is whether his conceptions of the relevant facts weigh with him only conditionally on his possession of a desire.

If we think of the requirements of morality as imposed by the circumstances of action, as they are viewed by agents, rather than by the associated "should" thoughts, we make it possible to defend the thesis that virtuous actions are dictated by non-hypothetical imperatives, without committing ourselves to the insane thesis that simply to say "You should . . ." to someone is enough to give him a reason for acting; as if, when he protested "But why should I?", it was sufficient to reply "You just should, that's all".

3. When we explain an action in terms of the agent's reasons, we credit him with psychological states given which we can see how doing what he did, or attempted, would have appeared to him in some favourable light. A full specification of a reason must make clear how the reason was capable of motivating; it must contain enough to reveal the favourable light in which the agent saw his projected action. We tend to assume that this is effected, quite generally, by the inclusion of a desire. (Of course a reason that includes a desire can be specified elliptically, when the desire is obvious enough not to need mentioning; as when we explain someone's taking an umbrella in terms of his belief that it is likely to rain.) However, it seems to be false that the motivating power of all reasons derives from their including desires.

Suppose, for instance, that we explain a person's performance of a certain action by crediting him with awareness of some fact that makes it likely (in his view) that acting in that way will be conducive to his interest. Adverting to his view of the facts may suffice, on its own, to show us the favourable light in which his action appeared to him. No doubt we credit him with an appropriate desire, perhaps for his own future happiness. But the commitment to ascribe such a desire is simply consequential on our taking him to act as he does for the reason we cite; the desire does not function as an independent extra component in a full specification of his reason, hitherto omitted by an understandable ellipsis of the obvious, but strictly necessary in order to show how it is that the reason can motivate him. Properly understood, his belief does that on its own. Thomas Nagel (in *The Possibility of Altruism,* pp. 29–30) puts the point like this:

> That I have the appropriate desire simply *follows* from the fact that these considerations motivate me; if the likelihood that an act will promote my future happiness motivates me to perform it now, then it is appropriate to ascribe to me a desire for my own future happiness. But nothing follows about the role of the desire as a condition contributing to the motivational efficacy of those considerations.

This passage is quoted in part, and its thesis endorsed, by Mrs Foot in "Reasons for Action and Desires".

Why should the reasons that move people to virtuous behaviour not be similar to the reasons that move them to prudent behaviour? To explain an action we regard as virtuous, we typically formulate a more or less complex characterization of the action's circumstances as we take the agent to have conceived them. Why should it not be the case, here too, that the agent's conception of the situation, properly understood, suffices to show us the favourable light in which his action appeared to him? If we credit him with a suitable desire, then, as before, that need be no more than a consequence of the fact that we take his conception of the circumstances to have been his reason for acting as he did; the desire need not function as an independent component in the explanation, needed in order to account for the capacity of the cited reason to influence the agent's will.

4. There may seem to be a difficulty: might not another person have exactly the same conception of the circumstances, but see no reason to act as the virtuous person does? If so, adverting to that conception of the situation cannot, after all, suffice to show us the favourable light in which the virtuous person saw his action. Our specification of his reason must, after all, have been elliptical; a full specification would need to add an extra psychological state to account for the action's attractiveness to him in particular—namely, surely, a desire.

We can evade this argument by denying its premise: that is, by taking a special view of the virtuous person's conception of the circumstances, according to which it cannot be shared by someone who sees no reason to act as the virtuous person does.

This may seem problematic. But if one concedes that a conception of the facts can constitute the whole of a reason for prudent behaviour, one is not at liberty to object to the very idea that a view of how things are might not need supplementing with a desire in order to reveal the favourable light in which someone saw some action; and a view with that property surely cannot be shared by someone who sees no reason to act in the way in question. If we allow this for prudence, why should we not allow it for morality too?

Suppose someone was incapable of seeing how a fact about the likely effect of an action on his own future could, on its own, constitute a reason for the action. On some suitable occasion, he might be unmoved by such a fact. It would not be wrong to say that an ordinarily prudent person, in parallel circumstances, would differ from him in having a certain desire. But according to the concession, the desire is not a further component, over and above the prudent person's conception of the likely effects of his action on his own future, in the explanation of his prudent behaviour. It is not that the two people share a certain neutral conception of the facts, but differ in that one, but not the other, has an independent desire as well, which combines with that neutral conception of the facts to cast a favourable light on his acting in a certain way. The desire is ascribable to the prudent person simply in recognition of the fact that his conception of the likely effects of his action on his own future by itself casts a favourable light on his acting as he does. So the admitted difference in respect of desire should be explicable, like the difference in respect of action, in terms of a more fundamental difference in respect of how they conceive the facts.

It is not clear that we really can make sense of the idea of someone who is otherwise rational but cannot see how facts about his future can, by themselves, constitute reasons for him to act in various ways. But to the extent to which the idea does make sense, it seems to be on just the lines we should expect: we picture him as someone with an idiosyncratic view of what it is for a fact to concern his own future. Perhaps he thinks of the person involved in such a fact as some future person, connected with the one who is currently deliberating by links of continuity and resemblance that are too tenuous, in his view, for it to be anything but arbitrary for the current deliberator to pay special attention to that future person's welfare. What is special about a prudent person is a different understanding of what it is for a fact to concern his own future. He sees things otherwise in the relevant area; and we comprehend his prudent behaviour by comprehending the relevant fragment of his world view, not by appealing to the desire that is admittedly ascribable to him. That is to be understood, no less than the behaviour is, in terms of the world view.

Why should it not be similar with explanations of virtuous behaviour in terms of the virtuous person's conceptions of situations in which he acts?

5. So far I have responded only *ad hominem* to qualms about the idea that a conception of how things are might constitute, on its

own, a reason for virtuous action. That is how it was conceded to be with prudential reasons, and there is no obvious argument that the possibility, once granted, should be restricted to prudential considerations. But presumably someone with sufficiently strong doubts about the case of morality will be encouraged to doubt the whole idea, and suppose that it cannot be so even with prudential reasons; he will not be impressed by the thought that, if granted there, the possibility cannot be dismissed out of hand for the case of morality.

I suppose the general doubt is on these lines. A view of how things are is a state or disposition of one's cognitive equipment. But the psychological states we are considering are to suffice, on their own, to show how certain actions appeared in a favourable light. That requires that their possession entails a disposition of the possessor's will. And will and belief—the appetitive and the cognitive—are distinct existences; so a state that presents itself as cognitive but entails an appetitive state must be, after all, only impurely cognitive, and contain the appetitive state as a part. If such a state strikes its possessor as cognitive, that is because he is projecting his states of will on to the world (a case of the mind's propensity to spread itself upon objects). The appetitive state should be capable in principle of being analysed out, leaving a neutrally cognitive residue. Thus where it appears that a conception of how things are exhausts an agent's reason for acting in a certain way, an analysed and less misleading formulation of the reason will be bipartite: it will specify, first, a neutral conception of the facts, available equally to someone who sees no reason to act in the way in question, and second, a desire, which combines with that conception of the facts to make the action attractive to its possessor.

This paper is primarily addressed to those who are vulnerable to the *ad hominem* argument. In their view, since the line of thought I have just sketched falsifies the workings of prudential explanations of behaviour, it simply cannot be generally right. In the rest of this section I shall make some remarks, not *ad hominem*, about the general issue; but a proper discussion is impossible here.

There is room for scepticism about whether it is acceptable to discount the appearances in the way the objection urges. Explanation of behaviour by reasons purports to show the favourable light in which an agent saw his action. If it strikes an agent that his reason for acting as he does consists entirely in his conception of the circumstances in which he acts, then an explanation that insists on analysing that seemingly cognitive state into a less problematically cognitive state combined with a separate desire, while it will show the action as attractive from the standpoint of the psychological states it cites, is not obviously guaranteed to get the favourable light right. If one accepts an explanation of the analysing sort, one will not be baffled by inability to find any point one can take the agent to have seen in behaving as he did; but what leaves one unpuzzled is not thereby shown to be a *correct* explanation.

The analysis will nevertheless seem compulsory, if the objection seems irresistible. If the world is, in itself, motivationally inert, and is also the proper province of cognitive equipment, it is inescapable that a strictly cognitive state—a conception of how things are, properly so called—cannot constitute the whole of a reason for acting. But the idea of the world as motivationally inert is not an independent hard datum. It is simply the metaphysical counterpart of the thesis that states of will and cognitive states are distinct existences, which is exactly what is in question.

If a conception of a set of circumstances can suffice on its own to explain an action, then the world view it exemplifies is certainly not the kind of thing that could be established by the methods of the natural sciences. But the notion of the world, or how things are, that is appropriate in this context is a metaphysical notion, not a scientific one: world views richer than that of science are not scientific, but not on that account unscientific (a term of opprobrium for answers other than those of science to science's questions). To query their status as world views on the ground of their not being scientific is to be motivated not by science but by scientism.

6. It is not to be denied that behaviour that is in fact virtuous can in some cases be found unsurprising through being what one would expect anyway, given an acceptably ascribed desire that is independently intelligible. That is why sheer bafflement at virtuous behaviour in general is very difficult to imagine. At some points even the rankest outsider would be able to attain a measure of comprehension of virtuous actions in terms of desires that people just naturally have: for instance the desire that people related to them in various ways should not suffer. Such coincidences constitute possible points of

entry for an outsider trying to work his way into appreciation of a moral outlook. Similarly, they perhaps partly explain how it is possible to acquire a moral outlook of one's own (not the same topic, since one can understand a moral outlook without sharing it).

What is questionable is whether there need *always* be an independently intelligible desire to whose fulfilment a virtuous action, if rational at all, can be seen as conducive.

Charitable behaviour aims at an end, namely the good of others. (See "Morality as a System of Hypothetical Imperatives", p. 165.) It does not follow that a full specification of the agent's reason for a charitable act would need to add a desire to his conception of the circumstances in which he acted. For prudent behaviour equally aims at an end, namely one's own future happiness. The desire for the good of others is related to charity as the desire for one's own future happiness is related to prudence; not, then, as a needed extra ingredient in formulations of reasons for acting. Rather, the desire is ascribed, as in the prudential case, simply in recognition of the fact that a charitable person's special way of conceiving situations by itself casts a favourable light on charitable actions. Of course a desire ascribed in this purely consequential way is not independently intelligible.

It does not seem plausible that any purely natural fellow-feeling or benevolence, unmediated by the special ways of seeing situations that are characteristic of charity as it is thought of above, would issue in behaviour that exactly matched that of a charitable person; the objects of a purely natural benevolence could not be guaranteed to coincide in all cases with the good of others as a possessor of the virtue would conceive it. It seems still less plausible that virtuous behaviour in general could be duplicated by means of the outcomes of independently intelligible desires.

Mrs Foot sometimes seems to suggest that if someone acts in a way he takes to be morally required, and his behaviour cannot be shown to be rational as a case of conformity to a hypothetical imperative, then he must be blindly obeying an inculcated code. (See "Reasons for Action and Desires", p. 155: "Perhaps we have been bewitched by the idea that we *just do* have reason to obey this part of our moral code". She does not endorse this thought, which is about honesty; but she seems to put it forward as the sole alternative to the thought that we should explain honest behaviour in terms of desires.) But if we deny that virtuous behaviour can always be explained as the outcome of independently intelligible desires, we do not thereby commit ourselves to its being mere obedience to a code. There need be no possibility of reducing virtuous behaviour to rules. In moral upbringing what one learns is not to behave in conformity with rules of conduct, but to see situations in a special light, as constituting reasons for acting; this perceptual capacity, once acquired, can be exercised in complex novel circumstances, not necessarily capable of being foreseen and legislated for by a codifier of the conduct required by virtue, however wise and thoughtful he might be.

On this view, independently intelligible desires will take an outsider only some of the distance towards full understanding of virtuous behaviour. In the first place, there will be some actions that simply cannot be explained as the outcomes of such desires. Second, if one sticks with explanations in terms of independently intelligible desires at the points of entry, where such explanations do make actions unpuzzling, one will not have the full picture even of those actions: if they manifest a virtuous person's distinctive way of seeing things, they must be explicable also in terms of exercises of that perceptual capacity, which need no supplementing with desires to yield full specifications of reasons. (This need not imply that the initial explanations, at the points of entry, were wrong. Someone can have two separate reasons for what he does; perhaps he can do it for both of them. If so, we need not suppose—as Kant perhaps did—that an action's being the outcome of a natural desire disqualifies it as a manifestation of virtue.)

§4 suggests that if someone could not see the force of prudential considerations, one might appropriately protest: "You don't know what it means for a fact to concern your future." Rather similarly, in urging behaviour one takes to be morally required, one finds oneself saying things like this: "You don't know what it means that someone is shy and sensitive." Conveying what a circumstance means, in this loaded sense, is getting someone to see it in the special way in which a virtuous person would see it. In the attempt to do so, one exploits contrivances similar to those one exploits in other areas where the task is to back up the injunction "See it like this": helpful juxtapositions of cases, descriptions with carefully chosen terms and carefully placed emphasis, and the like. (Compare, for instance, what one might do and say to someone who says "Jazz sounds to me like a mess, a mere welter of uncoordinated noise".) No such contrivances can be guaranteed success, in the sense that failure would show irrationality on the part of the audience. That, together with the importance of rhetorical skills to their successful deployment, sets them apart from the sorts of thing we typically regard as paradigms of argument. But these seem insufficient grounds for concluding that they are appeals to passion as opposed to reason: for concluding that "See it like this" is really a covert invitation to feel, quite over and above one's view of the facts, a desire that will combine with one's belief to recommend acting in the appropriate way.

Failure to see what a circumstance means, in the loaded sense, is of course compatible with competence, by all ordinary tests, with the language used to describe the circumstance; that brings out how loaded the notion of meaning involved in the protest is. Notice that, as the example of "shy and sensitive" illustrates, the language used to express a special reason-constituting conception of a situation need not be explicitly evaluative.

The question "Why should I conform to the dictates of morality?" is most naturally understood as asking for an extra-moral motivation that will be gratified by virtuous behaviour. So understood, the question has no answer. What may happen is that someone is brought to see things as a virtuous person does, and so stops feeling the need to ask it. Situation by situation, he knows why he should behave in the relevant ways; but what he now has is a set of answers to a different interpretation of the question.[1]

7. We have, then, an apparent contrast between two ways in which an agent's view of how things are can function in explaining his actions. In one, exemplified by the case of taking one's umbrella (§3), the agent's belief about how things are combines with an independently intelligible desire to represent the action as a good thing from the agent's point of view. In the other, a conception of how things are suffices on its own to show us the favourable light in which the action appeared. Beliefs about one's future well-being standardly operate in the second way, according to the concession of §3; so, ac-

---

[1]. See pp. 152-3 of D. Z. Phillips, "In Search of the Moral 'Must': Mrs Foot's Fugitive Thought"—an article from which I profited in writing this paper.

cording to the suggestion I am making in this paper, do moral reasons.

With reasons that function in the second way, it is not false that they weigh with people only if they have a certain desire. But that is just because the ascription of the desire in question follows from the fact that the reasons weigh as they do. It would be wrong to infer that the conceptions of situations that constitute the reasons are available equally to people who are not swayed by them, and weigh with those who are swayed only contingently on their possession of an independent desire. That would be to assimilate the second kind of reason to the first. To preserve the distinction, we should say that the relevant conceptions are not so much as possessed except by those whose wills are influenced appropriately. Their status as reasons is hypothetical only in this truistic sense: they sway only those who *have* them.

When we envisaged a person immune to the force of prudential considerations, we supposed that he might have an idiosyncratic understanding of what it was for a fact to concern his own future (§4). Particular facts about his own future, by themselves, would leave him cold. Now we might imagine equipping him with a separate desire, for the welfare of the future person he takes to be involved in the relevant facts. Then his conception of those facts might move him to action, with their influence conditional on his possession of that extra desire. But the resulting behaviour, only hypothetically called for by his conception of the facts, would match ordinary prudent behaviour only externally. It would be wrong to conclude that ordinary prudent behaviour is likewise only hypothetically commanded.

Similarly, someone who lacks a virtuous person's distinctive view of a situation might perhaps be artificially induced into a simulacrum of a virtuous action by equipping him with an independent desire. His conception of the situation would then be influencing his will hypothetically. But it would be wrong to conclude that a virtuous person's actions are likewise only hypothetically commanded by his conceptions of such situations. (§6 suggests, anyway, a special difficulty about the idea that virtuous behaviour might be thus artificially duplicated across the board.)

According to this position, then, a failure to see reason to act virtuously stems, not from the lack of a desire on which the rational influence of moral requirements is conditional, but from the lack of a distinctive way of seeing situations. If that perceptual capacity is possessed and exercised, it yields non-hypothetical reasons for acting. Now the lack of a perceptual capacity, or failure to exercise it, need show no irrationality. (It might be argued that not to have the relevant conception of one's own future, in the prudential case, would be irrational; but a parallel argument in the moral case would lack plausibility.) Thus we can grant Mrs Foot's premise—that it is possible without irrationality to fail to see reason to act as morality requires—without granting her conclusion—that moral requirements exert a rational influence on the will only hypothetically. The gap opens because we have undermined the assumption that a consideration can exert a rational influence on a will otherwise than hypothetically only if it is recognizable as a requirement by all rational people.

Mrs Foot thought her opponents would differentiate moral requirements from those of etiquette by claiming that moral requirements, unlike those of etiquette, are recognizable as requirements by all rational people; that is, that they are categorical imperatives in the sense stipulated by the assumption we have undermined. Obviously I am not here conforming to that expectation. In respect of not necessarily impressing any rational person, moral requirements and the requirements of etiquette are alike, and it is not my intention here to discuss in detail what makes them different. (Many actions performed for reasons of etiquette can be explained in terms of bewitchment by a code. There may be a residue of actions not explicable in that way. It does not seem to me to be obviously absurd, or destructive of the point of any distinction between categorical and hypothetical imperatives, to suppose that such residual actions might be most revealingly explained in terms of non-hypothetically reason-constituting conceptions of circumstances. One can attribute such conceptions to others without being compelled oneself; for one can appreciate how someone might see things a certain way without seeing them that way oneself.)

I have said nothing about where the line is to be drawn between hypothetical and non-hypothetical reasons for action. For purposes of exposition, I have assumed that when one explains taking an umbrella in terms of the agent's belief that it will probably rain, the reason specified needs supplementing with a desire. But it would not matter if someone insisted that what appears as a desire, in the most natural filling out of the reason, is actually better regarded as a cognitive state, a colouring of the agent's view of the world. If it is admitted that we can make sense of the idea of a reason of the second sort that I distinguished above, then there is content to the thesis that moral reasons are of that sort, even if it turns out that there are no reasons of the first sort.

Note that consequentially ascribed desires are indeed desires. Construing obedience to a categorical imperative as acting for a certain sort of reason, we can see the obedience as a case of doing what one wants. So subjection to categorical imperatives, even without the coincidences with natural desires that I mentioned in §6, need not be pictured as a grim servitude.

8. The strategy of this paper must raise the question whether I am treating prudential considerations as categorical imperatives. (It would be pleasant if Mrs Foot could be represented as holding that prudential imperatives are categorical and moral imperatives hypothetical.) The answer depends on which of Kant's characterizations of hypothetical imperatives we have in mind.

On the one hand, I interpret the concession of §3 as implying this: a prudent person's conception of facts about his own future exerts an influence on his will in its own right, not contingently upon his possession of an independent desire.

On the other hand, Kant's hypothetical imperatives are supposed to "declare a possible action to be practically necessary as a means to the attainment of something else that one wills (or that one may will)".[2] And it is certainly true that prudential considerations typically recommend actions as means to ends distinct from themselves.

Are not moral imperatives sometimes equally hypothetical in the second sense? Kant was committed to denying that moral considerations can recommend an action as a means to an end distinct from itself, but the denial seems desperately implausible. Perhaps the idea that one has to exclude means-end reasons from the sphere of virtue can be explained on the following lines. From the concession of §3,

2. *Groundwork of the Metaphysics of Morals*, p. 82.

we can see that if an action's rationality consists in its conduciveness to an end distinct from itself (the agent's future happiness, say), it does not follow that the willing of the distinct end is a desire intelligible independently of understanding the reason-constituting character of facts about such conduciveness. But though it does not follow, it would be natural to suppose it does. Kant's fundamental aim was to deny that the motivating capacity of moral considerations needs explaining from outside, in terms of desires that are not intrinsically moral—that is, to deny that moral requirements are hypothetical imperatives in the first sense. Given the natural error, he would think he had to deny that virtuous behaviour is ever rational as a means to a distinct end—that is, to deny that moral requirements are ever hypothetical imperatives in the second sense.

9. My suggestion, so far, has been this: one cannot share a virtuous person's view of a situation in which it seems to him that virtue requires some action, but see no reason to act in that way. The following possibility is still open: one sees reason to act in that way, but takes the reason to be outweighed by a reason for acting in some other way. But part of the point of claiming that the requirements of virtue are categorical imperatives may lie in a rejection of that possibility.

The rejection might stem from the idea that the dictates of virtue always outweigh reasons for acting otherwise. But I believe a more interesting ground for it is the idea that the dictates of virtue, if properly appreciated, are not weighed with other reasons at all, not even on a scale that always tips on their side. If a situation in which virtue imposes a requirement is genuinely conceived as such, according to this view, then considerations that, in the absence of the requirement, would have constituted reasons for acting otherwise are silenced altogether—not overridden—by the requirement.

"What shall it profit a man, if he shall gain the whole world, and lose his soul?" Obviously we are not meant to answer "The profits are outweighed by counterbalancing losses". The intended answer is "Nothing". At that price, whatever one might achieve does not count as profit. Or, in the terminology of reasons: the attractions of whatever wickedness might bring do not constitute some reason for wickedness, which is, however, overridden by the reasons against it; rather, given that they are achieved by wickedness, those attractive outcomes do not count as reasons at all.

10. Aristotle's thoughts about continence, incontinence, and virtue involve thinking of the status of the requirements of virtue on those lines. Perhaps the requirements are not exactly moral requirements, since Aristotle's notion of virtue is perhaps not exactly a moral notion. But his view may nevertheless usefully illustrate the structure of the position that I described in §9, and help to explain the distinction between silencing and overriding.

For Aristotle, if one needs to overcome an inclination to act otherwise, in getting oneself to act temperately, then one's action manifests continence rather than the virtue of temperance. Readers are apt to be puzzled about how they are meant to think of the virtue. Is the temperate person's libido somehow peculiarly undemanding? Does his inclination to sleep with someone he ought not to sleep with evaporate under the impact of the thought that he would not enjoy it at all (why ever not, unless he is not quite human?); or under the impact of the thought that his enjoyment would be counterbalanced by pangs of remorse?

In fact the idea is on these lines. The temperate person need be no less prone to enjoy physical pleasure than anyone else. In suitable circumstances it will be true that he would enjoy some intemperate action that is available to him. In the absence of a requirement, the prospective enjoyment would constitute a reason for going ahead. But his clear perception of the requirement insulates the prospective enjoyment—of which, for a satisfying conception of the virtue, we should want him to have a vivid appreciation—from engaging his inclinations at all. Here and now, it does not count for him as any reason for acting in that way.

Virtues such as temperance and courage involve steadfastness in the face of characteristic sorts of temptation, and it can seem impossible to register that fact without regarding them as cases of continence. Insisting nevertheless on the distinction between virtue and continence yields a view of these virtues that has a certain sublimity. Their proper manifestation is renouncing, without struggle, something that in the abstract one would value highly (physical pleasure, security of life and limb). The lack of struggle is ensured by keeping the attention firmly fixed on what Aristotle calls "the noble"; not by a weighing of attractions that leads to the conclusion that on balance the virtuous course is more desirable. (It is true that the competing course could not really satisfy a virtuous person. But that is not to say that he judges it on balance less desirable; it records a *consequence* of his conviction that in these circumstances the attractions of the competing course count for nothing.) Genuinely courageous behaviour, on this view, combines a lively awareness of risk, and a normal valuation of life and health (see *Nicomachean Ethics* 3.9), with a sort of serenity; taking harm to be, by definition, what one has reason to avoid, we can see the serenity as based on the belief, paradoxical in juxtaposition with the valuing of life and health, that no harm can come to one by acting thus.

This view of virtue obviously involves a high degree of idealization; the best we usually encounter is to some degree tainted with continence. But in a view of what genuine virtue is, idealization is not something to be avoided or apologized for.

It is evident that this view of virtue makes incontinence problematic. The weak incontinent person must conceive the circumstances of his action in a way that, in some sense, matches the way a virtuous person would conceive them, since he knows he is not acting as virtue demands. But the virtuous person conceives the relevant sorts of situation in such a way that considerations that would otherwise be reasons for acting differently are silenced by the recognized requirement. If the incontinent person has such a conception, how can those considerations make themselves heard by his will, as they do? Obviously continence poses a parallel difficulty.

The way out is to attenuate the degree to which the continent or incontinent person's conception of a situation matches that of a virtuous person. Their inclinations are aroused, as the virtuous person's are not, by their awareness of competing attractions: a lively desire clouds or blurs the focus of their attention on "the noble".

Curiously enough, if we approach incontinence on these lines, we entirely disarm one difficulty that threatens it on other approaches. (I owe this thought to David Wiggins.) Suppose we think of the incontinent person as failing to act on a judgement "all things considered", in which the motivating potential of alternative actions is registered by his counting their attractions, suitably weighted, as reasons for acting in those ways. The judgement will have to be that those reasons are outweighed by the force of the reason for the virtuous action. But now it seems mysterious how one of those alternative motivations can take charge. Why is its ability to move one not exhausted by the weight it is pictured as bringing to the scale? On the view I am describing, by contrast, the motivating potential of the competing attractions has not exerted any influence in forming the judgement that the person should have acted on—so that, as above, it might be expected to have used itself up there, and it is mysterious how it can still have energy to inject after it has been outweighed. The virtuous view of what should be done does not so much as take those attractions into account. So we can think of them as a potential source of motivating energy, not used up in the formation of the judgement. There can be a risk that the potential will be actualized, if the attractions are not insulated, by the clear perception of a silencing requirement, from engaging the inclinations.

A *caveat:* notice that the position is not that clear perception of any moral reason, however weak, silences any reasons of other sorts, however strong. The reasons that silence are those that mark out actions as required by virtue. There can be less exigent moral reasons, and as far as this position goes, they may be overridden.

11. In §8 I left moral and prudential considerations not sharply distinguished in the manner of their influence on the will. But the view that those moral reasons that count as imposing requirements are special, in the way I described in §9 and illustrated in §10, restores a distinction. On this view, to conceive some relevant fact about one's future as an ordinarily prudent person would is not, after all, *eo ipso* to take oneself to have a reason for the prudent behaviour that would normally be recommended by such a fact. If one is clearly aware of a moral requirement to behave differently, one will not take the prudential consideration as the reason it would otherwise be. (It is not plausible to suppose that perception of the moral requirement effects this by tampering with one's understanding of what it is for a fact to concern one's own future.) So prudential

considerations, on this view, are hypothetical imperatives in a new sense: their rational influence on the will is conditional, not on a desire, but on the absence of a clearly grasped moral requirement to do something else. Moral requirements, by contrast, are not conditional at all: neither on desires nor on the absence of other reasons.

ESSAY 5

Might There Be External Reasons?

1. This paper is directed to a question that has been posed by Bernard Williams, in his interesting and insufficiently discussed article "Internal and External Reasons". Statements to the effect that someone has reason to act in a specified way (say to φ), or that there is reason for someone to φ, are apparently susceptible of two sorts of interpretation. The first is the internal interpretation, on which the statement is falsified by the agent's lack of any "motive which will be served or furthered by his φ-ing" (p. 101).[1] The second is the external interpretation, on which that is not so. This is how things seem at first blush, but Williams argues for a scepticism about whether reason statements are ever true on the external interpretation.[2] That is the question I want to consider. The question is quite abstract and general, but it is obvious that it bears on a familiar problem that arises about ethical reasons in particular, in view of the evident possibility of being left cold by them. The implication of Williams's scepticism is that ethical reasons are reasons only for those for whom they are internal reasons: only for those who have motivations to which ethical considerations speak, or can be made to speak.

---

1. As will become clear immediately, this can be understood so as not to require that the agent is actually motivated towards φ-ing.
2. One might say: about whether there are any external reasons. Williams allows this sort of formulation (for instance in his title; I have followed suit in mine). But I shall follow him in treating this only as a convenience; nothing turns on whether we are looking for a classification of sorts of reasons for action or merely a classification of sorts of things that can be said.

2. It is a strength of Williams's argument that he bases it on a subtle and flexible conception of the materials available to the internal interpretation. On the crudest understanding of that interpretation, an agent would have a reason to φ only by virtue of having a desire such that φ-ing either is its satisfaction or is conducive to its satisfaction as means to end. I shall note two main ways in which Williams refines this.

First, about the role of desire. What is required if there is to be an internal reason is that the action in question is suitably related to an element in the agent's "subjective motivational set" (p. 102); and if the term "desire" is used for all such elements, we must be clear that this is only a "formal" (or, as one might say, philosopher's) usage. Subjective motivational sets are not restricted to what would ordinarily be called "desires"; they "can contain such things as dispositions of evaluation, patterns of emotional reaction, personal loyalties, and various projects, as they may be abstractly called, embodying commitments of the agent" (p. 105).

Second, about what it is for an action to be suitably related to an element in the agent's subjective motivational set. The crude view already allows that an agent can have a reason to φ without being actually motivated to φ, if he does not realize that φ-ing is a means to something he desires. The general idea is that one has reason to do what practical reasoning, starting from one's existing motivations, would reveal that one has reason to do—even if one has not realized that one has reason to do it. But the effect of the crude view is to limit the way in which practical reasoning can expand one's awareness of one's internal reasons; the expansion is restricted to cases where practical reasoning brings to light matters whose bearing on one's practical situation is, roughly speaking, technical.[3] Williams's refinement drops this exclusive concentration on means and ends. The conception of practical reasoning or deliberation involved in his version of the general idea is much less restricted; he sketches it only by means of examples. (Such a procedure is unavoidable, he suggests, since "there is an essential indeterminacy in what can be

---

3. Williams even suggests, on the basis of the fact that "the mere discovery that some course of action is the causal means to an end is not in itself a piece of practical reasoning" (p. 104), that the effect is to obliterate practical *reasoning* from the picture altogether.

counted a rational deliberative process" [p. 110].) He writes (p. 104):

> A clear example of practical reasoning is that leading to the conclusion that one has reason to φ because φ-ing would be the most convenient, economical, pleasant etc. way of satisfying some element in S [the agent's subjective motivational set], and this of course is controlled by other elements in S, if not necessarily in a very clear or determinate way. But there are much wider possibilities for deliberation, such as: thinking how the satisfaction of elements in S can be combined, e.g. by time-ordering; where there is some irresoluble conflict among the elements of S, considering which one attaches most weight to (which, importantly, does not imply that there is some one commodity of which they provide varying amounts); or, again, finding constitutive solutions, such as deciding what would make for an entertaining evening, granted that one wants entertainment.

One important ingredient in this freeing of the idea of practical rationality from restriction to satisfactions, and means to satisfactions, of given desires is that Williams is able to insist on the relevance of imagination to deliberation. By letting his imagination play on an outcome which he supposes he has reason to promote, an agent "may come to have some more concrete sense of what would be involved, and lose his desire for it"; conversely, "the imagination can create new possibilities and new desires" (p. 105).

So the idea is this: what one has reason to do, on the internal interpretation, is whatever one can conclude that one has reason to do by an exercise of practical reasoning, conceived on these unrestrictive lines. Practical reasoning is "a heuristic process, and an imaginative one" (p. 110). The significance of elements in one's subjective motivational set is not that one has reason to do only what is conducive to, or constitutes, their satisfaction, but that they "control" the thinking by which one determines what one has reason to do, in ways like those exemplified in the long quotation above: ways that it is impossible to codify in some simple theory.

3. Does this leave any room for the external interpretation? Williams argues, on the following lines, that it does not.

Any reason for action must be something that *could* explain someone's acting in the way for which it is a reason. If a reason did explain an action, the agent *would* have a motivation towards acting in the way in question—a motivation that the reason-giving explanation would spell out. But *ex hypothesi* an external reason statement can be true of someone without his actually having any motive that would be "served or furthered" by his doing what he is said to have a reason to do—not even one whose relevance to his doing that would need to be uncovered by deliberation. (This simply spells out the idea of the external interpretation.) We can reconcile this with the point that any reason, even an external one, must be potentially explanatory of action, on these lines. Consider an agent who is not motivated by an external reason. It must nevertheless be true that some consideration constitutes a reason for him to act in a certain way; his not being motivated by it is a matter of his not *believing*, of the consideration, that it is a reason to act in that way.[4] If he came to believe that, he would come to be motivated. That is, certainly, he would come to have an internal reason statement true of him. But this hypothetical internal reason need not pre-empt all the space an external reason might occupy: we can preserve the external reason if we can make sense of something that would be true throughout such a transition, and which is such that we can see how coming to believe it would be coming to have the motivation that makes the internal reason statement true.

So we need to consider the transition from not being motivated by a putatively external reason to being motivated by it. The question is whether we can make sense of this as coming to believe something that was true already in advance of the agent's being motivated. What "the external reasons theorist" needs, Williams says, is "that the agent should acquire the motivation *because* he comes to believe the reason statement, and that he should do the latter, moreover, because, in some way, he is considering the matter aright" (pp. 108–9).

At this point Williams makes a claim that is crucial for his argument (p. 109):

---

4. There are two possible cases here: one in which the consideration is in view, but not believed to constitute a reason, and one in which the consideration is not even in view, or, if in view, not in clear focus.

If the theorist is to hold on to these conditions, he will, I think, have to make the condition under which the agent appropriately comes to have the motivation something like this, that he should deliberate correctly; and the external reasons statement itself will have to be taken as roughly equivalent to, or at least as entailing, the claim that if the agent rationally deliberated, then, whatever motivations he originally had, he would come to be motivated to ϕ.

The effect of this is to represent the external reasons theorist as committed to returning an affirmative answer to Hume's question, whether reason alone can give rise to a motivation. The predicament itself determines an interpretation for "alone" here. As Williams describes his position, the external reasons theorist must envisage a procedure of correct deliberation or reasoning that gives rise to a motivation, but is not "controlled" by existing motivations, in the way that figures in the account of internal reasons; for, if the deliberation were thus "controlled" by existing motivations, the reason it brought to light would simply be an internal reason. So the external reasons theorist has to envisage the generation of a new motivation by reason, in an exercise in which the directions it can take are not determined by the shape of the agent's prior motivations—an exercise that would be rationally compelling whatever motivations one started from. As Williams says (p. 109), it is very hard to believe there could be a kind of reasoning that was pure in this sense—owing none of its cogency to the specific shape of pre-existing motivations—but nevertheless motivationally efficacious. If the rational cogency of a piece of deliberation is in no way dependent on prior motivations, how can we comprehend its giving rise to a new motivation?

4. But need the external reasons theorist fight on this ground?

Let us retrace our steps. We have to consider the transition from not being motivated by a supposedly external reason to being motivated by it. The external reasons theorist must suppose the agent acquires the new motivation by coming to believe the external reason statement. To be an external reason statement, that statement must have been true all along; in coming to believe it, the agent must be coming to consider the matter aright. The crucial question is this: why must the external reasons theorist envisage this transition to considering the matter aright as being effected by *correct deliberation*? He cannot make sense of the motivational effect of the transition by crediting it to deliberation "controlled" by prior motivations, since that would merely reveal the reason to be internal. So, if there must be deliberation—reasoning—that could bring about the transition, he needs to invent an application of reason in which it can impel people to action without owing its cogency to the specific shape of their prior motivations; and this is what Williams rightly says it is hard to believe in. The argument debars the external reasons theorist from supposing that there is no way to effect the transition except one that would not count as being swayed by reasons: for instance (p. 108), being persuaded by moving rhetoric, and, by implication (p. 110), inspiration and conversion. But what is the ground for this exclusion?

Williams's wording may seem to answer this question. To repeat a passage I have already quoted, he says that what the external reasons theorist needs is "that the agent should acquire the motivation *because* he comes to believe the reason statement, and that he should do the latter, moreover, because, in some way, he is considering the matter aright" (pp. 108–9). If "considering the matter aright" figures, as this suggests, in an *explanation* of the agent's coming to believe the reason statement, suited to reveal the transition as one to a *true* belief, it may seem that the phrase must single out and endorse something like a procedure of argument or reasoning. But in fact all that the external reasons theorist needs at that point in the argument—this is quite clear from the rephrasing of it in my last paragraph—is that *in* coming to believe the reason statement, the agent is coming to consider the matter aright. This leaves it quite open how the transition is effected.

It is worth emphasizing that there need be nothing philosophically mysterious about the notion of considering matters aright in this kind of context: no implication of a weird metaphysic, for instance, in which values or obligations are set over against our subjectivity, as independent of it as the shapes and sizes of things.[5] If we think of

---

5. Here I am in agreement with Simon Blackburn (see, e.g., chaps. 5 and 6 of *Spreading the Word*); although I do not think it is felicitous to represent the metaphysically undemanding notion of correctness or truth that is in question as a construction on an *anti*realistic base, as in Blackburn's projectivism.

ethical upbringing in a roughly Aristotelian way, as a process of habituation into suitable modes of behaviour, inextricably bound up with the inculcation of suitably related modes of thought, there is no mystery about how the process can be the acquisition, simultaneously, of a way of seeing things and of a collection of motivational directions or practical concerns, focused and activated in particular cases by exercises of the way of seeing things.[6] And if the upbringing has gone as it should, we shall want to say that the way of seeing things—the upshot, if you like, of a moulding of the agent's subjectivity—involves considering them aright, that is, having a correct conception of their actual layout. Here talking of having been properly brought up and talking of considering things aright are two ways of giving expression to the same assessment, one that would be up for justification by ethical argument.

Let me emphasize what is implicit in this last sentence: I am using the notion of proper upbringing only to defuse the threat of metaphysical peculiarity, not as a foundational element in some sort of ethical theory—as if we had independent access to what counts as a good ethical upbringing, and could use that to explain ethical truth as a property enjoyed by the judgements that a properly brought up person would make.

What if someone has not been properly brought up? In order to take seriously the idea that someone who has been properly brought up tends to consider matters aright in the relevant area, we surely do not need to embrace the massively implausible implication that someone who has not been properly brought up—someone who has slipped through the net, so to speak—can be induced into seeing things straight by directing some piece of *reasoning* at him. On the contrary, reasoning aimed at generating new motivations will surely stand a chance of working only if it appeals to something in the audience's existing motivational make-up, in something like the way exploited in Williams's account of the internal interpretation; and the trouble with someone who has in some radical way slipped through the net is that there may be no such point of leverage for

---

6. See *Nicomachean Ethics*, book 2; but no specific Aristotelian detail matters to the point I am making—what is in question is barely more than common sense. The terminology I have used to describe what I allege to be unmysterious in the light of Aristotelian common sense comes from David Wiggins: see "Deliberation and Practical Reason".

reasoning aimed at generating the motivations that are characteristic of someone who has been properly brought up. What it would take to get such a person to consider the relevant matters aright, we might plausibly suppose, is exactly the sort of thing that, according to Williams's argument, the external reasons theorist may not appeal to: something like conversion. Admittedly, it is not straightforwardly obvious how we should think of this, or some better substitute, as operating; the bare idea of conversion points at best to a schema for explanations of shifts of character, and the weight of the explanation in any real case would rest on our comprehension of the psychic efficacy of the specific converting factor (a religious experience, say). But it does not seem hopeless to suppose that at least sometimes we really might be able to understand on these lines how someone who had slipped through the net might suddenly or gradually become as if he had been properly brought up, with the interlocking collection of concerns and way of seeing things that he failed to acquire earlier. The idea of conversion would function here as the idea of an intelligible shift in motivational orientation that is exactly *not* effected by inducing a person to discover, by practical reasoning controlled by existing motivations, some internal reasons that he did not previously realize he had. But if its upshot *is* a case of considering matters aright, why should such a process not count as someone's being made aware of some *external* reasons, reasons that he had all along, for acting in the relevant ways?

It is plausible, then, that from certain starting-points there is no rational route—no process of being swayed by reasons—that would take someone to being as if he had been properly brought up. (Being properly brought up is not itself a rational route into being that way.) But this has no evident tendency to disrupt the natural connection between being that way and considering matters aright. So why not suppose that the kind of conversion I have envisaged might be a case of what the external reasons theorist needed: acquisition of a new motivation by way of acquiring correct beliefs?

5. Williams simply assumes what rules this out, that the external reasons theorist must envisage a transition to considering matters aright that would be effected by reasoning. This assumption is held in place by what Williams takes to be the only point of believing in

external reasons. According to Williams, the external reasons theorist wants to be able to bring a charge of *irrationality* against anyone who is not motivated in some direction that the theorist thinks he should be motivated in; "he wants any rational agent, as such, to acknowledge the requirement to do the thing in question" (p. 110).

There is certainly a recognizable temptation hereabouts. Moralists in particular are prone to suppose that there must be a knockdown argument, an appeal to unaided reason, which, if one could only find it and get people to listen, would force anyone capable of being influenced by reasons at all into caring about the sorts of things one ought to care about. In itself this might be no more than a harmless fantasy (although when the expectation of finding such an argument is disappointed, this can lead to morality's seeming problematic in ways that it should not).[7] What is in question at present, however, is a related temptation, which one can see that one should avoid however optimistic one is about the prospects for the knockdown argument: the temptation, lacking the knockdown argument as we all do, to talk as if the argument is out in the open and people who do not care about the sorts of things they ought to care about are flying in the face of it. Williams's excellent point is that an accusation of irrationality that is supposed to convey something on those lines is nothing but "bluff" (p. 111).[8]

As Williams notes, there are plenty of things that the internal reasons approach allows one to say against someone who is not motivated by the considerations one thinks he should be motivated by: for instance, "that he is inconsiderate, or cruel, or selfish, or imprudent; or that things, and he, would be a lot nicer if he were so motivated" (p. 110). (We can add: that the shape of his motivations reveals that he has not been properly brought up.) So what is the point of holding out for the right to make an accusation of irrationality as well, if it is not to bluff the person into mending his ways by means of a fraudulent suggestion that he is flouting considerations that anyone susceptible to reasons at all would be moved by? Perhaps the answer is "None"; it may be that calling a person "irrational" carries,

---

7. I use "morality" here as a mere variant on "ethics"; the point is not one about the special topic that Williams discusses in chap. 10 of *Ethics and the Limits of Philosophy*.

8. A similar point is made by Philippa Foot, in "Morality as a System of Hypothetical Imperatives". In Essay 4 above, I try to defend a version of the idea of the categorical imperative whose point would not lie in this kind of intellectual dishonesty.

beyond the possibility of cancellation, the illicit implication that he is unmoved by something that would move anyone capable of being moved by reasons at all. (I shall come back to this later.) But even if we renounce any right to direct an accusation of irrationality against a *person* when he is unmoved by considerations we think he should be moved by, that does not quite settle the question whether, as Williams puts it at one point (p. 111), "the only rationality of action is the rationality of internal reasons".

What is at issue here is the relation between the *explanatory* role of the concept of reason and a *critical* or *normative* dimension that it must have. Williams is considering this issue when he raises the question (pp. 102–3) whether someone who believes of some petrol that it is gin, and wants a gin and tonic, should be said to have a reason to mix the petrol with tonic and drink it. If he does that, we shall have an explanation, of the reason-giving kind, for his doing what he does. But Williams suggests that an internal reasons theorist should not say, on those grounds, that the person does have a reason to drink the stuff which is in fact petrol:

> It looks in the wrong direction, by implying in effect that the internal reason conception is only concerned with explanation, and not at all with the agent's rationality, and this may help to motivate a search for other sorts of reason which are connected with his rationality. But the internal reason conception is concerned with the agent's rationality. What we can correctly ascribe to him in a third-personal internal reason statement is also what he can ascribe to himself as a result of deliberation . . .

Here Williams is making room for a thought on these lines: the explanatory power of reason-giving explanations depends on there being a critical dimension to the concept of rationality. These explanations do not merely reveal actions as the outcome of some way— to whose detail we can be indifferent—in which the agent happens to be internally organized; that the operations of an internal organization from which an action is represented as flowing are recognizably the right kind of operations for the explanation to be of the reason-giving sort requires that they approximate sufficiently closely to something in the nature of an ideal.[9] Reason-giving explanations re-

---

9. Donald Davidson has written in this connection of the constitutive role of the concept of rationality (in its normative or critical application) in organizing our understanding of the concepts of common-sense psychology. See *Essays on Actions and Events*, especially

quire a conception of how things ideally would be, sufficiently independent of how any actual individual's psychological economy operates to serve as the basis for critical assessment of it. In particular, there must be a potential gap between the ideal and the specific directions in which a given agent's motivations push him.

Williams secures an independence that conforms to this abstract description, in the passage I have quoted, by his appeal to deliberation: what practical rationality requires of an agent is not simply read off from his specific motivations just as they stand (including, in Williams's example, a wish to drink some stuff that is in fact petrol), but is determined, from those motivations, by deliberation, whose capacity to correct and enrich the specific motivations one starts with is supposed to open up the necessary gap between actual and ideal.

But it is open to question whether this puts the *right* distance between the basis for criticism of the way an agent's actions flow from his psychological states, on the one hand, and the way his psychology happens to be, on the other.[10] Certainly the appeal to deliberation interposes some space between these things, but the standard is still, albeit with the indirection that that imposes, fixed by the agent's motivations as they stand. There is thus a sense in which it can be claimed that the resulting picture of the critical dimension of the concept of practical rationality is *psychologistic.* That term has become attached[11] to Frege's reproach against positions that treated the principles of logic, which we can think of as delineating an important part of the structure of theoretical rationality, as "laws of thought" rather than "laws of truth".[12] Frege's point was, in effect, that if logic is to be able to stand in judgement over the workings of

---

Essays 11 and 12. (The point comes out in the plausibility of saying that it would make no sense to suppose that an explanation was of the reason-giving sort while disallowing the question how *good* the reason is for which the agent is said to have acted. This suggests that Williams did not need to deny that the agent has a reason, in the case he describes: he could have made the essential point about the importance of the critical dimension of the concept of rationality by allowing that the agent has a reason, but insisting that the reason is open to objection.)

10. Of course it is not only (or even, perhaps, primarily) actions that can be criticized on the basis of a conception of rationality; but the topic of this paper is reasons for action in particular.

11. See Michael Dummett, *Frege: Philosophy of Language.*

12. See the opening of "Thoughts".

minds, it cannot be constructed out of mere facts about how psychological transitions take place. One reason, then, for doubting that "the only rationality of action is the rationality of internal reasons", quite distinct from the wish to browbeat people into (for instance, and especially) morality by a fraudulent accusation of irrationality, might be the idea that the critical dimension of the notion of practical rationality requires an analogous transcendence of the mere facts of individual psychology—even as corrected by the sort of deliberation that the internal reasons conception allows.

Beliefs are not rationally self-contained psychic phenomena, which could be aggregated just anyhow, with no restrictions on their interrelations and their relations to the subject's world, and still add up to a state of mind. Theoretical reason, both formal and substantive, puts limits on the attributions of belief that so much as make sense. It would get things back to front to think that an adequate conception of theoretical reason could be derivative from a set of supposedly independent data about the workings of minds. Now a point of this sort should be applicable to practical no less than to theoretical reason. Desires, in the broad "formal" sense of ingredients in subjective motivational sets, are similarly not rationally self-contained psychic phenomena, which can be unproblematically conceived as determinants, from the outside, of the shape that practical reason takes, for the individual agent whose desires they are.[13] But the idea that "the only rationality of action is the rationality of internal reasons" seems to involve thinking of the desires (in that sense) from which an individual agent starts in just this way.

In the context of this kind of refusal to find "the rationality of internal reasons" sufficient, the idea of not reasoning correctly might be glossed in terms of not giving a consideration the right weight in deliberation. On these lines, deliberating correctly would be giving all relevant considerations the force they are credited with in a correct picture of one's practical predicament. This yields a sense in which to believe an external reason statement is, as Williams indeed suggests it must be (p. 109), to believe that if the agent deliberated

---

13. See, again, Davidson, *Essays on Actions and Events*, especially Essays 11 and 12. Against the idea of desire as a self-standing phenomenon, so that particular desires stand in no need of a conception of rationality to underwrite their intelligibility, see G. E. M. Anscombe's well-known remarks about wanting a saucer of mud, in *Intention*, pp. 70–71.

correctly he would be motivated (of course not necessarily conclusively) in the direction in which the reason points.[14] But there is no implication, as in Williams's argument, that there must be a deliberative or rational procedure that would lead anyone from not being so motivated to being so motivated. On the contrary, the transition to being so motivated is a transition *to* deliberating correctly, not one effected *by* deliberating correctly; effecting the transition may need some non-rational alteration such as conversion.

Perhaps we can even give a sense to the accusation of irrationality within this framework. There would now be no question of a bluff, any more than one need be bluffing if one says, to someone who cannot find anything to appreciate in, say, twelve-tone music, "You are missing the reasons there are for seeking out opportunities to hear this music". (It might take something like a conversion to bring the reasons within the person's notice; there is no suggestion that he is failing to be swayed by something that would sway anyone capable of being influenced by reasons at all.) However, it is (at least) difficult to separate calling someone "irrational" from the suggestion that he is missing the force of something in the nature of an argument. (It would be odd to say that a person who finds no reasons to listen to twelve-tone music is irrational, even though one thinks that the reasons are there.) So far as I can see, scepticism about the adequacy of the internal reason conception has no need to insist on classifying people in these terms, and it is probably safest for it not to do so.

6. There is no question of my trying to establish the tenability of a position on these lines in this paper: my main point is only that, though Williams is surely right about the bluff he attacks, that does not show that the internal conception of practical reason gives us everything we want. In this section, I shall very briefly mention some possible different lines on which a scepticism about external reasons might be defended, and suggest responses to them.

---

14. This is essentially the point made by Brad Hooker, "Williams' Argument Against External Reasons"; he credits it to Robert Gay. Hooker does not question Williams's claim that the transition to being moved by an allegedly external reason would have to be effected by reasoning.

On the internal conception, practical reason can be, in a sense, content-neutral: deliberation is indifferent to the nature of the motivations that constitute input to it, and might be conceived as a procedure for imposing coherence and practical determinacy on whatever collection of prior motivations one presents it with. On an external conception, by contrast, practical reason is not something that can be equally well exemplified whatever the content of the motivations one begins with. If one is tempted to think that the content-neutrality of deductive rationality ought to generalize over all applications of reason, one will be inclined to see an argument for the internal conception here. But the argument would be no stronger than the case for generalizing that feature of deductive logic. And surely it is no more obvious that we should expect practical reason to be content-neutral than it is that we should expect, for instance, scientific reason to be so.[15]

Reasons must be capable of explaining actions; and it can seem that if we are to find that intelligible, we must conceive practical reason as directing the action-generating efficacy of a collection of motivations that are prior to it, and, as far as rational explanation goes, simply given. This idea is clearly congenial to the internal conception. But it rests on what looks like a misconception of the way actions are explained by reasons, one that assimilates that to the way events are explained by mechanical forces such as the tension in a tightly wound spring. One can be suspicious of this assimilation without threat to the thesis that reason-giving explanations are causal.[16] To respect the truism that reason-giving explanations work by revealing how actions are motivated, it is not necessary to picture motivations as antecedent quasi-mechanical sources of energy: in explaining an action, a reason-giving explanation can equally make the motivation of the action rationally intelligible, and there is no basis for insisting that this must be by way of representing that motivation as the upshot of reason's channelling a pre-rational motivational force in a certain direction.[17]

The opposition to psychologism I have described pictures practical predicaments as structured by collections of values that are indepen-

---

15. Williams himself would clearly have no sympathy with the idea of a purely *formal* account of practical reason.
16. For which see Davidson, "Actions, Reasons, and Causes".
17. See chap. 5 of Thomas Nagel, *The Possibility of Altruism*.

dent of any individual's motivational make-up, and this may seem to reintroduce the threat of a weird metaphysic which I discounted earlier. But this is a mistake. One way to avoid such a metaphysic is to regard values as reflections or projections of psychological facts involving affect or sentiment, and such a position might indeed have difficulties in accepting the kind of transcendence I have envisaged. But in order to acknowledge the constitutive connection of values to human subjectivity, it is not obligatory to suppose the genealogy of value can be unravelled, retrospectively, in such a way as to permit factoring out a contribution made by isolable facts about our individual psychology to the evaluative contours of our world. A sane subjectivism can allow that value transcends independently describable psychological fact.[18]

There may seem to be something suspect about the way I have exploited Williams's phrase "considering the matter aright". I suggested that when the supposed external reasons in question are ethical ones, the assessment expressed in "aright" would be grounded in ethical argument; and I meant argument internal to some specific ethical outlook, not argument that would somehow win over someone unmoved by what one wants to represent as external reasons. There is an intelligible temptation to suppose that such a use of "aright" cannot be more than bluster. That is indeed what it would be if it were meant somehow to impress outsiders, even in the absence of any ability to persuade them; that is Williams's point about bluff. But I have disavowed any aim of manipulating the notion like this. Nothing more would be in question, in any particular appeal to a determinate conception of how the relevant matters are rightly considered, than confidence in some part of an ethical outlook. (Ethical external reasons are not external to ethics.) This can seem a second-grade application of the concept of correctness, but it is open to question whether we can do better in any region of our thinking.[19] We do not conceive our values as owing their authenticity, and their relevance to what we do, to our motivational make-up or to anything in the psychological genesis of our coming to have them; and that, together with our managing to sustain confidence in them

---

18. See David Wiggins, "A Sensible Subjectivism?". It was the possibility of a subjectivism of this kind that I had in mind in my remark about projectivism in n. 5 above.

19. Against Williams's suggestion, in *Ethics and the Limits of Philosophy*, that natural science is in a relevantly different position, see my "Critical Notice".

through reflection, is all it takes for us to suppose they yield reasons that are not internal in the sense Williams explains. This sustaining of confidence is fraught with difficulties; but it is a mistake to let a supposed metaphysical insight, expressed in depreciating the sense of "aright" available in appraisal of ethical thinking, seem to add to them.

I began this section as if it were going to be something of a digression, but in fact I believe the last couple of paragraphs have touched on what is in one sense the heart of the matter. Williams's explicit argument has no deeper foundation than the assumption that the external reasons theorist wants to be entitled to find irrationality when someone is insensitive to the force of a supposed external reason; and in its naked form, the assumption seems too transparently flimsy to be the real basis for his conclusion. It is too easy to drive a wedge between irrationality and insensitivity to reasons that are nevertheless there: recall the case of not appreciating twelve-tone music. But perhaps we can begin to find it intelligible that this simple point goes missing if we locate the real foundation of the argument deeper down, in an idea on these lines: the notion of truth or objectivity, implicit in the appeal to "considering the matter aright" that the external reasons theorist needs, requires beliefs to be capable of being formed either under the causal control of the circumstances that render them true or as a result of exercising rationality conceived in purely procedural terms, as something that can be compelling without need of substantive presuppositions. Beliefs about values or obligations had better not fall under the first of these disjuncts, on pain of a weird metaphysic; so, according to this line of thought, they would have to fall under the second. I do not mean to suggest that starting here would make the argument against external reasons any stronger; on the contrary, we might just as well argue by *modus tollens* from the continued ease of driving the wedge to the conclusion that there must be something wrong with the disjunction. But there are familiar philosophical concerns about truth and objectivity whose operation, in some such form as this, might make it seem that Williams's starting assumption would have to be common ground.[20] All this, however, is off stage so far as Williams's article is concerned, and in another sense this section remains simply a digression.

---

20. The assumption seems to be conceded without question in Christine M. Korsgaard's acute discussion of Williams, in "Skepticism about Practical Reason".

7. Williams's argument depends crucially on the basic premise that a transition to a correct view of the reasons for acting that apply to an agent—to considering these matters aright—must be capable of being effected, for the agent, by reasoning. The internal reasons approach gives an account of such transitions that represents the possibilities for making them, and therefore the content of a correct view of reasons, as determined by the motivational orientation from which the agent in question begins. If one is suspicious of this account of how a correct view of reasons is determined, one's only recourse, given the basic premise, is to postulate a kind of reasoning that is practical but not shaped by the motivations of those who engage in it; this then looks like a supposed exercise of that bloodless or dispassionate Reason that stands opposed to Passion in a familiar and unprepossessing genre of moral psychology, one that Hume made it difficult to take seriously.

What I have been suggesting is that the basic premise distorts the issue. In order to urge that there is more substance to practical *reason* than the internal reasons conception allows, one need not seek to supplement the internal reasons picture of practical *reasoning*. This distinction enables us to decline the choice between, on the one hand, taking a correct view of an agent's reasons for acting to be determined (indirectly, via deliberation) by his "passions" as they stand—Williams's internal approach—and, on the other, taking it to be determined by dispassionate Reason—in effect, the only alternative Williams allows. We do not need to choose between conceiving practical reason psychologistically and conceiving it as an autonomous source of motivational energy over and above the "passions". This should begin to suggest a proper location for an investigation of practical reason that can accommodate the surely indubitable relevance of human psychology to what human beings have reason to do; the right way to think about this topic belongs between the individualistic psychologism of the internal reasons approach and the apsychologism, so to speak, of the only alternative that Williams's argumentative structure allows.[21]

---

21. I am grateful to Annette Baier and Paul Hurley for helpful comments on an earlier draft. T. M. Scanlon responded to a version of this paper that I delivered to the Eastern Division of the American Philosophical Association in December 1987, and his remarks have been very useful (though I have by no means met all his points). More recently, I have been greatly helped by comments from Jonathan Dancy.

ESSAY 6

Aesthetic Value, Objectivity, and the Fabric of the World

1. Aesthetic experience typically presents itself, at least in part, as a confrontation with value: an awareness of value as something residing in an object and available to be encountered. It thus invites the thought that value is, as J. L. Mackie puts it in his *Ethics: Inventing Right and Wrong*, "part of the fabric of the world" (p. 15). Mackie does not dispute, but indeed insists on, this phenomenological claim. But he contends that the appearance is illusory: value is not found in the world, but projected into it, a mere reflection of subjective responses.

Mackie's concern is primarily with ethical value, but he claims that "clearly much the same considerations apply to aesthetic and to moral values" (p. 15). In this paper I want to consider the plausibility of Mackie's thesis for the case of aesthetic value in particular.

The issue I mean to raise is not one about the significance of some putative range of peculiarly aesthetic, or perhaps more generally evaluative, vocabulary. It may well be true that a helpful critic rarely, if ever, makes an outright attempt to characterize the value which, in experiencing the works he discusses as they should be experienced, one should find in them (as the phenomenology of the experience tempts us to say). In that case explicitly evaluative terms are less than centrally important in the vocabulary of criticism. But this need not suggest that Mackie's thesis is not fundamental to aesthetics; for it remains plausible that the point of the critic's activity is to help his audience towards a proper experience of any work he discusses (an experience whose content he need not try to formulate explicitly), and thus that the critic's aim is, by a careful directing or focusing of the audience's attention to the work, to enable the audience to find for himself the value there is in it (still speaking as the phenomenology invites). The question Mackie raises—whether this is genuinely a matter of *finding*—has an interest for philosophical aesthetics that is quite independent of the mildly comical idea that the subject-matter of aesthetics is a set of judgements in which objects are explicitly appraised, ranked, or evaluated.

2. How should we interpret what our aesthetic experience purports, as it were, to tell us, when it represents value as part of the fabric of the world? What is the content of the appearance?

Mackie treats the thesis that value is in the world as interchangeable with the thesis that value is *objective* (see, e.g., p. 15). I believe this is not an innocuous variation of terminology; I think it insinuates, into Mackie's account of the content of value experience, a specific and disputable philosophical conception of the world (or the real, or the factual). This opens the possibility that when Mackie argues that the phenomenology of value experience embodies an error, his arguments involve a misconstrual of what the appearances invite us to believe.

The notion of objectivity that I think Mackie has in mind is one that would be explained by contrast with a suitable notion of subjectivity. A subjective property, in the relevant sense, is one such that no adequate conception of what it is for a thing to possess it is available except in terms of how the thing would, in suitable circumstances, affect a subject—a sentient being.[1] (Think of affective properties like amusingness, or sensory secondary qualities like colours, according to a familiar conception in which what it is to *be*, say, red is not adequately conceived independently of the idea of *looking* red; this would preclude identifying the property of being red with a categorical ground for something's disposition to look red in suitable circumstances.) What is objective, in the relevant sense, is what is not

---

1. I do not say that a subjective property is one that must be *analysed* in terms of its effects on subjects, because of the difficulty of seeing how it can be an *analysis* of, say, greenness to characterize it as a disposition to look *green* under suitable circumstances (and how else is the relevant effect to be described?). See §4 below.

subjective. Thus Mackie's implied doctrine that whatever is part of the fabric of the world is objective, if it is interpreted in this way, amounts to the doctrine that the world is fully describable in terms of properties that can be understood without essential reference to their effects on sentient beings. (Categorical grounds for affective or secondary properties can be part of the fabric of the world, on this view, even though the subjective properties they sustain cannot.)

Mackie cites two traditional reasons for holding that value is not in the world, the argument from relativity and the argument from queerness. (He supplements them with the claim that the illusion he takes them to reveal, embedded in the phenomenology of value experience, can be explained in terms of "patterns of objectification" (pp. 42–6).) Both arguments seem to owe their apparent cogency to the prior assumption that the world is objective in something like the sense I have just sketched.

Mackie's presentation of the argument from relativity (pp. 36–8) is partly spoiled by a tendency to slide between variation in valuings from one community to another, or within communities, and disagreement in valuings, as if those were the same thing. A shallow subjectivism might start from the thought that striking differences between, say, the artefacts of different cultures must result from a *disagreement* in valuings. This would yield an argument against any serious use, in this connection, of the notion of truth or the notion of the world: at most one of a pair of incompatible sets of valuings could match the world, and, since there is no unprejudiced way of telling which, we had better conclude that neither does. But this line of thought would be very crude. Our appreciating what we do need not preclude our supposing that there are different values, to which we are perhaps insensitive, in the artefacts of remote cultures—as if, when we take the value we find in the objects we appreciate to be really there in them, we use up all the room the world might afford for aesthetic merit to occupy. In fact it is remarkable, and heartening, to what extent, without losing hold of the sensitivities from which we begin, we can learn to find worth in what seems at first too alien to appreciate.

I think the argument Mackie intends is not this crude argument, but one that starts from the fact of *variation* in valuings (not necessarily amounting to disagreement), and turns on the claim that such variation is "more readily explained by the hypothesis that [the valuings] reflect ways of life than by the hypothesis that they reflect perceptions . . . of objective values" (p. 37).[2] Now the role of a way of life, in a plausible story about what presents itself as a sensitivity to the value in a particular range of aesthetic objects, is no doubt sufficiently analogous to the role of a specific sensory apparatus, in a plausible story about what presents itself as a sensitivity to (for instance) colours, to warrant the thought that the values are subjective in something like the sense suggested above.[3] But this rules out supposing that the sensitivity is just that—a capacity to detect and respond to something that is part of the fabric of the world—only if we make the prior assumption that nothing subjective, in that sense, is found in the world. The word "objective" is essential to Mackie's formulation of the hypothesis he wants us to reject; if "objective" were deleted, it would no longer seem so clear that we have to choose.[4]

As for the argument from queerness (pp. 38–42): there would indeed be something weird (to put it mildly) about the idea of a property that, while retaining the "phenomenal" character of experienced value, was conceived to be part of the world as objectively characterized. It would be as if we tried to construct a conception of amusingness that was fully intelligible otherwise than in terms of the characteristic human responses to what is amusing, but nevertheless contrived somehow to retain the "phenomenal" aspect of amusingness as we experience it in those responses.[5] But the phenomenology

---

2. I have omitted some words that suggest, again, the idea that the divergent perceptions would have to be in competition. Certainly any sensible cognitivism would have to make room for the thought that many of the experiences that purport to be perceptions of value are, as Mackie says, "seriously inadequate and badly distorted". But sheer variation does not itself justify that thought.
3. Membership of a community, or sympathetic understanding of its way of life, would constitute a point of view, in the extended sense that I am going to introduce in §3 below.
4. What emerges here is the possibility that explaining the perceptions as reflecting ways of life might not amount to explaining *away* what the perceptions purport to discover in reality.
5. I would sympathize with anyone who found this idea incoherent, whereas Mackie insists that his target is a thought that is coherent (though, of course, false). This might cast doubt on my interpretation of Mackie, were it not that this issue about coherence is duplicated in the case of Mackie's views about colour. Here he takes it to be coherent, though false, to suppose that there are colour properties that are not secondary but primary (that is, they characterize things independently of their effect on perceivers), but "resemble" colours as they figure in our experience (that is, they retain the "phenomenal" as

of value experience sets up this strain only if we insist on interpreting it in terms of a conception of the world as objective in the sense I have sketched.[6]

What emerges, then, is the prospect of a debate about whether it is compulsory to accept the equation of the world (what is real or factual) with what is objective in the relevant sense. If it is not compulsory, the phenomenology can be differently understood, so as to be, perhaps, immune to the traditional arguments. (And if there is no illusion to explain, Mackie's supplementation of the traditional arguments falls away as superfluous.)

When we consider aesthetic value in particular, there is a special advantage in shifting discussion away from Mackie's arguments to the question whether those arguments attack the right target. The issue is this: if we grant that we cannot construct a conception of aesthetic value that is detached from the idea of an experience of an object's seeming to have it, any more than we can construct a conception of amusingness that is detached from the idea of the responses that constitute finding something amusing, are we thereby debarred from supposing that we find aesthetic value (or amusingness) in the world? This is a general question about the status of properties that are not conceivable independently of sentient responses to them. Now the precise nature of the response in question can vary from case to case. And this means that we can let Mackie's harping on the queerness of, in particular, objective *prescriptivity* fade into the background; which is an improvement, since "prescrip-

---

pect of our ordinary notion of colours). Mackie rejects this thought on grounds of explanatory superfluity rather than queerness (though one might well suggest that an argument from queerness would be pretty effective against it). See Mackie's *Problems from Locke,* pp. 10–11, 18–19. I believe this idea of primary qualities that "resemble" colours as we see them can seem coherent only in the context of a quite disputable view of how colours figure in our experience; one that is at variance, moreover, with Mackie's official account of that matter.

6. I have ignored the epistemological component of Mackie's argument from queerness, where he claims that if one holds that value is in the world, one must postulate a special faculty ("intuition") to be what detects it. If the aim is, as Mackie takes it to be, to insist on the existence of primary qualities that "resemble" value properties as we experience them, it is hard to see how inventing a sense-like faculty would help. For surely values would seem to stand to any such faculty in the same sort of relation as that in which colours stand to the faculty of vision, thus remaining stubbornly non-primary.

tivity" suggests a specific response involving value's appeal to the *will*, and this is at best questionably appropriate for ethical value in general, and surely inappropriate for aesthetic value.

Mackie claims (p. 43) that the inclination to take value experience to be cognitive is less entrenched with aesthetic value than with moral value. This strikes me as exactly the reverse of the truth: and I think the reason is connected with the irrelevance, or near irrelevance, of the will to an account of aesthetic value. The phenomenology of value experience in general suggests a visual model for our dealings with value. In the moral case we are prone to be tempted away from that model by the distracting influence of the concept of choice or decision; whereas in the aesthetic case—so long as we are not corrupted by an easy philosophical assimilation—that temptation is not operative. (I think the temptation should be resisted in the moral case too, but that is another story.)

3. The conception of the world as objective, in something like the sense I have sketched, is given an explicit and highly illuminating discussion by Bernard Williams in *Descartes: The Project of Pure Enquiry*.[7] In this section I shall set out some salient features of Williams's discussion, with a view to raising the question whether the conception he describes can succeed in underwriting Mackie's metaphysically disparaging attitude to values.

The fundamental idea is the idea of the distinction between reality and appearance (see p. 241). The way the world really is must be distinguished from ways the world appears to be only because the recipient of the appearance occupies some local or parochial point of view.[8] An illustration of this distinction, with a literal application of the notion of a point of view, is afforded by the way we correct for the angle from which we are observing a plane surface when we form a judgement about its true shape.[9] But this use of the notion of

---

7. See especially pp. 241 and ff.
8. For the phrase "point of view" see, e.g., p. 245. Williams also uses, apparently interchangeably with the notion of a point of view, the notion of a perspective (see, e.g., p. 243). Ted Cohen persuaded me that this is a misuse of the notion of a perspective. But I think the attractiveness of the line of thought Williams sets out is not affected.
9. The illustration is not Williams's; he goes straight to the metaphorical use of the notion of a point of view.

a special point of view, as something requiring to be transcended if we are to achieve a conception of things as they are in themselves, lends itself naturally to metaphorical extension. Thus it is natural to think of possession of the special perceptual apparatus involved in colour vision as constituting a special point of view; and a generalization of this line of thought is what underlies the familiar philosophical thought that a description of the world as it really is would leave out the secondary qualities. Again, a description of something as amusing issues from a peculiarly human point of view, constituted, in this case, by certain "human tastes and interests" (p. 243); and a similar line of thought suggests that amusingness cannot belong to a description of things as they are in themselves.

Williams does not explicitly discuss the case of value as such. Perhaps amusingness is already an example of an aesthetic value. In any case, the evident analogy between relativity to tastes and interests and relativity to sensory peculiarities suggests a ready extension to value of the line of thought Williams spells out about secondary qualities.

It is natural to wonder whether the idea of transcending special points of view really makes sense. Surely any conception of reality we could achieve would still be *our* conception of reality, from a point of view we occupied; the idea of a view from nowhere is incoherent.[10] Williams notices this difficulty, and responds as follows (p. 244):

> ... there is no suggestion that we should try to describe a world without ourselves using any concepts, or without using concepts which we, human beings, can understand. The suggestion is that there are possible descriptions of the world using concepts which are not peculiarly ours, and not peculiarly relative to our experience. Such a description would be that which would be arrived at, as C. S. Peirce put it, if scientific enquiry continued long enough: it is the content of that "final opinion" which Peirce believed that enquiry would inevitably converge upon, a "final opinion ... independent not indeed of thought in general, but of all that is arbitrary and individual in thought".[11]

---

10. It is important to remember how far we are from a literal application of the notion of a point of view. The thought that there cannot be a view from nowhere is not the Berkeleyan thought that any conception of how things are must be a conception of how things would strike a possible perceiver.

11. The quotation is from "A Critical Review of Berkeley's Idealism", p. 82.

It is worth making explicit the distinctive character of the view of scientific enquiry that Williams here embraces. Scientific enquiry must be conceived as defined by a determinate method—one capable of yielding its practitioners some sort of assurance that they are on a path that, if properly followed, would lead at the limit to the ideal convergence Peirce envisaged. And scientific enquiry, so conceived, is taken to be a pure mode of investigation of the world, uncontaminated in itself by relativity to anything local or parochial. When a candidate mode of investigation of reality is such that its upshot is vulnerable to the line of thought exemplified in the discussion of secondary qualities, someone can always complain, about the view of reality that candidate yields, "That is merely how things strike *us*, constituted as we are". Facts about ourselves, additional to anything required of an investigator as such, prevent our achieving, in that way, an undistorted view of the world as it really is. But it is not so with scientific enquiry on the Peircean view that Williams endorses. Not that we cannot be engaged in scientific enquiry and still get reality wrong. But that will be because of our own fallibility; or perhaps because of our distance from the ideal end-point—perhaps there are some things we cannot get right until we are nearer getting everything right than we are. The method itself is conceived as intrinsically non-distorting; as a pure or transparent mode of access to reality.

So far we have been considering the conception of the world as it is in itself, that is, independently of the way it appears from this or that special point of view. What Williams calls "the absolute conception of reality" is something arrived at by extending the conception of the world as it is in itself so as to encompass and be able to explain the various appearances (see p. 245; the extension will be considered further in §4 below). Now Williams's need for something to play the role he envisages for scientific enquiry emerges very clearly from a dilemma with which he confronts the absolute conception of reality in an important earlier passage (pp. 64–7). If, on the one hand, the absolute conception does not involve any determinate substance (any determinate conception of things as being one way rather than another), but is a matter of conceiving the world merely as whatever it is of which the various particular appearances are appearances, then it would be self-deceptive to suppose we have anything against which we could assess, and in terms of which we could explain, the various appearances; as Williams puts it (p. 65), "the conception of an independent reality . . . slips out of the picture, leaving us only with a variety of possible representations to measure against each other, with nothing to mediate between them". If, on the other hand, we require the absolute conception to be a determinate conception of the way things are in themselves, then we are vulnerable to the worry that attaining such a conception is only attaining another particular point of view, so that all we have is a conception of how things appear from there—another appearance to add to the others, not something transcending appearance, in terms of which all appearances could be explained.

It seems clear that this dilemma can fail to be fatal to the absolute conception only if we take ourselves to be equipped with a pure or transparent mode of access to reality as it is in itself, such as is constituted by scientific enquiry on Williams's Peircean conception. (It was not inevitable that this abstract requirement should seem to be met by science, as opposed to, for instance, divine revelation; but in our culture the casting of science in the necessary role is overwhelmingly natural.) The idea that we have a transparent mode of access to reality can permit us to occupy something like the second horn of the dilemma. It entitles us to claim to have, if not "a determinate picture of what the world is like independent of any knowledge or representation in thought" (p. 65), at least a determinate picture of a determinate picture of what the world is like in itself,[12] and an assurance that at least the general shape of current science's (first-order) world view is on the right lines. And the conception of science as transparent blunts the point of the second horn as Williams presents the dilemma. The determinacy in the scientific picture of the world does not carry with it any vulnerability to the accusation that that picture is only how things appear from another point of view (the scientific point of view); scientific enquiry is conceived as progressively revealing to us reality as it is in itself. So the idea of a transparent mode of access to the world disarms the dilemma. And it seems clear that nothing else would serve; if the absolute conception is not to be

---

12. For the retreat to the second-order, compare Williams, p. 301: "a view of the world (or at least the coherent conception of such a view) which contains a theory of error: which can explain the possibility of rival views, and of itself".

empty (the first horn), it requires the idea of a mode of investigation that gives us the world itself, as that against which all mere representations of it are to be measured.

Williams himself does not use the absolute conception of reality in order to recommend an anti-cognitivist position about the properties that would be excluded from the Peircean description of the world. Indeed, he is explicit to the contrary about the case of colour (see p. 254, n. 19): his claim is not that we can know only what figures in its own right in the absolute conception of things, but only that our knowledge must be "comprehensibly related" to the absolute conception, and this allows, he says, the possibility of knowing that something is, say, green. But it would be unsurprising if this hospitality to an apparent cognitivism struck someone as a merely superficial terminological tolerance. (This would be particularly unsurprising in someone who was less cautious than Williams is committed to being about the precise manner in which the non-absolute parts of our knowledge—or, as such a person might prefer, "knowledge"—are to be comprehensibly related to the absolute conception of reality. I shall return to Williams's caution, about the case of colour in particular, in §4 below.) If the absolute conception is the frame within which all reflection on our cognitive dealings with the world must take place, then the contrast between reality and appearance is irresistibly brought into play—that is, after all, where we began—with secondary and affective qualities, and value, on the side of the appearances. Williams indeed speaks with apparent approval of "the idea . . . that the scientific picture presents the reality of which the secondary qualities, as perceived, are appearances" (p. 245). Perhaps it is only a matter of temperament whether one finds it natural at such a point, as Williams evidently does not, to say not just "appearances" but "mere appearances". In understanding the inclination to add "mere", we can understand how the thesis that all our knowledge must be comprehensibly related to the absolute conception might seem to leave no room for any substantive objection to Mackie's implied doctrine that what is *strictly* real, or part of the world, is objective. Perhaps this view might allow a more relaxed use of "world" or "reality" to pass muster on occasion, if explicitly recognized as non-strict. But the absolute conception cannot let such a relaxed use pass for all purposes, on pain of blurring the indispensable distinction between reality and appearance.

I conjecture, then, that what seems to justify Mackie's assumption that what is real, or part of the world, is objective—or perhaps what accounts for his not seeing that thesis as something for which a justification may be demanded—is something like the absolute conception of reality. But there is room for scepticism about the strength of any justification it can afford. I shall suggest two different grounds for scepticism in the two sections that follow.

4. The absolute conception owes what credentials it has, as the frame for all reflection about our cognitive relations with the world, to its explanatory aspirations. The conception of the world as it is in itself is not supposed to be a mere highest common factor, "the most that a set of very different observers could arrive at, like some cosmic United Nations resolution" (p. 244). Mere consensus could not by itself justify the claim to present the reality of which the non-agreed residues are appearances. The claim of the conception of the world as it is independently of observers (the objective conception of the world) to monopolize the "reality" side of the distinction between reality and appearance depends on the possibility of extending it so as to become the absolute conception: that is, extending it so as to embrace and explain the particular points of view it transcends. (See especially pp. 245–6.)

But there is room for doubt about this extension. Can the expansion to embrace the various local points of view be undertaken in the objective spirit that would be required for its upshot to sustain the correlation between objectivity and reality? Or would it necessitate—surely defeating the project—that we lapse back from trying to transcend particular points of view, in order to achieve an undistorted picture of reality as it is in itself, into unregenerately occupying the points of view that were to be transcended?

Take the case of colour. Williams considers an account of colour properties as dispositions to look red, green, etc., in certain circumstances; but he expresses scepticism about it, on the ground that "it leaves us with the discouraging task of explaining '. . . looks green' in some way which does not presuppose any prior understanding of '. . . is green'" (p. 243). This pessimism seems well placed; and what it amounts to is the thought that the content of the appearances to be explained in this case—how it is that things appear from the point of view in question—is not so much as intelligible except on the basis of occupying the point of view. (Not that one has to suppose always that things are coloured the way they appear to be. But only someone who has, or at least might have, a use for "... is green" can understand what it is for something to look green.) Thus an explanation of the appearances in this case would have to address itself exclusively to occupants of the point of view in question, on pain of unintelligibility in its formulation of its explicandum. And how could such an explanation help show us how to transcend that point of view, let alone help convince us that transcending it is necessary if we are to achieve a correct conception of our relation to reality?

Williams writes of "understanding ... , at a general and reflective level, why things *appear variously coloured* to various observers" (p. 242, my emphasis). Of course there is no disputing the possibility of such understanding, on the basis of information about the behaviour of light and the construction of visual equipment. But it seems to be an illusion to suppose that such understanding could still be forthcoming after we had definitively left behind a view of the world that represents colours as properties things have (it would be a mere pleonasm to say "really have"): in such a position, we would no longer understand what it was that we were supposed to be explaining. And it is mysterious how we are to be sustained in our resolve to abandon, or at least disparage, a point of view by a thought that is not thinkable anywhere else.

This is not a difficulty about the case of colours alone. Williams remarks that the problem about colours "is part of a larger question, how the partial views and local experiences are themselves to be related to the world as conceived in independence of them" (p. 244). The general idea is that in an overarching objective account (the absolute conception of reality), the subjective properties (such as colours) that figure in common-sense pictures of the world would be revealed as mere reflections of subjective responses to objective reality, "projected on to the description of the world" (p. 245). To achieve the overarching objective account, one needs to transcend the point of view from which a given range of subjective concepts appears to be required to describe how things are, while nevertheless retaining as objectively factual the use of those concepts, or something close enough to them to serve as a basis for the supposed projection, in describing the content of the experiences characteristic of that point of view. This would work if the occurrence of the relevant predicates in describing the content of the experiences were intelligible independently of understanding their use to say how (as one takes it) things are.[13] But that is just what Williams is sceptical of in the case of colour predicates; and the point of the scepticism cannot be confined to the case of colour, but applies quite generally to the relation between the notions of *appearing* thus and so and *being* thus and so. There is a general difficulty about the idea that we can firmly detach subjective properties from objects in the world, eschewing all need for the idea of an object's really possessing such a property, while retaining the thought that such properties "figure in our experience", so that we can regard them as projected on to the world from there.[14]

Williams returns later in the book to the question what is involved in incorporating states of consciousness into an objective conception of the world. In a strikingly illuminating passage, he draws a connection between the difficulties in a certain familiar model of self-knowledge, on the one hand, and a misguided attempt to locate the *contents* of states of consciousness in the objective world, on the other (p. 295):

> If I . . . revert to the third-personal or objective point of view, and try to form a conception from there of just what is in the world when A is in pain, the temptation is to try to write into the world, in some hazy way, the appropriate content of A's experience—as we might naturally, but too easily, say: the pain. But in taking the content of A's experience, and putting it into the world as a thing we can conceive of as there, we are in effect trying to abstract from *how it is for A*, the *how it is* and leave it as a fact on its own, which however has the mysterious property that it is available only to A, and can only be known directly

---

13. It is important that the predicates have to be *used* in describing the content of the experiences. I am not suggesting that there is a problem about the absolute conception's capacity to encompass, as a possible explicandum, someone's inclination to utter the word "green" when visually confronted with something. But that is not the same as crediting it with a capacity to encompass the fact that something *looks green* to someone.

14. The idea may be encouraged by the perennial temptation to fall into a traditional sense-datum view of perception, which allows the thought that phenomenal redness, say, is a genuine property of *something* in the objective world, namely some sense-data. (I think Mackie's talk of "resemblance"—see n. 5 above—really only makes sense in this sort of context, though it is not the theoretical framework in which Mackie claims to be operating.)

to *A*, though it can be conceived of, guessed at, and so on by others. But there must be a misconception here. The *only* perspective on the contents of *A*'s consciousness is the perspective of *A*'s consciousness. When *it is so for A* (e.g. *it hurts for A*), the only way of one's conceiving the appropriate *it is so* at all is that of adopting . . . *A*'s point of view and putting oneself imaginatively in a state which one expresses (if it can be verbally expressed) by saying, as *A, it is so* (e.g. *it hurts*).

But one can fully concede how perceptive this is, while remaining sceptical about what Williams aims to protect by distinguishing it from the misconception he discusses here: remaining sceptical, that is, about the claim that an objective conception of the world can embrace the relevant states of consciousness themselves—facts of Williams's form *it is so for A*, where the appropriate *it is so* has an essentially phenomenal character. It ought not to be controversial that such facts can be grasped from a *third-personal* point of view. But it does not follow that they are *objectively* graspable in a sense that affords any comfort to the absolute conception of reality. It seems inescapable to suppose that facts of the form in question are intelligible (third-personally, by all means) only at, or from, a sentient standpoint whose phenomenological character is sufficiently similar to that of the facts to be understood.[15] This is a claim about the difficulty of finding room in objective reality, not for the abstracted *it is so*, but for the composite *it is so for A*. And in the light of this claim, Williams's easy equation of "third-personal" with "objective" (which has to mean "independent of any special point of view") seems simply mistaken.

There is, then, a difficulty about the absolute conception's capacity to encompass the relevant subjective responses; and this raises a doubt about the absolute conception's capacity to justify the view

---

15. This has been argued by Thomas Nagel. See, e.g., his *Mortal Questions*, p. 172: "There is a sense in which phenomenological facts are perfectly objective: one person can know or say of another what the quality of the other's experience is. They are subjective, however, in the sense that even this objective ascription of experience is possible only for someone sufficiently similar to the object of ascription to be able to adopt his point of view—to understand the ascription in the first person as well as the third, so to speak." Nagel's point is not at all met, as Williams seems to imply at pp. 296–7, by the thought that the totality of objectively graspable facts may *determine* the facts about consciousness. That thought—which is indeed highly plausible—is quite compatible with the falsity of any physicalism strong enough to rule out attributive dualism.

that subjective properties reflect a projection of subjective responses on to the description of the world.[16]

5. The second ground for doubt is over the idea of scientific enquiry as a transparent mode of access to reality itself. Without falling into scepticism about the general reliability of science, one may well suspect that there is an element of philosophers' fantasy in the thought that the idea of science can yield a conception of an "Archimedean point" (Williams, p. 67), from which a comparison could be set up between particular representations of the world and the world itself.[17]

Surely whatever is substantive in any actual view of scientific method is itself part of a substantive view of what the world is like, which cannot escape being the product of a particular location in the history of science. One's beliefs about which sorts of transactions with the world yield knowledge of it are not prior to, but part of, one's beliefs about what the world is like; necessarily so, since the transactions themselves take place in the world. If a characterization of scientific method is to be general enough to be able to survive radical alterations in scientific theory, it needs to appeal to highly abstract notions like that of simplicity; and such notions acquire determinate content, and practical bite in the selection of one hypothesis as superior to others, only in the context of some specific beliefs. What looks simpler against one scientific background would look more complicated if the theory into which it is to be incorporated were different. This suggests a difficulty for the idea that scientific method can yield a conception of the Archimedean point. If we describe scientific method sufficiently abstractly not to seem vulnerable to accusations of historical parochialism (supposing we are worrying about Williams's dilemma at all), then the description will be insufficiently determinate to yield the idea of a standpoint from which to conceive the comparison between particular representations of the

---

16. I am not under the illusion that this section will have carried any conviction with anyone whose view of the mental is, in a broad sense, Cartesian. There is something to be said for including under this label the sort of physicalism Williams envisages at p. 297. The common feature, which makes the label not inappropriate, is an inability to accept the point Nagel insists on: namely that mental facts cannot be incorporated into a wholly objective conception of reality.

17. The idea of such a comparison is of course characteristic of traditional correspondence theories of truth.

world and the world itself (the idea of a determinate conception of the world as it is in itself). We shall be impaled on something like the first horn of Williams's dilemma. If, on the other hand, we make our account of scientific method substantive enough for it to be plausible that it counts as a representation of a determinate representation of the world, then we shall be impaled (again, supposing that we have a worry that makes us inclined to think this way at all) on the second horn of Williams's dilemma: "open to the reflection, once more, that that is only one particular representation of [the world], our own, and that we have no independent point of leverage for raising this into the absolute representation of reality" (p. 65).[18]

Williams seems to suppose that scepticism about the idea of the Archimedean point could issue only from a relativism whose ultimate tendency would be anti-scientific. A demand that the absolute conception is meant to satisfy is the demand "that we should be able to overcome relativism in our view of reality" (p. 301). Again, part of the point of the absolute conception is that it "would allow us, when we reflect on our representation of the world as being one among others, to go beyond merely assessing others, relativistically, from the standpoint of our own" (p. 211). It is hard to understand this except as suggesting that if we gave up the idea of the Archimedean point, we would leave ourselves uncomfortably vulnerable to some such thought as this: objectively speaking, there is nothing to choose between our own largely scientific view of the world and (say) some primarily animistic world view that we might have presented to us, as a possible alternative, by anthropological investigation. (We would be unable to combat the animistic world view except "relativistically, from the standpoint of our own".) But if this gave us any discomfort, it would depend on our incoherently combining conviction that the Archimedean point is unavailable with the thought that there ought still to be, so to speak, an "Archimedean" meaning that we could confer on the words "objectively speaking".[19]

---

18. Williams says (p. 246) that the absolute conception "is not something transcendental, but is an historical product of consciousness in the world". But it seems that there must be something transcendental about the idea of the view from the Archimedean point. If that view is "an historical product of consciousness in the world", then the thought of it does nothing to save us from the dilemma.

19. For a parallel point, see pp. 41–2 of Williams's own *Morality: An Introduction to Ethics*.

The right response to the claim that all our assessments of truth are made from the standpoint of a "conceptual system" that is inescapably our own is not to despair of our grip on reality but to say, with Hilary Putnam, "Well? We should use someone else's conceptual system?"[20] It is pointless to chafe at the fact that what we believe is what *we* believe. We can justify beliefs we hold about how things are (for instance, combat offered alternatives) only by appealing to what are in fact further beliefs we hold about how things are; but it would be a mistake to let this tend to undermine our confidence in the beliefs, or in their possession of a subject-matter largely independent of themselves—our confidence that we have reality more or less within our cognitive grasp. Occupation of the second horn of Williams's dilemma, unblunted by the idea of a somehow impersonal and ahistorical mode of access to reality, ought not to seem to threaten anything we should want to mean by Williams's thesis "knowledge is of what is there *anyway*" (p. 64).

This scepticism about the Archimedean point has no need to ally itself with the claim that the idea of convergent progress in science is a myth.[21] It is simply that convergence in science occupies a different position, in the right general picture of our relation to reality, from the one that Williams envisages. For Williams, the thesis that scientific enquiry converges on the truth plays a metaphysical role, in serving to introduce the idea of the Archimedean point. Once we have the idea of the Archimedean point, it is irresistible to suppose that all *genuine* truth about the world and our relation to it should be discernible from there. And since the Archimedean point has been introduced on the basis of the Peircean conception of scientific enquiry, we seem now to have been given a metaphysical foundation for the view that science constitutes the frame for all reflection on our relation to reality, and consequently a metaphysical justification for the projectivist rhetoric that seems forced on us if we try to say something suitable to such a frame about secondary qualities, affective qualities, and values. Without the Archimedean point, we can still usefully distinguish a scientifically objective component within a world view we can concede to be inescapably ours (giving up the as-

---

20. *Meaning and the Moral Sciences*, p. 32.
21. Williams considers this as a source of opposition to the absolute conception; see p. 248.

piration to render that component impersonal and ahistorical). There is nothing to prevent us from using whatever first steps towards Peircean convergence we think we can detect, in the history of science so far, as an internal check on the content of the objective component. This would be a scientific rather than metaphysical employment of the notion of scientific convergence. What we no longer have is a metaphysical reason to attribute to the objective component of our world view the status of a framework within which any philosophical reflection on the remainder of our view of reality must take place.

In short: the idea of the Archimedean point, in its Peircean version, appears to constitute a metaphysical underpinning for the tendency of science to arrogate to itself final authority over the use of the notion of the world (which is a metaphysical notion, not *ex officio* a scientific one); without the idea of the Archimedean point, that tendency stands revealed as nothing but a familiar scientism—which we can recognize as such without that relativistic disrespect for science itself that Williams rightly deplores.

6. Nothing I have said in this paper casts any doubt on the thesis that value is not objective in the sense I have attributed to Mackie. The point is, as I suggested earlier (§2), that if we can disconnect the notion of the world (or its fabric or furniture) from that notion of objectivity, then we make it possible to consider different interpretations of the claim that value is part of the world, a claim that the phenomenology of value experience has made attractive to philosophers and ordinary people. Of course this paper is at best a preliminary to that enquiry.[22]

22. In considering these different interpretations, we ought to contemplate the possibility that we might connect the notion of the world with *different* notions of objectivity. One such notion that might repay examination is one according to which an experience is of an objective reality if its object is independent of the experience itself. This is something we might make out to be true of particular experiences of value, even if what they experience is not independent of value experience in general. And we should ask ourselves whether something's being independent of each particular experience might not be enough to secure as much truth as we want for the thesis that "knowledge is of what is there anyway". Again, we ought to consider David Wiggins's suggestion that convergence need not be Peircean: that a notion of objectivity suitably explained in terms of a different notion of convergence does not, after all, exclude from objective reality all features that are subjective in the sense with which I have been concerned in this paper. (See "What Would Be a Substantial Theory of Truth?", especially at pp. 218–9.)

It would be pointless to pretend that the correlation between reality and that notion of objectivity is the only obstacle to taking the phenomenology of value experience at face value. I have already mentioned the difficulties posed by the relation that the experience of moral value apparently bears to the will (§2 above). A plausible connection between the experience of aesthetic value and the feeling of (in some sense) pleasure generates a problem about aesthetic value in particular, which might be summed up in this question: how can a mere *feeling* constitute an experience in which the world reveals itself to us? All I have done in this paper is to try to cast doubt on a line of thought that would prevent us from finding this question, and similar questions, so much as worth raising.

ESSAY 7

Values and Secondary Qualities[1]

1. J. L. Mackie insists that ordinary evaluative thought presents itself as a matter of sensitivity to aspects of the world.[2] And this phenomenological thesis seems correct. When one or another variety of philosophical non-cognitivism claims to capture the truth about what the experience of value is like, or (in a familiar surrogate for phenomenology[3]) about what we mean by our evaluative language, the claim is never based on careful attention to the lived character of evaluative thought or discourse. The idea is, rather, that the very concept of the cognitive or factual rules out the possibility of an undiluted representation of how things are, enjoying, nevertheless, the internal relation to "attitudes" or the will that would be needed for it to count as evaluative.[4] On this view the phenomenology of

---

1. This paper grew out of my contributions to a seminar on J. L. Mackie's *Ethics: Inventing Right and Wrong* that I had the privilege of sharing with Mackie and R. M. Hare in 1978. It was first published in a volume in Mackie's honour. I do not believe Mackie would have found it strange that I should pay tribute to a sadly missed colleague by continuing a strenuous disagreement with him.
2. See *Ethics: Inventing Right and Wrong*, pp. 31–5.
3. An inferior surrogate: it leads us to exaggerate the extent to which expressions of our sensitivity to values are signalled by the use of a special vocabulary. See Essay 6 above.
4. I am trying here to soften a sharpness of focus that Mackie introduces by stressing the idea of prescriptivity. Mackie's singleness of vision here has the perhaps unfortunate effect of discouraging a distinction such as David Wiggins has drawn between "evaluations" and "directives or deliberative (or practical) judgements" ("Truth, Invention, and the Meaning of Life", pp. 95–6). My topic here is really the former of these. (It may be, however, that the distinction does not after all matter in the way Wiggins suggests; see n. 46 below.)

value would involve a mere incoherence, if it were as Mackie says—a possibility that then tends (naturally enough) not to be so much as entertained. But, as Mackie sees, there is no satisfactory justification for supposing that the factual is, by definition, attitudinatively and motivationally neutral. This clears away the only obstacle to accepting his phenomenological claim; and the upshot is that non-cognitivism must offer to correct the phenomenology of value, rather than to give an account of it.[5]

In Mackie's view the correction is called for. In this paper I want to suggest that he attributes an unmerited plausibility to this thesis, by giving a false picture of what one is committed to if one resists it.

2. Given that Mackie is right about the phenomenology of value, an attempt to accept the appearances makes it virtually irresistible to appeal to a perceptual model. Now Mackie holds that the model must be perceptual awareness of *primary* qualities.[6] And this makes it comparatively easy to argue that the appearances are misleading. For it seems impossible—at least on reflection—to take seriously the idea of something that is like a primary quality in being simply *there*, independently of human sensibility, but is nevertheless intrinsically (not conditionally on contingencies about human sensibility) such as to elicit some "attitude" or state of will from someone who becomes aware of it. Moreover, the primary-quality model turns the epistemology of value into mere mystification. The perceptual model is no more than a model; perception, strictly so called, does not mirror the role of reason in evaluative thinking, which seems to require us to regard the apprehension of value as an intellectual rather than a merely sensory matter. But if we are to take account of this, while preserving the model's picture of values as brutely and absolutely

---

5. I do not believe Simon Blackburn's "quasi-realism" is a real alternative to this. (See, e.g., p. 358 of his "Truth, Realism, and the Regulation of Theory".) In so far as the quasi-realist holds that the values, in thinking and speaking about which he imitates the practices supposedly characteristic of realism, are *really* products of projecting "attitudes" into the world, he must have a conception of genuine reality—what the values lack and the things on to which they are projected have. And the phenomenological claim ought to be that *that* is what the appearances entice us to attribute to values.

6. See *Hume's Moral Theory*, pp. 32, 60–1, 73–4.

there, it seems that we need to postulate a faculty—"intuition"—about which all that can be said is that it makes us aware of objective rational connections; the model itself ensures that there is nothing helpful to say about how such a faculty might work, or why its deliverances might deserve to count as knowledge.

But why is it supposed that the model must be awareness of primary qualities rather than secondary qualities? The answer is that Mackie, following Locke, takes secondary-quality perception, as conceived by a pre-philosophical consciousness, to involve a projective error: one analogous to the error he finds in ordinary evaluative thought. He holds that we are prone to conceive secondary-quality experience in a way that would be appropriate for experience of primary qualities. So a pre-philosophical secondary-quality model for awareness of value would in effect be, after all, a primary-quality model. And to accept a philosophically corrected secondary-quality model for the awareness of value would be simply to give up trying to go along with the appearances.

I believe, however, that this conception of secondary-quality experience is seriously mistaken.

3. A secondary quality is a property the ascription of which to an object is not adequately understood except as true, if it is true, in virtue of the object's disposition to present a certain sort of perceptual appearance: specifically, an appearance characterizable by using a word for the property itself to say how the object perceptually appears. Thus an object's being red is understood as something that obtains in virtue of the object's being such as (in certain circumstances) to look, precisely, red.

This account of secondary qualities is faithful to one key Lockean doctrine, namely the identification of secondary qualities with "powers to produce various sensations in us".[7] (The phrase "perceptual appearance", with its gloss, goes beyond Locke's unspecific "sensations", but harmlessly; it serves simply to restrict our attention, as

---

7. *An Essay concerning Human Understanding*, 2.8.10.

Locke's word may not, to properties that are in a certain obvious sense perceptible.[8])

I have written of what property-ascriptions are *understood* to be true in virtue of, rather than of what they are true in virtue of. No doubt it is true that a given thing is red in virtue of some microscopic textural property of its surface; but a predication understood only in such terms—not in terms of how the object would look—would not be an ascription of the secondary quality of redness.[9]

Secondary-quality experience presents itself as perceptual awareness of properties genuinely possessed by the objects that confront one. And there is no general obstacle to taking that appearance at face value.[10] An object's being such as to look red is independent of its actually looking red to anyone on any particular occasion; so, notwithstanding the conceptual connection between being red and being experienced as red, an experience of something as red can count as a case of being presented with a property that is there anyway—there independently of the experience itself.[11] And there is no evident ground for accusing the appearance of being misleading. What would one expect it to be like to experience something's being such as to look red, if not to experience the thing in question (in the right circumstances) as looking, precisely, red?

On Mackie's account, by contrast, to take experiencing something as red at face value, as a non-misleading awareness of a property that really confronts one, is to attribute to the object a property that is "thoroughly objective",[12] in the sense that it does not need to be

---

8. Being stung by a nettle is an actualization of a power in the nettle that conforms to Locke's description, but it seems wrong to regard it as a perception of that power; the experience lacks a representational character that that would require. (It is implausible that looking red is intelligible independently of being red; combined with the account of secondary qualities that I am giving, this sets up a circle. But it is quite unclear that we ought to have the sort of analytic or definitional aspirations that would make the circle problematic. See Colin McGinn, *The Subjective View*, pp. 6-8.)

9. See McGinn, pp. 12-14.

10. Of course there is room for the concept of illusion, not only because the senses can malfunction but also because of the need for a modifier like my "in certain circumstances", in an account of what it is for something to have a secondary quality. (The latter has no counterpart with primary qualities.)

11. See the discussion of (one interpretation of the notion of) objectivity at pp. 77-8 of Gareth Evans, "Things Without the Mind". Throughout this section I am heavily indebted to this most important paper.

12. *Problems from Locke*, p. 18.

understood in terms of experiences that the object is disposed to give rise to; but which nevertheless resembles redness as it figures in our experience—this to ensure that the phenomenal character of the experience need not stand accused of misleadingness, as it would if the "thoroughly objective" property of which it constituted an awareness were conceived as a microscopic textural basis for the object's disposition to look red. This use of the notion of resemblance corresponds to one key element in Locke's exposition of the concept of a primary quality.[13] In these Lockean terms Mackie's view amounts to accusing a naive perceptive consciousness of taking secondary qualities for primary qualities.[14]

According to Mackie, this conception of primary qualities that resemble colours as we see them is coherent; that nothing is characterized by such qualities is established by merely empirical argument.[15] But is the idea coherent? This would require two things: first, that colours figure in perceptual experience neutrally, so to speak, rather than as essentially phenomenal qualities of objects, qualities that could not be adequately conceived except in terms of how their possessors would look; and, second, that we command a concept of resemblance that would enable us to construct notions of possible primary qualities out of the idea of resemblance to such neutral elements of experience. The first of these requirements is quite dubious. (I shall return to this.) But even if we try to let it pass, the second requirement seems impossible. Starting with, say, redness as it (putatively neutrally) figures in our experience, we are asked to form the notion of a feature of objects that resembles that, but is adequately conceivable otherwise than in terms of how its possessors would look (since if it were adequately conceivable only in those terms it would simply be secondary). But the second part of these instructions leaves it wholly mysterious what to make of the first: it precludes the required resemblance being in phenomenal respects, but it is quite unclear what other sense we could make of the notion of resemblance to redness as it figures in our experience. (If we find no other, we have failed to let the first requirement pass; redness as it

---

13. *An Essay concerning Human Understanding*, 2.8.15.
14. See *Problems from Locke*, p. 16.
15. See *Problems from Locke*, pp. 17–20.

figures in our experience proves stubbornly phenomenal.)[16] I have indicated how we can make error-free sense of the thought that colours are authentic objects of perceptual awareness; in the face of that, it seems a gratuitous slur on perceptual "common sense" to accuse it of this wildly problematic understanding of itself.

Why is Mackie resolved, nevertheless, to convict "common sense" of error? Secondary qualities are qualities not adequately conceivable except in terms of certain subjective states, and thus subjective themselves in a sense that that characterization defines. In the natural contrast, a primary quality would be objective in the sense that what it is for something to have it can be adequately understood otherwise than in terms of dispositions to give rise to subjective states. Now this contrast between objective and subjective is not a contrast between veridical and illusory experience. But it is easily confused with a different contrast, in which to call a putative object of awareness "objective" is to say that it is there to be experienced, as opposed to being a mere figment of the subjective state that purports to be an experience of it. If secondary qualities were subjective in the sense that naturally contrasts with this, naive consciousness would indeed be wrong about them, and we would need something like Mackie's Lockean picture of the error it commits. What is acceptable, though, is only that secondary qualities are subjective in the first sense, and it would be simply wrong to suppose this gives any support to the idea that they are subjective in the second.[17]

More specifically, Mackie seems insufficiently whole-hearted in an insight of his about perceptual experiences. In the case of "realistic" depiction, it makes sense to think of veridicality as a matter of resemblance between aspects of a picture and aspects of what it depicts.[18] Mackie's insight is that the best hope of a philosophically hy-

---

16. Compare pp. 56–7 of P. F. Strawson, "Perception and Its Objects".

17. This is a different way of formulating a point made by McGinn, *The Subjective View*, p. 121. Mackie's phrase "the fabric of the world" belongs with the second sense of "objective", but I think his arguments really address only the first. Pace p. 103 of A. W. Price, "Varieties of Objectivity and Values", I do not think the phrase can be passed over as unhelpful, in favour of what the arguments do succeed in establishing, without missing something that Mackie wanted to say. (A gloss on "objective" as "there to be experienced" does not figure in Price's inventory of possible interpretations, p. 10. It seems to be the obvious response to his challenge at pp. 118–9.)

18. I do not say it is correct: scepticism about this is very much to the point. (See Nelson Goodman, *Languages of Art*, chap. 1.)

gienic interpretation for Locke's talk of "ideas", in a perceptual context, is in terms of "intentional objects": that is, aspects of representational content—aspects of how things seem to one in the enjoyment of a perceptual experience.[19] Now it is an illusion to suppose, as Mackie does, that this warrants thinking of the relation between a quality and an "idea" of it on the model of the relation between a property of a picture's subject and an aspect of the picture. Explaining "ideas" as "intentional objects" should direct our attention to the relation between how things are and how an experience represents them as being—in fact identity, not resemblance, if the representation is veridical.[20] Mackie's Lockean appeal to resemblance fits something quite different: a relation borne to aspects of how things are by intrinsic aspects of a bearer of representational content—not how things are represented to be, but features of an item that does the representing, with particular aspects of its content carried by particular aspects of what it is intrinsically (non-representationally) like.[21] Perceptual experiences have representational content; but nothing in Mackie's defence of the "intentional objects" gloss on "ideas" would force us to suppose that they have it in that sort of way.[22]

19. See *Problems from Locke*, pp. 47–50.
20. When resemblance is in play, it functions as a palliative to lack of veridicality, not as what veridicality consists in.
21. Intrinsic features of experience, functioning as vehicles for aspects of content, seem to be taken for granted in Mackie's discussion of Molyneux's problem (*Problems from Locke*, pp. 28–32). The slide from talk of content to talk that fits only bearers of content seems to happen also in Mackie's discussion of truth, in *Truth, Probability, and Paradox*. There Mackie suggests that a formulation like "A true statement is one such that the way things are is the way it represents them as being" makes truth consist in a relation of correspondence (rather than identity) between how things are and how things are represented as being; pp. 56–7 come too late to undo the damage done by the earlier talk of "comparison", e.g. at pp. 50, 51. (A subject-matter for the talk that fits bearers is unproblematically available in this case; but Mackie does not mean to be discussing truth as a property of sentences or utterances.)
22. Indeed, this goes against the spirit of a passage about the word "content" at *Problems from Locke*, p. 48. Mackie's failure to profit from his insight emerges particularly strikingly in his remarkable claim (*Problems from Locke*, p. 50) that the "intentional object" conception of the content of experience yields an account of perception that is within the target area of "the stock objections against an argument from an effect to a supposed cause of a type which is never directly observed". (Part of the trouble here is a misconception of direct realism as a surely forlorn attempt to make perceptual knowledge unproblematic: *Problems from Locke*, p. 43.)

The temptation to which Mackie succumbs, to suppose that intrinsic features of experience function as vehicles for aspects of representational content, is indifferent to any distinction between primary and secondary qualities in the representational significance that these features supposedly carry. What it is for a colour to figure in experience and what it is for a shape to figure in experience would be alike, on this view, in so far as both are a matter of an experience's having a certain intrinsic feature. If one wants, within this framework, to preserve Locke's intuition that primary-quality experience is distinctive in potentially disclosing the objective properties of things, one will be naturally led to Locke's use of the notion of resemblance. But no notion of resemblance could get us from an essentially experiential state of affairs to the concept of a feature of objects intelligible otherwise than in terms of how its possessors would strike us. (I exploited a version of this point against Mackie's idea of possible primary qualities answering to "colours as we see them"; it tells equally against the Lockean conception of shapes.)

If one gives up the Lockean use of resemblance, but retains the idea that primary and secondary qualities are experientially on a par, one will be led to suppose that the properties attributed to objects in the "manifest image" are all equally phenomenal—intelligible, that is, only in terms of how their possessors are disposed to appear. Properties that are objective, in the contrasting sense, can then figure only in the "scientific image".[23] On these lines one altogether loses hold of Locke's intuition that primary qualities are distinctive in being both objective and perceptible.[24]

If we want to preserve the intuition, as I believe we should, then we need to exorcize the idea that what it is for a quality to figure in experience is for an experience to have a certain intrinsic feature: in fact I believe we need to reject these supposed vehicles of content altogether. Then we can say that colours and shapes figure in experience, not as the representational significance carried by features that are—being intrinsic features of experience—indifferently subjective

---

23. The phrases "manifest image" and "scientific image" are due to Wilfrid Sellars; see "Philosophy and the Scientific Image of Man".

24. This is the position of Strawson, "Perception and Its Objects" (and see also his "Reply to Evans"). I am suggesting a diagnosis, to back up McGinn's complaint, *The Subjective View*, p. 124.

(which makes it hard to see how a difference in respect of objectivity could show up in their representational significance); but simply as properties that objects are represented as having, distinctively phenomenal in the one case and not so in the other. (Without the supposed intrinsic features, we should be immune to the illusion that experiences cannot represent objects as having properties that are not phenomenal—properties that are adequately conceivable otherwise than in terms of dispositions to produce suitable experiences.)[25] What Locke infelicitously tried to yoke together, with his picture of real resemblances of our "ideas", can now divide into two notions that we must insist on keeping separate: first, the possible veridicality of experience (the objectivity of its object, in the second of the two senses I distinguished), in respect of which primary and secondary qualities are on all fours; and, second, the not essentially phenomenal character of some properties that experience represents objects as having (their objectivity in the first sense), which marks off the primary perceptible qualities from the secondary ones.

In order to deny that a quality's figuring in experience consists in an experience's having a certain intrinsic feature, we do not need to reject the intrinsic features altogether; it would suffice to insist that a quality's figuring in experience consists in an experience's having a certain intrinsic feature *together with* the quality's being the representational significance carried by that feature. But I do not believe that this yields a position in which accepting the supposed vehicles of content coheres with a satisfactory account of perception. This position would have it that the fact that an experience represents things as being one way rather than another is strictly additional to the experience's intrinsic nature, and so extrinsic to the experience itself (it seems natural to say "read into it"). There is a phenomenological falsification here. (This brings out a third role for Locke's resemblance, namely to obviate the threat of such a falsification by constituting a sort of intrinsic representationality: Locke's "ideas" carry

---

25. Notice Strawson's sleight of hand with phrases such as "shapes-as-seen", at p. 280 of "Reply to Evans". Strawson's understanding of what Evans is trying to say fails altogether to accommodate Evans's remark ("Things Without the Mind", p. 96) that "to deny that primary properties are *sensory* is not at all to deny that they are *sensible* or *observable*". Shapes as seen are *shapes*—that is, non-sensory properties; it is one thing to deny, as Evans does, that experience can furnish us with the concepts of such properties, but quite another to deny that experience can disclose instantiations of them to us.

the representational significance they do by virtue of what they are like, and this can be glossed both as "how they are intrinsically" and as "what they resemble".) In any case, given that we cannot project ourselves from features of experience to non-phenomenal properties of objects by means of an appeal to resemblance, it is doubtful that the metaphor of representational significance being "read into" intrinsic features can be spelled out in such a way as to avoid the second horn of our dilemma. How could representational significance be "read into" intrinsic features of experience in such a way that what was signified did not need to be understood in terms of them? How could a not intrinsically representational feature of experience become imbued with objective significance in such a way that an experience could count, by virtue of having that feature, as a direct awareness of a not essentially phenomenal property of objects?[26]

How things strike someone as being is, in a clear sense, a subjective matter: there is no conceiving it in abstraction from the subject of the experience. Now a motive for insisting on the supposed vehicles of aspects of content might lie in an aspiration, familiar in philosophy, to bring subjectivity within the compass of a fundamentally objective conception of reality.[27] If aspects of content are not carried by elements in an intrinsic structure, their subjectivity is irreducible. By contrast, one might hope to objectivize any "essential subjectivity" that needs to be attributed to not intrinsically representational features of experience, by exploiting a picture involving special access on a subject's part to something conceived in a broadly objective way—its presence in the world not conceived as constituted by the subject's special access to it.[28] Given this move, it becomes natural to

---

26. Features of physiologically specified states are not to the point here. Such features are not apparent in experience; whereas the supposed features that I am concerned with would have to be aspects of what experience is like for us, in order to function intelligibly as carriers for aspects of the content that experience presents to us. There may be an inclination to ask why it should be any harder for a feature of experience to acquire an objective significance than it is for a word to do so. But the case of language affords no counterpart to the fact that the objective significance in the case we are concerned with is a matter of how things (e.g.) *look* to be; the special problem is to prevent that "look" from having the effect that a supposed intrinsic feature of experience gets taken up into its own representational significance, thus ensuring that the significance is phenomenal and not primary.

27. See Thomas Nagel, "Subjective and Objective".

28. Compare Bernard Williams, *Descartes: The Project of Pure Enquiry*, p. 295.

suppose that the phenomenal character of the "manifest image" can be explained in terms of a certain familiar picture: one in which a confronted "external" reality, conceived as having only an objective nature, is processed through a structured "subjectivity", conceived in this objectivistic manner. This picture seems to capture the essence of Mackie's approach to the secondary qualities.[29] What I have tried to suggest is that the picture is suspect in threatening to cut us off from the *primary* (not essentially phenomenal) qualities of the objects that we perceive: either (with the appeal to resemblance) making it impossible, after all, to keep an essentially phenomenal character out of our conception of the qualities in question, or else making them merely hypothetical, not accessible to perception. If we are to achieve a satisfactory understanding of experience's openness to objective reality, we must put a more radical construction on experience's essential subjectivity. And this removes an insidious obstacle—one whose foundation is summarily captured in Mackie's idea that it is not simply wrong to count "colours as we see them" as items in our minds[30]—that stands in the way of understanding how secondary-quality experience can be awareness, with nothing misleading about its phenomenal character, of properties genuinely possessed by elements in a not exclusively phenomenal reality.

4. The empirical ground that Mackie thinks we have for not postulating "thoroughly objective features which resemble our ideas of secondary qualities"[31] is that attributing such features to objects is surplus to the requirements of explaining our experience of secondary qualities.[32] If it would be incoherent to attribute such features to objects, as I believe, this empirical argument falls away as

---

29. Although McGinn, in *The Subjective View*, is not taken in by the idea that "external" reality has only objective characteristics, I am not sure that he sufficiently avoids the picture that underlies that idea; see pp. 106–9. This connects with a suspicion that at pp. 9–10 he partly succumbs to a temptation to objectivize the subjective properties of objects he countenances. It is not as clear as he seems to suppose that, say, redness can be, so to speak, abstracted from the way things strike us by an appeal to relativity. His worry at pp. 132–6, that secondary-quality experience may after all be phenomenologically misleading, seems to betray the influence of the idea of content-bearing intrinsic features of experience.
30. See the diagram at *Problems from Locke*, p. 17.
31. *Problems from Locke*, pp. 18–19.
32. See *Problems from Locke*, pp. 17–18.

unnecessary. But it is worth considering how an argument from explanatory superfluity might fare against the less extravagant construal I have suggested for the thought that secondary qualities genuinely characterize objects; not because the question is difficult or contentious, but because of the light it casts on how an explanatory test for reality—which is commonly thought to undermine the claims of values—should be applied.

A *"virtus dormitiva"* objection would tell against the idea that one might mount a satisfying explanation of an object's looking red on its being such as to look red. The weight of the explanation would fall through the disposition to its structural ground.[33] Still, however, optimistic we are about the prospects for explaining colour experience on the basis of surface textures,[34] it would be obviously wrong to suppose that someone who gave such an explanation could in consistency deny that the object was such as to look red. The right explanatory test is not whether something pulls its own weight in the favoured explanation (it may fail to do so without thereby being explained away), but whether the explainer can consistently deny its reality.[35]

Given Mackie's view about secondary qualities, the thought that values fail an explanatory test for reality is implicit in a parallel that he commonly draws between them.[36] It is nearer the surface in his "argument from queerness",[37] and explicit in his citing "patterns of objectification" to explain the distinctive phenomenology of value experience.[38] Now it is, if anything, even more obvious with values than with essentially phenomenal qualities that they cannot be credited with causal efficacy: values would not pull their weight in any explanation of value experience even remotely analogous to the stan-

---

33. See McGinn, p. 14.
34. There are difficulties about how complete such explanations could aspire to be. See Price, "Varieties of Objectivity and Values", pp. 114–5; and Essay 6 above.
35. Compare pp. 206–8 of David Wiggins, "What Would Be a Substantial Theory of Truth?" The test of whether the explanations in question are consistent with rejecting the item in question is Wiggins's suggestion, in the course of a continuing attempt to improve the formulation there. I am indebted to discussion with him.
36. See, e.g., *Hume's Moral Theory*, pp. 51–2; *Ethics: Inventing Right and Wrong*, pp. 19–20.
37. *Ethics: Inventing Right and Wrong*, pp. 38–42.
38. *Ethics: Inventing Right and Wrong*, pp. 42–6. See also Simon Blackburn, "Rule-Following and Moral Realism"; and chap. 1 of Gilbert Harman, *The Nature of Morality*.

dard explanations of primary-quality experience. But reflection on the case of secondary qualities has already opened a gap between that admission and any concession that values are not genuine aspects of reality. And the point is reinforced by a crucial disanalogy between values and secondary qualities. To press the analogy is to stress that evaluative "attitudes", or states of will, are like (say) colour experience in being unintelligible except as modifications of a sensibility like ours. The idea of value experience involves taking admiration, say, to represent its object as having a property that (although there in the object) is essentially subjective in much the same way as the property that an object is represented as having by an experience of redness—that is, understood adequately only in terms of the appropriate modification of human (or similar) sensibility. The disanalogy, now, is that a virtue (say) is conceived to be not merely such as to elicit the appropriate "attitude" (as a colour is merely such as to cause the appropriate experiences), but rather such as to *merit* it. And this makes it doubtful whether merely causal explanations of value experience are relevant to the explanatory test, even to the extent that the question to ask is whether someone could consistently give such explanations while denying that the values involved are real. It looks as if we should be raising that question about explanations of a different kind.

For simplicity's sake, I shall elaborate this point in connection with something that is not a value, though it shares the crucial feature: namely danger or the fearful. On the face of it, this might seem a promising subject for a projectivist treatment (a treatment that appeals to what Hume called the mind's "propensity to spread itself on external objects").[39] At any rate the response that, according to such a treatment, is projected into the world can be characterized, without phenomenological falsification, otherwise than in terms of seeming to find the supposed product of projection already there.[40] And it would be obviously grotesque to fancy that a case of fear might be

---

39. *A Treatise of Human Nature*, 1.3.14. "Projectivist" is Blackburn's useful label; see "Rule-Following and Moral Realism", and "Opinions and Chances".

40. At pp. 180–1 of "Opinions and Chances", Blackburn suggests that a projectivist need not mind whether or not this is so; but I think he trades on a slide between "can . . . only be understood in terms of" and "our best vocabulary for identifying" (which allows that there may be an alternative, though it will be inferior).

explained as the upshot of a mechanical (or perhaps para-mechanical) process initiated by an instance of "objective fearfulness". But if what we are engaged in is an "attempt to understand ourselves",[41] then merely causal explanations of responses like fear will not be satisfying anyway.[42] What we want here is a style of explanation that makes sense of what is explained (in so far as sense can be made of it). This means that a technique for giving satisfying explanations of cases of fear—which would perhaps amount to a satisfactory explanatory theory of danger, though the label is possibly too grand—must allow for the possibility of criticism; we make sense of fear by seeing it as a response to objects that *merit* such a response, or as the intelligibly defective product of a propensity towards responses that would be intelligible in that way.[43] For an object to merit fear just is for it to be fearful. So explanations of fear that manifest our capacity to understand ourselves in this region of our lives will simply not cohere with the claim that reality contains nothing in the way of fearfulness.[44] Any such claim would undermine the intelligibility that the explanations confer on our responses.

The shared crucial feature suggests that this disarming of a supposed explanatory argument for unreality should carry over to the case of values. There is, of course, a striking disanalogy in the contentiousness that is typical of values; but I think it would be a mistake to suppose that this spoils the point. In so far as we succeed in achieving the sort of understanding of our responses that is in question, we do so on the basis of preparedness to attribute, to at least some possible objects of the responses, properties that would validate the responses. What the disanalogy makes especially clear is that the explanations that preclude our denying the reality of the special properties that are putatively discernible from some (broadly)

---

41. The phrase is from p. 165 of Blackburn, "Rule-Following and Moral Realism".
42. I do not mean that satisfying explanations will not be causal. But they will not be *merely* causal.
43. I am assuming that it is not a question of a theory according to which no responses of the kind in question *could* be well-placed. That would have a quite unintended effect. (See *Ethics: Inventing Right and Wrong*, p. 16.) Notice that it will not meet my point to suggest that calling a response "well-placed" is to be understood only quasi-realistically. Explanatory indispensability is supposed to be the test for the *genuine* reality supposedly lacked by what warrants only quasi-realistic treatment.
44. Compare Blackburn, "Rule-Following and Moral Realism", p. 164.

evaluative point of view are themselves constructed from that point of view. (We already had this in the case of the fearful, but the point is brought home when the validation of the responses is controversial.) However, the critical dimension of the explanations that we want means that there is no question of just any actual response pulling itself up by its own bootstraps into counting as an undistorted perception of the relevant special aspect of reality.[45] Indeed, awareness that values are contentious tells against an unreflective contentment with the current state of one's critical outlook, and in favour of a readiness to suppose that there may be something to be learned from people with whom one's first inclination is to disagree. The aspiration to understand oneself is an aspiration to change one's responses, if that is necessary for them to become intelligible otherwise than as defective. But although a sensible person will never be confident that his evaluative outlook is incapable of improvement, that need not stop him supposing, of some of his evaluative responses, that their objects really do merit them. He will be able to back up this supposition with explanations that show how the responses are well-placed; the explanations will share the contentiousness of the values whose reality they certify, but that should not prevent him from accepting the explanations any more than (what nobody thinks) it should prevent him from endorsing the values.[46] There is perhaps an air of bootstrapping about this. But if we restrict ourselves to explanations from a more external standpoint, at which values are not in our field of view, we deprive ourselves of a kind of

---

45. This will be so even in a case in which there are no materials for constructing standards of criticism except actual responses—something that is not so with fearfulness, although given a not implausible holism it will be so with values.

46. I can see no reason why we should not regard the contentiousness as ineliminable. The effect of this would be to detach the explanatory test of reality from a requirement of convergence (compare the passage from Wiggins cited in n. 35 above). As far as I can see, this separation would be a good thing. It would enable resistance to projectivism to free itself, with a good conscience, from some unnecessary worries about relativism. It might also discourage a misconception of the appeal to Wittgenstein that comes naturally to such a position. (Blackburn, at pp. 170–4 of "Rule-Following and Moral Realism", reads into Essay 10 below an interpretation of Wittgenstein as, in effect, making truth a matter of consensus, and has no difficulty in arguing that this will not make room for hard cases. But the interpretation is not mine.) With the requirement of consensus dropped, or at least radically relativized to a point of view, the question of the claim to truth of directives may come closer to the question of the truth status of evaluations than Wiggins suggests in "Truth, Invention, and the Meaning of Life".

intelligibility that we aspire to; and projectivists have given no reason whatever to suppose that there would be anything better about whatever different kind of self-understanding the restriction would permit.

5. It will be obvious how these considerations undermine the damaging effect of the primary-quality model. Shifting to a secondary-quality analogy renders irrelevant any worry about how something that is brutely *there* could nevertheless stand in an internal relation to some exercise of human sensibility. Values are not brutely there—not there independently of our sensibility—any more than colours are: though, as with colours, this does not prevent us from supposing that they are there independently of any particular apparent experience of them. As for the epistemology of value, the epistemology of danger is a good model. (Fearfulness is not a secondary quality, although the model is available only after the primary-quality model has been dislodged. A secondary-quality analogy for value experience gives out at certain points, no less than the primary-quality analogy that Mackie attacks.) To drop the primary-quality model in this case is to give up the idea that fearfulness itself, were it real, would need to be intelligible from a standpoint independent of the propensity to fear; the same must go for the relations of rational consequentiality in which fearfulness stands to more straightforward properties of things.[47] Explanations of fear of the sort I envisaged would not only establish, from a different standpoint, that some of its objects are really fearful, but also make plain, case by case, what it is about them that makes them so; this should leave it quite unmysterious how a fear response rationally grounded in awareness (unproblematic, at least for present purposes) of these "fearful-making characteristics" can be counted as being, or yielding, knowledge that one is confronted by an instance of real fearfulness.[48]

Simon Blackburn has written, on behalf of a projectivist sentimentalism in ethics, that "we profit . . . by realizing that a training of the feelings rather than a cultivation of a mysterious ability to spot the

---

47. Mackie's question (*Ethics: Inventing Right and Wrong*, p. 41) "Just what *in the world* is signified by this 'because'?" involves a tendentious notion of "the world".
48. See Price, "Varieties of Objectivity and Values", pp. 106–7, 115.

immutable fitnesses of things is the foundation of how to live".[49] This picture of what an opponent of projectivism must hold is of a piece with Mackie's primary-quality model; it simply fails to fit the position I have described.[50] Perhaps with Aristotle's notion of practical wisdom in mind, one might ask why a training of the feelings (as long as the notion of feeling is comprehensive enough) cannot *be* the cultivation of an ability—utterly unmysterious just because of its connections with feelings—to spot (if you like) the fitnesses of things; even "immutable" may be all right, so long as it is not understood (as I take it Blackburn intends) to suggest a "platonistic" conception of the fitnesses of things, which would reimport the characteristic ideas of the primary-quality model.[51]

Mackie's response to this suggestion used to be, in effect, that it simply conceded his point.[52] Can a projectivist claim that the position I have outlined is at best a notational variant, perhaps an inferior notational variant, of his own position?

It would be inferior if, in eschewing the projectivist metaphysical framework, it obscured some important truth. But what truth would this be? It will not do at this point to answer "The truth of projectivism". I have disarmed the explanatory argument for the projectivist's thin conception of genuine reality. What remains is rhetoric expressing what amounts to a now unargued primary-quality model for genuine reality.[53] The picture that this suggests for value experience—objective (value-free) reality processed through a moulded subjectivity—is no less questionable than the picture of secondary-quality experience on which, in Mackie at any rate, it is explicitly

---

49. "Rule-Following and Moral Realism", p. 186.

50. As Blackburn conceives moral realism, it evades the explanatory burdens that sentimentalism discharges, by making the world rich (compare p. 181) and picturing it as simply setting its print on us. Compare Mackie, *Ethics: Inventing Right and Wrong*, p. 22: "If there were something in the fabric of the world that validated certain kinds of concern, then it would be possible to acquire these merely by finding something out, by letting one's thinking be controlled by how things were." This saddles an opponent of projectivism with a picture of awareness of value as an exercise of pure receptivity; it prevents him from deriving any profit from an analogy with secondary-quality perception.

51. On "platonism", see Essay 10 below. On Aristotle, see M. F. Burnyeat, "Aristotle on Learning to be Good".

52. Price, "Varieties of Objectivity and Values", p. 107, cites Mackie's response to one of my contributions to the 1978 seminar (see n. 1 above).

53. We must not let the confusion between the two notions of objectivity that I distinguished in §3 above seem to support this conception of reality.

modelled. In fact I would be inclined to argue that it is projectivism that is inferior. Deprived of the specious explanatory argument, projectivism has nothing to sustain its thin conception of reality (that on to which the projections are effected) but a contentiously substantial version of the correspondence theory of truth, with the associated picture of genuinely true judgement as something to which the judger makes no contribution at all.[54]

I do not want to argue this now. The point I want to make is that even if projectivism were not actually worse, metaphysically speaking, than the alternative I have described, it would be wrong to regard the issue between them as nothing but a question of metaphysical preference.[55] In the projectivist picture, having one's ethical or aesthetic responses rationally suited to their objects would be a matter of having the relevant processing mechanism functioning acceptably. Now projectivism can of course perfectly well accommodate the idea of assessing one's processing mechanism. But it pictures the mechanism as something that one can contemplate as an object in itself. It would be appropriate to say "something one can step back from", were it not for the fact that one needs to use the mechanism itself in assessing it; but at any rate one is supposed to be able to step back from any naively realistic acceptance of the values that the first-level employment of the mechanism has one attribute to items in the world. How, then, are we to understand this pictured availability of the processing mechanism as an object for contemplation, separated off from the world of value? Is there any alternative to thinking of it as capable of being captured, at least in theory, by a set of principles for superimposing values on to a value-free reality? The upshot is that the search for an evaluative outlook one can endorse as rational

---

54. Blackburn uses the correspondence theorist's pictures for rhetorical effect, but he is properly sceptical about whether this sort of realism makes sense (see "Truth, Realism, and the Regulation of Theory"). His idea is that the explanatory argument makes a counterpart to the metaphysical favouritism characteristic of this sort of realism safely available to a projectivist about values. Deprived of the explanatory argument, this projectivism should simply wither away. (See "Rule-Following and Moral Realism", p. 165. Of course I am not saying that the thin conception of reality that Blackburn's projectivism needs is unattainable, in the sense of being unformulable. What we lack is reasons of a respectable kind to recognize it as a complete conception *of reality.*)

55. Something like this seems to be suggested by Price, "Varieties of Objectivity and Values", pp. 107–8.

becomes, virtually irresistibly, a search for such a set of principles: a search for a *theory* of beauty or goodness. One comes to count "intuitions" as respectable only in so far as they can be validated by an approximation to that ideal.[56] (This is the shape that the attempt to objectivize subjectivity takes here.) I have a hunch that such efforts are misguided; not that we should rest content with an "anything goes" irrationalism, but that we need a conception of rationality in evaluation that will cohere with the possibility that particular cases may stubbornly resist capture in any general net. Such a conception is straightforwardly available within the alternative to projectivism that I have described. I allowed that being able to explain cases of fear in the right way might amount to having a theory of danger, but there is no need to generalize that feature of the case; the explanatory capacity that certifies the special objects of an evaluative outlook as real, and certifies its responses to them as rational, would need to be exactly as creative and case-specific as the capacity to discern those objects itself. (It would be the same capacity: the picture of "stepping back" does not fit here.)[57] I take it that my hunch poses a question of moral and aesthetic taste, which—like other questions of taste—should be capable of being argued about. The trouble with

---

56. It is hard to see how a rational *inventing* of values could take a more piecemeal form.

57. Why do I suggest that a particularistic conception of evaluative rationality is unavailable to a projectivist? See Blackburn, "Rule-Following and Moral Realism", pp. 167–70. In the terms of that discussion, the point is that (with no good explanatory argument for his metaphysical favouritism) a projectivist has no alternative to being "a *real* realist" about the world on which he thinks values are superimposed. He cannot stop this from generating a quite un-Wittgensteinian picture of what *really* going on in the same way would be; which means that *he* cannot appeal to Wittgenstein in order to avert, as Blackburn puts it, "the threat which shapelessness poses to a respectable notion of consistency" (p. 169). So, at any rate, I meant to argue in Essay 10 below, to which Blackburn's paper is a reply. Blackburn thinks his projectivism is untouched by the argument, because he thinks he can sustain projectivism's metaphysical favouritism without appealing to "*real* realism", on the basis of the explanatory argument. But I have urged that this is an illusion. (At p. 181 Blackburn writes: "Of course, it is true that our reactions are 'simply felt' and, in a sense, not rationally explicable." He thinks he can comfortably say this because our conception of reason will go along with the quasi-realist truth that his projectivism confers on some evaluations. But how can one restrain the metaphysical favouritism a projectivist must show from generating some such thought as "This is not *real* reason"? If that is allowed to happen, a remark like the one I have quoted will merely threaten—like an ordinary nihilism—to dislodge us from our ethical and aesthetic convictions.)

projectivism is that it threatens to bypass that argument, on the basis of a metaphysical picture whose purported justification falls well short of making it compulsory. We should not let the question seem to be settled by what stands revealed, in the absence of compelling argument, as a prejudice claiming the honour due to metaphysical good taste.

ESSAY 8

Projection and Truth in Ethics

1. Projection is what the mind engages in when, as Hume puts the idea, it "spreads itself" on to the external world.[1] This image certainly seems to fit some ways of thinking and talking that we can be tempted into; consider for instance the confused notion that disgustingness is a property some things have intrinsically or absolutely, independently of their relations to us—a property of which our feelings of disgust constitute a kind of perception. That this notion is confused is of course no reason to suppose it cannot be true that something is disgusting. But the image of projection, figuring as it does in an explanation of how the confused notion comes about, might be useful in correcting a possible misconception of what such truth would amount to. My question in this paper is whether the image is well suited to a similar employment in the field of ethics.

In connection with the prospects for crediting ethical statements or judgements with truth, David Wiggins has pressed a distinction between what he calls "evaluations", on the one hand, and "directives or deliberative (or practical) judgements", on the other.[2] It is in relation to the former category that the attribution of truth is most immediately attractive; evaluations are not easily assimilated to, for instance, decisions what to do, but naturally strike us as correct or incorrect according to whether or not they accurately delineate the values that are to be found in their subject-matter. This feature of

---

1. See *A Treatise of Human Nature*, 1.3.14.
2. See "Truth, Invention, and the Meaning of Life", pp. 95–6.

evaluations makes them also the most immediately tempting field for an application of the idea of projection; the phenomenology that makes the attribution of truth attractive can seem well explained as the upshot of a projection of what Hume would call "sentiments" on to their objects. Without prejudice to the possibility of extending the discussion to Wiggins's other category, for the purposes of this paper I shall generally have evaluations in mind.

In the case of the supposedly absolute or intrinsic property of disgustingness, what projection leads to is error; one takes what one in fact spreads on to the external world to be something one finds in the world on to which one spreads it, something that is there anyway—that is, there independently of human or sentient responses to things. It may seem that any projective thinking must be metaphysically erroneous in this way; the associated "error theory" in ethics was embraced, as is well known, by J. L. Mackie.[3] But we have to take note of a different use of the image of projection, which has been elaborated in a number of writings by Simon Blackburn. The position Blackburn describes, and recommends for ethics in particular, is what he calls "quasi-realism". Quasi-realism aims to demonstrate that, starting from the claim that a mode of thinking (evaluation in our particular case) is projective, we can see how it can, without confusion, exemplify nevertheless all the twists of thought and speech that might seem to signal a fully realist metaphysic, although—since they are now provided for within a projectivist framework—it must be a mistake to suppose they signal any such thing.[4] According to Hume, when our "taste" is projected on to the world, it "raises in a manner a new creation".[5] Blackburn's proposal, in effect, is that this "new creation" can be sufficiently robust to underwrite the presence of the trappings of realism, so to speak, in thought and speech that is correctly understood as projective; and that participants in such thought and speech need not be led by those elements of it into missing its projective nature. We can be clear, even as we suppose that our judgements accurately delineate the contours of reality, that it is only the "new creation", a product of projection, that is in question.

3. See chap. 1 of his *Ethics: Inventing Right and Wrong*.
4. Among many other writings, see chaps. 5 and 6 of Blackburn's *Spreading the Word*.
5. *An Enquiry concerning the Principles of Morals*, Appendix I.

2. A tension arises in Blackburn's separation of projectivism from an error theory. (I mention this not to make it a problem for him, but to bring out a point that will be important in what follows.) To begin with at least, it is natural to put the projectivist thought, and Blackburn characteristically does put it, by saying that ethical commitments should not be understood as having truth-conditions. That would represent ethical remarks as statements about how things are, and according to projectivism they should be taken rather to express attitudes or sentiments.[6] But quasi-realism is supposed to make room for *all* the trappings of realism, including the idea that the notion of truth applies after all to ethical remarks. In that case, the original sharp contrast between putting forward a candidate for being true and expressing an attitude or sentiment cannot be right: a remark that expresses an attitude can also affirm a truth. Does this mean that projectivist quasi-realism is self-defeating?[7]

Not if we can distinguish what the projectivist starting-point rejects from what the quasi-realist conclusion establishes as acceptable. It may be tempting to suppose this can be done only if we discern two different *notions* of truth, one to figure in the projectivist denial that ethical statements can be true, and the other to figure in the quasi-realist reinstatement of ethical truth.[8] However, this is not how Blackburn resolves the tension.[9] What Blackburn does—and this is centrally important to the point I want to make—is to contrast an *unearned* appeal to the notion of truth, which is what the projectivist rejects, with an *earned* right to the use of the notion, which is what the quasi-realist reinstates. The point about the application of the notion of truth that quasi-realism is supposed to make available is that we do not merely help ourselves to it, but work for it.

The contrast—the unearned employment of the notion of truth that projectivism rejects—is a position that expands reality by mere postulation, beyond what the projectivist is comfortable with, to include an extra population of distinctively value-involving states of

---

6. See, e.g., *Spreading the Word*, pp. 167–71.
7. Blackburn raises the question whether "a projective approach is too good to be true" at p. 219 of *Spreading the Word*.
8. See Crispin Wright, "Realism, Anti-Realism, Irrealism, Quasi-Realism".
9. See *Spreading the Word*, p. 257: "Does this make moral commitments true in the same sense as others, or only in a different sense? I do not greatly commend the question."

affairs or facts. Corresponding to this, it purports to equip us with special cognitive faculties by whose exercise we become aware of this special field of knowable fact. These special cognitive faculties are vaguely assimilated to the senses, but no detailed account can be given of how they operate, such as might make it clear to us—as clear as it is in the case of the senses—how their exercise affords us access to the relevant range of circumstances. The assimilation to the senses gives this intuitionistic position the superficial appearance of offering an epistemology of our access to evaluative truth, but there is no substance behind this appearance.

How does projectivism improve on this rather clearly disreputable position?

The basic projectivist idea is that ethical remarks express not mysterious "cognizings" of evaluative facts, but attitudes. Now if that were the whole story, there would not be much prospect of a substantial notion of truth; think of the practice of expressing one's attitudes to various flavours of ice cream. But there is an extra ingredient to the story, which quasi-realism exploits. The attitudes are the upshot of sensibilities: that is, propensities to form various attitudes in response to various features of situations. Ethical sensibilities are themselves subject to attitudes of approbation or disapprobation; and—this is the crucial thing—these attitudes to sensibilities are a matter for argument and criticism.[10] We are not content simply to go along with the flow of our sensibilities as they stand, regardless of how they fare under critical scrutiny; and we are not at liberty to rank sensibilities at random and still be taken seriously as participants in ethical discussion. Truth, in a remark that has to be understood in the first instance as expressive of an attitude, can now be explained in terms of the fact that the sensibility from which the attitude issues stands up to the appropriate kind of criticism.

To complete the picture, we would need an account of the nature of the criticism to which ethical sensibilities are subject. In part the critical assessment in question is formal, involving requirements such as consistency. But there are also substantive constraints on whether a sensibility is acceptable. These derive—so Blackburn seems to suggest—from the function of ethical thought and speech in helping to

---

10. See *Spreading the Word*, p. 194.

secure such goods as social order and co-operation.[11] This sketch will serve for the present; as we shall see, a crucial issue opens up when one sets out to be less schematic.

3. It is hard to imagine that anyone would explicitly deny that if truth in ethics is available, it needs to be earned. It seems clear, moreover, that one would be deceiving oneself if one thought that those vague analogies with perception amounted to earning it. If the idea that truth must be earned is located as, precisely, a corrective to the unhelpful intuitionistic realism that Blackburn is primarily concerned to reject, it can seem to establish a conclusion about a metaphysical basis on which ethical truth must be worked for. Realism shirks the obligation, and the clear alternative is projectivism. But it is questionable whether that is the right setting in which to place the idea that truth must be earned.

Consider a view of the current predicament of ethics on the lines of Alasdair MacIntyre's in *After Virtue*. According to MacIntyre, the description of ethical language given by C. L. Stevenson—although it is not, as Stevenson claimed, a correct description of ethical language as such—has come to be true of the ethical language that is actually at our disposal. One crucial ingredient of Stevenson's picture is the implication that no substantial distinction can be drawn among methods of inducing people to change their minds on ethical matters, between making reasons available to them on the one hand and manipulating them in ways that have nothing in particular to do with rationality on the other. I do not want to go into the question whether MacIntyre is right in contending that we now lack the means to draw such distinctions; the point is that if he is right, then clearly there is no prospect of achieving, in ethical thought with its present conceptual resources, anything we could count as truth in any serious sense. No doubt it is always possible for anyone to use "It is true that . . ." as an indication of willingness on his own part

---

11. See, e. g., *Spreading the Word*, pp. 192, 197. I think Blackburn would regard Hume's treatment of the artificial virtues as a model of the kind of thing that would be required in a full version of the quasi-realist project, constructing truth out of an account of how projective thinking can allow for a substantial notion of better and worse ways of doing it.

to affirm whatever follows "that". But if MacIntyre's Stevensonian picture is correct, we lack what a more substantial notion of truth seems plainly to require, a conception of better and worse ways to think about ethical questions that connects with the idea that there are reasons for being of a certain mind on a question. Contrast the suggestion that there is nothing to ethical thinking but rationally arbitrary subjective stances and whatever power relations might be exploited to shift people's ethical allegiances.[12]

Earning the notion of truth, in the face of this sort of suggestion, would thus be a matter of arguing that we do after all have at our disposal a conception of reasons for ethical thinking that is sufficiently rich and substantial to mark off rationally induced improvements in ethical stances from alterations induced by merely manipulative persuasion.

Positions like MacIntyre's suggest a quite different context for the thought that the availability of truth in ethics is something it would take work to establish. The problem about truth in ethics, viewed in this context, is not that it fails to be as the intuitionist realist supposes, so that establishing its availability requires a different metaphysical basis. The problem is that a question is raised whether our equipment for thinking ethically is suited only for mere attitudinizing—whether our ethical concepts are too sparse and crude for ethical thought to seem an exercise of reason, as it must if there is to be room in it for a substantial notion of truth.[13] It is really not clear why addressing a problem of this sort should seem to require a metaphysical move at all.

---

12. I am not suggesting that any ethical thought and language of which an account that is in some sense emotivist is true must dissolve such distinctions: compare *Spreading the Word*, p. 197. (I have not questioned that ethical thought and speech engages our affective nature, and I suppose that is an emotivist insight.) But Stevenson's account does dissolve such distinctions; so it affords a good picture of a kind of threat in the face of which earning truth should seem a good thing to attempt. (If MacIntyre is right, earning truth would involve a conceptual reform.)

13. This requires me to take issue with Blackburn when he says such things as the following (p. 181 of "Rule-Following and Moral Realism"): "Of course, it is true that our reactions are 'simply felt' and, in a sense, not rationally explicable. But we should not be too worried about reason here. In general, reason follows where truth leads." By my lights this is the wrong way round. If we could not convince ourselves that our rankings of sensibilities were capable of being grounded in reason (as Blackburn's appealing, when he finds it useful, to argument and criticism suggests they are), there would not be any reason to suppose that we had regained an application for the notion of truth.

4. It may still seem that, even if earning truth in the face of this sort of challenge to its availability requires something other than an explicitly metaphysical move, namely vindicating the richness and robustness of the conception of reasons for ethical judgements that our conceptual resources equip us with, nevertheless, as soon as we concede that attaining truth is not simply a matter of "cognizing" evaluative facts, we must have implicitly adopted a projectivist metaphysic. This appearance reflects an assumption that, at the metaphysical level, there are just two options: projectivism and the unattractive intuitionistic realism that populates reality with mysterious extra features and merely goes through the motions of supplying an epistemology for our supposed access to them. But the assumption is questionable.

The point of the image of projection is to explain certain seeming features of reality as reflections of our subjective responses to a world that really contains no such features. Now this explanatory direction seems to require a corresponding priority, in the order of understanding, between the projected response and the apparent feature: we ought to be able to focus our thought on the response without needing to exploit the concept of the apparent feature that is supposed to result from projecting the response. In the sort of case I cited at the beginning, it is plausible that this requirement is met. Disgust and nausea, we can plausibly suppose, are self-contained psychological items, conceptualizable without any need to appeal to any projected properties of disgustingness or nauseatingness. (No doubt a full explanation of the psychological phenomena would group things together in terms of their tendency to produce those responses, but those tendencies are not properties that need to be explained as projections of the responses.) The question, now, is this: if, in connection with some range of concepts whose application engages distinctive aspects of our subjective make-up in the sort of way that seems characteristic of evaluative concepts, we reject the kind of realism that construes subjective responses as perceptions of associated features of reality and does no work towards earning truth, are we entitled to assume that the responses enjoy this kind of explanatory priority, as projectivism seems to require?

It may help to consider a non-ethical case in which an intuitionistic realism is obviously unattractive, and in which Blackburn proceeds as if projectivism is obviously correct: the case of the comic or funny. To begin with at least, this looks like a good field for a projective account. But what exactly is it that we are to conceive as projected on to the world so as to give rise to our idea that things are funny? "An inclination to laugh" is not a satisfactory answer;[14] projecting an inclination to laugh would not necessarily yield an apparent instance of the comic, since laughter can signal, for instance, embarrassment just as well as amusement. Perhaps the right response cannot be identified except as amusement; and perhaps amusement cannot be understood except as finding something comic. I need not take a view on whether this is correct. But if it is correct, there is a serious question whether we can really *explain* the idea of something's being comic as a *projection* of that response. The suggestion is that there is no self-contained prior fact of our subjective lives that could enter into a projective account of the relevant way of thinking; in the only relevant response, the conceptual apparatus that figures in the relevant way of thinking is already in play. No doubt the propensity to laugh is in some sense a self-contained prior psychological fact. But differentiating some exercises of that unspecific propensity as cases of *amusement* is something we have to learn, and if the suggestion is correct, this learning is indistinguishable from coming to find some things comic. Surely it undermines a projective account of a concept if we cannot home in on the subjective state whose projection is supposed to result in the seeming feature of reality in question without the aid of the concept of that feature, the concept that was to be projectively explained. And surely this scepticism cannot tend in the direction of a relapse into the intuitionistic sort of realism.

Blackburn himself is remarkably casual about this. I know only one place where he discusses the question whether this kind of consideration poses a problem for projectivism; and in that place he simply asserts that there is no problem for projectivism if the only way to describe a supposedly projected subjective response is in terms of seeming to find the supposed upshot of projecting it in something one confronts.[15] I think this reflects the assumption I mentioned ear-

---

14. Compare Blackburn's "Errors and the Phenomenology of Value", p. 9.
15. This is at pp. 180–1 of "Opinions and Chances". Blackburn makes the point that it would not be surprising, given a projectivist view, that "our best vocabulary for identifying the reaction should be the familiar one using the predicates we apply to the world we have spread". This seems right; once we have done the spreading, the resulting way of

lier, that if we are not realists of the unsatisfactorily intuitionistic sort then we cannot but be projectivists.

Blackburn's view of the available options is well summed up in these words of his (they apply to morality in particular, but the structure is quite general):

> The projectivist holds that our nature as moralists is well explained by regarding us as reacting to a reality which contains nothing in the way of values, duties, rights and so forth; a realist thinks it is well explained only by seeing us as able to perceive, cognize, intuit, an independent moral reality. He holds that the moral features of things are the parents of our sentiments, whereas the Humean holds that they are their children.[16]

Realism here is the unsatisfactory position that helps itself to an unearned notion of truth. So if the choice is the one Blackburn offers in this passage, it seems compulsory to opt for regarding the "features of things" that are in question as children of our sentiments rather than their parents. There is no room to raise a problem about whether the sentiments have the requisite explanatory independence. But why do we have to limit ourselves to those two options? What about a position that says the extra features are neither parents nor children of our sentiments, but—if we must find an apt metaphor from the field of kinship relations—siblings?[17] Such a view would be appropriate for amusement and the comic, if that case is as I have suggested it might be. Denying that the extra features are prior to the relevant sentiments, such a view distances itself from the idea that they belong, mysteriously, in a reality that is wholly independent of our subjectivity and set over against it. It does not follow that the

---

talking will no doubt seem more natural to us than any other. But that is not the same as saying that there is *no* alternative way of identifying the response. And if there is no alternative way, then there is no way of saying what has happened, in detail, in terms of the image of projection, and it is obscure why we should allow *that* to be consistent with projectivism.

16. "Rule-Following and Moral Realism", pp. 164–5. It may be worth mentioning in passing that the idea of rights as children of our sentiments seems an over-simplification of Hume's view.

17. See David Wiggins, "Truth, Invention, and the Meaning of Life", at p. 106; and for an elaboration of the thought there expressed that "an adequate account of these matters will have to treat psychological states and their objects as equal and reciprocal partners", see "A Sensible Subjectivism?".

sentiments have a priority. If there is no comprehending the right sentiments independently of the concepts of the relevant extra features, a no-priority view is surely indicated. There are two possible ways of not being an intuitionistic realist, and the image of projection really fits only one of them.

In the case of the comic, the threat in the face of which it would be necessary to earn truth—if one wanted to—would not be that any persuasion seems indistinguishable from manipulation; argument is not an important ingredient in that part of our lives. (The attempt to persuade someone that something is funny is typically self-defeating.) But there is a sameness underlying this difference. In both cases, the threat to a substantial notion of truth lies in the idea that there is nothing really to choose between different sensibilities, and that any convergence is best thought of as a mere coincidence of subjectivities rather than agreement on a range of truths—the sort of view that would be natural if everyone came to prefer one flavour of ice cream to any other. And in both cases, the threatening thought can be put like this: different sensibilities cannot be ranked according to whether there are better *reasons* for one sensibility's response than another's. Whether or not the sensibilities are conceived as typically altered by argument, so that the issue can be whether persuading someone counts as giving him reasons to change his mind, the challenge can be put as a query whether a mode of thought that engages subjective responses allows for a sufficiently substantial conception of reasons for exercises of it to be capable of truth.

The interest of the no-priority view, now, is that it opens up the possibility that it might be respectable to *use* the apparently world-describing conceptual resources with which we articulate our responses, in earning truth in one of the relevant areas. Blackburn's simpler structure of options suggests we must deny ourselves those resources, on pain of lapsing back into a bald intuitionism. A serious projective quasi-realism about the comic would construct a conception of what it is for things to be really funny on the basis of principles for ranking senses of humour that would have to be established from outside the propensity to find things funny. The contrasting idea would be that we might regard our conception of greater and less refinement and discrimination in senses of humour as derivative from an understanding of what it is for things to be really funny—something we can acceptably aim to elaborate from within the propensity to find things funny. The concept of the comic is not a device for a rationally isolated grouping of items, things whose satisfaction of it we take to be simply a matter of their eliciting the appropriate reaction from us; having the concept involves at least inklings of a place it occupies in a rationally interconnected scheme of concepts, and we should aim to exploit such inklings in working out an aesthetic, so to speak, of humour. A ranking of sensibilities would flow from that, rather than being independently constructed (from what materials?)[18] and used to deliver verdicts on when things are really comic. Of course we might not be able to squeeze much in the way of rankings of senses of humour out of our understanding of the funny. And anything on these lines that we did come up with would be liable, as such constructions always are, to accusations of fraud, on behalf of people whose senses of humour we represented as blunter than they might be. We would need to take great care to be sure that we were not merely projectively conferring a bogus objectivity on the deliverances of a sensibility that was in fact rationally on a par with any other. But, although we must of course acknowledge the risks and do our best to guard against them, we would not be guaranteed to fall into self-deception of this sort, simply by virtue of working from within.

The no-priority view allows, then, that it might be possible to do something recognizable as earning truth by focusing on the funny itself. The idea of what is really funny need not be explained in terms of an independently established conception of what makes a sense of humour more discriminating. This contrasts with a constraint that seems to be implicit in a serious projectivism, according to which the idea of a superior discernment has to be made clear without exploiting exercises of the way of thinking that is to be explained as projective, so that it is available for use in certifying some such exercises as (quasi-realistically) true.

---

18. This is a serious question for anyone who is sympathetic to a quasi-realist projectivism about the comic. Much of what is ordinarily appealed to in ranking objects for amusement is suitably external but just for that reason not obviously relevant to *this* issue; for instance jokes that one may deplore as being "in bad taste" (usually on moralistic grounds) are not thereby shown not to be extremely *funny*. It seems highly implausible that we could extract out of the function of the sense of humour (if we knew it) something that would even seem to do the sort of work in a quasi-realist ranking of sensibilities that Blackburn seems to suggest is done in the ethical case by the function of ethical thinking.

Analogously in the ethical case; here again, the possibility of the no-priority view brings out that we do not need to choose between, on the one hand, lapsing into intuitionism—simply helping ourselves to truth—and, on the other, disallowing ourselves, in earning truth, the conceptual equipment that projectivism sees as the product of projection. Earning truth is a matter of supplying something that really does what is merely pretended by the bogus epistemology of intuitionism. Instead of a vague attempt to borrow the epistemological credentials of the idea of perception, the position I am describing aims, quite differently, at an epistemology that centres on the notion of susceptibility to reasons. The threat to truth is from the thought that there is not enough substance to our conception of reasons for ethical stances. When we try to meet this threat, there is no reason not to appeal to all the resources at our disposal, including all the ethical concepts we can lay our hands on, so long as they survive critical scrutiny; and there need be no basis for critical scrutiny of one ethical concept except others, so the necessary scrutiny does not involve stepping outside the point of view constituted by an ethical sensibility.

Notice that this does not make it a foregone conclusion that the threat will be satisfactorily met; MacIntyre's picture of our present predicament, for instance, cannot be ruled out without actually looking into the resources we still have. Aiming to meet the threat from within is not helping ourselves to ethical truth in the manner of an intuitionistic realism; and it would be quite wrong to suppose that it is helping ourselves to ethical truth in the different sense that the issue is prejudged in favour of truth's being attainable.

5. Blackburn has purported to respond to the suggestion that truth in ethics might be earned from within ethical thinking, and similarly in other areas where an issue about projection arises. His claim is that such a suggestion merely shirks a plainly necessary explanatory task: one in which

> we try to place the activity of moralizing, or the reaction of finding things funny . . . In particular we try to fit our commitments in these areas into a metaphysical understanding of the kinds of fact the world contains: a metaphysical view which can properly be hostile to an unanalysed and *sui generis* area of moral or humorous . . . facts. And relative to this interest, answers which merely cite the truth of various

such verdicts are quite beside the point. This . . . is because there is no theory connecting these truths to devices whereby we know about them—in other words, no way of protecting our right to [conditionals of the form "If it hadn't been the case that p, I would not be committed to p"].[19]

This passage raises several questions. I shall end this paper by making three points about it.

First, note how the passage still strikes the note of theft as against honest toil, as if the target were still the kind of intuitionism that merely helps itself to a novel range of facts. This looks quite unwarranted once it is clear that there are three positions and not just two. The suggestion is not that we "merely cite the truth"—presumably alleged to be detected by some mysterious quasi-sensory capacities—of specific ethical verdicts, or judgements to the effect that something is funny. The aim is to give an account of how such verdicts and judgements are located in the appropriate region of the space of reasons. No particular verdict or judgement would be a sacrosanct starting-point, supposedly immune to critical scrutiny, in our earning the right to claim that some such verdicts or judgements stand a chance of being true. That is not at all to say that we must earn that right from an initial position in which *all* such verdicts or judgements are suspended at once, as in the projectivist picture of a range of responses to a world that does not contain values or instances of the comic.

The second point relates to the "metaphysical understanding" that Blackburn mentions. This fixes an inventory of "the kinds of fact the world contains". It fixes also, in parallel, a conception of the kinds of cognitive occurrence that can constitute access to facts; nothing will serve except what can be conceived in terms of the impact on us of the world as the "metaphysical understanding" understands it. That is why one is not allowed to count as protecting one's right to a conditional of the form "If it had not been the case that p, I would not have become committed to the belief that p", if one establishes that one would not have arrived at the belief that p had it not been for good reasons for it, with the excellence of the reasons vindicated from within the relevant way of thinking.

---

19. "Errors and the Phenomenology of Value", pp. 17–18: I have supplied the material in square brackets from p. 16.

But how good are the credentials of a "metaphysical understanding" that blankly excludes values and instances of the comic from the world in advance of any philosophical enquiry into truth?[20] Surely if the history of philosophical reflection on the correspondence theory of truth has taught us anything, it is that there is ground for suspicion of the idea that we have some way of telling what can count as a fact, prior to and independent of asking what forms of words might count as expressing truths, so that a conception of facts could exert some leverage in the investigation of truth. We have no point of vantage on the question what can be the case, that is, what can be a fact, external to the modes of thought and speech we know our way around in, with whatever understanding of what counts as better and worse execution of them our mastery of them can give us. If there is enough substance to that understanding to enable us to rule out positions like MacIntyre's with a clear conscience, that is what it is for truth to be attainable in such thought and speech, and so much the worse for any prior "metaphysical understanding" that holds that there cannot be facts of that kind.[21] It is

---

20. Blackburn is extraordinarily unconcerned with this question. See *Spreading the Word*, p. 39, where "the best philosophical problems" are said to arise when "we get a sense of what the world is like, what it must be like", and cannot find room in it for something that we are loath to give up: for instance, "consciousness, agency, causation, or value". Blackburn does not raise the question where we get this sense, and what its credentials might be. Similarly at p. 146: "Once such doubts are felt—motivated in whatever way—a number of attitudes are possible." Again there is a striking lack of concern with the origin of the doubts, and this leaves no room for addressing the question of their merits. It is as if any bit of philosophy that comes naturally to us must be all right, ahead of any inquiry into why it comes naturally to us. (In Essay 7 above, I consider and reject the suggestion that the favouritism of the "metaphysical understanding" might be defended on the basis of a conception of the real as what is explanatorily indispensable. Blackburn's purported response, in "Errors and the Phenomenology of Value", pp. 17–18, still takes the "metaphysical understanding" not to need defending; the response does not make contact with its purported target.)

21. Blackburn considers (see *Spreading the Word*, p. 236) the thesis that "there is no way in which any mind can step back from its own system of belief, survey without its benefit a reality the system aims to depict, and discover whether it is doing well or badly". I am not sure I understand his attitude to this thesis. In the chapter from which I have quoted those words, he considers (as in the passage under discussion in my text) only "correspondence conditionals" with directly causal underpinnings—cases where we can take quite literally the idea of reality making an impact on us. It would surely be a mistake to suppose that when we cite such causal underpinnings for the idea that we are capable of attaining the truth in some area, we are somehow managing after all to step outside reliance on the best we can do, from within our "system of belief", to afford reasons for bits of it. And one might think this thought ought to neutralize the inclination to connect truth

a matter for diagnosis and exorcism, not something that can be allowed without further ado to be a good starting-point for a philosophy of ethics or humour. To reiterate the first point, we need not be frightened out of this line by the bogey of "an unanalysed and *sui generis* area of moral or humorous . . . facts". That is what one gets if one accepts a familiar "metaphysical understanding"—one that is in fact quite dubious even in the areas where it is most tempting—with its picture of facts and our access to them, and then tries to accommodate exercises of ethical sensibilities or senses of humour within its framework; but that was never the proposal.

The third point is about "placing" ethics or humour. I have been suggesting that an undefended "metaphysical understanding" cannot impose binding intellectual obligations on anyone. But that is not to say there are no good questions in this general vicinity. Consider the world as natural science describes it. It is plausible (although not beyond dispute) that that "world" would not contain moral values or instances of the comic. (This is no concession to the "metaphysical understanding"; what is missing is a reason to suppose that natural science has a foundational status in philosophical reflection about truth—that there can be no facts other than those that would figure in a scientific understanding of the world.) Now there is no reason not to raise the question how ethics or humour relate to the scientifically useful truth about the world and our dealings with it. There is no reason to dispute that a good answer to such questions might contribute to our making ourselves intelligible to ourselves in a way that we ought to find desirable. Finding things funny, for instance, can seem, from a certain fully intelligible perspective, a peculiar and even mysterious aspect of our lives, quite unlike, say, being able to tell what shapes things have, or even what colours things have. Anything that alleviated this sense of mystery would be welcome, and it

---

with *causally* underwritten "correspondence conditionals" in particular. That is just one shape that rationally underwritten "correspondence conditionals" can take. Blackburn, however, writes (pp. 247–8) as if a thought on the lines of the one I have just expressed involves a "gestalt-switch" akin to Idealism, and in competition with ascribing to objects and facts "their independence of us and our beliefs". It seems to me quite clear that there is no competition here. I am accordingly led to wonder if Blackburn is, in some submerged way, conceiving the causal impact on us of some facts as a way in which after all the World Itself—what we would like to get a glimpse of head on, if we could only "step back"—penetrates the veil of our "system of belief" and gets through to us.

would be anti-intellectual or obscurantist to deny that. What is unclear, however, is why it seems so obvious to Blackburn that this kind of consideration supports projectivism. No doubt reflections about the benefits of co-operation and social order go some distance towards "placing" ethics—making it intelligible that we inculcate ethical sensibilities in our young, trying to give ethics the importance to them that we believe is proper. (It is not at all obvious what might play an analogous role with senses of humour.) But we do not need to suppose such "placing" functions by allowing us to make sense of a range of subjective responses to a world that contains nothing valuable, or funny—responses that we can then see as projected on to that world so as to generate the familiar appearances. What we "place" need not be the sort of sentiments that can be regarded as parents of apparent features; it may be pairs of sentiments and features reciprocally related—siblings rather than parents and children.

There is surely something right about the Humean idea of a "new creation"—the idea of a range of seeming states of affairs that would not be as they are if it were not for the distinctive affective colouration of our subjectivity. What does not follow is that the seeming states of affairs can be understood as creatures of independently intelligible operations of our affective nature. These seeeming objectivities need not be a shadow or reflection of a self-contained subjectivity: understanding the genesis of the "new creation" may be understanding an interlocking complex of subjective and objective, of response and feature responded to. And in that case it is a mistake to think we can illuminate the metaphysics of these matters by appealing to the image of projection.

ESSAY 9

Two Sorts of Naturalism[1]

1. Philippa Foot has long urged the attractions of ethical naturalism. I applaud the negative part of her point, which is to reject various sorts of subjectivism and supernaturalist rationalism. But I doubt whether we can understand a positive naturalism in the right way without first rectifying a constriction that the concept of nature is liable to undergo in our thinking. Without such preliminaries, what we make of ethical naturalism will not be the radical and satisfying alternative to Mrs Foot's targets that naturalism can be. Mrs Foot's writings do not pay much attention to the concept of nature in its own right, and this leaves a risk that her naturalism may seem to belong to this less satisfying variety. I hope an attempt to explain this will be an appropriate token of friendship and admiration.

2. I begin with a claim about how not to read Aristotle, whose ethical outlook is obviously naturalistic in some sense. There is an Aristotelian notion of what is necessary as that without which good cannot be attained.[2] It can be tempting to suppose that when Aristotle relates human virtue to nature he is, in effect, exploiting that notion in order to validate the appeal of ethical considerations to reason. The idea is that the appeal is validated on the ground that the virtues are necessary in that sense, with the necessity founded in indepen-

---

1. This paper was written for a Festschrift for Philippa Foot.
2. *Metaphysics* Δ5, 1015a22–6.

dent facts, underwritten by nature, about what it is for a human life to go well. But I think any such reading of Aristotle's intentions is quite wrong.

It is striking that that notion of necessity does not figure in Aristotle's own talk about the virtues. A quick reading of Aristotle's ethics may give the impression that this is only a verbal absence. Surely he represents happiness as a good unattainable without the virtues? But if we are to ground the appeal of ethical considerations to reason by exploiting the claim that the virtues are something without which good cannot be attained, the grounding must invoke a dependence within the sphere of the practical. The good in question—what figures as "happiness" in our translations—must be independently recognizable as such. But Aristotle explains "happiness" as "acting well", with "well" glossed as "in accordance with the virtues".[3] The good he represents as unattainable without the virtues just is virtuous activity. And we obviously cannot help ourselves to the thesis that virtuous activity is a good while we are suspending judgement as to whether ethical considerations really appeal to reason, as we must if we are to exploit nature to establish that the appeal is genuine. There is no promise here of founding the rational appeal of ethical considerations on a claim of natural necessity.

Of course decent people (like us) think acting in accordance with the virtues is, as such, a good. So we can say we need the virtues, since without them we cannot attain that good. But if we say that, we are not pointing to any dependence within the sphere of what has a claim on practical reason. To say "We need the virtues" is just to say that ethical considerations constitute genuine reasons for acting, not to give the outline of a grounding for that claim.

I think the reading of Aristotle I am rejecting is mostly held in place by inability to see any alternative. I hope the rest of this essay will help to dislodge it.[4] But I can mention a couple of exegetical points in advance.

The reading makes it difficult to place an attractive thesis of Aristotle's, to the effect that virtuous actions are—presumably rightly—seen by a virtuous person as worth performing *for their own sake*.[5]

---

3. See *Nicomachean Ethics* (henceforth *NE*) 1.7.
4. See also Essay 1 above.
5. See *NE* 2.4. For the idea that a virtuous person gets this kind of thing right, see, for instance, *NE* 3.4.

On the reading I am rejecting, when Aristotle says the good for human beings is a life of activity in accordance with the virtues, he must mean that a life of virtuous activity is recognizably good, as such, only derivatively; it is non-derivatively recognizable as good not under the description "a life of virtuous activity", but under some description that displays an independent appeal to reason—an appeal we can see that the life so specified has, even while we are suspending judgement on whether reason requires virtuous activity. But how can this cohere with the suggestion that virtuous action as such recommends itself to a rational will?

Similarly, consider the thesis that a virtuous person acts "for the sake of the noble".[6] A virtuous action's appeal to reason—which a virtuous person gets right—consists in the action's being noble. This goes well with the suggestion that virtuous action appeals to reason in its own right, not as needed to secure some good whose status as such can be recognized independently of whether virtue's demands on reason are genuine. A virtuous action's appeal to reason is captured by an evaluation, "noble", which is internal to the standpoint of someone who already accepts that virtue's demands on reason are real. Accepting that, and accepting that "for the sake of the noble" gives a reason for acting, are the same thing.

3. Just how convincing a grounding for the appeal of ethical considerations to reason is available anyway, from the claim that human beings need the virtues if their life is to go well? Would this claim be like the claim that wolves need a certain sort of co-operativeness if their life is to go well?

Suppose some wolves acquire reason. I mean this as something one might say in Greek with the word *"logos"*. What the wolves acquire is the power of speech, the power of giving expression to conceptual capacities that are rationally interlinked in ways reflected by what it makes sense to give as a reason for what.

I have spoken of wolves rather than of a lone wolf, and this bypasses one of the difficulties one might have about whether the supposition is really intelligible. Other difficulties remain: Wittgenstein's

---

6. See, e.g., *NE* 3.7.

aphorism "If a lion could talk, we could not understand him"[7] is very much to the point, and we should add that if we could not understand him, that ought to undermine our confidence that we were entitled to suppose talking was what he was doing.[8] But for my purposes, it does not matter whether it is genuinely intelligible that wolves (or lions) might acquire *logos*; it will be enough if we can get as far as pretending that it is.

A rational wolf would be able to let his mind roam over possibilities of behaviour other than what comes naturally to wolves. Aside from the fact that it comes within the scope of our pretence, that may seem obvious, and indeed it is. Even so, it reflects a deep connection between reason and freedom; we cannot make sense of a creature's acquiring reason unless it has genuinely alternative possibilities of action, over which its thought can play. We cannot intelligibly restrict the exercise of conceptual powers to merely theoretical thinking, on the part of something whose behaviour, if any, flows from a brutely natural aspect of its total make-up, uncontaminated by its conceptual powers—so that it might conceive "its own" behaviour if any (it could not be its own in any very strong sense) as just another phenomenon in the world it conceptualizes. An ability to conceptualize the world must include the ability to conceptualize the thinker's own place in the world; and to find the latter ability intelligible, we need to make room not only for conceptual states that aim to represent how the world anyway is, but also for conceptual states that issue in interventions directed towards making the world conform to their content.[9] A possessor of *logos* cannot be just a knower, but must be an agent too; and we cannot make sense of *logos* as manifesting itself in agency without seeing it as selecting between options, rather than simply going along with what is going to happen anyway.

---

7. *Philosophical Investigations*, p. 223.
8. See Donald Davidson, "On the Very Idea of a Conceptual Scheme".
9. This formulation fits representations of states of affairs in the world apart from the subject, entering into the aetiology of action aimed at bringing them about; and also representations of the subject's projected interventions themselves. It is a question over which I shall not pause whether a conceptual scheme could have no concepts of the exercise of agency except those constructed out of the concept-schema *bringing it about that* . . . .

This is to represent freedom of action as inextricably connected with a freedom that is essential to conceptual thought. The physical make-up of the animal who is the thinker and agent sets limits on these freedoms, and contingent deficiencies of imagination (inborn or conditioned) may restrict their actual exercise more stringently yet. No doubt the question how imaginative a rational wolf might be is too wildly counterfactual to be worth bothering with. But that does not matter. The point is that something whose physical make-up left no free play in how it manifested itself in interactions with the rest of reality, or something whose physical make-up, although it left such free play, somehow precluded the development of the imagination required to contemplate alternatives, could not acquire reason. This does not depend on pretences about lions or wolves.

Suppose now that a rational wolf finds himself in a situation in which some behaviour would come naturally to him: say playing his part in the co-operative activity of hunting with the pack. Having acquired reason, he can contemplate alternatives; he can step back from the natural impulse and direct critical scrutiny at it. We cannot allow ourselves to suppose that God, say, might confer reason on wolves, but stop short of his giving them the materials to step back and frame the question "Why should I do this?".

But once this critical question has arisen, how can it help to appeal to what wolves need? "Why should I pull my weight?", says our reflective wolf, wondering whether to idle through the hunt but still grab his share of the prey. Suppose we respond, truly enough: "Wolves need to pool their energies, if their style of hunting is to be effective." If our wolf has stepped back from his natural impulse and taken up the critical stance, why should what we say impress him?

A statement to the effect that wolves need such-and-such is what Michael Thompson calls "an Aristotelian categorical".[10] The logical powers of such statements are peculiar. Consider the example "Human beings have thirty-two teeth".[11] There is a truth we can state in those terms; but from that truth, together with the fact that I am a human being, it does not follow that I have thirty-two teeth. (In fact it is false.) Similarly, from "Wolves need such-and-such" and the

---

10. See "The Representation of Life".
11. Discussed by G. E. M. Anscombe in "Modern Moral Philosophy".

fact that he is a wolf, our wolf cannot conclude that he needs such-and-such. Of course this logical weakness of "Aristotelian categoricals" raises no practical problem for an ordinary non-rational wolf: the way what wolves need impinges on his behaviour is not by an inference to what *he* needs. But the point makes a difference when we imagine a rational wolf wondering what to do.

One difference reason would make is to bring the facts about what wolves need to conceptual awareness, and so make them available to serve as rational considerations. But what converts what animals of one's species need into potential rational considerations is precisely what enables a rational animal to step back and view those considerations from a critical standpoint. So when they become potential reasons, their status as reasons is, by the same token, opened to question. And now it matters that the predicate of an "Aristotelian categorical" about the species cannot be deductively transferred to its individual members. The deliberative question reason enables our wolf to ask is not about wolves in general but about himself: "What should I do?" And the deductive impotence of the "Aristotelian categorical" brings out that what wolves need is not guaranteed a rational bearing on his question; and this even if he never forgets that he is a wolf. Reason does not just open our eyes to our nature, as members of the animal species we belong to; it also enables and even obliges us to step back from it, in a way that puts its bearing on our practical problems into question.

With the onset of reason, then, the nature of the species abdicates from a previously unquestionable authority over the behaviour of the individual animal. We are supposed to be looking for a grounding for the genuineness of the demands that virtue purports to make on reason, and while the search is on we may not appeal to those demands. This can easily leave the individual interest of the deliberator looking like the only candidate to take over the vacant throne. It would not be surprising if the deliberating wolf thought reason requires him to transcend his wolfish nature in pursuit of his individual interest, exploiting the less intelligent wolves who continue to let their lives be structured by what wolves need. No doubt the transcendence can be only partial, since the idea that free-riding might be a good plan depends on its being a way to secure things that naturally matter to wolves, such as plenty of meat to eat, not having to exert oneself if one can avoid it, and so forth. But a deliberating wolf might still take large parts of the natural pattern in the life of wolves to have no rational bearing on what he should do.

He might adopt a Calliclean or Nietzschean stance, regarding the less intelligent wolves whom he proposes to exploit as degenerate. This involves reconceiving the project of partially transcending his nature as a project of properly realizing his nature. After all, he has not stopped being a wolf, and reason, which seems to him to dictate the project, has become part of his nature. (It is part of our nature.) The concept of nature figures here, without incoherence, in two quite different ways: as "mere" nature, and as something whose realization involves transcending that. This wolf has no need to deny those facts about the nature—the "mere" nature—of wolves that underlie the claim that a good wolf is one who pulls his weight in the hunt. In fact he must agree that most wolves had better not behave as he proposes to; but that is all right, because he is not preaching to the herd, or rather, in this case, the pack. There is nothing he is denying or overlooking about the natural patterns of life among wolves. Of course he may be quite wrong in thinking his project is workable, or in thinking it will be satisfactory to him, wolf that he is. But perhaps he is not wrong; and if he is, we cannot show him he is by reaffirming the facts about what wolves need. There is nothing there that he needs to dispute.

So even if we grant that human beings have a naturally based need for the virtues, in a sense parallel to the sense in which wolves have a naturally based need for co-operativeness in their hunting, that need not cut any ice with someone who questions whether virtuous behaviour is genuinely required by reason.

4. It would be a mistake to think Aristotle might be invulnerable to this point, because he has a thick "pre-modern" conception of nature. The point is structural; it does not depend on the content of any particular conception of the needs that nature underwrites. As soon as we conceive nature in a way that makes it begin to seem sensible to look there for a grounding for the rationality of virtuous behaviour, the supposed grounding is in trouble from the logical impotence of "Aristotelian categoricals". Reason enables a deliberating agent to step back from *anything* that might be a candidate to ground its putative requirements. This is a problem for Aristotle on

readings like that of Bernard Williams, who thinks Aristotle had a conception of nature, no longer available to us, in which it could serve as an Archimedean point for justifying ethics.[12]

Perhaps Aristotle missed the impotence of "Aristotelian categoricals". But it is surely better to try out the thought that his naturalism simply does not promise to validate putative rational requirements. That he is not concerned about grounding is anyway strongly suggested by the fact that he addresses his ethical lectures only to people who have been properly brought up.[13]

We find it difficult not to want a foundation, but that is because of a location in the history of thought that separates us from Aristotle. To understand his naturalism correctly, we need to achieve a willed immunity to some of the influence of our intellectual inheritance, an influence of which Aristotle himself was simply innocent. That way, we can stop supposing the rationality of virtue needs a foundation outside the formed evaluative outlook of a virtuous person.

5. The most striking occurrence in the history of thought between Aristotle and ourselves is the rise of modern science. I want to suggest that a dubious philosophical response to that has made it difficult for modern readers to take the measure of Greek naturalism.

It is a commonplace that modern science has given us a disenchanted conception of the natural world. A proper appreciation of science makes it impossible to retain, except perhaps in some symbolic guise, the common mediaeval conception of nature as filled with meaning, like a book containing messages and lessons for us.[14] The tendency of the scientific outlook is to purge the world of meaning—the object of reason, in an old sense that is threatened by just this development.[15]

Hume is the prophet *par excellence* of this tendency, although he is quite unconscious of the historical explanation for it. Reason, Hume insists, does not find meaning or intelligible order in the world; rather, whatever intelligible order there is in our world-

---

12. See chap. 3 of *Ethics and the Limits of Philosophy*.
13. *NE* 1.4, 1095b4–6.
14. For an elaboration of this, see chap. 1 of Charles Taylor, *Hegel*.
15. With an eye to what is to come, let me remark that the relevant notion of reason includes what Kant calls "understanding".

picture is a product of the operations of mind, and those operations are themselves just some of what goes on in nature, in itself meaninglessly, as it were.

From this standpoint, Kant looks like a desperate reactionary. He insists that intelligible order is found in the world, but he makes this out only by reconstruing the world as partly constituted by mind. This looks like an image of Hume's picture in a distorting medium. It looks inferior, by the lights of what seems a merely sane naturalism, in that it conceives the meaning-yielding operations of mind transcendentally rather than as part of nature. And it looks unconvincing in its insistence that the order is there to be found; it seems to undermine that by suggesting that we constitute the order ourselves.

This view of the Kantian alternative provokes an understandable recoil. A familiar response is to retain Hume's picture of the meaning-yielding operations of mind, but to discard his responsiveness to scepticism, which keeps Hume himself from a scientistic realism. According to the sort of outlook I mean, reality is exhausted by the natural world, in the sense of the world as the natural sciences are capable of revealing it to us. Part of the truth in the idea that science disenchants nature is that science is committed to a dispassionate and dehumanized stance for investigation; that is taken to be a matter of conforming to a metaphysical insight into the character of reality as such. (The fact that the natural sciences reveal the world as intelligible has to be glossed over somehow; I shall return to this in §7 below.) Any candidate feature of reality that science cannot capture is downgraded as a projection, a result of mind's interaction with the rest of nature.[16]

Against this background, it will seem that a putative operation of the intellect can stand up to reflective scrutiny only if its products can be validated on the basis of the facts of nature, conceived in the disenchanted way that is encouraged by modern science. For if we are to understand what is in question as an operation of the intellect at all, we must make room for objectivity: for there to be a difference between being right and seeming right.[17] And science has presented itself as the very exemplar of access to objective truth.

---

16. This Humean image has been recommended by Simon Blackburn in a number of places; see, for instance, *Spreading the Word*, chaps. 5 and 6.

17. See Wittgenstein, *Philosophical Investigations* §258.

This will go for practical reason as much as any other putative operation of the intellect. Hume himself does not officially recognize a practical employment of reason. But we can graft a notion of practical reason into the neo-Humean position I am describing if we can make out a notion of correctness in practical thinking that is suitably grounded in facts of nature. Hume himself suggests that correctness in practical thinking can be grounded only in individual wants and likings, conceived as brute unassessable facts; that is why he cannot see any substantial practical role for reason. But in the neo-Humean position there is no need for this subjectivistic conception of the possibilities. The basic picture is that putative reasons need to be grounded in facts of disenchanted nature (nature no longer construed as addressed to us). And those facts can include such things as what animals of a particular species need in order to do well in the sort of life they naturally live.

6. It can easily seem, now, that an appeal to such facts is the only way to try to make out that ethical considerations make real demands on reason. Given the conception of nature we have arrived at, we have a forced choice between this and an unpalatable dilemma.

If we confine ourselves to the realm of nature, the only alternative to this appeal to needs (or interests) is some version of the subjectivism we can find in Hume himself. But in its pure form that gives up the project of certifying that ethical considerations genuinely constitute reasons. It is true that there are descendants of the Humean outlook, such as prescriptivism, that purport to execute the project. The idea is to superimpose some quasi-Kantian formal or structural requirements of reason on pro-attitudes (or something to that effect), conceived as in themselves—were it not for the superimposition of reason—capable of fastening on anything at all. But Mrs Foot has argued, convincingly, that the underlying conception of pro-attitudes (or whatever) in this picture makes no sense.[18] The envisaged superimposition of reason yields an appearance of objectivity, but it comes too late to make any difference to that.

Perhaps we need not confine ourselves to the realm of nature? But then we are conceiving reason as a foreign power, ordering our ani-

---

18. See especially the first part of "Moral Beliefs".

mal nature about from outside the natural world. Our lives are mysteriously split, somehow taking place both in nature and in some alien realm in which reason operates.[19] This sort of overt supernaturalism is of course hard to take seriously. It, too, has been a target of effective polemic from Mrs Foot: no one has done more than she to expose the uselessness of a conception of reason as somehow authoritative over us from outside our natural attitudes and inclinations.[20]

What I have sketched here can look like a cogent argument by elimination, forcing us to try to ground the rationality of ethics in something like what it is for the life of the species to go well.[21] Williams's reading of Aristotle fits here in a way, as a response to the fact that such a grounding has its own problems (§3 above), which means that the framework of available options is under stress. It is as if, barring subjectivism, the appeal to the supernatural has to show up somewhere, and only in a primitive conception of nature could it pass unnoticed that something supernatural is being smuggled into nature.[22]

But there is still the option of looking for a position that disclaims any need for foundations. Following this through, we shall see that we do not need to accept the conception of nature that organizes this inventory of available positions.

7. The neo-Humean outlook I have described (§5 above), freed from Hume's subjectivism and sympathy for scepticism, can seem sheer

---

19. In "Plato's heaven", perhaps. In fact I believe it is quite unfair to Plato to represent him as a supernaturalist about reason in this way. Plato is a naturalist of the Aristotelian sort, with a penchant for vividly realized pictorial presentations of his thought.

20. See especially "Morality as a System of Hypothetical Imperatives".

21. For the suggestion of such an argument, see Foot, "Hume on Moral Judgement". In that paper she recommends the thesis that "moral virtues are qualities necessary if men are to get on well in a world in which they are frightened, tempted by pleasure and liable to hurt rather than help each other". Her ground is that this is the way to preserve Hume's opposition to a supernatural conception of reason, while avoiding his lapse into subjectivism.

22. This is the context in which to understand David Wiggins's remark that "Aristotelian Eudaemonism" attributes an "unconvincing speaking part" to nature: "Truth, Invention, and the Meaning of Life", p. 134. (See also *Sameness and Substance,* p. 187, with pp. 183–4.) The "speaking part" Wiggins thinks Aristotle assigns to nature must be either the role for ordinary nature that I considered in §3, which is unconvincing for the sorts of reasons I canvassed there; or a role for a supposed special Aristotelian super-nature, such as figures in Williams's reading, which is unconvincing because we know now that nature is not like that.

common sense, if the only alternative is the mysteries of transcendental idealism. But this assessment misses an essential Kantian insight.

Empiricist realists insist on the intellectual respectability of certain cognitive states: those that register direct observation, however that is conceived, and those that result from however much natural science they allow to derive intellectual respectability from that of observation. We need not bother with the different options; the essential point is that, whatever the details, an acceptable world-picture consists of articulable, conceptually structured representations. Their acceptability resides in their knowably mirroring the world; that is, representing it as it is.

Well and good; I do not believe that thought need attract our suspicion.[23] But note that if we retain it, we cannot suppose that intelligible order has completely emigrated from the world we take to be mirrored by intellectual states in ground-level good standing, the standing on the basis of which the standing of any other intellectual states is to be established. We have to suppose that the world has an intelligible structure, matching the structure in the space of *logos* possessed by accurate representations of it.[24] The disenchantment Hume applauds can seem to point to a conception of nature as an ineffable lump, devoid of structure or order. But we cannot entertain such a conception. If we did, we would lose our right to the idea that the world of nature is a world at all (something that breaks up into things that are the case), let alone the world (everything that is the case).[25] Hume himself, innocent of the very idea of conceptual articulation, is oblivious of this point; his modern successors lack his excuse.[26]

---

23. Compare Richard Rorty, *Philosophy and the Mirror of Nature*. Rorty suggests that mirror imagery is suspect in its own right; but I think what follows accommodates his good point without jettisoning such imagery.

24. I am deliberately being very unspecific here. Kant himself claims to have been nudged into transcendental philosophy by a recoil from Hume's treatment of causation in particular. But a thought of the general shape I am describing might cohere with a quasi-Humean disbelief that causal connections are an aspect of the way *logos* as it were permeates the world; this possibility finds expression in Wittgenstein's *Tractatus Logico-Philosophicus*.

25. See *Tractatus* §1.

26. There is a temptation, which presumably issues from an inkling of the trouble this point makes, to suppose empiricism can dispense with mirroring or accurate representation, and make do instead with an idea like that of organizing. This would be congenial to the thought that intelligible order is, across the board, imposed rather than found. On this, see Davidson, "On the Very Idea of a Conceptual Scheme".

Kant has this point, but his picture contains a version of the fully disenchanted item that lies at the end of Hume's path, something brutely alien to the space of *logos*. Thus the thesis that the world of nature cannot be constitutively independent of the space in which thought operates becomes the thesis that the world of nature is, transcendentally speaking, a joint product of the structure of subjectivity and an ineffable "in itself" that is fully independent of that structure. This is quite unsatisfying: it looks like a displacement of the objectivity we wanted in the world of nature to a place in the overall picture where it is no use to us—for the ineffable "in itself" is, by Kant's own showing, nothing to us. About the world of nature, we are fobbed off with idealism; and it is really no consolation to be told (with at best questionable intelligibility anyway) that it is only transcendentally speaking that that world is in part a product of subjectivity.[27]

This is what makes it seem common sense to detranscendentalize Kant's structure of joint determination by subjectivity and the "in itself". The perfectly describable empirical world takes over the role played in Kant's structure by the ineffable "in itself", the role of objective member of a pair of determinants. It is not now intelligible order as such that is jointly produced by such a pair of determinants, since the empirical world already has that, of itself as it were. But all other intelligible order, all other meaning or value, beyond what is required for the natural facts to be articulable, is conceived as partly a reflection of our subjectivity. In such a position, it is natural to say, in Humean style, that the surplus of meaning or value is projected on to objective reality from its subjective source. So transcendental idealism triggers a recoil, representing itself as common sense, into an empiricistic realism about nature, with any other features of a world view conceived as projections.

But mirroring cannot be *both* faithful, so that it adds nothing in the way of intelligible order, *and* such that in moving from what is mirrored to what does the mirroring, one moves from what is brutely alien to the space of *logos* to what is internal to it. That is no reason to give up the idea that empirical thought can mirror the natural world.[28] But if we keep the idea of accurate representation, we

---

27. For an eloquent expression of this point, see Barry Stroud's contribution to the symposium "The Disappearing 'We'".
28. See n. 23 above.

cannot shirk the consequence, which we might put by saying that the natural world is in the space of *logos*. The ineffable "in itself" in Kant's picture performs the function of satisfying a felt need to recognize something wholly alien to subjectivity; and Kant's insight is that the natural world, just because it is not ineffable, cannot take over that function.

It may now seem that we are trapped between a rock and a hard place: between Kant's insight and the repulsiveness of the sort of idealism that says we make the world. But that is not so. The insight degenerates into that sort of idealism only because Kant keeps a role in his picture for the ineffable "in itself", the item that lies at the terminus of the process of expelling intelligibility from the world for which Hume acts as cheerleader. In fact Kant goes beyond Hume here, in extrapolating from the disenchantment of nature. The insight saves him from supposing there is a viable conception of nature as what we are left with when all intelligibility has been expelled, but he does find that terminal item another role, and that is what introduces idealism. The thesis that the world of nature is internal to the space of *logos,* in which thought has its being, becomes an affirmation of idealism only because the structure of subjectivity is conceived as a joint determinant of the intelligible structure of the world of nature, along with the "in itself". If the "in itself" drops out, the thesis that the natural world is in the space of *logos* need not seem to be a form of the thesis that thought makes the world.

This puts us in a position to focus on the insight, without being distracted by the fear of picturing nature as our creation. We should not conceive the disenchanted natural world as a satisfyingly detranscendentalized surrogate for the "in itself". Since it is a world, the natural world is not constitutively independent of the structure of subjectivity. It is a mistake to conceive objectivity in terms of complete independence from subjectivity. We miss the point if, retaining the hankering that that idea expresses, we nod in the direction of Kant's lesson that the "in itself" is nothing to us, but think we can fasten on the disenchanted natural world as the next best thing. Kant's own thinking comes to wreck because of a vestige of the hankering; what it is after is repositioned but not dislodged by the insight, which cannot achieve its proper form in an environment in which the hankering persists. The real lesson is that we ought to exorcize the hankering. It is a splendid thing to find out the facts of disenchanted nature, but not because that is as close as we can come to knowing the "in itself".

Why is our wish to acknowledge a role for the "in itself" so obstinate? I am suggesting, in effect, that it kept Kant himself, who almost saw through it, from a proper appreciation of his own insight. The role of science in our culture is not immediately the explanation. Science does not itself lay claim to enshrining metaphysical truth; it takes philosophers to make such claims on its behalf. More to the point is an intelligible wish to avoid responsibility. If something utterly outside the space of *logos* forces itself on us, we cannot be blamed for believing what we do.[29] Our position in history makes available to us the idea of the world as science reveals it; that means that in our case the wish to disclaim responsibility has a concrete and determinate object to fasten on. (The rise of modern science would also be central in an account of why we are especially prone to feel the responsibility of thought as a burden.)

There is no need to deny that what science reveals is special, in a way that is brought out by the point about disenchantment. In discarding the mediaeval conception of nature as a book, science indeed unmasked projective illusions, and it is essential to how scientific investigation rightly conceives its topic that it should be on guard against such illusions. The investigative stance of science discounts for the effects of features of the investigator, even his humanity. That is why the world as science reveals it does not contain secondary qualities. More generally, what science aims to discover is the nature of reality in so far as it can be characterized in absolute terms: the content of the view from nowhere, in Thomas Nagel's evocative phrase.[30] And the practice of science is not a mere quirk of our culture, on a par with, say, chess. Thanks to science, we know far more about the world, and understand it far better, than the mediaevals did, and it does not undermine the fact that this is an objective improvement to say (true though it is) that we make these assessments from our present standpoint, which includes the hard-won idea of

---

29. Rorty, *Philosophy and the Mirror of Nature*, has suggestive things to say about this.

30. Nagel, *The View from Nowhere*. On "absolute", see chap. 8 of Bernard Williams, *Descartes: The Project of Pure Enquiry*; also chap. 8 of his *Ethics and the Limits of Philosophy*.

disenchanted nature as the province of scientific understanding.[31] But it is one thing to recognize that the impersonal stance of scientific investigation is a methodological necessity for the achievement of a valuable mode of understanding reality; it is quite another thing to take the dawning grasp of this, in the modern era, for a metaphysical insight into the notion of objectivity as such, so that objective correctness in any mode of thought must be anchored in this kind of access to the real.[32] And it is simply a confusion if one is encouraged in this thought by the idea that what science uncovers is the nearest we can come to the "in itself". The detranscendentalized analogue of Kant's picture that empiricist realism amounts to is not the educated common sense it represents itself as being; it is shallow metaphysics.

8. I have been trying to explain how an understandable recoil from Kant's philosophy of nature encourages the idea that all intellectual respectability, including whatever intellectual respectability can be possessed by exercises of practical reason, must in the end be grounded on correctness about the disenchanted natural world. The upshot is that the philosophy of nature, which aims to deal with how the world comes to expression in *logos,* as it were swallows up the philosophy of practice, which aims to deal with how *logos* comes to expression in the world.

Kant's own philosophy of practice is of course a separate enterprise, in a way we can perhaps understand on this basis: it reflects the thought I have been representing as having a debilitating effect on his philosophy of nature. He keeps something wholly alien to subjectivity in the picture, and that means the philosophy of nature has to take the following general shape: although empirically speaking we find meaning or intelligible order in the world, transcendentally speaking we co-operate with the "in itself" to make it. The idea of making meaning fits action, so perhaps we can understand Kantian philosophy of practice as shaped by the thought that there is a general lesson to be learned here: all making of meaning has a tran-

---

31. See Williams's reaction to Rorty, at pp. 137–8 of *Ethics and the Limits of Philosophy;* compare *Descartes: The Project of Pure Enquiry,* p. 248, n. 21. To undermine the metaphysical pretensions of "the absolute conception of reality", one need not say, as Rorty likes to, the sort of thing that provokes this response.
32. See Taylor, "Theories of Meaning", especially at pp. 290–1.

scendental aspect. Meaning is not in nature, on the disenchanted conception, and transcendental philosophy attempts to show us how to live with the thought that the disenchanted conception of nature is indispensable to what has become our paradigm for intellectual respectability. In the philosophy of nature, we have the idea that behind an empirical transaction in which a fact impresses itself on a knowing subject, perhaps causally, there lies a transaction between subjectivity and the "in itself" that constitutes the fact—a transaction that cannot be causal, since causation operates within the constituted empirical world. In the philosophy of practice, we have the roughly corresponding idea that behind the causal goings-on involved in an action, there is a transcendental injection of meaning into the world from outside: necessarily not a causal transaction for the same reason. The correspondence is only rough, because the meaning injected by the transcendental operation involved in action is as it were a second dose; what this meaning is injected into is not the "in itself", but the empirical world, to whose constitution subjectivity has already made a transcendental contribution.

If the meaning action has by virtue of being the expression of *logos* is injected into the natural world from outside, the *logos* that expresses itself in action cannot be part of the natural world. So Kant's philosophy of practice needs to reject naturalistic ways of giving substance to practical reason. The central concept must be the concept of pure practical reason, constrained only by considerations of form. If we supposed that correctness in practical reason might be non-formally determined, that would deprive practical reason of its capacity to be the transcendental originator of the meaning of action.

Rehearsing these features of Kant's philosophy of practice may reinforce the temptation to think a recoil into a neo-Humean naturalism is common sense: if we want to recognize practical reason, we must construct the requisite idea of getting things right out of the facts of disenchanted nature. But none of this further detail undermines the fact that that sort of naturalism loses Kant's insight. I have suggested how we can extricate the insight from transcendental idealism in the philosophy of nature; what happens if we extend the implications into the philosophy of practice?

The recipe was to rid ourselves of the hankering to acknowledge something brutely alien to subjectivity. If we can manage that, we can stop supposing that behind the finding of meaning in the empirical world with which the philosophy of nature deals, there is a transcendental making of meaning. But then the philosophy of nature no longer contains grounds for insisting that the making of meaning with which the philosophy of practice deals must be transcendentally conceived. We can go on taking action to be the making of meaning, to be practical *logos* expressing or realizing itself, but we no longer need to think of practical *logos* as external to nature. But we should now be past the idea that we must construct a notion of correctness in exercises of practical reason out of facts available to natural science. So we can bring practical reason back into nature; but what we bring back into nature is practical reason still conceived in a somewhat Kantian fashion, as something that does not need certification from outside itself.

A good way to begin to appreciate the shape of the possibility that opens up here is by reflecting on the concept of second nature, which is all but explicit in Aristotle's account of the acquisition of virtue of character. Virtue of character embodies the relevant proper state of practical *logos,* what Aristotle calls *"phronēsis"*—"practical wisdom", in the translation of W. D. Ross.[33] The concept of second nature registers that we do not need to conceive practical reason as subject only to formal constraints. What it is for the practical intel-

---

33. See *NE*, book 2. Many modern commentators separate *phronēsis* from the formed character—second nature—that is Aristotle's concern in that book: they take his view to be that *phronēsis* (an intellectual virtue) equips one's reason to issue the right orders to one's formed character, the point of character-formation being that it makes one's second nature willing in its obedience to reason's commands. (For a very clear example of such a reading, see John M. Cooper, "Some Remarks on Aristotle's Moral Psychology".) But 2.4, with the requirement that the virtuous person chooses virtuous actions for their own sake, suggests that Aristotle conceives the topic of book 2, officially the moulding of character, as already including the proper shaping of the practical intellect. And 6.13 does not compel the idea that character takes orders from reason, as opposed to the idea that the moulding of character *is* (in part) the shaping of reason. The architectonic device of 1.13, dividing the virtues into virtues of character and intellectual virtues, leaves open the possibility that Aristotle means it to become clear, as the doctrine unfolds, that the division is not exclusive. The contrary reading of Aristotle is shaped, I believe, by the anachronistic importation of a quasi-Kantian extra-natural conception of practical reason. (Cooper would object that the conception of reason as autonomous, constituted independently of the natural motivational propensities that are moulded into virtues of character, is not modern, as I am suggesting, since, even if its presence in Aristotle is disputable, its presence in the Stoics is not. I think this reflects a philosophical misreading of Stoicism, but I cannot go into that here.) See, further, Essay 2 above.

lect to be as it ought to be, and so equipped to get things right in its proper sphere, is a matter of its having a certain determinate non-formal shape. The practical intellect's coming to be as it ought to be is the acquisition of a second nature, involving the moulding of motivational and evaluative propensities: a process that takes place in nature. The practical intellect does not dictate to one's formed character—one's nature as it has become—from outside. One's formed practical intellect—which is operative in one's character-revealing behaviour—just is an aspect of one's nature as it has become.

9. In Kant, the critique of theoretical reason and the critique of practical reason are somewhat separate enterprises. The former yields a picture of how the world comes to expression in *logos;* the latter handles the way *logos* expresses itself in the world. But we are now equipped to consider a version of the upshot of the first critique that fits both these topics.

Consider again the thesis that the world is not constitutively independent of subjectivity, which has its being in the space of *logos.* So far I have discussed this thesis exclusively in connection with theoretical reason. But the very idea of thought—the exercise of intellect—presupposes a notion of objectivity that we can gloss in terms of a distinction between being right and seeming right.[34] And the idea of the world, as it figures in that vestigially Kantian thesis, need not amount to more than an expression of that notion of objectivity. Practical thought aspires to objectivity in that general sense no less than theoretical thought does; it could not be thought, as opposed to, say, attitudinizing, if it did not. If we let the vestigially Kantian thesis embrace that point, our conception of the world, in the sense of what *logos* aims to represent accurately, expands to include features that practical *logos,* if equipped to get things right in its proper sphere, takes to justify its expressings of itself in action—rightly, since it is equipped to get things right.[35]

One supposed ground for doubt that practical thought should be allowed its aspiration to objectivity, in that general sense, is that

---

34. See n. 17 above.
35. I believe this is the sort of framework within which we should start to understand Aristotle's difficult notion of practical truth: see *NE* 6.2.

practical thought does not aspire to a kind of truth that one could conceive in terms of mirroring the disenchanted natural world. An empiricistic naturalism restricts us to the following options for ethics: deny that ethical truth would have to be practical, or, if we hold on to the idea of ethical truth, if any, as a species of practical truth, either force practical truth into the form of mirroring disenchanted nature or else—for those who doubt that that is feasible—renounce the aspiration to ethical truth: for instance embrace a position like emotivism, but there are more sophisticated ways of taking this last option.[36] But I have insisted that this empiricistic naturalism is metaphysically shallow.

This expansion of the notion of the world is the point of at least one version of what has come to be called "ethical realism". One misses the point if one takes the position to represent ethical investigation as a kind of para-science, as in J. L. Mackie's "argument from queerness",[37] or (more subtly) in Bernard Williams's idea that ethical realism would have to suppose—what is indeed implausible—that there is a prospect of convergence on ethical questions that could be explained in the sort of way we can explain convergence on scientific questions.[38] That is how the rhetoric of ethical realism would need to be understood if someone produced it in the context of the sort of empiricistic naturalism whose shallowness I am trying to bring out. But that is simply the wrong environment for the idea. The only similarity there needs to be between ethics and science, for ethical realism properly understood to be acceptable, is that in both of them it can be rational to say of a conclusion that *logos* itself compels it (to echo Plato's Socrates).

There is no need to deny that *logos* compels conclusions in science in a special way: the conclusion that *logos* compels is not only that things are thus and so, but also that investigation has led to that con-

---

36. See Williams, *Ethics and the Limits of Philosophy*, pp. 170–1, on confidence rather than knowledge as a model for ethical conviction. Williams's idea that a knowledge model is unavailable reflects his adherence to the empiricistic naturalism I am attacking. He does not suggest that practical thought needs to renounce an aspiration to get things right; and he is rightly concerned with the fragility of that aspiration in our modern intellectual milieu. But he never considers the role, in bringing about that fragility, of the empiricistic naturalism he himself continues to take for granted.

37. See chap. 1 of *Ethics: Inventing Right and Wrong*.

38. See chap. 8 of *Ethics and the Limits of Philosophy*.

clusion because of the causal influence of the fact that things are thus and so. There is no analogue to that in ethics. But this cannot exempt scientific truth from the need to establish its status by recommending itself to *logos*. And *logos* has, everywhere, only its own lights to go by; the role of causation, in scientific thought's well-grounded conception of itself, does not rescue scientific thought from Neurath's boat. Empiricistic naturalism misses the significance of the fact that the Neurathian "predicament" is quite general. If one protests that science is in the same boat, that tends to be misconceived as expressing a relativistic refusal to accept that science is objectively special.[39] Science is indeed objectively special, and ethical realism does not require us to unlearn its lessons, as if we were to try to regain the mediaeval conception of nature as a book. But it is a mistake to think we cannot show proper respect for science unless we suppose that truth about disenchanted nature is the sole context in which the material good standing of an exercise of intellect can be directly apparent, so that any good standing that is not that must be either merely formal or indirectly grounded on such truth. Good standing is, everywhere, for *logos* to pronounce on, using whatever standards it can lay hands on; nothing but bad metaphysics suggests that the standards in ethics must be somehow constructed out of facts of disenchanted nature.

I have insisted that the point does not involve debunking the scientific way of understanding nature. And it is part of my correction to Kant that exercises of the practical intellect do not impinge on nature from outside. So there can be nothing against looking for a scientific explanation of the place of, say, ethical discourse in disenchanted nature. There might be a question whether the disenchanted conception of nature contains the resources to recognize the topic as discourse, as expressive of thought. But we need not worry about that; in any case the availability of such an explanation would not *compete* with inquiry into how well supported by reasons a particular bit of such discourse is. The sheer possibility of doing science here cannot show that there is no room for a mode of assessment

---

39. See n. 31 above. At p. 218 of *Ethics and the Limits of Philosophy* Williams finds it "revealing" that, in Essay 3 above, I trace scepticism about objectivity in ethics to a "philistine scientism". I think the point is that he takes me to share the anti-scientific relativism he finds in Rorty.

that might certify what is expressed as a thought that is simply correct, without needing to base that correctness on the thought's relation to extra-ethical reality.[40]

10. Holding firm to the thought that the second nature acquired in moral education is a specific shaping of practical *logos*, we can register the point I made by means of the parable about rational wolves (§3 above). Moral education does not merely rechannel one's natural motivational impulses, with the acquisition of reason making no difference except that one becomes self-consciously aware of the operation of those impulses. In imparting *logos*, moral education enables one to step back from any motivational impulse one finds oneself subject to, and question its rational credentials. Thus it effects a kind of distancing of the agent from the practical tendencies that are part of what we might call his first nature.

Nature controls the behaviour of a non-rational animal. It seemed that reason compels nature to abdicate that authority, leaving a void that self-interest seemed fitted to fill. But now we can see that the way reason distances one from first nature need not invite a *coup d'état* from self-interest. In acquiring one's second nature—that is, in acquiring *logos*—one learned to take a distinctive pleasure in acting in certain ways, and one acquired conceptual equipment suited to characterize a distinctive worthwhileness one learned to see in such actions, that is, a distinctive range of reasons one learned to see for acting in those ways. If the second nature one has acquired is virtue, the rationality of virtue simply is not in suspense, though it is always open to reflective questioning. The dictates of virtue have acquired an authority that replaces the authority abdicated by first nature with the onset of reason. (It cannot be the same authority, because everything is now open to reflective questioning.) It is not that the dictates of virtue fill what would otherwise be a void; they are in po-

---

40. Simon Blackburn has persistently argued as if the sheer possibility of asking scientific questions about ethics would establish the correctness of a neo-Humean projectivism. See, e.g., "Errors and the Phenomenology of Value". This is just one more expression of the empiricistic naturalism I am attacking.

sition already, before any threat of anarchy can materialize. The alteration in one's make-up that opened the authority of nature to question is precisely the alteration that has put the dictates of virtue in place as authoritative.

Any second nature of the relevant kind, not just virtue, will seem to its possessor to open his eyes to reasons for acting. What is distinctive about virtue, in the Aristotelian view, is that the reasons a virtuous person takes himself to discern really are reasons; a virtuous person gets this kind of thing right.[41] Aristotle himself is notably unconcerned to defend, against potential competitors, the way things look to the kind of person he thinks of as virtuous. And we should not play that fact down; one thing it reflects is his immunity to the metaphysical sources of our modern diffidence about such things. But, without abandoning a fundamentally Aristotelian outlook, we can let the question arise whether the space of reasons really is laid out as it seems to be from the viewpoint of a particular shaping of practical *logos*. What we must insist is that there is no addressing the question in a way that holds that apparent layout in suspense, and aims to reconstruct its correctness from a vantage-point outside the ways of thinking one acquired in ethical upbringing. This allows for radical ethical reflection, as Aristotle himself seems not to. But, like any reflection about the credentials of a seeming aspect of *logos*, this reflection must be Neurathian; we cannot escape the burden of reflective thought—the obligation to weigh, by the best lights we have, the credentials of considerations purporting to appeal to reason—by a fantasy of having some suitable first-natural facts force themselves on us in a way that would bypass the need for thought.[42]

---

41. See n. 5 above.

42. In *Aristotle's First Principles*, Terence Irwin reads Aristotle as a "metaphysical realist", as opposed to an "internal realist", and takes him to have the idea of a kind of dialectic that somehow breaks out of inherited conceptual schemes into contact with the real. My phrase "by the best lights we have" reflects the sort of thing Aristotle says about ordinary dialectic, which I believe is the only sort of dialectic Aristotle envisages. We cannot but start from what we find ourselves already thinking, and any thoughts of others that we can understand. "Metaphysical realism", and the doubt Irwin ascribes to Aristotle whether a procedure that fits that description could attain objective truth, make no sense except as a confused response to Kant. The anxiety about objectivity that Irwin attributes to Aristotle makes no sense before the modern era, in which it can seem to be alleviated by a scientistic metaphysic.

Of course first nature matters. It matters, for one thing, because the innate endowment of human beings must put limits on the shapings of second nature that are possible for them. This is not just because a shaping of second nature involves a moulding of prior motivational tendencies. It also involves the imparting of practical reason; and reason is inherently open to reflective questions about the rational credentials of the way it sees things. Not that people do not often embrace without reflection a conceptual organization of the sphere of ethical conduct that has been imparted to them by their elders; but if what is in question really is something conceptual, it is essential to it that reflection can break out at any time. People come unstuck from a traditional ethical outlook when reflection does break out, and they come to think, rightly or wrongly, that they have seen through the outlook's pretensions of rational cogency. If something is to be an intelligible candidate for being the way second nature should be, it must at least be intelligible that the associated outlook could seem to survive this reflective scrutiny. And there are limits on the courses reflection can intelligibly take, which come out in limits on what can be intelligible in the way of statements that purport to express part of such reflection. We can vividly bring out the bearing on reflection of these limits on intellible speech if we conceive reflection as a communal activity. But even if one engages in reflection by oneself, one must be able to convey one's thought to others (which is not the same as convincing them of it), on pain of its being in doubt whether what one has engaged in was really thought at all. And one source of these limits on intelligibility is first nature.[43]

First nature matters not only like that, in helping to shape the space in which reflection must take place, but also in that first-natural facts can be part of what reflection takes into account. This is where we can register the relevance of what human beings need in order to do well, in a sense of "doing well" that is not just Aristotle's "acting in accordance with the virtues". Consider a rational wolf whose acquisition of practical reason included being initiated into a tradition in which co-operative behaviour in the hunt is regarded as admirable, and so as worth going in for in its own right. What wolves need might figure in a bit of reflection that might help reas-

---

43. This is Wiggins's point in writing of the "enabling role" that he contrasts with the "unconvincing speaking part".

sure him that when he acquired a second nature with that shape, his eyes were opened to real reasons for acting. The reflection would be Neurathian, so it would not weigh with a wolf who has never acquired such a mode of valuation of conduct, or one who has come unstuck from it. And there would be no irrationality in thus failing to be convinced. But this need not undermine the reassurance, if the reflection that yields it is self-consciously Neurathian. The point stands that what members of one's species need is not guaranteed to appeal to practical reason. But the point is harmless to the genuine rationality of virtue, which is visible (of course!) only from a standpoint from which it is open to view.

It is important that when the connections between virtue and doing well—in a sense that is not Aristotle's "acting in accordance with the virtues", a sense that is not itself shaped by ethical concerns—do figure in a reflective reassurance about an ethical outlook, they operate at one remove from the subject's rational will. What directly influences the will is the valuations of actions that have come to be second nature. This point helps us to cope satisfactorily with the fact that virtue sometimes requires self-sacrifice. Mrs Foot considers this matter with special reference to justice;[44] but the point is not restricted to specifically other-regarding virtues, and I shall discuss how it arises in the case of courage.

The connection of courage with doing well, in the relevant sense, is that human beings need courage if they are to stick to their worthwhile projects, in the face of the motivational obstacle posed by danger. Something on those lines belongs in the reflective background for a second nature that values courageous actions.[45] But we should not try to picture such a consideration as what directly engages the will of a courageous person. If we do, we risk losing our hold on how it can be rational to face danger, even in the interest of something one values deeply, if one's own death is a possible upshot. The point of courage was supposed to be that one needs it to ensure that one sticks to one's projects. How can this point not be undermined

---

44. See part II of "Moral Beliefs". (In that paper, she thought she had to argue that justice is something anyone needs in his dealings with his fellows; but see the renunciation in the added note, pp. 130–1.)

45. This helps explain why there is nothing morally admirable in facing danger for its own sake, with no independently sensible project thus protected from abandonment.

by a probability, even a slight one, that if one acts courageously one will no longer be around to have any projects, let alone stick to them?

Transposing Mrs Foot's discussion of justice to this case suggests the response that courageousness is primarily a matter of being a certain kind of person. One cannot be that kind of person but stand ready to rethink the rational credentials of the motivations characteristic of being that kind of person, on occasions when acting on those motivations is in some way unattractive; part of what it is to be that kind of person is not to regard those credentials as open to question on particular occasions. That response is exactly right. But it works only in the context of the point that the general human need for courage stands at one remove from the rational will of a person engaged in courageous behaviour. Without that context, the response looks like a recommendation to abandon reason—which surely does examine the rational credentials of actions one by one—in favour of blind adherence to a policy. Within that context, the damage that acts of virtue can do to one's interests is unproblematic: the point of a particular courageous action lies not in the fact that human beings in general need courage, focused, as it were, on the circumstances at hand, but in the fact that this action counts as worth-while in its own right, by the lights of a conceptual scheme that is second nature to a courageous person.

11. Finding a way to preserve Kant's insight leads, I have claimed, to a conception of reason that is, in one sense, naturalistic: a formed state of practical reason is one's second nature, not something that dictates to one's nature from outside. But the conception is not naturalistic in the sense of purporting to found the intellectual credentials of practical reason on facts of the sort that the natural sciences discover.

To use the rhetoric of ethical realism, second nature acts in a world in which it finds more than what is open to view from the dehumanized stance that the natural sciences, rightly for their purposes, adopt. And there is nothing against bringing this richer reality under the rubric of nature too. The natural sciences do not have exclusive rights in that notion; and the added richness comes into view, not through the operations of some mysteriously extra-natural power, but because human beings come to possess a second nature.

Nature, on this richer conception, is to some extent autonomous with respect to nature on the natural-scientific conception. Correctness in judgements about its layout is not constituted by the availability of a grounding for them in facts of first nature; it is a matter of their coming up to scratch by standards internal to the formed second nature that is practical *logos*. Of course the autonomy is not total; facts about what human beings need in order to get on well, on a first-natural conception of what getting on well is for human beings, figure in the reflective background of specific shapings of second nature (see §10 above). This should be seen as a case of a relation that Wittgenstein draws to our attention, between our concepts and the facts of nature that underlie them. The concepts would not be the same if the facts of (first) nature were different, and the facts help to make it intelligible that the concepts are as they are, but that does not mean that correctness and incorrectness in the application of the concepts can be captured by requirements spelled out at the level of the underlying facts.

Nature, on the neo-Humean conception, can be pictured as the content of the view from nowhere. This conception can find goodness in nature, provided it is not goodness visible only to a human subject. What doing well is for a tree, and what doing well is for a wolf, are topics that a neo-Humean naturalism can embrace; they are not erased from nature by discounting the effects of a specifically human perspective, because the relevant assessment of good and bad is not relative to human projects and interests. (For my present purposes, we can ignore a physicalism that refuses to count plant or animal flourishing as a subject for natural science.) When this kind of naturalism considers what doing well is for a human being, a human perspective can no longer be irrelevant, but that is a mere peculiarity of the particular topic in view. The metaphysical rules do not change; the account of what doing well is for a human being can be shaped by a human perspective only in so far as what shapes the perspective can be supposed to figure in nature as seen from nowhere, or from God's point of view. So in forming a suitable conception of what doing well is for a human being, one must discount any valuations and aspirations that are special to one's historical or cultural situation: anything one cannot regard as characteristic of human beings as such. To work one's way back to endorsing the specific conception of reasons that constitutes a historically concrete ethical outlook, one would have to hope that the concrete detail can be represented as an application, suitable for just these cultural circumstances, of prior truths about what it is for human beings as such to do well.

Contrast the naturalism that makes play with second nature. Any actual second nature is a cultural product; this is true whether or not it is aware of itself as such. (Some outlooks are informed—as Aristotle's is not—by a lively sense of alternative possibilities for human life, lived out in cultures other than one's own.) The more putative ethical reasons for acting one can represent as enjoining no more than a culturally specific realization of what doing well is for human beings as such, the less vulnerable one will be to a certain kind of loss of confidence. But there is nothing to suggest that confidence in a particular region of an ethical outlook is misplaced unless it can be given that treatment. Whether confidence is in order or not is for second nature itself to assess, exploiting whatever materials for critical reflection are available: including, so long as they stand up to Neurathian scrutiny, concepts that are part of its specific cultural inheritance.

Radical critical reflection is open-ended, and confidence is inherently fragile. But there is also a peculiarly modern threat to confidence, posed by neo-Humean naturalism itself. Neo-Humean naturalism requires confidence to be grounded in facts of first nature, and it is not difficult to make the materials available for such grounding look inadequate—in effect, to make the sheer fact that ethical thinking is not science into a problem for the rational credentials of ethical thinking.

It is true that Callicles, for instance, in Plato's *Gorgias*, exploits the notion of nature, but that is no problem for my claim that the threat I am talking about is peculiarly modern. Callicles exemplifies only the standing fragility of confidence. He does not invite us to realize that first nature cannot ground a conventional ethical outlook. Rather, he disputes the conception of *second* nature embodied in a conventional ethical outlook, on grounds that are internal to practical *logos,* such as that a life of conventional virtue is slavish.

The presence of Callicles in Plato's work shows Plato's interest in people who have come unstuck from an inherited ethical outlook, even to the extent of becoming confident that it is a manipulative fraud. Aristotle, by contrast, gives no sign that he is so much as aware that ethical confidence is fragile, let alone concerned about the fact. He simply stipulates, in effect, that he is addressing only people in whom the value scheme he takes for granted has been properly ingrained.[46] In Williams's reading, this reflects a conviction on Aristotle's part that the virtues he lists are necessary for proper realization of human nature as it would figure in an accurate depiction of the view from nowhere—a thesis that Williams rightly says we cannot now believe, about any list of virtues, even ones we ourselves admire and aspire to. (See §4 above.) I think the only interesting thing it reflects is rather Aristotle's enviable immunity to that peculiarly modern threat to confidence. If it is a fact that Aristotle did not share the concern of Plato (who had that immunity too) with the perennial fragility of confidence, it is a superficial fact—perhaps the result of a propensity towards smugness. And by my lights, Williams's reading is a historical monstrosity; it attributes to Aristotle a felt need for foundations, and a conception of nature as where the foundations must be, that make sense only as a product of modern philosophy, and then represents him as trying to satisfy the need with an archaic picture of nature.[47] According to Williams, modernity has lost a foundation for ethics that Aristotle was still able to believe in.[48] But what has happened to modernity is rather that it has fallen into a temptation, which we can escape, to wish for a foundation for ethics of a sort that it never occurred to Aristotle to supply it with.[49]

12. There is no purely formal notion of practical reason such as Kant envisaged: something that could enforce the claims of virtue on the rational will of anyone at all, no matter what his motivational

---

46. See n. 13 above.

47. I find ironic the superior note Williams sounds when he remarks, of my use of a non-Aristotelian virtue in discussing an Aristotelian conception of virtue, in Essay 3 above, that it shows that I am "unconcerned . . . about history" (*Ethics and the Limits of Philosophy*, p. 218). I am unabashed about abstracting from Aristotle's substantive ethical views; it seems obvious that if anything in Aristotle's ethics can still live for us, it is his moral psychology, as a potential frame for a more congenial list of virtues. Where lack of concern with history, or getting history wrong, matters is in a reading of the moral psychology.

48. See p. 53 of *Ethics and the Limits of Philosophy*, where Williams says that this supposed loss is the state of affairs on which the argument of his book is going to turn.

49. Williams's book is an attempt to show us how to live with the lack of foundations. It cannot be ultimately satisfactory, by my lights, because he does not unmask the modern philosophy that makes the lack of foundations look like a problem in the first place; his own conception of the metaphysical status of science (see chap. 8) is a version of that very philosophy.

make-up. That is one way of putting the point of "Morality as a System of Hypothetical Imperatives". This impotence of Kantian practical reason leaves untouched virtue's grip on the rational wills of volunteers in the army of duty,[50] those who care about the goods achieved by virtuous conduct. So far, so good. What was disquieting about Mrs Foot's position in that paper was the further suggestion—implicit in putting the anti-Kantian point by reversing Kant's own terms—that virtue's appeal to reason, when it has any, is on a par with the appeal to reason of the actions necessary to achieve any goal one happens to care about, say building the biggest ever matchstick model of St. Paul's. This suggestion seemed to be simply a corollary of the negative point, because the thought that one *should* care about the goods achieved by virtuous conduct seemed to involve the elusive notion of a practical application of reason that would speak to anyone whatever he cared about.

The neo-Humean naturalism I have been considering in this paper might seem exactly suited to respond to this discomfort. It promises to underwrite the thought that one *should* care about the ends achievable by virtuous conduct, not in the mysterious purely formal way that Kant envisaged, but in a way that bases the rational appeal of virtue on material facts. But my point in §3 above can be put by saying that, even though this picture has no truck with the Kantian idea that a rational motivation could be spun out of formal requirements without material motivational input, it still runs foul of a version of the admirable negative point of "Morality as a System of Hypothetical Imperatives". This picture loses the good point that is made by speaking of volunteers in duty's army; it suggests that reason does after all order all human beings to join up, just as Kant thought, even if some are deaf to the command. But the material base of the construction is not guaranteed to appeal to reason; practical reason distances an agent from his natural motivational impulses.

Aristotelian naturalism satisfies all the desiderata that are in play here. Those who serve in duty's army do not just happen to care about certain ends; we can say that reason reveals the dictates of virtue to them as genuine requirements on a rational will. The reason

---

50. For this image, see *Virtues and Vices*, p. 170.

that effects this revelation is their acquired second nature. That this opens their eyes to real reasons for acting is argued not formally but materially, on the basis of Neurathian reflection that starts from the substantive view of the space of reasons opened up to them by their ethical upbringing. This makes it obviously wrong to expect right reason to be capable of issuing commands to just anyone, whatever his motivational make-up. On these lines, we can have it that those who serve in duty's army are kept loyal not by goals they happen to pursue but by reason's dictates as they rightly see them; but this talk of rightness does not require us to invent a way in which reason can be conceived as imposing these dictates on just anyone—neither Kant's formal way nor the material way offered by neo-Humean naturalism.

One might be tempted to object that this represents the soldiers in duty's army as conscripts, not volunteers. But reason did not order them to join up; they were not in a position to hear its orders until they were already enrolled. It is their continuing service that is obedience to reason's categorical demands. I put it this way to emphasize that the position has a distinctly Kantian flavour, though it is entirely free of formalism and supernaturalism.

I relish the fact that what I am urging in this paper can be put by saying that it takes reflection on Kant, of all people, to show us the way to an acceptable picture of the relation of reason to nature: to show us the way to an acceptable naturalism. Naturalism of the neo-Humean variety seems doomed to oscillate between the idea that the attractions of virtuous conduct just happen to appeal to some people, like the attractions of stamp-collecting, and the idea that the appeal of virtue to reason can be grounded on first nature, which I have claimed is unsatisfactory. It might be objected that we do not need reflection on Kant to see our way past this; by my own showing, reflection on Aristotle should suffice. But modern readers will always be prone to misinterpret Aristotle if they read him without first immunizing themselves against the damaging effects of modern philosophy; and I do not think we can do that without working our way through Kant's thinking, realizing what went wrong, but recognizing what was right.

ESSAY 10

Non-Cognitivism and Rule-Following[1]

1. Non-cognitivists hold that ascriptions of value should not be conceived as propositions of the sort whose correctness, or acceptability, consists in their being true descriptions of the world; and, correlatively, that values are not found in the world, as genuine properties of things are. Such a position should embody a reasoned restriction on the sort of proposition that does count as a description (or at worst misdescription) of reality: not merely to justify the exclusion of value-ascriptions, but also to give content to the exclusion—to explain what it is that value judgements are being said not to be. In fact presentations of non-cognitivist positions tend to take some suitable conception of the descriptive, and of the world, simply for granted. In this paper, if only to provoke non-cognitivists to explain how I have missed their point, I want to bring out into the open the nature of a conception that might seem to serve their purpose, and to suggest that there is room for doubt about its serviceability in this context.

According to the conception I have in mind, how things really are is how things are in themselves—that is, independently of how they strike the occupants of this or that particular point of view. With a literal interpretation of the notion of a point of view, this idea under-

---

1. Much of §3 of this paper is adapted from Essay 3 above. I first delivered a version of this paper at a conference in Oxford, and Simon Blackburn commented (a version of his comments was published as "Rule-Following and Moral Realism"); I benefited from his comments in revising the paper for publication.

pins our correcting for perspective when we determine the true shapes of observed objects. But the idea lends itself naturally to various extensions.

One such extension figures in the thought, familiar in philosophy, that secondary qualities as we experience them are not genuine features of reality. If, for instance, someone with normal human colour vision accepts that the world is as his visual experience (perhaps corrected for the effects of poor light and so forth) presents it to him, then the familiar thought has it that he is falling into error. This is not merely because the appropriate sensory equipment is not universally shared. That would leave open the possibility that the sensory equipment enables us to detect something that is really there anyway, independently of how things appear to us. But the familiar thought aims to exclude this possibility with the claim that the appearances can be satisfyingly explained away. If, that is, we suppose that how things really are can be exhaustively characterized in primary quality terms, then we can explain why our colour experience is as it is without representing it as strictly veridical: the explanation reveals the extent to which the world as colour experience presents it to us is mere appearance—the extent to which colour vision fails to be a transparent mode of access to something that is there anyway.[2]

Now an analogy between colour experience and (so to speak) value experience seems natural. We can learn to make colour classifications only because our sensory equipment happens to be such as to give us the right sort of visual experience. Somewhat similarly, we can learn to see the world in terms of some specific set of evaluative classifications, aesthetic or moral, only because our affective and attitudinative propensities are such that we can be brought to care in appropriate ways about the things we learn to see as collected together by the classifications. And this might constitute the starting-point of a parallel argument against a naive realism about the values we find ourselves impelled to attribute to things.[3]

There is an extra ingredient that threatens to enter the argument about values and spoil the parallel. In the argument about colours,

---

2. There is an excellent discussion of this line of thought (though more sympathetic to it than I would want to be) in Bernard Williams, *Descartes: The Project of Pure Enquiry*, chap. 8. (I shall not pause to criticize the application to secondary qualities.)
3. The parallel is suggested by Williams, when, at p. 245, he writes of "concepts . . . which reflect merely a local interest, taste or sensory peculiarity".

we are led to appeal to the explanatory power of a description of the world in primary-quality terms, in order to exclude the suggestion that colour vision is a mode of awareness of something that is there anyway. The parallel suggestion, in the case of values, would be that the members of some specific set of values are genuine features of the world, which we are enabled to detect by virtue of our special affective and attitudinative propensities. And it might be thought that this suggestion can be dismissed out of hand by an appeal to something with no analogue in the argument about secondary qualities; namely, a philosophy of mind that insists on a strict separation between cognitive capacities and their exercise, on the one hand, and what eighteenth-century writers would classify as passions or sentiments, on the other.[4] The suggestion involves thinking of exercises of our affective or conative natures either as themselves in some way percipient, or at least as expanding our sensitivity to how things are; and the eighteenth-century philosophy of mind would purport to exclude this *a priori*.

But perhaps this gets things the wrong way round. Do we actually have any reason to accept the eighteenth-century philosophy of mind, apart from a prior conviction of the truth of non-cognitivism?[5] The question is at least awkward enough to confer some attractions on the idea of a route to non-cognitivism that bypasses appeal to the eighteenth-century philosophy of mind, and proceeds on a parallel with the argument about secondary qualities, claiming that the character of our value experience can be satisfyingly explained on the basis of the assumption that the world—that is, the world as it is anyway (independently of value experience, at any rate)[6]—does not contain values. (I shall return to a version of the eighteenth-century philosophy of mind later: §4 below.)

How is the explanatory claim made out? Typically, non-cognitivists hold that when we feel impelled to ascribe value to something, what is actually happening can be disentangled into two compo-

---

4. Compare J. L. Mackie, *Ethics: Inventing Right and Wrong*, p. 22.
5. Compare Mackie, pp. 40–1.
6. The non-cognitivist's conception of the world is not exhausted by primary-quality characterizations. (See David Wiggins, "Truth, Invention, and the Meaning of Life", pp. 119–22.) So his notion of the world as it is anyway is not the one that figures in the argument about secondary qualities. What is wanted, and what my parenthesis is intended to suggest, is an analogy, rather than an addition, to the secondary-quality argument.

nents. Competence with an evaluative concept involves, first, a sensitivity to an aspect of the world as it really is (as it is independently of value experience), and, second, a propensity to a certain attitude—a non-cognitive state that constitutes the special perspective from which items in the world seem to be endowed with the value in question. Given the disentangling, we could construct explanations of the character of value experience on the same general lines as the explanations of colour experience that we have in mind when we are tempted by the argument about secondary qualities: occupants of the special perspective, in making value judgements, register the presence in objects of some property they authentically have, but enrich their conception of this property with the reflection of an attitude.[7]

2. Now it seems reasonable to be sceptical about whether the disentangling manoeuvre here envisaged can always be effected; specifically, about whether, corresponding to any value concept, one can always isolate a genuine feature of the world—by the appropriate standard of genuineness: that is, a feature that is there anyway, independently of anyone's value experience being as it is—to be that to which competent users of the concept are to be regarded as responding when they use it: that which is left in the world when one peels off the reflection of the appropriate attitude.

Consider, for instance, a specific conception of some moral virtue: the conception current in a reasonably cohesive moral community. If the disentangling manoeuvre is always possible, that implies that the extension of the associated term, as it would be used by someone who belonged to the community, could be mastered independently of the special concerns that, in the community, would show themselves in admiration or emulation of actions seen as falling under the concept. That is: one could know which actions the term would be applied to, so that one would be able to predict applications and withholdings of it in new cases—not merely without oneself sharing

---

7. This formulation fits Mackie's error theory, rather than the different sort of non-cognitivism exemplified by R. M. Hare's prescriptivism (see, e.g., *Freedom and Reason*), in which ordinary evaluative thinking has enough philosophical sophistication not to be enticed into the projective error of which Mackie accuses it. But the idea could easily be reformulated to suit Hare's position; this difference between Hare and Mackie is not relevant to my concerns in this paper.

the community's admiration (there need be no difficulty about that), but without even embarking on an attempt to make sense of their admiration. That would be an attempt to comprehend their special perspective; whereas, according to the position I am considering, the genuine feature to which the term is applied should be graspable without benefit of understanding the special perspective, since sensitivity to it is singled out as an independent ingredient in a purported explanation of why occupants of the perspective see things as they do. But is it at all plausible that this singling out can always be brought off?

Notice that the thesis I am sceptical about cannot be established by appealing to the plausible idea that evaluative classifications are supervenient on non-evaluative classifications. Supervenience requires only that one be able to find differences expressible in terms of the level supervened upon whenever one wants to make different judgements in terms of the supervening level.[8] It does not follow from the satisfaction of this requirement that the set of items to which a supervening term is correctly applied need constitute a kind recognizable as such at the level supervened upon. In fact supervenience leaves open this possibility, which is just the possibility my scepticism envisages: however long a list we give of items to which a supervening term applies, described in terms of the level supervened upon, there may be no way, expressible at the level supervened upon, of grouping just such items together. Hence there need be no possibility of mastering, in a way that would enable one to go on to new cases, a term that is to function at the level supervened upon, but is to group together exactly the items to which competent users would apply the supervening term.[9] Understanding why just those things belong together may essentially require understanding the supervening term.

---

8. Compare Hare, *Freedom and Reason*, p. 33, on the thesis of universalizability: "What the thesis does forbid us to do is to make different moral judgements about actions which we admit to be exactly or relevantly similar." In chap. 2, Hare claims that this thesis of universalizability just is the thesis that evaluative concepts have "descriptive" meaning (which is Hare's version of the thesis I am sceptical about); see p. 15. The identification is undermined by my remarks about supervenience.

9. The point is not merely that the language may lack such a term, a gap that might perhaps be filled by coining one. (See Hare, "Descriptivism".) What I am suggesting is that such a coinage might not be learnable except parasitically on a mastery of the full-blown evaluative expression.

I shall reserve till later (§5) the question whether there may be a kind of non-cognitivist who can happily concede this possibility. Meanwhile it is clear that the concession would at any rate preclude explaining the relation between value experience and the world as it is independently of value experience in the manner I described above (§1). And actual non-cognitivists typically assume that they must disallow the possibility I have envisaged.[10] They may admit that it is often difficult to characterize the authentic property (according to their standards of authenticity) that corresponds to an evaluative concept; but they tend to suppose that there *must* be such a thing, even if it cannot be easily pinned down in words. Now there is a profoundly tempting complex of ideas about the relation between thought and reality that would make that "must" seem obvious. But one strand in Wittgenstein's thought about "following a rule" is that the source of the temptation is the desire for a security that would actually be quite illusory.

3. A succession of judgements or utterances, to be intelligible as applications of a single concept to different objects, must belong to a practice of going on *doing the same thing*. We tend to be tempted by a picture of what that amounts to, on the following lines. What counts as doing the same thing, within the practice in question, is fixed by its rules. The rules mark out rails along which correct activity within the practice must run. These rails are there anyway, independently of the responses and reactions a propensity to which one acquires when one learns the practice itself; or, to put the idea less metaphorically, it is in principle discernible, from a standpoint independent of the responses that characterize a participant in the practice, that a series of correct moves in the practice is really a case of going on doing the same thing. Acquiring mastery of the practice is pictured as something like engaging mental wheels with these objectively existing rails.

The picture comes in two versions. In one, the rules can be formulated, as a codification of the practice in independently accessible

---

10. See Hare, *Freedom and Reason*, chap. 2. Mackie, at p. 86, objects to the idea that a corresponding value-neutral classification is (as in Hare's position) part of the *meaning* of an evaluative term, but evidently in the context of assuming that there must be such a corresponding classification.

terms. Mastery of the practice is conceived as knowledge, perhaps implicit, of what is expressed by these formulations; and running along the rails is a matter of having one's actions dictated by proof of their correctness within the practice, with these formulations as major premises. Sometimes, however, a practice of concept-application resists codification otherwise than trivially (as in "It is correct to call all and only red things 'red'"), and in such cases we tend to resort to the other version of the picture. Here we appeal to grasp of a universal, conceiving this as a mechanism of an analogous sort: one that, like knowledge of an explicitly stateable rule, constitutes a capacity to run along a rail that is independently there.

Extending a number series is an example of going on doing the same thing that should constitute an ideal case for this picture. Each correct move in a series of responses to the order "Add 2" is provably correct, as in what seems the clearest version of the picture. But in fact the idea that the rules of a practice mark out rails traceable independently of the reactions of participants is suspect even in this apparently ideal case; and if we insist that wherever there is going on in the same way there must be rules that can be conceived as marking out such independently traceable rails, we reveal a misconception of the sort of case in which correctness within a practice can be given the kind of demonstration we count as proof.

We can begin working up to this conclusion by coming to appreciate the emptiness, even in what should be the ideal case, of the psychological component of the picture: that is, the idea that grasp of a rule is a matter of having one's mental wheels engaged with an independently traceable rail. The picture represents understanding of, for instance, the instruction "Add 2"—command of the rule for extending the series 2, 4, 6, 8, . . . — as a psychological mechanism that, apart from mistakes, churns out the appropriate behaviour with the sort of reliability that, say, a clockwork mechanism might have. If someone is extending the series correctly, and one takes this to be because he has understood the instruction and is complying with it, then, according to the picture, one has hypothesized that the appropriate psychological mechanism, the engagement with the rails, underlies his behaviour. (This would be an inference analogous to that whereby one might postulate a physical mechanism underlying the behaviour of an inanimate object.)

But what manifests understanding of the instruction, so pictured? Suppose we ask the person what he is doing, and he says "Look, I'm adding 2 each time". This apparent manifestation of understanding will have been accompanied, whenever it occurs, by at most a finite fragment of the potentially infinite range of behaviour that we want to say the rule dictates. The same goes for any other apparent manifestation of understanding. Thus the evidence we have at any point for the presence of the pictured state is compatible with the supposition that, on some future occasion for its exercise, the behaviour elicited by the occasion will diverge from what we would count as correct, and not simply because of a mistake. Wittgenstein dramatizes this "possibility" with the example of the person who continues the series, after 1000, with 1004, 1008, . . . (*Philosophical Investigations* (henceforth "*PI*"), §185). Suppose a divergence of the 1004, 1008, . . . type turned up, and we could not get the person to admit that he was simply making a mistake; that would show that his behaviour hitherto was not guided by the psychological conformation we were picturing as guiding it. The pictured state, then, always transcends any grounds there may be for postulating it.

There may be a temptation to protest as follows: "This is nothing but a familiar inductive scepticism about other minds. After all, one knows in one's own case that one's behaviour will not come adrift like that." But this objection is mistaken in itself, and it misses the point of the argument.

First, if what it is for one's behaviour to come adrift is for it suddenly to seem that everyone else is out of step, then any sceptical conclusion the argument were to recommend would apply in one's own case just as much as in the case of others. (Imagine the person who goes on with 1004, 1008, . . . saying in advance "I know in my own case that my behaviour will not come adrift".) If there is any scepticism involved, it is not especially about *other* minds.

Second, it is anyway a mistake to construe the argument as making a sceptical point: that one does not know that others' behaviour (or one's own, once we have made the first correction) will not come adrift. The aim is not to suggest that we should be in trepidation lest "possibilities" of the 1004, 1008, . . . type be realized.[11] We are in fact confident that they will not, and the argument aims, not to undermine this confidence, but to change our conception of its ground and nature. Our picture represents the confident expectation as

---

11. Nor even that we really understand the supposition that such a thing might happen; see Barry Stroud, "Wittgenstein and Logical Necessity".

based on whatever grounds we have via the mediation of the postulated psychological mechanism. But we can no more find the putatively mediating state manifested in the grounds for our expectation (say about what someone else will do) than we can find manifested there the very future occurrences we expect. Postulating the mediating state is an idle intervening step; it does nothing to underwrite the confidence of our expectation.

(Postulating a mediating brain state might indeed figure in a scientifically respectable argument, vulnerable only to ordinary inductive scepticism, that some specifically envisaged train of behaviour of the 1004, 1008, . . . type will not occur; and our picture tends to trade on assimilating the postulation of the psychological mechanism to this. But the assimilation is misleading. Consider this variant of Wittgenstein's case: on reaching 1000, the person goes on as we expect, with 1002, 1004, . . . , but with a sense of dissociation from what he finds himself doing; it feels as if something like blind habit has usurped his reason in controlling his behaviour. Here the behaviour is kept in line, no doubt, by a brain state; but the person's sense of how to extend the series correctly shows a divergence from ours, of the 1004, 1008, . . . type. Of course we confidently expect this sort of thing not to happen, just as in the simpler kind of case. But a physically described mechanism cannot underwrite confidence in the future operations of someone's sense of what is called for; and once again postulating a psychological mechanism would be an idle intervening step.)[12]

What, then, is the ground and nature of our confidence? Stanley Cavell has described the view Wittgenstein wants to recommend as follows:

> We learn and teach words in certain contexts, and then we are expected, and expect others, to be able to project them into further contexts. Nothing insures that this projection will take place (in particular, not the grasping of universals nor the grasping of books of rules), just as nothing insures that we will make, and understand, the same projections. That on the whole we do is a matter of our sharing routes of interest and feeling, senses of humor and of significance and of fulfilment, of what is outrageous, of what is similar to what else, what a rebuke,

---

12. In the context of a physicalistic conception of mind, this paragraph will be quite unconvincing; this is one of the points at which a great deal more argument is necessary.

what forgiveness, of when an utterance is an assertion, when an appeal, when an explanation—all the whirl of organism Wittgenstein calls "forms of life." Human speech and activity, sanity and community, rest upon nothing more, but nothing less, than this. It is a vision as simple as it is difficult, and as difficult as it is (and because it is) terrifying.[13]

The terror of which Cavell writes at the end of this marvellous passage is a sort of vertigo, induced by the thought that there is nothing that keeps our practices in line except the reactions and responses we learn in learning them. The ground seems to have been removed from under our feet. In this mood, we are inclined to feel that the sort of thing Cavell describes is insufficient foundation for a conviction that some practice really is a case of going on in the same way. What Cavell offers looks, rather, like a congruence of subjectivities not grounded as it would need to be to amount to the sort of objectivity we want if we are to be convinced that we are *really* going on in the same way.

It is natural to recoil from this vertigo into the picture of rules as rails. But the picture is only a consoling myth elicited from us by our inability to endure the vertigo. It consoles by seeming to put the ground back under our feet; but we see that it is a myth by seeing, as we did above, that the pictured psychological mechanism gives only an illusory security. (Escaping from the vertigo would require seeing that this does not matter; I shall return to this.)

The picture has two interlocking components: the idea of the psychological mechanism correlates with the idea that the tracks we follow are objectively there to be followed, in a way that transcends the reactions and responses of participants in our practices. If the first component is suspect, the second component should be suspect too. And it is.

In the numerical case, the second component is a kind of platonism. The idea is that the relation of our arithmetical thought and language to the reality it characterizes can be contemplated, not only from the midst of our mathematical practices, but also, so to speak, from sideways on—from a standpoint independent of all the human activities and reactions that locate those practices in our "whirl of

---

13. *Must We Mean What We Say?*, p. 52.

organism"; and that it would be recognizable from the sideways perspective that a given move is the correct move at a given point in the practice: that, say, 1002 really does come after 1000 in the series determined by the instruction "Add 2". It is clear how this platonistic picture might promise to reassure us if we suffered from the vertigo, fearing that the Wittgensteinian vision threatens to dissolve the independent truth of arithmetic into a collection of mere contingencies about the natural history of man. But the picture has no real content.

We tend, confusedly, to suppose that we occupy the external standpoint envisaged by platonism, when we say things we need to say in order to reject the reduction of mathematical truth to human natural history. For instance, we deny that what it is for the square of 13 to be 169 is for it to be possible to train human beings so that they find such-and-such calculations compelling. Rather, it is because the square of 13 really *is* 169 that we can be brought to find the calculations compelling. Moved by the vertigo, we are liable to think of remarks like this as expressions of platonism. But this is an illusion. To suppose that such a remark is an expression of platonism is to suppose that when we utter the words "the square of 13 is 169", in the context "It is because ... that we can be brought to find the calculations compelling", we are speaking not from the midst of our merely human mathematical competence but from the envisaged independent perspective instead. (As if, by a special emphasis, one could somehow manage to speak otherwise than out of one's own mouth.) We cannot occupy the independent perspective that platonism envisages; and it is only because we confusedly think we can that we think we can make any sense of it.

If one is wedded to the picture of rules as rails, one will be inclined to think that to reject it is to suggest that, say, in mathematics, anything goes: that we are free to make mathematics up as we go along.[14] But none of what I have said casts any doubt on the idea that the correctness of a move, in a mathematical case of going on doing the same thing, can be proved—so that it is compulsory to go on like that. The point is just that we should not misidentify the perspective from which this necessity is discernible. What is wrong is to suppose that when we describe someone as following a rule in ex-

---

14. See Michael Dummett, "Wittgenstein's Philosophy of Mathematics". For a corrective, see Stroud, "Wittgenstein and Logical Necessity".

tending a series, we characterize the output of his mathematical competence as the inexorable workings of a machine: something that could be seen to be operating from the platonist's standpoint, the standpoint independent of the activities and responses that make up our mathematical practice. The fact is that it is only because of our own involvement in our "whirl of organism" that we can understand a form of words as conferring, on the judgement that some move is the correct one at a given point, the special compellingness possessed by the conclusion of a proof. So if dependence on the "whirl of organism" induces vertigo, then we should feel vertigo about the mathematical cases as much as any other. No security is gained by trying to assimilate other sorts of case to the sort of case in which a hard-edged proof of correctness is available.

Consider, for instance, concepts whose application gives rise to hard cases, in this sense: there are disagreements, which resist resolution by argument, as to whether or not a concept applies.[15] If one is convinced that one is in the right on a hard case, one will find oneself saying, as one's arguments tail off without securing acceptance, "You simply aren't seeing it", or "But don't you see?" (compare *PI* §231). One will then be liable to think oneself confronted by a dilemma.

On the first horn, the inconclusiveness of the arguments results merely from a failure to get something across. This idea has two versions, which correspond to the two versions of the picture of rules as rails. According to the first version, it is possible, in principle, to spell out a universal formula that specifies, in unproblematic terms, the conditions under which the concept one intends is correctly applied. If one could only find the words, one could turn one's arguments into hard-edged proofs. (If the opponent refused to accept the

---

15. Blackburn objected that the central "rule-following" passages in Wittgenstein discuss cases where following the rule is a matter of course. There are no hard cases in mathematics. In the end I do not mind if my remarks about hard cases correspond to nothing in Wittgenstein. They indicate (at least) a natural way to extend some of Wittgenstein's thoughts. Where hard cases do occur, the agreement that constitutes the background against which we can see what happens as, e.g., disputes about genuine questions cannot be agreement in judgements as to the application of the concepts themselves; compare *PI* §242. What matters is, for instance, agreement about what counts as a reasonable argument; consider how lawyers recognize competence in their fellows, in spite of disagreement over hard cases.

major premise, that would show that he had not mastered the concept one intended; in that case his inclination not to accept one's words would reveal no substantive disagreement.) According to the second version, the concept is not codifiable (except trivially), and one's problem is to use words as hints and pointers, in order to get one's opponent to divine the right universal. (This is really only a variant of the first version. The idea is that if one could only convey which universal was at issue, the opponent would have a sort of non-discursive counterpart to the formulable proof envisaged in the first version; and as before, if he grasped what one was trying to get across and still refused to accept one's conclusion, that would show that there was no substantive disagreement.)

If neither of these alternatives seems acceptable, then one is pushed on to the second horn of the dilemma by this thought: if there is nothing such that to get it across would either secure agreement or show that there was no substantive disagreement in the first place, then one's conviction that one is genuinely making an application of a concept (genuinely going on in some same way) is a mere illusion. The case is one that calls, not for finding the right answer to some genuine question, but rather for a freely creative decision as to what to say.

In a hard case, the issue seems to turn on that appreciation of the particular instance whose absence is deplored, in "You simply aren't seeing it", or which is (possibly without success) appealed to, in "But don't you see?" The dilemma reflects a refusal to accept that a genuine issue can really turn on no more than that; it reflects the view that a putative judgement that is grounded in nothing firmer than that cannot really be a case of going on as before. This is a manifestation of our vertigo: the idea is that there is not enough there to constitute the rails on which a genuine series of applications of a concept must run. But it is an illusion to suppose one is safe from vertigo on the first horn. The illusion is the misconception of the mathematical case: the idea that provable correctness characterizes exercises of reason in which it is, as it were, automatically compelling, without dependence on our partially shared "whirl of organism". The dilemma reflects a refusal to accept that when the dependence that induces vertigo is out in the open, in the appeal to appreciation, we can genuinely be going on in the same way; but the paradigm with which the rejected case is unfavourably compared has the same dependence, only less obviously. Once we see this, we should see that we make no headway, in the face of the discouraging effects of the vertigo, by trying to assimilate all cases to the sort of case where proofs are available. We should accept that sometimes there may be nothing better to do than to appeal explicitly to a hoped-for community of human response. This is what we do when we say "Don't you see?" (though there is a constant temptation to misconceive this as a nudge towards grasp of the universal).

Once we have felt the vertigo, then, the picture of rules as rails is only an illusory comfort. What is needed is not so much reassurance—the thought that after all there is solid ground under us—as not to have felt the vertigo in the first place. Now if we are simply and normally immersed in our practices, we do not wonder how their relation to the world would look from outside them, and feel the need for a solid foundation discernible from an external point of view. So we would be protected against the vertigo if we could stop supposing that the relation to reality of some area of our thought and language needs to be contemplated from a standpoint independent of that anchoring in our human life that makes the thoughts what they are for us.[16]

At any rate, it is a bad move to allow oneself to conceive some area of thought from the extraneous perspective at which vertigo threatens, but then suppose one can make oneself safe from vertigo with the idea that rules mark out rails discernible from that external point of view. Just such a move—seeing the anthropocentricity or ethnocentricity of an evaluative outlook as generating a threat of vertigo, but seeking to escape the threat by finding a solid, externally recognizable foundation—would account for insistence (compare §2 above) that any respectable evaluative concept must correspond to a classification intelligible from outside the evaluative outlook within which the concept functions.[17]

---

16. This is not an easy recipe. Perhaps finding out how to stop being tempted by the picture of the external standpoint would be the discovery that enables one to stop doing philosophy when one wants to (compare *PI* §133).

17. The idea of rules as rails seems to pervade chap. 2 of Hare's *Freedom and Reason*. Hare argues there that evaluative words, if used with "that consistency of practice in the use of an expression which is the condition of its intelligibility" (p. 7), must be governed by principles that connect their correct application to features of value-independent reality (that which can be descriptively characterized, in Hare's sense of "descriptively"). Hare

The idea that reflecting on the relation between thought and reality requires the notion of an external standpoint is characteristic of a philosophical realism that is often considered in a different, more epistemologically oriented context, and in areas where we are not inclined to question whether there are facts of the matter at all. This realism chafes at the fallibility and inconclusiveness of all our ways of finding out how things are, and purports to confer a sense on "But is it *really* so?" in which the question does not call for a maximally careful assessment by our lights, but is asked from a perspective that transcends the limitations of our cognitive powers. Thus this realism purports to conceive our understanding of what it is for things to be thus and so as independent of our limited abilities to find out whether they are. An adherent of this sort of realism will tend to be impressed by the line of thought sketched in §1 above, and hence will tend to fail to find room for values in his conception of the world; whereas opposition to this kind of realism about the relation, in general, between thought and reality makes a space for realism, in a different sense, about values.[18]

4. I want now to revert to the eighteenth-century philosophy of mind, which I mentioned and shelved in §1 above, and consider one way in which it connects with the line of thought I have been discussing.

What I have in mind is an argument for non-cognitivism that goes back at least to Hume (though I shall formulate it in rather un-Humean terms).[19] It has two premises. The first is to the effect that ascriptions of moral value are action-guiding, in something like this

---

mentions Wittgenstein, but only as having introduced "'family resemblance' and 'open texture' and all that" (p. 26) into "the patter of the up-to-date philosophical conjurer" (p. 7). It is hard to resist the impression that Hare thinks we can respect everything useful that Wittgenstein said, even while retaining the essentials of the picture of rules as rails, simply by thinking of the mechanism as incompletely rigid and difficult to characterize in precise terms.

18. I distinguish opposition to the realism that involves the idea of the external standpoint from anti-realism in the sense of Michael Dummett, which is the positive doctrine that linguistic competence consists in dispositions to respond to circumstances recognizable whenever they obtain. (See my "Anti-Realism and the Epistemology of Understanding".)

19. See *A Treatise of Human Nature*, 3.1.1.

sense: someone who accepts such an ascription may (depending on his opportunities for action) *eo ipso* have a reason for acting in a certain way, independently of anything else being true about him. The second premise is this: to cite a cognitive propositional attitude—an attitude whose content is expressed by the sort of proposition for which acceptability consists in truth—is to give at most a partial specification of a reason for acting; to be fully explicit, one would need to add a mention of something non-cognitive, a state of the will or a volitional event. Clearly, it would follow that ascriptions of value, however acceptable, can be at most in part descriptive of the world.

The key premise, for my purposes, is the second. Notice that if this premise is suspect, that casts doubt not only on the non-cognitivism to which one would be committed if one accepted both premises, but also on a different position that rejects the non-cognitivist conclusion, and, keeping the second premise as a fulcrum, dislodges the first. This different position might merit Hare's label "descriptivism", meant as he means it—something that is not true of the anti-non-cognitivism I would defend, which retains the first premise.[20] (A version of descriptivism, without general insistence on the second premise—exceptions are allowed in the case of reasons that relate to the agent's interest—but with a restricted form of it used to overturn the first premise, is found in some of the writings of Philippa Foot.)[21]

I suspect that one reason why people find the second premise of the Humean argument obvious lies in their inexplicit adherence to a quasi-hydraulic conception of how reason explanations account for action. The will is pictured as the source of the forces that issue in the behaviour such explanations explain. This idea seems to me a radical misconception of the sort of explanation a reason explanation is; but it is not my present concern.

---

20. As Hare uses the word "descriptive", a descriptive judgement is, by definition, not action-guiding. Hare does not consider a resistance to non-cognitivism that accepts the first premise of the Humean argument.
21. See especially *Virtues and Vices*, p. 156. From the point of view of a resistance to non-cognitivism that accepts the first premise of the Humean argument, the difference between non-cognitivism and descriptivism tends to pale into insignificance, by comparison with the striking fact that they share a conception of the world according to which knowing how things are in the world cannot by itself move us to action.

A different justification for the second premise might seem to be afforded by a line of thought obviously akin to what I have been considering; one might put it as follows. The rationality that a reason explanation reveals in the action it explains ought, if the explanation is a good one, to be genuinely there: that is, recognizable from an objective standpoint, conceived (compare §3) in terms of the notion of the view from sideways on—from outside any practices or forms of life partly constituted by local or parochial modes of response to the world. This putative requirement is not met if we conceive value judgements in the way I would recommend: the ascription of value that one cites in giving an agent's reason for an action, so far from revealing the rationality in the action to an imagined occupier of the external standpoint, need not even be intelligible from there. By contrast, insistence on the second premise might seem to ensure that the requirement can be met. For on this view an explanation of an action in terms of a value judgement operates by revealing the action as the outcome of an unproblematically cognitive state plus a non-cognitive state—a desire, in some suitably broad sense;[22] and if we think someone's possession of the desires in question could be recognized from a standpoint external to the agent's moral outlook, then it might seem that those desires would confer an obvious rationality, recognizable from that objective standpoint, on actions undertaken with a view to gratifying them.

I shall make two remarks about this line of thought.

First, I expressed scepticism (in §2) about the possibility of mastering the extension of a value concept from the external standpoint (so that one could move to understanding the value concept by tacking on an evaluative extra). The scepticism obviously recurs here, about the possibility of grasping, from the external standpoint, the content of the envisaged desires. On this view there is a set of desires, a propensity to which constitutes the embracing of a particular moral outlook; if the content of this set can be grasped from the external standpoint, then the actions required by that moral stance are in theory classifiable as such by a sheer outsider. This amounts to the assumption that a moral stance can be captured in a set of externally

---

22. Either, as in non-cognitivism, accepting a moral judgement really is a composite state including a desire; or, as in descriptivism, the moral judgement is itself strictly cognitive, but it makes the behaviour intelligible only in conjunction with a desire.

formulable principles—principles such that there could in principle be a mechanical (non-comprehending) application of them that would duplicate the actions of someone who puts the moral stance into practice. This assumption strikes me as merely fantastic.[23]

Second, the underlying line of thought inherits whatever dubiousness is possessed by its relatives in, say, the philosophy of mathematics. (See §3, but I shall add a little here.)

Consider the hardness of the logical "must". One is apt to suppose that the only options are, on the one hand, to conceive the hardness platonistically (as something to be found in the world as it is anyway: that is, the world as characterized from a standpoint external to our mathematical practices); or, on the other (if one recoils from platonism), to confine oneself to a catalogue of how human beings act and feel when they engage in deductive reasoning. (Taking this second option, one might encourage oneself with the thought: at least all of this is objectively there.) On the second option, the hardness of the logical "must" has no place in one's account of how things really are; and there must be a problem about making room for genuine rationality in deductive practice, since we conceive that as a matter of conforming our thought and action to the dictates of the logical "must". If one recoils from platonism into this second position, one has passed over a fully satisfying intermediate position, according to which the logical "must" is indeed hard (in the only sense we can give to that idea), and the ordinary conception of deductive rationality is perfectly acceptable; it is simply that we must avoid a mistake about the perspective from which the demands of the logical "must" are perceptible. (As long as the mistake is definitely avoided, there is something to be said for calling the intermediate position a species of platonism.)[24]

Now it is an analogue to this intermediate position that seems to me to be most satisfying in the case of ethics. The analogue involves insisting that moral values are there in the world, and make demands

---

23. See Essay 3 above.
24. This passage (*Remarks on the Foundations of Mathematics* VI.49) seems to be an expression of the intermediate position:

> What you say seems to amount to this, that logic belongs to the natural history of man. And that is not combinable with the hardness of the logical "must".
> But the logical "must" is a component part of the propositions of logic, and these are not propositions of human natural history.

on our reason. This is not a platonism about values (except in a sense analogous to that in which the intermediate position about the logical "must" might be called a species of platonism); the world in which moral values are said to be is not the externally characterizable world that a moral platonism would envisage.[25] Non-cognitivism and descriptivism appear, from this point of view, as different ways of succumbing to a quite dubious demand for a more objective conception of rationality. If we accept the demand, then they will indeed seem the only alternatives to a full-blown moral platonism. But in the logical case, we should not suppose that recoiling from platonism commits us to some kind of reduction of the felt hardness of the logical "must" to the urging of our own desires.[26] In the ethical case too, we should not allow the different option that the intermediate position affords to disappear.[27]

5. Non-cognitivism, as I see it, invites us to be exercised over the question how value experience relates to the world, with the world conceived as how things are anyway—independently, at least, of our value experience being as it is. The non-cognitivism I have been concerned with assumes that evaluative classifications correspond to kinds into which things can in principle be seen to fall independently of an evaluative outlook. Thereby it permits itself to return an answer to the question that clearly does not undermine the appearance that evaluative thinking is a matter of the genuine application of concepts. As one's use of an evaluative term unfolds through time, one is genuinely (by the non-cognitivist's lights) going on in the same way. Admittedly, the non-cognitive ingredient in what happens

---

25. So this position does not commit the error that Mackie finds in cognitivism about values. (It is a fascinating question whether Plato himself was a moral platonist in the sense that is in play here, involving committing Mackie's error. I am myself inclined to think he was not.)

26. On these lines: "perceiving" that a proposition is, say, a conclusion by *modus ponens* from premises one has already accepted, since it constitutes having a reason to accept the proposition, is really an amalgam of a neutral perception and a desire (compare non-cognitivism); or the perception constitutes having a reason only in conjunction with a desire (compare descriptivism). I am indebted here to S. L. Hurley here.

27. For the suggestion that Wittgenstein's philosophy of mathematics yields a model for a satisfactory conception of the metaphysics of value, see Wiggins, "Truth, Invention, and the Meaning of Life", pp. 128–30.

makes the case more complex than our usual paradigms of concept-application. But the non-cognitive extra, repeated as the practice unfolds, is seen as a repeated response to some genuinely same thing (something capturable in a paradigmatic concept-application): namely, membership in some genuine kind. To put it picturesquely, the non-cognitive ingredient (an attitude, say) can, without illusion by the non-cognitivist's lights, see itself as going on in the same way. Given that, the whole picture looks sufficiently close to the usual paradigms of concept-application to count as a complex variant of them. But I have suggested that the assumption on which the possibility of this partial assimilation depends is a prejudice, without intrinsic plausibility.

Might non-cognitivism simply disown the assumption?[28] If what I have just written is on the right track, it can do so only at a price: that of making it problematic whether evaluative language is close enough to the usual paradigms of concept-application to count as expressive of judgements at all (as opposed to a kind of sounding off). Failing the assumption, there need be no genuine same thing (by the non-cognitivist's lights) to which the successive occurrences of the non-cognitive extra are responses. Of course the items to which the term in question is applied have, as something genuinely in common, the fact that they elicit the non-cognitive extra (the attitude, if that is what it is). But that is not a property to which the attitude can coherently be seen as a response. The attitude can see itself as going on in the same way, then, only by falling into a peculiarly grotesque form of the alleged illusion: projecting itself on to the objects, and then mistaking the projection for something it finds and responds to in them. So it seems that, if it disowns the assumption, non-cognitivism must regard the attitude as something that is simply felt (causally, perhaps, but not rationally explicable); and uses of evaluative language seem appropriately assimilated to certain sorts of exclamation, rather than to the paradigm cases of concept-application.

Of course there are some who will not find this conclusion awkward.[29] But anyone who finds it unacceptable, and is sympathetic to the suggestion that the disputed assumption is only a prejudice, has

---

28. Blackburn pressed this question.
29. I mean those who are content with a view of values on the lines of, e.g., A. J. Ayer, *Language, Truth and Logic*, chap. 6.

reason to suspect that the non-cognitivist is not asking the right question. It is not that we cannot make sense of the non-cognitivist's conception of a value-free world; nor that we cannot find plausible some account of how value experience relates to the world so conceived (causally, no doubt). But if we resist both the disputed assumption and the irrationalistic upshot of trying to read an account of the relation between value experience and the world so conceived, not based on the disputed assumption, as an account of the real truth about the conceptual content of the experience, then we must wonder about the credentials of the non-cognitivist's question. If we continue to find it plausible that asking how value experience relates to the world should yield a palatable account of the content of value experience, we must wonder whether the world that figures in the right construal of the question should not be differently conceived, without the non-cognitivist's insistence on independence from evaluative outlooks.[30] In that case the non-cognitivist's anxiety to maintain that value judgements are not descriptive of *his* world will seem, not wrong indeed, but curiously beside the point.

30. The pressure towards conceiving reality as objective, transcending how things appear to particular points of view, is not something to which it is clearly compulsory to succumb in all contexts, for all its necessity in the natural sciences. See Thomas Nagel, "Subjective and Objective".

PART III

ISSUES IN WITTGENSTEIN

ESSAY 11

Wittgenstein on Following a Rule[1]

These things are finer spun than crude hands have any inkling of.
(RFM VII-57.)[2]

1. We find it natural to think of meaning and understanding in, as it were, contractual terms.[3] Our idea is that to learn the meaning of a word is to acquire an understanding that obliges us subsequently—if we have occasion to deploy the concept in question—to judge and speak in certain determinate ways, on pain of failure to obey the dictates of the meaning we have grasped; that we are "committed to certain patterns of linguistic usage by the meanings we attach to expressions".[4] According to Crispin Wright, the burden of

---

1. This paper originated in an attempt to respond to Simon Blackburn, "Rule-Following and Moral Realism"; I was also stimulated, in writing the first draft, by an unpublished paper of Blackburn's, a revised version of which is Blackburn, "The Individual Strikes Back". I benefited from comments on the first draft from Margaret Gilbert, Susan Hurley, Saul Kripke, David Lewis, Christopher Peacocke, Philip Pettit, David Wiggins, and Crispin Wright, who also kindly let me see a draft of his "Kripke's Wittgenstein", a forerunner of his "Kripke's Account of the Argument against Private Language".
2. I shall use *"RFM"* for Wittgenstein, *Remarks on the Foundations of Mathematics*.
3. See p. 19 of Crispin Wright, *Wittgenstein on the Foundations of Mathematics*.
4. Wright, p. 21. This idea of commitment to patterns must be treated with care if we are not to falsify the intuition. The most straightforward sort of case, on which it is familiar that Wittgenstein concentrates, is the continuation of a numerical series. Here it is natural to think of the correct expansion of the series as constituting a pattern to which understanding of its principle commits one. In the general case, the "pattern" idea is the idea of a series of things that, given the way the world develops, it would be correct to say if one chose to express a given concept; outside the series-expansion case, this idea is obviously metaphorical at best, since what it is correct to say with the use of a given concept,

Wittgenstein's reflections on following a rule, in his later work, is that these natural ideas lack the substance we are inclined to credit them with: "there is in our understanding of a concept no rigid, advance determination of what is to count as its correct application".[5]

If Wittgenstein's conclusion, as Wright interprets it, is allowed to stand, the most striking casualty is a familiar intuitive notion of objectivity. The idea at risk is the idea of things being thus and so anyway, whether or not we choose to investigate the matter in question, and whatever the outcome of any such investigation. That idea requires the conception of how things could correctly be said to be anyway—whatever, if anything, we in fact go on to say about the matter; and this notion of correctness can only be the notion of how the pattern of application that we grasp, when we come to understand the concept in question, extends, independently of the actual outcome of any investigation, to the relevant case. So if the notion of investigation-independent patterns of application is to be discarded, then so is the idea that things are, at least sometimes, thus and so anyway, independently of our ratifying the judgement that that is how they are. It seems fair to describe this extremely radical consequence as a kind of idealism.[6]

We may well hesitate to attribute such a doctrine to the philosopher who wrote:

> If one tried to advance *theses* in philosophy, it would never be possible to debate them, because everyone would agree to them. (*PI* §128.)[7]

---

even supposing a determinate state of affairs one aims to describe, depends on what other concepts one chooses to express in the same utterance. (The non-metaphorical kernel is simply the idea that the meaning of what one says is a matter of the conditions under which it would be true.) It is important, also, not to falsify the connection between the patterns and meaningfulness—e.g., by suggesting that the idea is that making sense depends on *conforming* to the appropriate commitments. Tracing out the patterns is what the "pattern" idea takes consistently speaking the truth to be; to make sense (in an affirmation) one needs to do no more than felicitously make as if to be doing what one takes that to require. (See, further, n. 46 below.)

5. *Wittgenstein on the Foundations of Mathematics*, p. 21. "Rigid" will call for comment; see n. 21 below.

6. Wright does this at p. 252 of "Strict Finitism". See also pp. 246–7 of his "Anti-Realist Semantics: The Role of *Criteria*".

7. I shall use "*PI*" for Wittgenstein, *Philosophical Investigations*. Stanley Cavell's correction of the usual reading of this passage, at pp. 33–4 of *The Claim of Reason*, does not make it any easier to reconcile with Wright's view of Wittgenstein.

Notice that the destructive effect of the doctrine goes far beyond Wittgenstein's hostility to the imagery of mathematical platonism, in which mathematics is pictured as "the natural history of mathematical objects" (*RFM* II-40). The remarks about rule-following are not confined to mathematics; on Wright's reading they would undermine our ordinary intuitive conception of natural history, literally so called—the very model on which that suspect platonist picture of mathematics is constructed.

More specific grounds for doubting the attribution might be derived from passages like this (*PI* §195):

> "But I don't mean that what I do now (in grasping a sense) determines the future use *causally* and as a matter of experience, but that in a *queer* way, the use itself is in some sense present."—But of course it is, 'in *some* sense'! Really the only thing wrong with what you say is the expression "in a queer way". The rest is all right. . . .[8]

What this suggests is something we might anyway have expected: that Wittgenstein's target is not the very idea that a present state of understanding embodies commitments with respect to the future, but rather a certain seductive misconception of that idea.

Not that Wright merely ignores such passages. His claim is that Wittgenstein seems *almost* to want to deny all substance to the "pattern" idea; what he attributes to Wittgenstein is not an outright abandonment of the idea but a reinterpretation of it.[9] Wright's view is that the intuitive contractual picture of meaning and understanding can be rendered innocuous—purged of the seductive misconception—by discarding the thought that the patterns are independent of our ratification. Later (§§5, 7, 10) I shall suggest that this purged version of the intuitive picture is not recognizable as a picture of meaning and understanding at all, and is not correctly attributed to Wittgenstein. But for the present, let me note only that Wright's reinterpretation, precisely by denying the ratification-independence of the patterns, leaves the intuitive conception of objectivity untenable, in the way I described above. So we are bound to wonder whether the concession that Wright envisages Wittgenstein making to the

---

8. See also, e.g., *PI* §§187, 692, 693.
9. See *Wittgenstein on the Foundations of Mathematics*, pp. 21, 227.

"pattern" idea can account satisfactorily for Wittgenstein's reassuring tone in his response to the interlocutor of *PI* §195.

2. In Wright's view, then, the butt of Wittgenstein's reflections on rule-following is the idea that understanding an expression is "grasp of a pattern of application, conformity to which requires certain determinate verdicts in so far unconsidered cases" (p. 216). But (p. 216):

> We have to acknowledge . . . that the "pattern" is, strictly, inaccessible to definitive explanation. For, as Wittgenstein never wearied of reminding himself, no explanation of the use of an expression is proof against musunderstanding; verbal explanations require correct understanding of the vocabulary in which they are couched, and samples are open to an inexhaustible variety of interpretations. So we move towards the idea that understanding an expression is a kind of "cottoning on"; that is, a leap, an inspired guess at the pattern of application which the instructor is trying to get across.

The pictured upshot of this "leap" is something idiolectic. So the suggestion is that the "pattern" idea comes naturally to us, in the first instance, in the shape of "the idea that each of us has some sort of privileged access to the character of his own understanding of an expression; each of us knows of an idiolectic pattern of use, for which there is a strong presumption, when sufficient evidence has accumulated, that it is shared communally" (p. 217).[10]

What is wrong with this idea? Wright's answer is this:

> . . . *whatever* sincere applications I make of a particular expression, when I have paid due heed to the situation, will seem to me to conform with my understanding of it. There is no scope for a distinction here between the fact of an application's seeming to me to conform with the way in which I understand it and the fact of its really doing so.[11]

---

10. See also pp. 32, 354.
11. Ibid.; see also p. 36. Compare *PI* §258: "One would like to say: whatever is going to seem right to me is right. And that only means that here we can't talk about 'right'." (See §14 below.)

Now we are naturally inclined to protect the intuitive view that thoughts and utterances make sense by virtue of owing, or purporting to owe, allegiance to conceptual commitments. So, given that idiolectic understanding cannot make room for the "pattern" idea, it is tempting to appeal to communal understanding. But (the argument that Wright ascribes to Wittgenstein continues) this cannot rehabilitate the "pattern" idea. For (p. 218):

> Suppose that one of us finds himself incorrigibly out of line concerning the description of a new case. We have just seen that he cannot single-handed, as it were, give sense to the idea that he is at least being faithful to his *own* pattern; that is, that he recognises how he must describe the new case if he is to remain faithful to his own understanding of the relevant expressions. How, then, does his disposition to apply the expression to a new case become, properly speaking, recognition of the continuation of a pattern if it so happens that he is *not* out of line, if it so happens that there is communal agreement?

The trouble is that there is a precise parallel between the community's supposed grasp of the patterns that it has communally committed itself to and the individual's supposed grasp of his idiolectic commitments. Whatever applications of an expression secure communal approval, just those applications will seem to the community to conform with its understanding of the expression.[12] If we regard an individual as aiming to speak a communal language, we take account of the possibility that he may go out of step with his fellows; thus we make room for an application of the notion of error, and so of right and wrong. But it is only going out of step with one's fellows that we make room for; not going out of step with a ratification-independent pattern that they follow. So the notion of right and wrong that we have made room for is at best a thin surrogate for what would be required by the intuitive notion of objectivity. That would require the idea of concepts as authoritative; and the move away from idiolects has not reinstated that idea. In sum (p. 220):

> None of us unilaterally can make sense of the idea of correct employment of language save by reference to the authority of securable com-

---

12. One would like to say: whatever is going to seem right to *us* is right. And that only means that here we can't talk about "right".

munal assent on the matter; and for the community itself there is no authority, so no standard to meet.

3. According to Wright, then, Wittgenstein's reflections are directed, in the first instance, against the idea that a determinate practice can be dictated by a personal understanding—something that owes no allegiance to a communal way of going on. On the surface, at least, there is a point of contact here with Saul Kripke's influential reading of the remarks on rule-following, which I shall now outline.[13]

Suppose one is asked to perform an addition other than any one has encountered before, either in the training that gave one one's understanding of addition or in subsequently trying to put one's understanding into practice.[14] In confidently giving a particular answer, one will naturally have a thought that is problematic: namely—to put it in terms that bring out the point of contact with Wright's reading—that in returning this answer one is keeping faith with one's understanding of the "plus" sign. To show how this thought is problematic, Kripke introduces a sceptic who questions it. The natural idea is that one's understanding of "plus" dictates the answer one gives. But what could constitute one's being in such a state? Not a disposition: no doubt it is true that answering as one does is an exercise of a disposition that one acquired when one learned arithmetic, but the relation of a disposition to its exercises is in no sense contractual—a disposition is not something to which its exercises are faithful.[15] But nothing else will serve either: for—to quote Kripke's summary of a rich battery of argument—"it seems that no matter what is in my mind at a given time, I am free in the future to interpret it in different ways" (p. 107). That is, whatever piece of mental furniture I cite, acquired by me as a result of my training in arithmetic, it is open to the sceptic to point out that my present performance keeps

---

13. See Kripke, *Wittgenstein on Rules and Private Language*. Wright notes the parallel at p. 249 of "Strict Finitism"; although he takes issue with Kripke in "Kripke's Account of the Argument against Private Language".

14. Where I say "other", Kripke has "larger". This makes the scepticism perhaps more gripping, but the difference is inessential.

15. This is the gist of the excellent discussion at Kripke, *Wittgenstein on Rules and Private Language*, pp. 22–37.

faith with it only on one interpretation of it, and other interpretations are possible. So it cannot constitute my understanding "plus" in such a way as to dictate the answer I give. Such a state of understanding would require not just the original item but also my having put the right interpretation on it. But what could constitute my having put the right interpretation on some mental item? And now the argument can evidently be repeated.

The upshot of this argument is a "sceptical paradox", which, according to Kripke (pp. 69–71), Wittgenstein accepts: there is no fact that could constitute my having attached one rather than another meaning to the "plus" sign.

It may well seem that if Wittgenstein concedes this much to Kripke's sceptic, he has renounced the right to attribute meaning to expressions at all. According to Kripke, however, Wittgenstein offers a "sceptical solution" to the "sceptical paradox". A "sceptical solution" to a sceptical problem is one that "begins . . . by conceding that the sceptic's negative assertions are unanswerable" (p. 66). The essentials of the "sceptical solution" are as follows.

First, we must reform our intuitive conception of meaning, replacing the notion of truth-conditions with some notion like that of justification conditions. Kripke quotes with approval (p. 73) a claim of Michael Dummett's: "The *Investigations* contains implicitly a rejection of the classical (realist) Frege-*Tractatus* view that the general form of explanation of meaning is a statement of the truth conditions."[16] The "sceptical paradox", which we are to accept, is that there is no fact that could constitute my having attached one rather than another determinate meaning to the "plus" sign. We are inclined to understand this as a concession that I have attached *no* determinate meaning to the "plus" sign: but the suggestion is that this is only because we adhere, naively, to the superseded truth-conditional conception of meaning—applied, in this case, to the claim "I have attached a determinate meaning to the 'plus' sign".

Second, when we consider the justification conditions of the statements in which we express the idea that someone attaches some determinate meaning to an expression (the conditions under which we

---

16. "Wittgenstein's Philosophy of Mathematics", p. 348.

affirm such statements, and the roles they play in our lives), we see that we can make sense of them in terms of their use to record acceptance of individuals into the linguistic community. (The thesis that we can make sense of the idea of meaning only in that connection is the core of Kripke's interpretation of the Private Language Argument.)

Now there is room for doubt about how successful this "sceptical solution" can be. The exegetical framework within which it is constructed—the Dummettian picture of the transition between the *Tractatus* and the *Investigations*—is not beyond dispute. But without opening that issue (which I shall touch on below: §§10, 11, 14), we can note that when Dummett expresses his doubts about the "realist" (truth-conditional) conception of meaning (which are supposed to be in the spirit of the later Wittgenstein's doubts about the *Tractatus*), it is typically by pressing such questions as this: "What could constitute someone's possession of the sort of understanding of a sentence that 'realism' attributes to him?" The implication is that, failing a satisfactory answer, no one could possess that sort of understanding.[17] It is natural to suppose that if one says "There is no fact that could constitute its being the case that P", one precludes oneself from affirming that P; and this supposition, so far from being a distinctively "realist" one, plays a central role in the standard arguments *against* "realism". Given this supposition, the concession that Kripke says Wittgenstein makes to the sceptic becomes a *denial* that I understand the "plus" sign to mean one thing rather than another. And now—generalizing the denial—we do seem to have fallen into an abyss: "the incredible and self-defeating conclusion, that all language is meaningless" (p. 71). It is quite obscure how we could hope to claw ourselves back by manipulating the notion of accredited membership in a linguistic community.

4. In any case, Kripke's thesis that Wittgenstein accepts the "sceptical paradox" seems a falsification. Kripke (see p. 7) identifies the "sceptical paradox" he attributes to Wittgenstein with the paradox Wittgenstein formulates in the first paragraph of *PI* §201:

---

17. See especially Dummett, "What Is a Theory of Meaning? (II)".

This was our paradox: no course of action could be determined by a rule, because every course of action can be made out to accord with the rule. The answer was: if everything can be made out to accord with the rule, then it can also be made out to conflict with it. And so there would be neither accord nor conflict here.

But §201 goes on with a passage for which Kripke's reading makes no room:

> It can be seen that there is a misunderstanding here from the mere fact that in the course of our argument we give one interpretation after another; as if each one contented us at least for a moment, until we thought of yet another standing behind it. What this shews is that there is a way of grasping a rule which is *not* an *interpretation,* but which is exhibited in what we call "obeying the rule" and "going against it" in actual cases.

What could constitute my understanding, say, the "plus" sign in a way with which only certain answers to given addition problems would accord? Confronted with such questions, we tend to be enticed into looking for a fact that would constitute my having put an appropriate *interpretation* on what I was told and shown when I was instructed in arithmetic. Anything we hit on as satisfying that specification contents us only "for a moment"; then it occurs to us that whatever we have hit on would itself be capable of interpretation in such a way that acting in conformity with it would require something quite different. So we look for something that would constitute my having interpreted the first item in the right way. Anything we come up with as satisfying that specification will in turn content us only "for a moment"; and so on: "any interpretation still hangs in the air along with what it interprets, and cannot give it any support" (*PI* §198). Kripke's reading has Wittgenstein endorsing this reasoning, and consequently willing to abandon the idea that there is anything that constitutes my understanding an expression in some determinate way. But what Wittgenstein clearly claims, in the second paragraph of §201, is that the reasoning is vitiated by "a misunderstanding". The right response to the paradox, Wittgenstein in effect tells us, is not to accept it but to correct the misunderstanding on which it depends: that is, to realize "that there is a way of grasping a rule which is *not* an *interpretation*".

The paradox of §201 is one horn of a dilemma with which the misunderstanding presents us. Suppose we are not disabused of the misunderstanding—that is, we take it that our problem is to find a fact that constitutes my having given some expression an interpretation with which only certain uses of it would conform. In that case, the attempt to resist the paradox of §201 will drive us to embrace a familiar mythology of meaning and understanding, and this is the second horn of the dilemma. My coming to mean the expression in the way I do (my "grasping the rule") must be my arriving at an interpretation; but it must be an interpretation that is not susceptible to the movement of thought in the sceptical line of reasoning—not such as to content us only until we think of another interpretation standing behind it.

> What one wants to say is: "Every sign is capable of interpretation; but the *meaning* mustn't be capable of interpretation. It is the last interpretation." (*Blue Book*, p. 34.)[18]

Understanding an expression, then, must be possessing an interpretation that cannot be interpreted—an interpretation that precisely bridges the gap, exploited in the sceptical argument, between the instruction one received in learning the expression and the use one goes on to make of it. The irresistible upshot of this is that we picture following a rule as the operation of a super-rigid yet (or perhaps we should say "hence") ethereal machine.

> How queer: It looks as if a physical (mechanical) form of guidance could misfire and let in something unforeseen, but not a rule! As if a rule were, so to speak, the only reliable form of guidance. (*Zettel* §296.)[19]

One of Wittgenstein's main concerns is clearly to cast doubt on this mythology. But his attacks on the mythology are not, as Kripke suggests, arguments for acceptance of the "sceptical paradox".[20]

---

18. Compare *Zettel*, §231.
19. There is a good description of the mythological ideas expressed here, with a wealth of citations of relevant passages, in Gordon Baker, "Following Wittgenstein: Some Signposts for *Philosophical Investigations* §§143–242".
20. See *Wittgenstein on Rules and Private Language*, pp. 65, 69: Kripke cannot distinguish rejecting the "superlative fact" of *PI* §192—rejecting the mythology—from refusing

That would be so if the dilemma were compulsory; but the point of the second paragraph of PI §201 is precisely that it is not. The mythology is wrung from us, in our need to avoid the paradox of the first paragraph, only because we fall into the misunderstanding; the attack on the mythology is not support for the paradox, but rather constitutes, in conjunction with the fact that the paradox is intolerable, an argument against the misunderstanding.

It is worth noting two points about the second horn of the dilemma that correspond to two aspects of Wright's reading of Wittgenstein.

First, if we picture an interpretation that would precisely bridge the gap between instruction and competent use, it seems that it can only be one that each person hits on for himself—so that it is at best a fortunate contingency if his interpretation coincides with the one arrived at by someone else subjected to the same instruction, or with the one intended by the instructor.

> "But do you really explain to the other person what you yourself understand? Don't you get him to *guess* the essential thing? You give him examples,—but he has to guess their drift, to guess your intention." (*PI* §210.)

This is clearly the basis in Wittgenstein for Wright's remarks (quoted in §2 above) about "the idea that understanding an expression is a kind of 'cottoning on'; that is, a leap, an inspired guess at the pattern of application which the instructor is trying to get across".

Second, a concomitant of the picture of the super-rigid machine is a picture of the patterns as sets of rails. (See, for instance, *PI* §218.) At each stage, say in the extending of a series, the rule itself determines what comes next, independently of the techniques that we learn in learning to extend it; the point of the learning is to get our practice of judging and speaking in line with the rule's impersonal dictates. (An omniscient God would not need to do mathematics in order to know whether "777" occurs in the decimal expansion of π;

---

to countenance a fact in which my attaching a determinate meaning to "plus" consists—accepting the paradox.

see *RFM* VII-41.) Now this conception figures regularly in Wright's formulations of the "pattern" idea:

> ... the pattern extends *of itself* to cases which we have yet to confront ...

> ... the investigation-independent truth of statements requires that their truth is settled, *autonomously and without the need for human interference,* by their meanings and the character of the relevant facts.[21]

It is clear, again, that these formulations have a basis in Wittgenstein's polemic against the second horn of the dilemma. A remark like "I give the rule an extension" (*RFM* VI-29) is meant as a corrective of the inclination to say "The rule extends of itself". (And "even God can determine something mathematical only by mathematics": *RFM* VII-41.)

5. In Wright's reading, as I said (§§1 and 2 above), Wittgenstein's point is that the natural contractual conception of understanding should not be discarded, but purged of the idea—which it must incorporate if the intuitive notion of objectivity is to have application—that the patterns to which our concepts oblige us are ratification-independent. I expressed a suspicion (in §1 above) that this purging would not leave a residue recognizable as a conception of meaning and understanding at all, or recognizable as something that Wittgenstein recommends. I want now to begin on an attempt to back up this suspicion.

At *PI* §437 Wittgenstein writes:

> A wish seems already to know what will or would satisfy it; a proposition, a thought, what makes it true—even when that thing is not there at all! Whence this *determining* of what is not yet there? This despotic demand? ("The hardness of the logical must.")

Note the parenthesis: clearly he thinks that the discussion in which this passage occurs—dealing with the relation between wishes or ex-

---

21. Wright, *Wittgenstein on the Foundations of Mathematics*, p. 216, and "Strict Finitism", p. 250, both with my emphasis. "Rigid", at *Wittgenstein on the Foundations of Mathematics*, p. 21 (which I quoted in §1 above), is an expression of the same idea—Wright does not mean "rigid" as opposed to, say, "vague" (see Baker,"Following Wittgenstein", pp. 40–1).

pectations and their fulfilment, and the relation between orders and their execution—raises the same issues as his reflections on the continuation of a series.[22] We can bring out the connection by focusing on the case of orders and their execution: it is natural to say that the execution of an order is faithful to its meaning, and in saying this we clearly express a version of the idea that we express when we say that the competent continuation of a series is faithful to its principle.

What would Wright's reading of Wittgenstein be like, transposed to this case? Something on these lines (compare §2 above). The temptation to say that my execution of an order conforms with my understanding of it arises primarily out of a conception of my understanding as idiolectic—something that cannot be definitively conveyed to someone else, so that it is at best a happy contingency if it coincides with the understanding of the order possessed by the person who issued it. On reflection, however, we should realize that this is an illusion: we cannot make sense of anything that would constitute an essentially personal understanding of an order, but would nevertheless impose genuine constraints on what I did in "execution" of it. For whatever I "sincerely" did would seem to be in conformity with my supposed personal understanding of the order. We naturally want to protect the intuitive notion of an action's fulfilling an order; so we are tempted at this point to appeal to the idea of my membership in a linguistic community. This does make room for my going wrong. But all that my going wrong can amount to is this: my action does not secure the approval of my fellows, or is not what they would do in attempted fulfilment of such an order. When the community does approve, that is not a matter of its collectively recognizing the conformity of my action to an antecedent communal understanding of the order: for this supposed communal understanding would be in exactly the same position as my supposed idiolectic understanding. We cannot hold, then, that the community "goes right or wrong", by the lights of its understanding, when it awards my action the title "execution of the order"; "rather, it just goes".

Given the correspondence (which I noted in §4 above) between aspects of Wright's reading and aspects of Wittgenstein's polemic against the second horn of the dilemma, it is not surprising that part,

22. See Kripke, *Wittgenstein on Rules and Private Language*, pp. 25–6, n. 19.

at least, of this transposed version of Wright's reading should neatly fit parts of Wittgenstein's discussion. Consider, for instance, *PI* §460:

> Could the justification of an action as fulfilment of an order run like this: "You said 'Bring me a yellow flower', upon which this one gave me a feeling of satisfaction; that is why I have brought it"? Wouldn't one have to reply: "But I didn't set you to bring me the flower which should give you that sort of feeling after what I said!"?

It seems correct and illuminating to understand this as an attack on the idea that the understanding I act on is essentially idiolectic.[23]

Taken as a whole, however, I think this reading gets Wittgenstein completely wrong. I can perhaps begin to explain my disbelief with this remark: it would have been fully in character for Wittgenstein to have written as follows:

> Could the justification of an action as fulfilment of an order run like this: "You said 'Bring me a yellow flower', upon which the one received approval from all the bystanders; that is why I have brought it"? Wouldn't one have to reply: "But I didn't set you to bring the flower which should receive approval from everyone else after what I said!"?

In his later work, Wittgenstein returns again and again to trying to characterize the relation between meaning and consensus. If there is anything that emerges clearly, it is that it would be a serious error, in his view, not to make a radical distinction between the significance of, say, "This is yellow" and the significance of, say, "This would be called 'yellow' by (most) speakers of English" (see, for instance, *Zettel* §§428–431). And my transposed version of Wright's reading seems to leave it mysterious, at best, why this distinction should be so important.

It may appear that the answer is both obvious and readily available to Wright: "To say 'This would be called "yellow" by speakers of English' would not be to *call* the object in question 'yellow', and that is what one does when one says 'This is yellow'." But this would

---

23. That is, the passage is of a piece with the passage from *PI* §258 that I quoted in n. 11 above. This suggestion does not compete with, but rather complements, Kripke's suggestion (pp. 25–6, n. 19) that the passage refers obliquely to Russell's treatment of desire in *The Analysis of Mind*.

merely postpone the serious question: does Wright's reading of Wittgenstein contain the means to make it intelligible that there should so much as *be* such an action as calling an object "yellow"? The picture Wright offers is, at the basic level, a picture of human beings vocalizing in certain ways in response to objects, with this behaviour (no doubt) accompanied by such "inner" phenomena as feelings of constraint, or convictions of the rightness of what they are saying. There are presumably correspondences in the propensities of fellow members of a linguistic community to vocalize, and to feel comfortable in doing so, that are unsurprising in the light of their belonging to a single species, together with similarities in the training that gave them the propensities. But at the basic level there is no question of shared commitments—of the behaviour, and the associated aspects of the streams of consciousness, being subject to the authority of anything outside themselves. ("For the community itself there is no authority, so no standard to meet.") How, then, can we be entitled to view the behaviour as involving, say, calling things "yellow", rather than a mere brute meaningless sounding off?

The thought that is operative here is one Kripke puts by saying: "The relation of meaning and intention to future action is *normative, not descriptive*" (p. 37). It is a thought Wright aims to respect. This is the point of his aspiration not to discard the contractual conception of meaning, but only to purge it of the idea of ratification-independence. But the purging yields the picture of what I have been calling "the basic level"; and at that level Wright's picture has no room for norms, and hence—given the normativeness of meaning—no room for meaning. Wright hopes to preserve a foothold for a purified form of the normativeness implicit in the contractual conception of meaning, by appealing to the fact that individuals are susceptible to communal correction. It is problematic, however, whether the picture of the basic level, once entertained as such, can be prevented from purporting to contain *the real truth* about linguistic behaviour. In that case its freedom from norms will preclude our attributing any genuine substance to the etiolated normativeness Wright hopes to preserve. The problem for Wright is to distinguish the position he attributes to Wittgenstein from one according to which the possibility of going out of step with our fellows gives us the *illusion* of being subject to norms, and consequently the *illusion* of entertaining and expressing meanings.

6. Moved by the insight that meaning relates normatively to linguistic behaviour, Kripke—like Wright—reads Wittgenstein as concerned to preserve a role for the intuitive contractual conception. But Kripke's Wittgenstein locates that conception only in the context of the "sceptical solution"—a response to a supposedly accepted "sceptical paradox". Applied to the case of orders and their execution, Kripke's "sceptical paradox" will take this form: there is nothing that constitutes my understanding an order in a way with which only acting in a certain determinate manner would conform. And, here as before (compare §4 above), it is open to question whether, once that much is conceded to scepticism, a "sceptical solution" can avert the destructive effect that the concession threatens to have.

In any case, this line of interpretation gets off on the wrong foot, when it credits Wittgenstein with acceptance of a "sceptical paradox", so that a "sceptical solution" would be the best that could be hoped for. Just as in the case of the continuation of a series, the reasoning that would lead to this "sceptical paradox" starts with something Wittgenstein aims to show up as a mistake: the assumption, in this case, that the understanding on which I act when I obey an order must be an interpretation. The connection with the thought of *PI* §201 is made clear by this juxtaposition (*RFM* VI-38):

> How can the word "Slab" indicate what I have to do, when after all I can bring any action into accord with any interpretation?
>
> How can I follow a rule, when after all whatever I do can be interpreted as following it?

The parallel can be extended (see §4 above). If we assume that understanding is always interpretation, then the need to resist the paradox of *PI* §201 drives us into a fantastic picture of how understanding mediates between order and execution. Consider, for instance, *PI* §431:

> "There is a gulf between an order and its execution. It has to be filled by the act of understanding."
>
> "Only in the act of understanding is it meant that we are to do THIS. The order—why, that is nothing but sounds, ink-marks.—"[24]

---

24. Compare the passage from *Blue Book*, p. 34, that I quoted in §4 above.

The act of understanding, conceived in terms of hitting on an interpretation that completely bridges the gulf between an order and its execution, demands to be pictured as setting up a super-rigid connection between the words and the subsequent action (hence the allusion, in *PI* §437, to "the hardness of the logical must"). It is this idea that Wittgenstein is mocking in *PI* §461:

> In what sense does an order anticipate its execution? By ordering *just that* which later on is carried out?—But one would have to say "which later on is carried out, or again is not carried out." And that is to say nothing.
>
> "But even if my wish does not determine what is going to be the case, still it does so to speak determine the theme of a fact, whether the fact fulfils the wish or not." We are—as it were—surprised, not at anyone's knowing the future, but at his being able to prophesy at all (right or wrong).
>
> As if the mere prophecy, no matter whether true or false, foreshadowed the future; whereas it knows nothing of the future and cannot know less than nothing.

And the parallel goes further still. When we are tempted to conceive the understanding of an order in this way, what we have in mind is something essentially personal: a guess at the meaning of the person who issued the order. This idea is Wittgenstein's target in, for instance, *PI* §433:

> When we give an order, it can look as if the ultimate thing sought by the order has to remain unexpressed, as there is always a gulf between an order and its execution. Say I want someone to make a particular movement, say to raise his arm. To make it quite clear, I do the movement. This picture seems unambiguous until we ask: how does he know *he is to make this movement?*—How does he know at all what use he is to make of the signs I give him, whatever they are?—Perhaps I shall now try to supplement the order by means of further signs, by pointing from myself to him, making encouraging gestures, etc.. Here it looks as if the order were beginning to stammer.
>
> As if the signs were precariously trying to produce understanding in us.—But if we now understand them, by what token do we understand?

If we read Wittgenstein in Kripke's way, we shall take Wittgenstein's mockery of these ideas as argument in favour of the "sceptical paradox"—the thesis that there is nothing that could constitute my understanding an order in a determinate way. That is what the mockery would amount to if there were no options besides the paradox and the ideas that Wittgenstein mocks. But Wittgenstein's point is that this dilemma seems compulsory only on the assumption that understanding is always interpretation; his aim is not to shift us from one horn of the dilemma to the other, but to persuade us to reject the dilemma by discarding the assumption on which it depends.

7. Having diagnosed the dilemma as resting on the mistaken idea that grasping a rule is always an interpretation, Wittgenstein goes on, famously, to say (*PI* §202):

> And hence also 'obeying a rule' is a practice. And to *think* one is obeying a rule is not to obey a rule. Hence it not possible to obey a rule 'privately': otherwise thinking one was obeying a rule would be the same thing as obeying it.

The diagnosis prompts the question "How can there be a way of grasping a rule which is not an interpretation?", and I think the thesis that obeying a rule is a practice is meant to constitute the answer to this question. That is, what mediates the inference ("hence also") is this thought: we have to realize that obeying a rule is a practice if we are to find it intelligible that there is a way of grasping a rule which is not an interpretation. (The rest of §202—the crystallization into two sentences of the Private Language Argument—is offered as a corollary.)

There is another formulation of the same line of thought in *PI* §198:

> "Then can whatever I do be brought into accord with the rule?"—Let me ask this: what has the expression of a rule—say a sign-post—got to do with my actions? What sort of connexion is there here?—Well, perhaps this one: I have been trained to react to this sign in a particular way, and now I do so react to it.
>
> "But that is only to give a causal connexion: to tell how it has come about that we go by the sign-post; not what this going-by-the-sign really consists in."—On the contrary; I have further indicated that a

person goes by a sign-post only in so far as there exists a regular use of sign-posts, a custom.[25]

This passage opens with an expression of the paradox formulated in the first paragraph of §201. Then Wittgenstein introduces the case of sign-posts, in order to adumbrate the diagnosis that he is going to state more explicitly in §201. When I follow a sign-post, the connection between it and my action is not mediated by an interpretation of sign-posts that I acquired when I was trained in their use. I simply act as I have been trained to.[26] This prompts an objection, which might be paraphrased on these lines: "Nothing in what you have said shows that what you have described is a case of following a rule; you have only told us how to give a causal explanation of certain bit of (what might as well be for all that you have said) mere behaviour." The reply—which corresponds to the first sentence of §202—is that the training in question is initiation into a custom. If it were not that, then the account of the connection between sign-post and action would indeed look like an account of nothing more than brute movement and its causal explanation; our picture would not contain the materials to entitle us to speak of following (going by) a sign-post.[27]

Now how exactly is this to be understood?

Wittgenstein's concern is to exorcize the insidious assumption that there must be an interpretation that mediates between an order, or the expression of a rule given in training, on the one hand, and an action in conformity with it, on the other. In his efforts to achieve this, he is led to say such things as "I obey the rule *blindly*" (*PI* §219). This is of a piece with his repeated insistence that the agreement that is necessary for the notion of following a rule to be applicable is not agreement in opinions:

"So you are saying that human agreement decides what is true and what is false?"—It is what human beings *say* that is true and false; and

---

25. I have ventured to change the punctuation in the second paragraph, in order to make the dialectical structure of the passage clearer.
26. Compare *PI* §506: "The absent-minded man who at the order 'Right turn!' turns left, and then, clutching his forehead, says 'Oh! right turn' and does a right turn.—What has struck him? An interpretation?"
27. Compare *RFM* VI-43.

they agree in the *language* they use. That is not agreement in opinions but in form of life. (*PI* §241.)[28]

I take it that at least part of the point of this passage is that an opinion is something for which one may reasonably be asked for a justification; whereas what is at issue here is below that level—the "bedrock" where "I have exhausted the justifications" and "my spade is turned" (*PI* §217). The thought is clear in *RFM* VI-28:

> Someone asks me: What is the colour of this flower? I answer: "red".— Are you absolutely sure? Yes, absolutely sure! But may I not have been deceived and called the wrong colour "red"? No. The certainty with which I call the colour "red" is the rigidity of my measuring-rod, it is the rigidity from which I start. When I give descriptions, *that* is not to be brought into doubt. This simply characterizes what we call describing.
>
> (I may of course even here assume a slip of the tongue, but nothing else.)
>
> Following according to the rule is FUNDAMENTAL to our language-game. It characterizes what we call description.

Again (*RFM* VI-35):

> How do I know that the colour that I am now seeing is called "green"? Well, to confirm it I might ask other people, but if they did not agree with me, I should become totally confused and should perhaps take them or myself for crazy. That is to say: I should either no longer trust myself to judge, or no longer react to what they say as to a judgement.
>
> If I am drowning and I shout "Help!", how do I know what the word Help means? Well, that's how I react in this situation.—Now *that* is how I know what "green" means as well and also know how I have to follow the rule in the particular case.[29]

What Wittgenstein is trying to describe is a use of language in which what one does is "to use an expression without a justification" (*PI* §289; compare *RFM* VII-40). One may be tempted to protest: when I say "This is green", in the sort of case he envisages, I do have a justification, namely that the thing in question is green.

---

28. See also *RFM* VI-30, VI-9.
29. With "Well, that's how I react in this situation", compare *PI* §217: ". . . I am inclined to say: 'This is simply what I do.'"

But how can I justify the use of an expression by repeating it? It is thoughts of this sort that lead Wittgenstein to say (*On Certainty* §204):

> Giving grounds, however, justifying the evidence, comes to an end;— but the end is not certain propositions' striking us immediately as true, i.e. it is not a kind of *seeing* on our part; it is our *acting*, which lies at the bottom of the language-game.[30]

Now there is a temptation to understand this on the following lines. At the level of "bedrock" (where justifications have come to an end), there is nothing but verbal behaviour and (no doubt) feelings of constraint. Presumably people's dispositions to behaviour and associated feelings match in interesting ways; but at this ground-floor level there is no question of shared commitments—everything normative fades out of the picture.

This is the picture of what I called "the basic level" that is yielded, in Wright's reading, by the rejection of ratification-independence (see §5 above). I expressed disbelief that a position in which this is how things are at the basic level can accommodate meaning at all. If it is true that a failure to accommodate meaning is the upshot of the position, then it can be attributed to Wittgenstein only at the price of supposing that he does not succeed in his aims. But we are now equipped to see that the attribution falsifies his intentions. When he describes the "bedrock" use of expressions as "without justification", he nevertheless insists (to complete the quotation from *PI* §289):

> To use an expression without a justification does not mean to use it without right.[31]

And it seems clear that the point of this is precisely to prevent the leaching out of norms from our picture of "bedrock"—from our picture, that is, of how things are at the deepest level at which we may

---

30. It is worth noting how paradoxical "it is not a kind of seeing" can seem in the case of such uses of language as saying that something is green. For an illuminating discussion of Wittgenstein's stress on acting as "lying at the bottom of the language-game", see Peter Winch, "Im Anfang war die Tat".

31. Or "wrongfully" (*RFM* VII-30). For a discussion of the translation of "zu Unrecht", see Kripke, p. 74, n. 63.

sensibly contemplate the place of language in the world. To quote again from *RFM* VI-28:

> Following according to the rule is FUNDAMENTAL to our language-game.

By Wittgenstein's lights, it is a mistake to think we can dig down to a level at which we no longer have application for normative notions (like "following according to the rule"). Wright's picture of the basic level, so far from capturing Wittgenstein's view, looks like a case of succumbing to a temptation that he is constantly warning against:

> The difficult thing here is not, to dig down to the ground; no, it is to recognize the ground that lies before us as the ground. (*RFM* VI-31.)

Wittgenstein's problem is to steer a course between a Scylla and a Charybdis. Scylla is the idea that understanding is always interpretation. This idea is disastrous because embracing it confronts us with the dilemma of §4 above: the choice between the paradox that there is no substance to meaning, on the one hand, and the fantastic mythology of the super-rigid machine, on the other. We can avoid Scylla by stressing that, say, calling something "green" can be like crying "Help!" when one is drowning—simply how one has learned to react to this situation. But then we risk steering on to Charybdis—the picture of a basic level at which there are no norms; if we embrace that, I have suggested, then we cannot prevent meaning from coming to seem an illusion. The point of *PI* §198, and part of the point of §§201-202, is that the key to finding the indispensable middle course is the idea of a custom or practice. How can a performance both be nothing but a "blind" reaction to a situation, not an attempt to act on an interpretation (avoiding Scylla); and be a case of going by a rule (avoiding Charybdis)? The answer is: by belonging to a custom (*PI* §198), practice (*PI* §202), or institution (*RFM* VI-31).

Until more is said about how exactly the appeal to communal practice makes the middle course available, this is only a programme for a solution to Wittgenstein's problem. But even if we were at a loss as to how he might have thought the programme could be executed (and I shall suggest that we need not be: see §§10 and 11 below), this would be no ground for ignoring the clear textual evidence that the programme is Wittgenstein's own.

8. What I have claimed might be put like this: Wittgenstein's point is that we have to situate our conception of meaning and understanding within a framework of communal practices. Kripke's reading credits Wittgenstein with the thesis that the notion of meaning something by one's words is "inapplicable to a single person considered in isolation" (p. 79). The upshot is similar, then; and it cannot be denied that the insistence on publicity in Kripke's reading corresponds broadly with a Wittgensteinian thought. But it makes a difference how we conceive the requirement of publicity to emerge.

In my reading, it emerges as a condition for the intelligibility of rejecting a premise—the assimilation of understanding to interpretation—that would present us with an intolerable dilemma. So there are three positions in play: the two horns of the dilemma, and the community-oriented conception of meaning that enables us to decline the choice. Kripke conflates two of these, equating the paradox of *PI* §201—the first horn of the dilemma—with Wittgenstein's conclusion; only so can he take it that when Wittgenstein objects to the "superlative fact" of *PI* §192, he is embracing the paradox of §201.[32] But this is quite wrong. The paradox that Wittgenstein formulates at §201 is not, as Kripke supposes, the mere "paradox" that if we consider an individual in isolation, we do not have the means to make sense of the notion of meaning (something we might hope to disarm by appealing to the idea of a linguistic community). It is the genuine and devastating paradox that meaning is an illusion. Focusing on the individual in isolation from any linguistic community is not the way we fall into this abyss; it is, rather, an aspect of the way we struggle not to, so long as we retain the assumption that generates the dilemma. (See §4 above, on the idiolectic implications of the second horn.) The fundamental trouble is that Kripke makes nothing of Wittgenstein's concern to reject the assimilation of understanding to interpretation; and the nemesis of this oversight is the unconvincingness (see §3 above) of the "sceptical solution" on which Kripke's Wittgenstein must rely.

9. Kripke suggests (p. 3) that, in the light of *PI* §202, we should take it that the essentials of the Private Language Argument are contained

---

32. See n. 20 above.

in the general discussion of rule-following, rather than in the section of the *Investigations* that begins at §243, where it has been more usual to look. I cannot accept Kripke's view that the Private Language Argument is a corollary of the "sceptical solution"; but his structural proposal can be detached from that.

Kripke remarks (pp. 79–80) that the lesson of Wittgenstein's reflections on rule-following is particularly counter-intuitive in two areas: mathematics and talk of "inner" facts. This remark is still true after we have corrected Kripke's account of what the lesson is. In the case of mathematics, the difficulty is that we tend to construe the phenomenology of proof as a matter of glimpses of the super-rigid machinery in operation. In the case of talk of "inner" facts, the difficulty lies in the temptation to suppose that one knows what one means from one's own case (*PI* §347). How can one's linguistic community have any bearing on the matter—beyond its control over the circumstances in which one gave oneself one's private ostensive definitions? Kripke's illuminating suggestion is that the passages usually regarded as containing the Private Language Argument are not rightly so regarded; the argument is essentially complete by *PI* §202, and the familiar passages (§§258, 265, 293, and so forth) are attempts to dissipate this inclination to cite talk of "inner" facts as a counter-example to its conclusion.

This implies that whether those familiar passages carry conviction is, in a sense, irrelevant to the cogency of Wittgenstein's argument. If the inclination to regard talk of "inner" facts as a counter-example persists through them, that by itself cuts no ice. And we are now in a position to see what would be needed in order to undermine the argument. One would need to show either that one or the other of the horns of the dilemma can be comfortably occupied, or that it is not the case that the assimilation of understanding to interpretation, which poses the dilemma, can be resisted only by locating meaning in a framework of communal practices.

If the target of Wittgenstein's reflections is the assimilation of understanding to interpretation, we should expect the areas where his conclusion is peculiarly counter-intuitive to be areas where we are strongly inclined to be comfortable with that assimilation. In the mathematical case, we are particularly prone to the assimilation because—as I remarked above—we are especially inclined to accept its natural accompaniment, the picture of the super-rigid machine.

What about talk of "inner" facts? We are strongly tempted, in this context, to think there could be a private grasp of a concept—something by which, for all its privacy, it would make sense to think of judgements and utterances as constrained. What Wittgenstein's argument, as I read it, requires is the diagnosis that we are here toying with the picture of an interpretation (placed by us on a private ostensive definition)—that it is only so that we can contrive to conceive the matter in terms of concepts and judgements at all. It is true that this pictured interpretation does not readily succumb to the softening effect of the sceptical reasoning—"one interpretation after another, as if each one contented us at least for a moment, until we thought of yet another standing behind it" (*PI* §201). We imagine that in this case we can picture an interpretation that stays hard—one that comprehensively bridges the gap between the private ostensive definition and the judgements that we picture it as dictating. But there cannot be exceptions to the thesis that no interpretation can bridge the gap between the acquisition of a concept and its subsequent employment. It is this, I think that Wittgenstein is trying to make vivid for us in the battery of passages of which the following might stand as an epitome:

> Always get rid of the idea of the private object in this way: assume that it constantly changes, but that you do not notice the change because your memory constantly deceives you (*PI* p. 207).[33]

The idea that a private interpretation can be immune to the softening effect must be an illusion. If we conceive such an interpretation as comprehensively filling the gap, whatever the gap turns out to be, we deprive of all substance the hardness that we picture it as having.

It may be tempting to locate a weakness, in the argument I attribute to Wittgenstein, in the claim that we can steer between Scylla and Charybdis only by appealing to the practice of a community. If it is the notion of a practice that does the work, can we not form a conception of the practice of an individual that would do the trick?[34]

---

33. See, e.g., *PI* §§258, 265, 270. See Anthony Kenny, "The Verification Principle and the Private Language Argument".

34. Simon Blackburn presses what is in effect this question, in "The Individual Strikes Back".

But if one is tempted by this thought, one must search one's conscience to be sure that what one has in mind is not really, after all, the picture of a private interpretation; in which case one is not, after all, steering between Scylla and Charybdis, but resigning oneself to Scylla, leaving oneself fully vulnerable to the line of argument that I have just sketched.[35]

10. Wright's reading of Wittgenstein hinges on this conditional: if possession of a concept were correctly conceived as grasp of a (ratification-independent) pattern, then there would be no knowing for sure how someone else understands an expression. This conditional underlies Wright's conviction that, when we entertain the "pattern" idea,

> ... the kind of reflective grasp of meaning appealed to is essentially *idiolectic*—it is a matter of each of us discerning the character of his own understanding of expressions. There is no temptation to claim a reflective knowledge of features of *others'* understanding of a particular expression—except against the background of the hypothesis that it coincides with one's own.[36]

We can summarize Wright's reading by saying that he takes Wittgenstein to propound a *modus tollens* argument with the conditional as major premise. Thus: the idea of knowledge of idiolectic meaning is an illusion; therefore possession of a concept cannot be correctly conceived as grasp of a (ratification-independent) pattern.

The basis of this argument is, as Wright points out, "the fundamental anti-realist thesis that we have understanding only of concepts of which we can distinctively manifest our understanding" (p. 221). Wright would ground both premises of the *modus tollens* argument on anti-realism. The justification for the minor premise (see §2 above) is that the picture of an idiolectic rule makes no room for a distinction between actually conforming and merely having the impression that one is conforming. In Wright's reading the thought

---

35. In this section I have aimed to describe only the *structure* of the Private Language Argument. A fuller account of how it works would require, in addition, discharging the unfinished business noted at the end of §7 above. See especially §11 below.

36. Wright, *Wittgenstein on the Foundations of Mathematics*, p. 354. A footnote adds: "Or with one's understanding of another specified expression."

here is an anti-realist one: that in an idiolectic context one could not distinctively manifest—not even with a manifestation to oneself—a difference in one's understanding of "I am actually conforming" and "I have the impression of conforming".[37] What underlies the major premise—the conditional—is the anti-realist conception of what it is to manifest understanding to others.

According to that conception, the behaviour that counts as manifesting understanding to others must be characterizable, in such a way as to display its status as such a manifestation, without benefit of a command of the language in question. Without that proviso, the "manifestation challenge" that anti-realists direct against the truth-conditional conception of meaning would be trivialized.[38] The challenge would hold no fears for the truth-conditional conception if one were allowed to count as satisfying the requirement of manifestation by such behaviour as saying—manifestly, at least to someone who understands the language one is speaking—that such-and-such is the case. So the distinctive manifestations allowed by anti-realism consist, rather, in such behaviour as assenting to a sentence in such-and-such circumstances.[39]

Now what—besides itself—could be fully manifested by a piece of behaviour, or a series of pieces of behaviour, described in accordance with the anti-realist requirement?[40] Perhaps the behaviour would license us to attribute a disposition; but how can we extrapolate to a determinate conception of what the disposition is a disposition to do? Our characterization of the manifesting behaviour is not allowed to exploit understanding of the language in question; so even if, in

---

37. This is how Wright thinks the Private Language Argument is to be understood. Note that the requirement of manifestation is not initially imposed, in this line of thought, as a requirement of *public* manifestation. We are supposed to be brought to see that public manifestation is what is required in consequence of an independent (non-question-begging) critique of the idea of idiolectic understanding. On the structure of Wright's reading, see §14 below.

38. For the terminology "manifestation challenge", see Wright, "Realism, Truth-Value Links, Other Minds and the Past", pp. 112-3. For the substance of the challenge, see, e.g., Dummett, *Frege: Philosophy of Language*, p. 467.

39. It is actually an illusion to think that this kind of characterization of behaviour conforms to the anti-realist requirement: see my "Anti-Realism and the Epistemology of Understanding". But in the course of arguing, as I am, that the programme is misconceived in principle, there is no point in jibbing at the details of its purported execution.

40. For "fully" see Dummett, *Frege: Philosophy of Language*, p. 467.

our innocence, we start out by conceiving that as grasp of "a network of determinate patterns",[41] we are debarred from extrapolating along the pathways of the network. It seems clear that within the rules of this game any extrapolation could only be inductive, which means that if we accept the requirement that understanding be fully manifested in behaviour, no extrapolation is licensed at all. The upshot is this: the anti-realist requirement of manifestation precludes any conception of understanding as grasp of a network of patterns. And this is precisely the conclusion Wright draws.[42]

The obstacle to accepting this argument is the normative character of the notion of meaning. As I have granted, Wright aims to accommodate that: he would insist that his conclusion is not that concepts have no normative status, but that the patterns they dictate are not independent of our ratification. But the trouble is (see §§5 and 7) that the denial of ratification-independence, by Wright's own insistence, yields a picture of the relation between the communal language and the world in which norms are obliterated. And once we have this picture, it seems impossible simply to retain alongside it a different picture, in which the openness of an individual to correction by his fellows means that he is subject to norms. The first picture irresistibly claims primacy, leaving our openness to correction by our fellows looking like, at best, an explanation of our propensity to the illusion that we are subject to norms. If this is correct, it turns

---

41. Wright, *Wittgenstein on the Foundations of Mathematics*, p. 220.
42. At least in *Wittgenstein on the Foundations of Mathematics*. Contrast "Strawson on Anti-Realism", p. 294: ". . . supppose [someone] has this knowledge: of every state of affairs criterially warranting the assertion, or denial, of 'John is in pain', he knows in a practical sense both that it has that status and under what conditions it would be brought out that its status was merely criterial; that is, he knows the 'overturn-conditions' of any situation criterially warranting the assertion, or denial, of 'John is in pain'. *No doubt we could not know for sure* that someone had this knowledge; but the stronger our grounds for thinking that he did, the more baffling would be the allegation that he did not grasp the assertoric content of 'John is in pain'." (My emphasis.) Here Wright contemplates maintaining a version (formulated in terms of criteria) of the idea that understanding is grasp of a pattern of use, and accordingly opts—as his overall position indeed requires—for the other horn of this dilemma: the thesis, namely, that one cannot have certain knowledge of the character of someone else's understanding. What is remarkable is Wright's insouciance about this move: it openly flouts the fundamental motivation of anti-realism, which is what Wright is supposed to be defending against Strawson in the passage I have quoted. It seems clear that the contrasting position of *Wittgenstein on the Foundations of Mathematics* is the only one an anti-realist can consistently occupy.

Wright's argument on its head: a condition for the possibility of finding real application for the notion of meaning at all is that we reject anti-realism.

I think this transcendental argument against anti-realism is fully cogent. But it is perhaps unlikely to carry conviction unless supplemented with a satisfying account of how anti-realism goes wrong. (Providing this supplementation will help to discharge the unfinished business that I noted at the end of §7.)

11. According to anti-realism, people's sharing a language is constituted by appropriate correspondences in their dispositions to linguistic behaviour, as characterized without drawing on command of the language, and hence not in terms of the contents of their utterances. The motivation for this thesis is admirable: a recoil from the idea that assigning a meaning to an utterance by a speaker of one's language is forming a hypothesis about something concealed behind the surface of his linguistic behaviour. But there are two possible directions in which this recoil might move one. One—the anti-realist direction—is to retain the conception of the surface that makes the idea natural, and resolutely attempt to locate meaning on the surface, so conceived. That this attempt fails is the conclusion of the transcendental argument. The supplementation that the argument needs is to point out the availability of the alternative direction: namely, to reject the conception of the surface that anti-realism shares with the position it recoils from. According to this different view, the outward aspect of linguistic behaviour—what a speaker makes available to others—must be characterized in terms of the contents of utterances (the thoughts they express). Of course such an outward aspect cannot be conceived as made available to just anyone; command of the language is needed in order to put one in direct cognitive contact with that in which someone's meaning consists.[43] (This might seem to represent command of the language as a mysterious sort of X-ray vision; but only in the context of the rejected conception of the surface.)

Wittgenstein warns us not to try to dig below "bedrock". But it is difficult, in reading him, to avoid acquiring a sense of what, as it

---

43. See my "Anti-Realism and the Epistemology of Understanding".

were, lies down there: a web of facts about behaviour and "inner" episodes, describable without using the notion of meaning. One is likely to be struck by the sheer contingency of the resemblances between individuals on which, in this vision, the possibility of meaning seems to depend, and hence impressed by an apparent precariousness in our making sense of one another.[44] There is an authentic insight here, but one that is easily distorted; correcting the distortion will help to bring out what is wrong with the anti-realist construal of Wittgenstein.

The distorted version of the insight can be put as a dilemma, on these lines. Suppose that, in claiming a "reflective knowledge" of the principle of application of some expression, I claim to speak for others as well as myself. In that case my claim (even if restricted to a definitely specified other: say my interlocutor in a particular conversation) is indefinitely vulnerable to the possibility of an unfavourable future. Below "bedrock" there is nothing but contingency; so at any time in the future my interlocutor's use of the expression in question may simply stop conforming to the pattern that I expect. And that would retrospectively undermine my present claim to be able to vouch for the character of his understanding. So I can claim to know his pattern now only "against the background of the hypothesis that it coincides with [my] own".[45] If, then, we retain the conception of understanding as grasp of patterns, the feeling of precariousness becomes the idea that what we think of as a shared language is at best a set of corresponding idiolects, with our grounds for believing in the correspondence no better than inductive. The only alternative—the other horn of the dilemma—is, with Wright, to give up the conception of understanding as grasp of (ratification-independent) patterns. This turns the feeling of precariousness into the idea that I cannot know for sure that my interlocutor and I will continue to march in step. But on this horn my present claim to understand him is not undermined by that concession: my understanding him now is a matter of our being in step now, and does not require a shared pattern extending into the future.

---

44. See *Wittgenstein on Rules and Private Language*, p. 97; compare Cavell, *Must We Mean What We Say?*, p. 52, and Essay 10 above.

45. Wright, *Wittgenstein on the Foundations of Mathematics*, p. 354.

What is wrong with this, in Wittgensteinian terms, is that it conflates propositions at (or above) "bedrock" with propositions about the contingencies that lie below. (See, for instance, *RFM* VI-49.) Its key thought is that, if I claim to know someone else's pattern, I bind myself to a prediction of the uses of language that he will make in various possible future circumstances, with these uses characterized in sub-"bedrock" terms. (That is why coming to see the contingency of the resemblances, at this level, on which meaning rests is supposed to induce appreciation that knowledge of another person's pattern could at best be inductive.) But when I claim understanding of someone else, and construe this as knowledge of the patterns to which his present utterance owes allegiance, what I claim to know is not that in such-and-such circumstances he will do so and so, but rather at most that that is what he will do if he sticks to his patterns.[46] And that is not a prediction at all. (Compare *RFM* VI-15.)

It is true that a certain disorderliness below "bedrock" would undermine the applicability of the notion of rule-following. So the underlying contingencies bear an intimate relation to the notion of rule-following—a relation that Wittgenstein tries to capture by saying "It is as if we had hardened the empirical proposition into a rule" (*RFM* VI-22). But recognizing the intimate relation must not be allowed to obscure the difference of levels.[47] If we respect the difference of levels, what we make of the feeling of precariousness will be as follows. When I understand another person, I know the rules he is going by.

---

46. Even this is too much. It passes muster where the "pattern" idea is least metaphorical, namely in the case of continuation of a series. But in the general case, the idea of a corpus of determinate predictions to which a claim of present understanding would commit one is absurd. (See n. 4 above.) The point I am making here is a version of one that Rush Rhees makes, in terms of a distinction between the general practice of linguistic behaviour and the following of rules, at pp. 55–6 of "Can There Be a Private Language?". It disarms, as an objection to Wittgenstein, the insightful remarks of Jerry A. Fodor, *The Language of Thought*, pp. 71–2.

47. The difference of levels is the subject of Wittgenstein's remarks about "the limits of empiricism": *RFM* III-71, VII-17, VII-21. (The source of the phrase is Russell's paper of that name.) See Wright, *Wittgenstein on the Foundations of Mathematics*, p. 220. I think the point of the remarks is, very roughly, that empiricism can deal only with what is below "bedrock"; the limits of empiricism (which "are not assumptions unguaranteed, or intuitively known to be correct: they are ways in which we make comparisons and in which we act": *RFM* VII-21, compare *On Certainty* §204, quoted in §7 above) lie above it (outside its reach), at "bedrock" level. Wright, by contrast, seems to interpret the passages as if Wittgenstein's view were that for all its limits empiricism contained the truth.

My right to claim to understand him is precarious, in that nothing but a tissue of contingencies stands in the way of my losing it. But to envisage its loss is not necessarily to envisage its turning out that I never had the right at all. The difference of levels suffices to drive a wedge between these; contrast the second horn of the above dilemma, on which inserting the wedge requires abandonment of the idea that mutual understanding is mutual knowledge of shared commitments.[48]

Anti-realists hold that initiation into a common language consists in acquisition of linguistic propensities describable without use of the notion of meaning. They thereby perpetrate exactly the conflation of levels against which Wittgenstein warns; someone's following a rule, according to anti-realism, is constituted by the obtaining of resemblances, describable in sub-"bedrock" terms, between his behaviour and that of his fellows. Not that anti-realists would put it like that: it is another way of making the same point to say that they locate "bedrock" lower than it is—not accommodating the fact that "following according to the rule is FUNDAMENTAL to our language-game" (*RFM* VI-28; see §7 above). If, by contrast, we satisfy the motivation of anti-realism in the different way that I distinguished above, then we refuse to countenance sub-"bedrock" (meaning-free) characterizations of what meaning something by one's words consists in, and thus respect Wittgenstein's distinction of levels.

We make possible, moreover, a radically different conception of what it is to belong to a linguistic community. Anti-realists picture a community as a collection of individuals presenting to one another exteriors that match in certain respects. They hope to humanize this bleak picture by claiming that what meaning consists in lies on those exteriors as they conceive them. But the transcendental argument reveals this hope as vain. A related thought is this: if regularities in the verbal behaviour of an isolated individual, described in norm-free terms, do not add up to meaning, it is quite obscure how it could somehow make all the difference if there are several individuals with

---

48. Christopher Peacocke, at p. 88 of "Rule-Following: The Nature of Wittgenstein's Arguments", implies that statements about rule-following *supervene*, in Wittgenstein's view, on sub-"bedrock" statements. There may be an acceptable interpretation of this; but on the most natural interpretation, it would make statements about rule-following vulnerable to future loss of mutual intelligibility in just the way I am objecting to.

matching regularities.[49] The picture of a linguistic community degenerates, then, under anti-realist assumptions, into a picture of a mere aggregate of individuals whom we have no convincing reason not to conceive as opaque to one another. If, on the other hand, we reject the anti-realist restriction on what counts as manifesting one's understanding, we entitle ourselves to this thought: shared membership in a linguistic community is not just a matter of matching in aspects of an exterior that we present to anyone whatever, but equips us to make our minds available to one another, by confronting one another with a different exterior from that which we present to outsiders.

Wittgenstein's problem was to explain how understanding can be other than interpretation (see §7 above). This non-anti-realist conception of a linguistic community gives us a genuine right to the following answer: shared command of a language equips us to know one another's meaning without needing to arrive at that knowledge by interpretation, because it equips us to hear someone else's meaning in his words. Anti-realists would claim this right too, but the claim is rendered void by the merely additive upshot of their picture of what it is to share a language. In the different picture I have described, the response to Wittgenstein's problem works because a linguistic community is conceived as bound together, not by a match in mere externals (facts accessible to just anyone), but by a capacity for a meeting of minds.

When we had no more than an abstract characterization of Wittgenstein's response, as an appeal to the notion of communal

---

49. Blackburn writes ("Rule-Following and Moral Realism", p. 183): "... we can become gripped by what I call a *wooden* picture of the use of language, according to which the only fact of the matter is that in certain situations people use words, perhaps with various feelings like 'that fits', and so on. This wooden picture makes no room for the further fact that in applying or withholding a word people may be conforming to a pre-existent rule. But just because of this, it seems to make no room for the idea that in using their words they are expressing judgments. Wittgenstein must have felt that publicity, the fact that others do the same, was the magic ingredient turning the wooden picture into the full one. It is most obscure to me that it fills this role: a lot of wooden persons with propensities to make noises is just more of whatever one of them is." It will be apparent that I have a great deal of sympathy with this complaint. Where I believe Blackburn goes wrong is in thinking it tells against Wittgenstein himself, as opposed to the position that Wittgenstein has been saddled with by a certain set of interpreters (among whom I did not intend to enrol myself in Essay 10 above, the paper to which Blackburn is responding).

practice, there seemed to be justice in this query: if the concept of a communal practice can magic meaning into our picture, should not this power be credited to the concept of a practice as such—so that the practice of an individual might serve just as well? (See §7 above.) But if Wittgenstein's position is the one I have described in this section, it is precisely the notion of a *communal* practice that is needed, and not some notion that could equally be applied outside the context of a community. The essential point is the way in which one person can know another's meaning without interpretation. Contrary to Wright's reading, it is only because we *can* have what Wright calls "a reflective knowledge of features of *others'* understanding of a particular expression"[50] that meaning is possible at all.[51]

12. Wittgenstein's reflections on rule-following attack a certain familiar picture of facts and truth, which I shall formulate like this. A genuine fact must be a matter of the way things are in themselves, utterly independently of us. So a genuinely true judgement must be, at least potentially, an exercise of pure thought; if human nature is necessarily implicated in the very formation of the judgement, that precludes our thinking of the corresponding fact as properly independent of us, and hence as a proper fact at all.[52]

We can find this picture of genuine truth compelling only if we either forget that truth-bearers are such only because they are meaningful, or suppose that meanings take care of themselves, needing, as it were, no help from us. This latter supposition is the one that is relevant to our concerns. If we make it, we can let the judging subject, in our picture of true judgement, shrink to a locus of pure thought,

---

50. *Wittgenstein on the Foundations of Mathematics*, p. 354.

51. If I am right to suppose that any merely aggregative conception of a linguistic community falsifies Wittgenstein, then it seems that the parallel Kripke draws with Hume's discussion of causation (independently proposed by Blackburn, "Rule-Following and Moral Realism", pp. 182–3) is misconceived. Wittgenstein's picture of language contains no conception of the individual such as would correspond to the individual cause-effect pair, related only by contiguity and succession, in Hume's picture of causation.

52. The later Wittgenstein may have (perhaps unjustly) found a form of this picture in the *Tractatus*. On the relation between the later work and the *Tractatus,* see Peter Winch, "Introduction: The Unity of Wittgenstein's Philosophy", especially the very illuminating discussion at pp. 9–15.

while the fact that judging is a human activity fades into insignificance.

Now Wittgenstein's reflections on rule-following undermine this picture by undermining the supposition that meanings take care of themselves. A particular performance, "inner" or overt, can be an application of a concept—a judgement or a meaningful utterance—only if it owes allegiance to constraints that the concept imposes. And being governed by such constraints is not being led, in some occult way, by an autonomous meaning (the super-rigid machinery), but acting within a communal custom. The upshot is that if something matters for one's being a participant in the relevant customs, it matters equally for one's being capable of making any judgements at all. We have to give up that picture of genuine truth, in which the maker of a true judgement can shrink to a point of pure thought, abstracted from anything that might make him distinctively and recognizably one of us.

It seems right to regard that familiar picture as a kind of realism. It takes meaning to be wholly autonomous (one is tempted to say "out there"); this is reminiscent of realism as the term is used in the old debate about universals. And it embraces an extreme form of the thesis that the facts are not up to us; this invites the label "realism" understood in a way characteristic of more recent debates. But if we allow ourselves to describe the recoil from the familiar picture as a recoil from realism, there are two points that we must be careful not to let this obscure.

First: the recoil has nothing to do with rejection of the truth-conditional conception of meaning, properly understood. That conception has no need to camouflage the fact that truth-conditions are necessarily given by us, in a language that we understand. When we say "'Diamonds are hard' is true if and only if diamonds are hard", we are just as much involved on the right-hand side as the reflections on rule-following tell us we are. There is a standing temptation to miss this obvious truth, and to suppose that the right-hand side somehow presents us with a possible fact, pictured as a unconceptualized configuration of things in themselves. But we can find the connection between meaning and truth illuminating without succumbing to that temptation.

Second: the recoil is from an extreme form of the thesis that the facts are not up to us, not from that thesis in any form whatever.

What Wittgenstein's polemic against the picture of the super-rigid machine makes untenable is the thesis that possessing a concept is grasping a pattern of application that extends *of itself* to new cases. (See §4 above.) In Wright's reading, that is the same as saying that it deprives us of the conception of grasp of ratification-independent patterns. But rejection of ratification-independence obliterates meaning altogether (see §§5, 7, 10 above). In effect, the transcendental argument shows that there *must* be a middle position. Understanding is grasping patterns that extend to new cases independently of our ratification, as is required for meaning to be other than an illusion (and—not incidentally—for the intuitive notion of objectivity to have a use); but the constraints imposed by our concepts do not have the platonistic autonomy with which they are credited in the picture of the super-rigid machinery.

As before (compare §11 above), what obscures the possibility of this position is the "anti-realist" attempt to get below "bedrock". Wright suggests that the emergence of a consensus on whether, say, to call some newly encountered object "yellow" is subject to no norms. That is indeed how it seems if we allow ourselves to picture the communal language in terms of sub-"bedrock" resemblances in behaviour and phenomenology. But if we respect Wittgenstein's injunction not to dig below the ground, we must say that the community "goes right or wrong" according to whether the object in question is, or is not, *yellow*; and nothing can make its being yellow, or not, dependent on our ratification of the judgement that that is how things are. In Wittgenstein's eyes, as I read him, Wright's claim that "for the community itself there is no authority, so no standard to meet" can be, at very best, an attempt to say something that cannot be said but only shown. It may have some merit, conceived in that light; but attributing it to Wittgenstein as a doctrine can yield only distortion.

Wittgenstein writes, at *RFM* II-61:

> Finitism and behaviourism are quite similar trends. Both say, but surely, all we have here is. . . . Both deny the existence of something, both with a view to escaping from a confusion.[53]

---

53. Kripke discusses this passage at pp. 106–7; but I believe his attribution to Wittgenstein of the "sceptical paradox" and the "sceptical solution" prevents him from fully appreciating its point.

The point about finitism is this. It recoils, rightly, from the mythology of the super-rigid machinery—the patterns that extend of themselves, without limit, beyond any point we take them to. But it equates this recoil with rejecting any conception of patterns that extend, without limit, beyond any such point. This is like the behaviourist idea that in order to escape from the confused idea of the mental as essentially concealed from others behind behaviour, we have to reject the mental altogether. The idealism that Wright reads into Wittgenstein seems to be another similar trend. (Clearly the remark does not applaud the trends it discusses.)

13. In this section I want to mention two sets of passages in Wittgenstein of which we are now placed to make better sense than Wright can.

First: in Wright's reading, the "pattern" idea is inextricably connected with the picture of idiolectic understanding. But this does not seem to be how Wittgenstein sees things. Wittgenstein does not scruple to say that a series "is defined . . . by the training in proceeding according to the rule" (*RFM* VI-16). And at *Zettel* §308 he writes:

> Instead of "and so on" he might have said: "Now you know what I mean." And his explanation would simply be a *definition* of the expression "following the rule +1" . . .

Again, *PI* §208 and the remarks that follow it contain a sustained attack on the idea that successfully putting someone through the sort of training that is meant to "point beyond" the examples given (see §208) is getting him "to *guess* the essential thing" (*PI* §210). For Wright, when these passages reject the picture of a leap to a personal understanding, they should be *eo ipso* rejecting the "pattern" idea. But Wittgenstein combines criticism of the "leap" picture with conceding (§209) how natural it is to think of our understanding as reaching beyond all the examples given. (Wright would construe this concession in terms of his purged version of the "pattern" idea. But we can make sense of what Wittgenstein says without saddling him with the problems generated by denial of ratification-independence.)

Second: Wittgenstein sometimes (for instance at *PI* §151) discusses the idea that one can grasp the principle of a series, or a meaning, "in a flash". Wright suggests that the idea of this "flash" can be nothing but the idea of a leap to a purely personal understanding.[54] But I see no reason to accept that Wittgenstein intends this identification. In fact, the suggestion casts a gratuitous slur on his phenomenological perceptiveness. The idea that the meaning of an expression can be present in an instant is just as tempting about someone else's meaning as it is about one's own; and Wittgenstein is perfectly aware of this:

> When someone says the word "cube" to me, for example, I know what it means. But can the whole *use* of the word come before my mind, when I *understand* it in that way? (*PI* §139; compare §138.)

Wright's view must be that the intended answer to this question is "No"—that Wittgenstein intends to show up as an illusion the idea that one can grasp someone else's pattern in a flash. But the only illusion that Wright explains to us in this neighbourhood is the illusion of supposing that one could have an idiolectic grasp of a pattern. So Wright's Wittgenstein owes us something for which we search the writings of the actual Wittgenstein in vain: an explanation of how it is that we not only fall into that illusion but misconceive its character—mistaking what is in fact the supposition that we can guess at someone else's pattern for (what seems on the face of it very different) the supposition that we can hear it in his utterances.

We are now placed to see that this latter supposition is not, in Wittgenstein's view, an illusion at all. "Grasping the whole use in a flash" is not to be dismissed as expressing an incorrigibly confused picture—the picture of a leap to an idiolectic understanding—but to be carefully understood in the light of the thesis that there is a way of grasping a rule which is not an interpretation. In that light, we can see that there is nothing wrong with the idea that one can grasp in a flash the principle of a series one is being taught; and equally that there is nothing wrong with the idea that one can hear someone else's meaning in his words. The "interpretation" prejudice insidiously tempts us to put a fantastic mythological construction on these conceptions; the right response to that is not to abandon the conception but to exorcize the "interpretation" prejudice and so return them to sobriety. ("Really the only thing wrong with what you say is the expression 'in a queer way'": *PI* §195.)

---

54. *Wittgenstein on the Foundations of Mathematics*, pp. 30–1.

At *PI* §534, Wittgenstein writes:

> Hearing a word in a particular sense. How queer that there should be such a thing!
>
> Phrased *like this*, emphasized like this, heard in this way, this sentence is the first of a series in which a transition is made to *these* sentences, pictures, actions.
>
> ((A multitude of familiar paths leads off from these words in every direction.))[55]

What are these "familiar paths"? Presumably, for instance, continuations of the conversation that would make sense: not, then, "patterns" in precisely the sense with which we have been concerned (which would be, as these paths would not, cases of "going on doing the same thing"), but they raise similar issues. Suppose that, in describing a series of utterances that in fact constitutes an intelligible conversation, we conform to the anti-realist account of how meaning must be manifested. We shall have to describe each member of the series without drawing on command of the language in question. Such a description will blot out the relations of meaning between the members of the series, in virtue of which it constitutes an intelligible conversation; what is left will be, at best, a path that one could trace out inductively (whether predicting or retrodicting).[56] Wright's demonstration that anti-realism cannot countenance ratification-independent patterns should work for these "familiar paths" too. An anti-realist cannot extrapolate, from what is done in his presence on an occasion, along paths marked out by meaning; and inductive extrapolation is against the rule that we must restrict ourselves to what is fully manifested in linguistic behaviour. It is obscure to me what

---

55. The last sentence is quoted from *PI* §525. A related passage is *PI* II.xi: the connection between the topics of seeing an aspect and "experiencing the meaning of a word" is drawn explicitly at pp. 214, 215.

56. At pp. 130–1 of "What Is a Theory of Meaning? (II)", Dummett writes: "We do not expect, nor should we want, to achieve a deterministic theory of meaning for a language, even one which is deterministic only in principle: we should not expect to be able to give a theory from which, together with all other relevant conditions (the physical environment of a speaker, the utterances of other speakers, etc.), we could predict the exact utterances of any one speaker, any more than, by a study of the rules and strategy of a game, we expect to be able to predict actual play." But in the context of the anti-realist restriction, all that this can mean is that we must content ourselves with weaker relations of the same general kind (inductively traceable, not meaning-dependent) as those that would be involved in a theory of the deterministic sort we are to renounce.

interpretation of the passage I have quoted is available to Wright. What seems to be the case is that anti-realism, by, in effect, looking for "bedrock" lower than it is, blocks off the obvious and surely correct reading: that hearing a word in one sense rather than another is hearing it in one position rather than another in the network of possible patterns of making sense that we learn to find ourselves in when we acquire mastery of a language.

14. We can centre the issue between Wright's reading and mine on this question: how does Wittgenstein's insistence on publicity emerge? In my reading, the answer is this: it emerges as a condition of the possibility of rejecting the assimilation of understanding to interpretation, which poses an intolerable dilemma. In Wright's reading, the answer is this: it emerges as the only alternative left, after the notion of idiolectic understanding has been scotched by a self-contained argument that is epitomized by this passage (*PI* §258):

> ... One would like to say: whatever is going to seem right to me is right. And that only means that here we can't talk about "right".

Wright takes the thought here to be an anti-realist one, to the effect that the distinction between being right and seeming right is shown to be empty, in the idiolectic case, by the impossibility of manifesting a grasp of it, even to oneself. (See §10 above.) Given this, I suppose Wright takes it that sheer consistency requires construing the appeal to the community, shown to be obligatory by virtue of being the only remaining possibility, in an anti-realist way.

Now it is true that the idiolectic conception of understanding is a corollary of the second horn of the dilemma. (See §4 above.) So my reading need not exclude a self-contained argument against that idea, constituting part of the demonstration that the dilemma is intolerable. On such a view, the insistence on publicity would emerge twice over: first as a direct implication of the self-contained argument, and second, indirectly, as required by the rejection of the dilemma. In fact I think this complexity is unnecessary. Wittgenstein has plenty to say against the second horn of the dilemma—the picture of the super-rigid machine—without needing, for his case against it and therefore against accepting the dilemma, the envisaged self-contained argument against this corollary. And I have explained (in §9 above) how passages like the one I quoted above from *PI* §258, which Wright takes as formulations of the self-contained argument, are intelligible in the context of the second, indirect route to the requirement of publicity. But the real flaw in Wright's reading, in my view, is not that it countenances the first route, but that it omits the second. Like Kripke (see §8 above), Wright makes nothing of Wittgenstein's concern—which figures at the centre of my reading— to attack the assimilation of understanding to interpretation.

This oversight shows itself in Wright's willingness to attribute the following line of thought to Wittgenstein:

> ... the investigation-independent truth of statements requires that their truth is settled, autonomously and without the need of human interference, by their meanings and the character of the relevant facts. For a complex set of reasons, however, no notion of meaning can be legitimised which will play this role ... the meaning of a statement, if it is to make the relevant autonomous contribution towards determining that statement's truth-value, cannot be thought of as fully determined by previous uses of that statement or, if it is a novel statement, by previous uses of its constituents and by its syntax; for those factors can always be reconciled with the statement's having any truth-value, no matter what the worldly facts are taken to be. The same goes for prior phenomenological episodes—imagery, models—in the minds of the linguistically competent. Nothing, therefore, in the previous use of the statement, or of its constituents, or in the prior streams of consciousness of competent speakers, is, if its meaning is in conjunction with the facts to determine its truth-value, sufficient to fix its meaning. So what does?[57]

This is essentially the argument that generates the paradox of *PI* §201; and it can be attributed to Wittgenstein only at the cost of ignoring, like Kripke, that section's second paragraph.

The result of the oversight is that, whereas Wittgenstein's key thought is that the dilemma must be avoided, Wright's reading leaves the dilemma unchallenged. Wittgenstein obviously attacks the

---

57. "Strict Finitism", p. 250. Note also *Wittgenstein on the Foundations of Mathematics*, p. 22, where Wright identifies the second speaker in the dialogue of *RFM* I-113 ("However many rules you give me—I give a rule which justifies *my* employment of your rules") with Wittgenstein himself; and p. 216 (a passage I quoted in §2 above), where it is the susceptibility of all explanations to unintended *interpretations* that is said to push us into the idea of understanding as essentially idiolectic.

second horn of the dilemma—the picture of the super-rigid machinery. The consequence of leaving the dilemma unchallenged is thus to locate Wittgenstein on its first horn—embracing the paradox of §201. This disastrous upshot does not, of course, correspond to Wright's *intentions* in his interpretation of Wittgenstein. (Contrast Kripke, who can be content to attribute acceptance of the paradox of §201 to Wittgenstein because he misses its devastating character.) Nevertheless, it is where his reading leaves us (see §§5, 7, 10 above): a fitting nemesis for its inattention to Wittgenstein's central concern.

The villain of the piece—what makes it impossible for Wright to accommodate Wittgenstein's insistence that understanding need not be interpretation—is the anti-realist conception of our knowledge of others. (See §§11 and 12 above. Contrary to what, at the beginning of this section, I took Wright to suppose, the cogency of a passage like *PI* §258, against the picture of idiolectic understanding, is quite unconnected with the anti-realist view of what it is to manifest understanding to others.) From Wright's reading, then, we can learn something important: that there cannot be a position that is both anti-realist and genuinely hospitable to meaning, and that the construal of Wittgenstein as the source of anti-realism, often nowadays taken for granted, is a travesty.

ESSAY 12

Meaning and Intentionality in Wittgenstein's Later Philosophy

1. Suppose someone correctly understands the meaning of, say, "Add 2". Her understanding must be something with which, if she is aiming to put that understanding into practice and has reached "996, 998, 1000" in writing out the resulting series, only writing "1002" next will *accord*. It seems essential to be able to make this kind of use of notions like that of accord if we are to be entitled to think in terms of meaning and understanding at all. In sections of the *Philosophical Investigations*[1] that have come to be regarded as central, and elsewhere in his later work, Wittgenstein is clearly concerned with difficulties we can fall into in trying to maintain our hold on this kind of use of notions like that of accord. (See §§198, 201.)

These passages have become increasingly familiar, largely under the impetus of Saul Kripke's celebrated reading of them.[2] Many of the ingredients for a proper reading are now well understood. But I believe the thrust of Wittgenstein's reflections is often misconceived. The result is that in spite of the recent surge of attention, this part of his legacy is still not widely available to contemporary philosophy. In this paper, I shall offer a brief and dogmatic overview, in the hope that, in the absence of qualification and nuance, the overall lines of a way to place Wittgenstein's later thinking can stand out more clearly.

---

1. Subsequent references not otherwise signalled will be to this work.
2. Saul A. Kripke, *Wittgenstein on Rules and Private Language*.

2. There is a quite general link between the idea of understanding or grasp of a meaning, on the one hand, and the idea of behaviour classifiable as correct or incorrect in the light of the meaning grasped, that is, classifiable as in accord with the meaning grasped or not, on the other. Wittgenstein concentrates on the case of extending a series of numbers in the light of one's understanding of the principle of the series. In that case, given where one has got to in the series, there is nothing but the relevant understanding for one's behaviour to accord with or not as the case may be. (The understanding may be of instructions for continuing the series; or, in the absence of explicit instructions, simply of the principle of the series.) Contrast the ordinary use of an expression whose meaning suits it for describing the empirical world. Here, if one's utterance is to be correct, it needs to be faithful not only to the meaning of the expression but also to the layout of the empirical world. The series-extension case isolates the way in which grasped meanings in particular give a normatively characterizable shape to the space of options within which behaviour is undertaken; so it brings that point into especially clear focus. But the point applies to understanding quite generally.

3. Suppose we ask: what could someone's grasp of, say, the meaning of the instruction "Add 2" consist in, given that it would need to bear this normative relation to her behaviour?

In order to get the difficulties going, we need to feel the attractions of a certain conception of the region of reality in which we would most naturally look for someone's grasp of a meaning—intuitively, that person's mind. The conception is one according to which such regions of reality are populated exclusively with items that, considered in themselves, do not sort things outside the mind, including specifically bits of behaviour, into those that are correct or incorrect in the light of those items. According to this conception, the contents of minds are items that, considered in themselves, just "stand there like a sign-post", as Wittgenstein puts it (§85). Considered in itself, a sign-post is just a board or something similar, perhaps bearing an inscription, on a post. Something so described does not, as such, sort behaviour into correct and incorrect—behaviour that counts as following the sign-post and behaviour that does not. What does sort behaviour into what counts as following the sign-post and what does not is not an inscribed board affixed to a post, considered in itself, but such an object *under a certain interpretation*—such an object interpreted as a sign-post pointing the way to a certain destination.

If we conceive the contents of the mind on the model of sign-posts, considered in themselves, we seem to need a parallel move. It does not matter what item we might at first have been inclined to pick out, from the inventory we are restricting ourselves to, as a plausible candidate for being what someone's grasp of the meaning of "Add 2" consists in. Whatever it is, considered in itself it cannot be what we hoped it would be, since it just "stands there like a sign-post". What we need is not that item, whatever it was, considered in itself, but that item under the right interpretation.

But now we are in trouble. On our present way of thinking, someone's understanding the instruction, or the principle of the series, would need to involve her putting the right interpretation on something; only so can we get the concept of accord into play, as we need to in order to get the concept of understanding into play. (It does not matter what we suppose she puts the interpretation on: perhaps just the instruction itself as she heard it.) But there is just as much reason for asking what her putting the right interpretation on something could consist in as there was for asking, in the first place, what her understanding "Add 2" could consist in. And it is just as plausible that we would need to look for the answer to this second question in a region of reality populated by items that, considered in themselves, just "stand there" as it was in the case of the original question.

The idea of interpretation seemed hopeful because it promised to enable us to attribute, to items that are in themselves normatively inert, a derivative power to impose a normative classification on items in the world outside the mind—thus bringing into play the application for the concept of accord that seems to be required if the concepts of meaning and understanding are to get a grip. Although no behaviour counts as following (acting in accord with) an inscribed board affixed to a post, considered merely as such, nevertheless when such an object is interpreted as a sign-post pointing the way to a certain destination, it is determined that going in a certain direction counts as following the sign-post—acting in accord with its instructions for reaching that destination. The hope was that we could exploit this normativity-introducing effect of the idea of interpretation quite generally.

But the hope is bound to be disappointed. As long as the restricted inventory of items we can appeal to, in answering our questions as to what this or that consists in, is in force, the problem that the idea of interpretation was supposed to meet merely duplicates itself. It does not matter what item, from the restricted inventory, we pick on as a plausible candidate to be what someone's putting the right interpretation on, say, the heard instruction "Add 2" (or on anything else) might consist in. Whatever it is, it cannot be what we hoped it would be, since considered in itself it in turn just "stands there like a sign-post". We might be tempted to require putting the right interpretation on the item that was supposed to be an interpretation, but that is clearly to embark on a regress, which looks as if it must be hopeless. The item that is supposed to be the right interpretation of the first putative interpretation will shrink in its turn, under the requirement of fitting into the restricted inventory of available items, into something that just "stands there". So the very idea of a person's understanding, as something that determines a distinction between behaviour that is in accord with the understanding and behaviour that is not, comes under threat.

4. Kripke gives a gripping exposition of this threatened regress of interpretations, and it is beyond question that the regress is one of the ingredients for a proper understanding of Wittgenstein's point.

But Kripke's reading goes beyond identifying the threat and giving it vivid expression. On Kripke's account, Wittgenstein rescues the idea of understanding by abandoning the idea that someone's grasping a meaning is a *fact* about her. According to Kripke's Wittgenstein, as soon as we look for a fact about a person that is what her grasping a meaning consists in, we are doomed to have any appearance that what we pick on might be the right sort of fact—specifically that it might have the right sort of normative links with her behaviour—crumble before our eyes under the impact of the regress of interpretations. So we should conclude that there can be no such fact. This claim, that there can be no fact in which someone's understanding something consists, is a "sceptical paradox".

Kripke's suggestion, on Wittgenstein's behalf, is that a "sceptical solution" can free this "sceptical paradox" of such devastating implications as that nobody understands anything. The "sceptical solution" sharply distinguishes something we can have, a story about social practices of mutual recognition and so forth, which can underwrite a conception of correctness in attributions of understanding, from something that the "sceptical paradox" says we cannot have, a story about facts in which the truth of such attributions would consist.

After the first burst of discussion of Kripke, many readers would agree that this apparatus of "sceptical paradox" and "sceptical solution" is not a good fit for Wittgenstein's texts. In §201, Wittgenstein says:

> This was our paradox: no course of action could be determined by a rule, because every course of action can be made out to accord with the rule. The answer was: if everything can be made out to accord with the rule, then it can also be made out to conflict with it. And so there would be neither accord nor conflict here.
>
> It can be seen that there is a misunderstanding here from the mere fact that in the course of our argument we give one interpretation after another; as if each one contented us at least for a moment, until we thought of yet another standing behind it. What this shews is that there is a way of grasping a rule which is *not* an *interpretation*.

This looks like a proposal, not for a "sceptical solution" to a "sceptical paradox" locked into place by an irrefutable argument, as in Kripke's reading, but for a "straight solution": a solution that works by finding fault with the reasoning that leads to the paradox. The paradox Wittgenstein mentions at the beginning of this passage is not something we have to accept and find a way to live with, but something we can expose as based on "a misunderstanding".

The villain of the piece, Wittgenstein here suggests, is the idea that the notion of accord could be available in the way we need only by courtesy of an application for the notion of interpretation. And there is no hint that when we try to escape the temptation to think we can get accord into the picture only by appealing to interpretation, we are supposed to be helped by ridding ourselves of the inclination to think of grasp of a rule or a meaning as a *fact* about the person who grasps it. If we can manage to follow Wittgenstein's direction to think of a grasp of a rule *(eine Auffassung einer Regel)* that is not an interpretation, that will ensure that we do not even start on the regress of interpretations. And it will do so in a way that leaves us perfectly at liberty, at least as far as these considerations are concerned, to think of the grasp of a rule that is in question as a fact about the person who enjoys it, if it pleases or helps us to do so.[3]

5. Kripke's reading of how the regress of interpretations threatens the very idea of understanding turns on this thesis: "no matter what is in my mind at a given time, I am free in the future to interpret it in different ways" (p. 107). This presupposes that whatever is in a person's mind at any time, it needs interpretation if it is to sort items outside the mind into those that are in accord with it and those that are not. There are always other possible interpretations, and a different interpretation, imposing a different sorting, may be adopted at a different time. Considered in themselves, that is, in abstraction from any interpretations, things in the mind just "stand there".

This presupposition endorses the restricted conception of what a person can strictly speaking have in mind that I mentioned when I introduced the regress of interpretations (§3 above). The presupposition determines that it is only under an interpretation of something in someone's mind that the question can so much as arise whether an extra-mental item accords with that thing. And then the regress of interpretations makes it impossible to privilege an interpretation under which the "right" extra-mental items count as according with the mental thing we started with, whatever it was. Given the connection between accord and understanding, it follows that whatever is in someone's mind at any time, its being in her mind cannot be what constitutes her understanding something in a determinate way.

Now if the shift from a "sceptical solution" to a "straight solution" (§4 above) leaves this presupposition about the nature of possible contents of minds in place, it makes for what looks like only an insignificant divergence from Kripke.

Kripke in effect assumes that the only way someone's understanding something could even seem to be a fact about her would be if one

---

3. In any case, separating the question whether something is a fact from the question whether some assertoric utterance would be correct seems foreign to the later Wittgenstein; see, e.g., §136. The objection against Kripke that §201 seems to point to a "straight solution" was made independently and more or less simultaneously by a number of writers, including me in Essay 11 above.

thought her understanding was a matter of her having something in mind. He finds in Wittgenstein an argument, based on the presupposition, to show that a person's having something in mind cannot constitute her understanding something, on pain of the regress of interpretations. And he concludes on Wittgenstein's behalf that a person's understanding something cannot be a fact about her. According to Kripke's Wittgenstein, we must stop conceiving attributions of understanding as candidates for truth, in a sense that brings into play facts or states of affairs in which their truth would consist. Instead we must locate a conception of what it is for such attributions to be correct, not involving their being in line with the facts, within an account of a social practice of mutual recognition and acceptance.

If we move to a "straight solution", we shall no longer suppose it helps to deny that someone's understanding something is a fact about her. But if we leave Kripke's presupposition about the nature of things in the mind unchallenged, we shall still be precluded from supposing that the facts that the "straight solution" allows us to countenance are constituted by the person's having something in her mind. And then, when we ask what they *are* constituted by, it will be overwhelmingly natural to appeal to the very same sorts of social practices that figure in Kripke's "sceptical solution", not now as a substitute for saying what fact about the person constitutes her understanding, but as affording an account of what that fact is. On this sort of view, Kripke's error was just to suppose that the only facts about a person that could even be candidates for constituting her understanding something would be facts consisting in her having something in mind. Someone's occupying a suitable social status can be a fact about her, and, on this reading, it can constitute her understanding something, without trouble from the regress of interpretations. According to this reading, the way to follow Wittgenstein's instruction to think of "a way of grasping a rule which is *not* an *interpretation*" is to reconceive what sort of fact or state of affairs someone's grasping a rule is. Instead of conceiving it as a state of affairs involving her having something in mind, we should conceive it as a state of affairs involving her occupying a position in a community.

But now it seems a merely notational issue whether we count a story about social recognition and the like, with Kripke, as a "sceptical solution", replacing any picture of a fact or state of affairs in which someone's understanding consists, or as a "straight solution", saying in a regress-proof way what the relevant facts or states of affairs come to. The important thing is surely what is common between these positions, namely the idea that to avoid the regress, we must deny that a person's understanding could be her having something in mind.

6. We get a more radical divergence from Kripke, however, if we suppose that the thrust of Wittgenstein's reflections is to cast doubt on the master thesis: the thesis that whatever a person has in her mind, it is only by virtue of being interpreted in one of various possible ways that it can impose a sorting of extra-mental items into those that accord with it and those that do not.

It is really an extraordinary idea that the contents of minds are things that, considered in themselves, just "stand there". We can bring out how extraordinary it is by noting that we need an application for the concept of accord, and so run the risk of trouble from the regress of interpretations if we accept the master thesis, not just in connection with grasp of meaning but in connection with intentionality in general. An intention, just as such, is something with which only acting in a specific way would accord. An expectation, just as such, is something with which only certain future states of affairs would accord. Quite generally, a thought, just as such, is something with which only certain states of affairs would accord.[4]

Suppose I am struck by the thought that people are talking about me in the next room. The supposition implies that only a state of affairs in which *people are talking about me in the next room* would be in accord with my thought. Now the master thesis implies that whatever I have in my mind on this occasion, it cannot be something to whose very identity that normative link to the objective world is essential. It is at most something that *can* be interpreted in a way that introduces that normative link, although it can also be interpreted differently. ("I am free in the future to interpret it in different ways.") Considered in itself it has no relations of accord or conflict to matters outside my mind, but just "stands there". The regress of

---

4. In passages like §437, Wittgenstein discusses the way intentional concepts such as the concepts of wish and thought can raise versions of the problems about making room for the notion of accord that he considers elsewhere in connection with "grasping a rule".

interpretations will then preclude conceiving the thought, considered as something to whose identity it is essential that it is to the effect *that people are talking about me in the next room,* as something I have in my mind at all. What I have in my mind is at most a potential vehicle for the significance in question, in the sort of way in which a sentence, considered as a phonetic or inscriptional item, is a vehicle for a significance that it can be interpreted as bearing.

We can extrapolate from the case of meaning and understanding to philosophical strategies that might purport to make this conclusion harmless—not, as it seems at first sight, a threat to the very idea that I might be struck by a specific thought. According to a "sceptical solution", it was a mistake to think there needed to be a fact to the effect that this is what I think, which would have to be a matter of my having something in mind; instead we should explain the correctness of attributing that thought to me in terms of my occupying a certain position in a social framework. According to a "straight solution" on the lines of the one I described in §5 above, a fact to the effect that this is what I think would not have to be a matter of my having something in mind; such a fact can be identified with my occupying a certain position in a social framework. If we supposed that the master thesis was compulsory, that would make us need such contrivances. Philosophers have devoted impressive ingenuity to elaborating their counterparts in the case of meaning and understanding.

But when we evaluate the master thesis, it is important not to be sidetracked by a premature admiration for such philosophical ingenuity. The master thesis is not just a piece of common sense, which we can sensibly leave unquestioned while we look in Wittgenstein for philosophical contrivances aimed at freeing it of paradoxical implications; or perhaps while we complain, with Crispin Wright, of a "quietism" that leads Wittgenstein to shirk elaborating such contrivances, although he supposedly reveals problems that require them.[5] The master thesis implies that what a person has in mind, strictly speaking, is never, say, *that people are talking about her in the next room* but at most something that *can* be interpreted as having that content, although it need not. Once we realize that that is

---

5. This complaint is expressed in several recent writings of Wright's; see, e.g., his "Critical Notice of Colin McGinn, *Wittgenstein on Meaning*", especially pp. 304–5.

what the master thesis implies, it should stand revealed as quite counter-intuitive, not something on which a supposed need for constructive philosophy could be convincingly based.

It is surely uncharacteristic of Wittgenstein to leave such a thesis, which is obviously philosophically motivated, unchallenged, and work towards, or, with a quietism that would evidently be unwarranted in this context, shirk working towards, ways of answering the philosophical questions that must look urgent if the thesis is accepted: questions such as "How is meaning possible?", or more generally "How is intentionality possible?" A more Wittgensteinian lesson to learn from his manipulation of the regress of interpretations is that we need a diagnosis of why we are inclined to fall into the peculiar assumption, crystallized in the master thesis, that makes such questions look pressing. Given a satisfying diagnosis, the inclination should evaporate, and the questions should simply fall away. There is no need to concoct substantial philosophical answers to them. The right response to "How is meaning possible?" or "How is intentionality possible?" is to uncover the way of thinking that makes it seem difficult to accommodate meaning and intentionality in our picture of how things are, and to lay bare how uncompulsory it is to think in that way.

7. Wittgenstein's reflections on meaning and understanding bring into prominence an image of meaning as a collection of super-hard rails that our minds engage with when we come to understand anything. It is obvious that this sort of imagery figures in Wittgenstein's texts as a target. We need to see how the tendency to resort to such imagery connects with the threatened regress of interpretations.

The germ of the imagery is clearly expressed in a passage in *The Blue Book* (p. 34):

> What one wants to say is: "Every sign is capable of interpretation; but the *meaning* mustn't be capable of interpretation. It is the last interpretation."

The effect of the regress of interpretations is that we lose our entitlement to the idea that a grasped meaning imposes demands on a person's behaviour. We allow ourselves to think that meaning's demands on behaviour must be mediated by an interpretation; nothing else could bring accord and conflict into the picture, if we start with something that just "stands there". But then we realize that whatever we have hit on as what is to be the mediating interpretation, it is itself something that can be interpreted otherwise than so as to make the right bits of behaviour count as correct. Now we can no longer appeal to a mediating interpretation to make it intelligible how the space of behavioural possibilities acquires a normative shape. To postulate another mediating interpretation, imposing the right interpretation on the first mediating interpretation, is clearly to embark on a regress. The hardness—the demandingness—of the demands ("the hardness of the logical must", §437) seems to disappear.

Now the right move in response to this is to realize that we should not suppose we have to start with something that just "stands there". We should not suppose that the normative surroundings of the concept of understanding can be in place only thanks to there being a role for the concept of interpretation. Contrast the way of thinking expressed in the *Blue Book* passage. That way of thinking attempts to keep the hardness of the demands, in the face of how the regress of interpretations threatens to soften them, while leaving unquestioned the idea that the normative surroundings of the concept of understanding can be in place only thanks to there being a role for the concept of interpretation. The right move is not even to start on the regress of interpretations; but the *Blue Book* passage suggests we can start on the regress but bring it to a harmless stop, by conceiving meaning as "the last interpretation".

It should be obvious on reflection that we cannot disarm the regress of interpretations like this. There is nothing in the idea that meaning can stop the regress, once we have let it begin, except a recipe for an imagistic pseudo-conception of meaning in terms of super-rigid machinery. It must be self-deceptive to suppose that this is a way to regain an authentic understanding of meaning's normative reach into the objective world.

Now one thing that is labelled by the word "platonism", in a contemporary philosophical usage whose relation to Plato we need not consider, is this imagery of super-rigid machinery. As I said, it is obvious that platonism in this sense comes under attack from Wittgenstein.

But the label "platonism" is also used for ideas that are simply part of the conception of meaning as reaching normatively into the objective world: for instance the idea that the meaning of, say, an instruction for extending a numerical series determines what is correct at any point in the series, in advance of anyone's working out the series to that point, so that the meaning constitutes a standard of correctness for what any calculator or group of calculators does or might do. Putting the idea picturesquely, we can say that the meaning reaches forward in the series ahead of anyone who actually works the series out, and is so to speak already there waiting for such a person, ready to stand in judgement over her performance, at any point she reaches in the series. The standards of correctness embodied in a grasped meaning are, as Crispin Wright puts it, ratification-independent.

No doubt this kind of picture *may* be an expression of the self-deceptive thinking that seeks to stop the regress of interpretations by conceiving meaning as "the last interpretation". But the idea of ratification-independence is, as I said, just part of the idea of meaning's normative reach—the idea expressed by the relevant use of the notion of accord. The idea of ratification-independence need not come into play in the context of the self-deceptive attempt to let the regress of interpretations begin but come to a harmless stop. The idea of ratification-independence need have no connection with the regress of interpretations, over and above the fact that it is part of the general way of thinking that the regress threatens. If the threat posed by the regress is properly disarmed by discarding the master thesis, as opposed to the ineffectual response of conceiving meaning as "the last interpretation", then ratification-independence, detached from that ineffectual response, can fall into place as simply part of a way of thinking that we are now able to take in our stride. There seemed to be problems about the normative reach of meaning, but since they depended on a thesis that we have no reason to accept, they stand revealed as illusory.

The question "How is it possible for meaning to reach ahead of any actual performance?" is just a specific form of the question "How is it possible for the concept of accord to be in place in the way that the idea of meaning requires it to be?" The Wittgensteinian response is not that these are good questions, calling for constructive philosophy to answer them. The Wittgensteinian response is to draw attention to a defect in the way of thinking that makes it look as if there are problems here.

We misread Wittgenstein if we let the elasticity of the term "platonism" induce us to lump the very idea of ratification-independence (and the like) in with the imagery whose sole point is a self-deceptive attempt to let the regress of interpretations begin but ensure that it does no harm. The effect of lumping these things together is that, on the basis of Wittgenstein's patent hostility to that imagery, we are led to suppose he finds the very idea of ratification-independence (and the like) problematic. But we cannot cite Wittgenstein's authority for supposing that the very idea of ratification-independence (and the like) is problematic.

8. Commentators often suggest that the concept of *custom* and its cognates figure in Wittgenstein as elements in a constructive philosophical response to questions like "How is meaning possible?" According to some versions of this reading, Wittgenstein actually gives the response; according to others, he points towards it but does not give it, out of a quietism that must stand exposed as inappropriate by the sheer fact that the questions are (supposedly) good ones. I am committed to regarding this as a misreading.[6]

The role of the concept of custom in Wittgenstein's thinking is crystallized in this central text (§198):[7]

> "Then can whatever I do be brought into accord with the rule?"—Let me ask this: what has the expression of a rule—say a sign-post—got to do with my actions? What sort of connexion is there here?—Well, perhaps this one: I have been trained to react to this sign in a particular way, and now I do so react to it.
>
> "But that is only to give a causal connexion: to tell how it has come about that we go by the sign-post; not what this going-by-the-sign really consists in."—On the contrary; I have further indicated that a person goes by a sign-post only in so far as there exists a regular use of sign-posts, a custom.

This passage starts by formulating the threat posed by the regress of interpretations to the very idea of accord between a rule and the

---

6. I now think Essay 11 above is too hospitable to this kind of reading.
7. I have changed the punctuation in the second paragraph, in a way that brings out what I take to be the dialectical flow of the passage.

performances that count as following it. I have been urging that we should avoid the threat by not letting the regress start—by not letting it seem that the concept of interpretation must be in play if the concept of accord is to be secured its application. The passage suggests that we can avoid that appearance by insisting on a bit of common sense about following a sign-post. When one follows an ordinary sign-post, one is not acting on an *interpretation*. That gives an overly cerebral cast to such routine behaviour. Ordinary cases of following a sign-post involve simply acting in the way that comes naturally to one in such circumstances, in consequence of some training that one underwent in one's upbringing. (Compare §506: "The absent-minded man who at the order 'Right turn!' turns left, and then, clutching his forehead, says 'Oh! right turn' and does a right turn.— What has struck him? An interpretation?") But if we give this corrective to an over-mentalizing of the behaviour, perpetrated by giving the concept of interpretation an unwarranted role in our conception of it, we run the risk of being taken to overbalance in the opposite direction, into under-mentalizing the behaviour—adopting a picture in which notions like that of accord cannot be in play, because the behaviour is understood as nothing but the outcome of a causal mechanism set up by the training. Such a picture might fit an acquired automatism, in which there is no question of *acting on an understanding* of the sign-post's instructions at all. Wittgenstein averts this risk, that if we exploit the concept of training to exorcize the idea of interpretation, we shall lose our entitlement to the idea of understanding as well, by adding another bit of common sense, that the training is initiation into a custom.

If the concept of custom figured here as the beginning of a constructive philosophical account of how the meaning of sign-posts, and our understanding of their meaning, are constituted, the custom that Wittgenstein mentions would need to be characterizable in terms that do not presuppose meaning and understanding. But the concept of custom can do the work it does here without being capable of being put to that sort of philosophical service. The concept of custom can do the work it does here even if the only answer to the question "What custom?" is "The custom of erecting and following sign-posts", or perhaps more specifically "The custom of erecting and following sign-posts of just this style and configuration"; that is, an answer that, with the talk of *following,* simply presupposes the supposedly problematic notion of accord. What made the notion of accord seem problematic was the regress of interpretations, and the first move in the passage, the appeal to training, has ensured that we need not begin on the regress of interpretations. The point of the appeal to custom is just to make sure that that first move is not misunderstood in such a way as to eliminate accord, and with it understanding, altogether.

Readers of Wittgenstein often suppose that when he mentions customs, forms of life, and the like, he is making programmatic gestures towards a certain style of positive philosophy: one that purports to make room for talk of meaning and understanding, in the face of supposedly genuine obstacles, by locating such talk in a context of human interactions conceived as describable otherwise than in terms of meaning or understanding. But there is no reason to credit Wittgenstein with any sympathy for this style of philosophy. When he says "What has to be accepted, the given, is—so one could say—forms of life" (p. 226), his point is not to adumbrate a philosophical response, on such lines, to supposedly good questions about the possibility of meaning and understanding, or intentionality generally, but to remind us of something we can take in the proper way only after we are equipped to see that such questions are based on a mistake. His point is to remind us that the natural phenomenon that is normal human life is itself already shaped by meaning and understanding. As he says: "Commanding, questioning, recounting, chatting, are as much part of our natural history as walking, eating, drinking, playing" (§25).

If one reads Wittgenstein as offering a constructive philosophical account of how meaning and understanding are possible, appealing to human interactions conceived as describable in terms that do not presuppose meaning and understanding, one flies in the face of his explicit view that philosophy embodies no doctrine, no substantive claims. This view of philosophy is what Wright describes as quietism. Wright takes Wittgenstein to have uncovered some good philosophical problems about meaning and understanding. Reasonably enough in view of that, Wright cannot see how a quietistic hostility to constructive philosophy can be warranted: if Wittgenstein reveals tasks for philosophy, he cannot appeal to what now looks like an adventitiously negative view of philosophy's scope to justify not engaging with those tasks. Other interpreters actually credit

Wittgenstein with a substantive "social pragmatist" philosophy of meaning. Wright is less optimistic about what can be found in the texts, which he takes to hold back from substantive philosophy, in line with Wittgenstein's quietistic conception of the nature of philosophy. In Wright's view the texts contain at most a programme for the supposedly needed philosophy of meaning. Wright reads Wittgenstein in a way that respects his disavowal of constructive ambitions, but he makes that disavowal a point of criticism, based on the uncovering of philosophical problems that is supposed to be a Wittgensteinian achievement.

Contrast the style of reading I have outlined here. There is indeed room to complain that Wittgenstein reveals a need for something that he does not give, or does not give enough of. But what we might ask for more of is not a constructive account of how human interactions make meaning and understanding possible, but rather a diagnostic deconstruction of the peculiar way of thinking that makes such a thing seem necessary. It would be good to say something about how the diagnosis should go in detail, but this paper is not the place for that.

ESSAY 13

One Strand in the Private Language Argument

1. This paper belongs in a general investigation of dualism of conceptual scheme and pre-conceptual given: that is, of the philosophical temptation to suppose that the conceptual structures that figure in experience (to put it neutrally) are the result of our imposing conceptual form on something received in pre-conceptual shape—intuitions, in a roughly Kantian sense. It is becoming a familiar suggestion in modern philosophy that this dualism is a mistake. Wilfrid Sellars has long opposed "the Myth of the Given";[1] and the dualism has more recently been attacked by Donald Davidson[2] and Richard Rorty.[3]

Hostility to the dualism has been fairly widely promoted in connection with "outer" experience—again in a roughly Kantian sense. But if this hostility is well placed, the dualism ought to be equally wrong about purely "inner" experience: pains, tickles, and the like. Trying to take the point quite generaly, we ought to look with favour on a thesis on these lines: nothing can count as an episode in a stream of consciousness unless it has (already, we might say) a conceptual shape, an articulable experiential content. There is an intelligible inclination to resist this thesis on the basis of the dualism: a temptation, that is, to regard conceptual structures as the upshots of our conceptualizing pre-conceptual intuitions, and then (as is natural enough once one has this framework in place) to say that it is the

---

1. See, e.g., "Empiricism and the Philosophy of Mind".
2. See "On the Very Idea of a Conceptual Scheme".
3. See "The World Well Lost".

intuitions that occur in the stream of consciousness—that the conceptual structures are a commentary on the stream of consciousness, not its ingredients. And this temptation should be no less unhealthy in this application of the idea to "inner" experience than its counterpart for the case of "outer" experience.

These considerations suggest a way of understanding the motivation for the position that Wittgenstein attacks in the sections of *Philosophical Investigations* (henceforth *PI*) that are known as the Private Language Argument. The idea is that the "private linguist" succumbs to a version of the dualism of scheme and given: his thought is, as above, that a stream of consciousness is made up of non-conceptual items that justify conceptualizations of them. If we see things like this, the idea of private *language* seems to be an infelicitous way of trying to satisfy the underlying motivation; the "private linguist" aims to represent as linguistically capturable, and so as a case of articulable, concept-involving awareness, something that one really wants, when one is in this philosophical mood, only in the form of necessarily inarticulate confrontation with the pre-conceptual given. This may seem to represent the "private linguist" as more self-deceived than is credible, but the temptations in this area are very powerful.[4]

I do not mean to suggest that Wittgenstein sees his polemic in precisely these terms, as an application of a general rejection of the dualism. Opposition to the dualism makes good sense of some of what he says. I think it leaves some of what he says unexplained, and some looking positively mistaken.

2. Intuitions ought to be points at which what Sellars has called "the logical space of reasons" is impinged on by what lies outside it. What is pre-conceptually given has to be outside the space of reasons, since it is not in conceptual shape and therefore not capable of standing in rational relations to anything. But it has to be such that

---

4. It may be worth comparing the elementary propositions of *Tractatus Logico-Philosophicus*. On one reading, elementary propositions are a limiting case of articulate expression: the nearest one could come (as one might suppose) to a direct contact between language and extra-conceptual reality while nevertheless preserving the articulation that language must have. (But this reading of the *Tractatus* is contentious.) Closer to home, consider *PI* §§379–81 (of which more below).

being given some of it can be conceived as happening inside the space of reasons, since getting a piece of the given is supposed to constitute a *ground* or *justification* for our lowest-level conceptualizations. Now one way of coming at why the dualism is a supect framework for thinking about experience is through the thought that nothing can play both these roles. And, though this point is most familiar in application to "outer" experience,[5] it is quite general. The application to purely "inner" experience is explicitly made by Rorty in the following passage, in which Rorty is aiming to expound a Wittgensteinian point:

> ... unless there were such a thing as typical pain behavior we would never be able to teach a child the meaning of, for example, "toothache". More generally, ... the way in which the pre-linguistic infant knows that it has a pain is the way in which the record-changer knows the spindle is empty, the plant the direction of the sun, and the amoeba the temperature of the water. But this way has no connection with what a language-user knows when he knows what pain is ... The mistake which Wittgenstein exposed was to assume that we learn what a pain is in the second sense by casting linguistic garb over our knowledge of what pain is in the first sense—by clothing our direct acquaintance with special felt, incommunicable qualities in words ...

Rorty goes on to identify "the mistake which Wittgenstein exposed" as "the notion that knowledge in the first sense—the sort manifested by behavioral discrimination—is the 'foundation' (rather than simply one possible causal antecedent) of knowledge in the second sense".[6]

What Rorty says here about knowing the meaning of "toothache" can be easily transposed into parallel remarks about possessing the concept of toothache; then his point can be put as one about the relation between pre-conceptually felt pain and episodes of pain that belong in full-fledged streams of consciousness, conceived as necessarily in conceptual shape. The fundamental point is the distinction between foundations and (mere) causal antecedents: non-conceptual pain (in pre-linguistic infants) is a causal antecedent of the ability to have conceptually structured pain episodes, not a continuing ingredient in them that grounds the conceptual structures involved. Put like

---

5. For a good exposition, see Michael Williams, *Groundless Belief*.
6. *Philosophy and the Mirror of Nature*, pp. 110–1.

this, Rorty's point perfectly fits the reading of Wittgenstein I am recommending.

Rorty seems to me, however, to spoil the point somewhat by putting it in unnecessarily provocative surroundings. No useful purpose is served by crediting the pre-linguistic infant with *knowing* that it has a pain, rather than simply with *feeling* pain. Putting the matter as Rorty does, in terms of two sorts of knowing, naturally encourages the behaviouristic remarks he makes about the supposed first sort, so that the record-changer naturally seems a straightforward example of the same sort of thing, with feeling not in question at all. This paves the way for a thesis Rorty embraces later (pp. 188–92), that crediting pre-linguistic (or non-linguistic) awareness, for instance feelings of pain, to "babies and the more attractive sorts of animal" (p. 189) is "a courtesy extended potential or imagined fellow-speakers of our language" (p. 190): a matter of, for instance, how easy we find it, perhaps with self-conscious fancifulness, to imagine something asking us for help. But if we insist that the issue—the area where we are vulnerable to philosophical temptations that need to be resisted—concerns the relation between non-linguistic *feelings* and concept-involving awareness, then the record-changer, and perhaps the amoeba, seem to be an irrelevance. We need not yet be falling into the philosophical confusion that Rorty is rightly concerned to expose if we claim that attributing pain to pre-linguistic infants is not a courtesy, an exercise of fancy, but an acknowledgement of a plain fact. Pain can be non-fancifully attributed to things to which things matter—"subjects of significance", in a phrase of Charles Taylor's.[7] (It matters itself, in an obvious way, and it is connected in obvious ways to other things that matter.) Whether something is a subject of significance at all, and more specifically whether it feels pain (ever, or on some occasion), is a question of, in a broad sense, biology (this is without prejudice to the possibility of synthesized life)—not something to do with how attractive we find it. Rorty is led to say otherwise by the fear that if one allows pre-linguistic awareness as a fact, one will lay oneself open to the idea that it *grounds* the conceptual structures that figure in episodes of concept-involving awareness; that is the idea he is concerned, following Wittgenstein, to resist. But there is overkill here: the distinction

---

7. See "The Concept of a Person".

between foundations and mere causal antecedents suffices to make the point, in a way that is consistent with claiming that pre-linguistic and non-linguistic pain are not a matter of courtesy.

If we refrain from this overkill, there is room for a project of making the process of initiation into the space of reasons (the space of concepts) intelligible. Without thinking of pre-linguistic awareness as something that persists into a life of concept-involving awareness, serving, in its occurrences as an element in such a life, to supply grounds for conceptualizations, we can nevertheless think of it as a substratum on which the capacity for concept-carried awareness is constructed. It may help that we can begin with things that are already subjects of significance, when we try to make sense of the transition to being subjects of significance in a stronger sense.

3. If we read Wittgenstein in this framework, we may want to query his sureness of foot in passages like this (*PI* §304):

> "And yet you again and again reach the conclusion that the sensation itself is a *nothing*."—Not at all. It is not a *something*, but not a *nothing* either! The conclusion was only that a nothing would serve just as well as a something about which nothing could be said. We have only rejected the grammar which tries to force itself on us here.

Or this (§293):

> The thing in the box has no place in the language-game at all; not even as a *something* . . . That is to say: if we construe the grammar of the expression of sensation on the model of 'object and designation' the object drops out of consideration as irrelevant.

On the view I am suggesting, Wittgenstein could, and perhaps should, have said something more like this. The sensation (the pain, say) is a perfectly good something—an object, if you like, of concept-involving awareness. What is a nothing (and this is simply a nothing, not "not a something, but not a nothing either") is the supposed pre-conceptual *this* that is supposed to ground our conceptualizations (the item we want to gesture at, when it is pointed out that "pain" and "sensation" are words of our common language, with an inarticulate noise: §261). The episode of consciousness comes to us in already conceptual shape; it is not a question of our imposing conceptual shape on a given *this*. But that is no reason to suggest that the conceptual content of the episode of consciousness cannot be parsed in terms of a classification of a something ("the sensation itself": the pain) as the kind of something it is.

Wittgenstein's willingness to say that the sensation is "not a something" is a response to a thought one might put (in order to register the point but not encourage that response) like this: in the kind of case in question we have at best a *limiting case* of the model of object and designation—a limiting case of the idea of an object that we can designate and classify. The idea of encountering a particular is in place here *only because* the experience involves a concept (*pain*, say, or *toothache*): the particular has no status except as what is experienced as instantiating the concept.[8] So the idea of encountering a particular in this application lacks a kind of independent robustness that we can credit it with in other applications.

The peculiarity of this case induces P. F. Strawson to raise the following highly instructive worry: given that the objects of this kind of experience are not independent of our awareness of them (as seems indeed to be the case), what secures it that the experiences have the complexity of structure that they must have to be even minimally concept-involving? What saves the recognitional or classificatory element that must be present in a minimally conceptual content from being "absorbed into" the item recognized?[9] This question presupposes that the "item recognized"—one element in a minimal particular/general or subject/predicate structure, to be thought of as correlated with another element that expresses a classification of it, or a recognition of it as belonging to a kind—is unproblematically present in these cases. But from Wittgenstein's point of view this is the wrong way round. At *PI* §290 Wittgenstein's interlocutor says "But isn't the beginning the sensation—which I describe?" This expresses, surely for purposes of criticizing it, what seems to be precisely the presupposition of Strawson's question: the idea that the "item recognized" (the sensation) is present anyway, independently of being brought under a concept ("described")—which is something that

---

8. It may be said at this point that no concept need be recognized as being in play except the concept of, say, *being in* pain or *having* toothache—a concept that is instantiated by the *person*. This is in line with letting the sensation, as a particular, drop out of consideration as irrelevant. What I am trying to suggest is that this is overkill; we can take Wittgenstein's good point without needing this move.

9. *The Bounds of Sense*, pp. 100–1.

happens later. The sensation is here being conceived as an intuition, in a more or less full-blown Kantian sense. This is plainly the cast of thought that makes Strawson's worry about "absorption" seem urgent: it is hard now to see how a recognitional or classificatory element in a conceptual content could be anything but an optional extra, dispensable without disrupting the status of the episode as an experience. But in fact, if there is a risk of "absorption" in Wittgenstein, it is the other way round: what risks disappearing is not the recognitional or classificatory element in a minimal conceptual content, but the "item recognized"—and sometimes that item does seem to disappear, as when it is said not to be a something. But Wittgenstein's best moves in this area are more subtle.

To the interlocutor of §290, Wittgenstein responds:

> Perhaps this word "describe" tricks us here. I say "I describe my state of mind" and "I describe my room". You need to call to mind the differences between the language-games.

Notice that the suggestion here is not that "describe" is wrong, but simply that it needs to be handled with care. The notion of a limiting case of a particular/general or subject/predicate structure, as I put it a moment ago, is a way of keeping "describe" without implying the idea that Wittgenstein is clearly trying to avoid: that what describing here amounts to is bringing under a concept an item that is there in consciousness anyway, whether or not any conceptual structure is in place. §290 goes on like this:

> What I do is not, of course, to identify my sensation by criteria [this *would* be a matter of bringing an independently encountered item under a concept]: but to repeat an expression. But this is not the *end* of the language-game: it is the beginning.

We can transpose the thought that is expressed here in terms of language use into a parallel thought relating to the employment of concepts. The point then emerges like this: in the relevant cases an already conceptual episode is the *first* thing that happens in the space of reasons; its coming to be the case that some conceptual structure is in place is not the end of some transition within the space of reasons—the transition that a conceptualization of a prior nonconceptual item would supposedly be—but the beginning of everything relevant that happens in that space. Once this is clear, there is no need to suppose that the "repeating of an expression" that is "the beginning of the language-game" cannot be thought of as a case of description—a limiting case of bringing an object under a concept.

One thing that emerges here is that there is room for an innocuous form of the thought that when I truthfully say "I am in pain" I have a justification. The justification is the fact that I am in pain—that, to put it in terms of item recognized and expression of what it is recognized to be, what I feel is a pain.[10] This does not contradict the point Wittgenstein is making when he says (*PI* §289, with a different use of "justification") that this kind of remark is a case of using a word without a justification. His point is to reject the idea that I have a justification that points to something within the space of reasons, but further back than the conceptual episode: namely my being presented with the sensation, conceived as a pre-conceptual *this*, which I then classify "by criteria" or "according to rules" (compare §292). It does no violence to this point if we seek to preserve a sense in which the conceptual episode itself constitutes a justification for a remark that makes its conceptual content explicit.

§293 implies that it is a mistake to "construe the grammar of the expression of sensation on the model of 'object and designation'", and I have in effect been suggesting that if this is meant to convey that sensations are not objects of reference (as the context—"not even . . . a something"—certainly indicates), then the diagnosis is not quite right.

It is not difficult to find a germ of truth in the remark. If we take the description of external objects (compare §290) as the paradigmatic field of application for the model of "object and designation", then to apply the model to the expression of sensation would be to make precisely the mistake that Wittgenstein, as I read him, is concerned to expose. For when an external object figures in one's thought, it is there for one's thinking anyway, independently of the specific predication that one's thought makes concerning it, and this is exactly not so with a sensation. On this account, the correct point is not that sensations are not objects of reference, but that they are not objects of reference in the way external objects are (and in employing the model of "object and designation", one naturally gravitates to the latter kind of case).

---

10. The implied equivalence here may seem suspect, but see n. 8 above.

There is a deeper point to be made about the model of "object and designation". One can be tempted to take what I have just said about the case of external objects—that they are there for one's thinking anyway, independently of what one thinks about them—as encouragement for the idea that reference is a point where a remarkable contact between Thought (conceptually structured) and World (brutely external to anything conceptual) is effected. What is wrong with this, to put it telegraphically, is that it involves forgetting or denying a point of Frege's that we can put like this: even if an object is there for one's thinking independently of what one predicates of it in thought, it nevertheless figures in one's thought *as something*—"under a mode of presentation". The effect of reaffirming this is to restore reference to its proper place as a point of unremarkable contact between—if you like—thought and world. But if someone wants to keep the capital letters (the idea of a remarkable feat of linkage), the case of reference to "inner" objects, conceived as far as possible on the model of reference to external objects, is a good case to focus on: the bad analogy has the object there for one's thinking independently of anything one predicates of it in one's thought, and since there is in this case nothing besides what one predicates of it in one's thought to yield an answer to the question "*As what* does it figure in one's thought?", this can seem like a particularly clear or pure case of the remarkable contact between thought and something radically alien to the conceptual. That this is quite wrong is, I believe, a way of putting Wittgenstein's point. The point does not seem to be happily expressed by the remark about "object and designation": what we are dealing with here—the wish to keep the capital letters—is a construal of "object and designation" that is dubious anywhere, in a way that Wittgenstein himself seems to want to bring out elsewhere, notably in the discussion of the Augustinian picture of language, ostensive definition, and so forth, in the early sections of the *Investigations*. Those sections are well known to contain much prefiguring of the "private language" sections, which must be meant at least in part to apply their moral; I have been suggesting, in effect, that Wittgenstein may not have fully thought through the connection he was driving at.[11]

---

11. For some related suggestions, see pp. 16–18 of Peter Winch, "Introduction: The Unity of Wittgenstein's Philosophy".

4. In the passage I have quoted, Rorty shows an excellent appreciation of the negative thesis that is the heart of Wittgenstein's position, on the reading I am endorsing. He is, I believe, less convincing about what this leaves it open to us to say; and it is instructive to follow this through. There are two points here. First, Rorty embraces a highly subtle form of the sort of materialism that leads less circumspect thinkers to say that what makes ascriptions of sensations true is neurophysiological events. Second, Rorty suggests that one's special authority in ascribing sensations to oneself amounts to nothing but the fact that one's linguistic community takes one's word for it on such matters; this is a way of *not* allowing the authority to have a basis in the fact that it is one's *own* sensation that is in question. I shall expand a little on each of these points.

5. Rorty explains his version of materialism in terms of the fantasy of the Antipodeans, who use neurophysiological descriptions of themselves and others in something like the sorts of situation where we use sensation talk.[12] He expresses his materialism by claiming that "no predictive or explanatory or descriptive power would be lost if we had spoken Antipodean all our lives" (p. 120). Rorty avoids a thesis on these lines: "What pains really are, or would be if there were any, is . . . [filled in with a specification of a 'mental' essence]; so, given the claim about the power of Antipodean, there are no pains." (That would be an eliminative materialism.) He also avoids a thesis on these lines: "What pains really are is such-and-such neurophysiological events." (That would be a reductive or identity-theory materialism.) This manifests a well-placed scepticism about the sort of essentialism both these positions share (signalled by the fact that plausible formulations of them begin with "What pains really are is . . .").[13]

But Rorty never looks critically at the basically materialistic claim that the Antipodean language would involve no "loss of power". (This is what, if combined with the essentialistic impulse he deplores,

---

12. See *Philosophy and the Mirror of Nature*, chap. 2.
13. See pp. 118–21.

induces the seeming need to choose between those two familiar varieties of materialism.)

I think we should question whether this claim really has any plausibility. Is there really anything in favour of supposing that, say, "It hurts" is simply a "place-holder" for something like "Such-and-such a bundle of neurons is jangling"—that something like the latter might, in some future neurophysiology, acquire the *same* explanatory power that the former now has?[14] (This is not an expression of armchair scepticism about the development of neurophysiology. Maybe a neurophysiological replacement might succeed in explaining what were in some sense the same explananda; but this leaves wide open what would be the crucial question, whether it would be the same *explanation.*) Rorty's bland and unargued pronouncement to the contrary[15] must reflect his seeing no option besides this materialism, on the one hand, and, on the other, the conception of sensations expressed in "But isn't the beginning the sensation?" But there is another option: the thin ("limiting case") application of the model of object and designation that I have been trying to describe. This allows an innocuous continuation, without materialistic implications, of the apparently essentialistic opening "What pains really are is . . .": namely *"pains!"*[16]

---

14. See pp. 81, 83.
15. See the "plausible prediction" on p. 115.
16. One way of protesting against Rorty's claim that a shift to Antipodean would lose us no explanatory power is to say: "The explanatory power of talking about pain must be unavailable to any discourse as objectivistic as neurophysiology is (rightly) committed to being." Something prevents Rorty from making anything of this; he cannot understand protests about subjectivity as anything except insisting on incorrigibility, misconceived as involving confrontation with wispy or insubstantial entities (see, e.g., pp. 28–31, 83–8). The defenders of subjectivity whom Rorty actually considers are partly to blame for this; but the first sentence of this footnote is not an appeal to incorrigibility. Rorty's version of materialism is also partly sustained by a disputable view of how much Quine has shown. It is quite close to Rorty's own use of Quine to suggest that Quine's good point, in objecting to philosophical employments of an analytic/synthetic distinction, is simply a form of opposition to the dualism of scheme and content. At pp. 101–2, n. 11, Rorty, in a Quinean spirit, rebukes Sellars for going on conceiving what he liberates from the Myth of the Given as "logically privileged access" rather than, as in, for instance, Armstrong, "empirically privileged access" (*sc.* access to what is in fact literally inside one). But the idea of "language-game-theoretically privileged access"—to, for instance, pains, conceived not as "really" neurophysiogical occurrences but in terms of the thin application of the model of object and designation—is perfectly consistent with Quine's good point.

6. Rorty expresses his view about first-person authority in remarks like this: "assertions are justified by society rather than by the character of the inner representations they express."[17] This is, of course, reminiscent of the "community interpretation" of Wittgenstein.[18] It is a ticklish question what exactly the role of the community in Wittgenstein is; the "community interpretation" has met with severe criticism.[19] We may be helped to make some headway on this question if we notice that the interlocutor voice in the *Investigations* is at least once induced to take Wittgenstein to be fobbing us off with an appeal to the community, in place of an unaccountably withheld acknowledgement of first-person authority; this elicits the following protest (§386):

> "But why have you so little confidence in yourself? Ordinarily you always know well enough what it is to 'calculate'. So if you say you have calculated in imagination, then you will have done so . . . And further: you do not always rely on the agreement of other people; for you often report that you have seen something no one else has."

What Rorty speaks of is not simply "relying on the agreement of other people". But Rorty's idea should strike the interlocutor as similarly refusing to acknowledge what the interlocutor thinks is special about self-awareness. Rorty's idea is that the special status of one's say-so should not be seen as amounting to anything more than the fact that our language-game requires other people to defer to what one says on these matters; it should not be seen as in any way grounded in the fact that it is one's own inner life that one is pronouncing on. It is a felt threat of being deprived of this latter conception that elicits the interlocutor's protest; and reliance on the agreement of others is the best the interlocutor can come up with as what Wittgenstein must be proposing as a substitute.

Here too, Rorty's starting-point is a good thought, namely that the conception of sensation expressed in "But isn't the beginning the sensation?" is useless. If that were all that could seem to warrant the idea that one's special authority comes from the fact that it is

---

17. See pp. 173–82; the quotation is from p. 174. Compare also p. 191, on "the Sellarsian notion that the inside of people and quasi-people is to be explained by what goes on outside (and, in particular, by their place in our community) rather than conversely".
18. See especially Saul A. Kripke, *Wittgenstein on Rules and Private Language*.
19. See G. P. Baker and P. M. S. Hacker, *Scepticism, Rules, and Language*.

one's own experience to which one is giving expression, then so much the worse for the idea. Mention of the community, whether in the interlocutor's rather crude style or in Rorty's much subtler version, might then seem a natural way to fill what would threaten to constitute a gap.

But I believe Wittgenstein's aim hereabouts is rather different. Wittgenstein's aim is not to substitute *something else,* the community's conferring of authority on individuals, for the idea of a special relation to the subject-matter of their remarks, as that which makes them specially authoritative in making them. Wittgenstein's aim is, rather, to disarm a temptation to think that the latter idea requires *queer* items or states of affairs.[20]

Now there is a threat of queerness that Wittgenstein engages with here—in the context of questions about first-person authority—that simply never comes into view in Rorty's discussion. The only threatened queerness that Rorty ever sees looming in this context is a kind of wispiness or ghostliness, imported by a misconception of incorrigibility or "privileged access".[21] The quite different threat I have in mind is something I can best introduce in contexts where intentionality is in play.[22] (The threat is of wider scope, as will emerge; but it is easiest to appreciate if we start with the application to cases involving intentionality.) This threat is under discussion in a series of remarks that come after the interlocutor's complaint that I have just quoted from §386.

> ... But I do have confidence in myself—I say without hesitation that I have done this sum in my head, have imagined this colour. The difficulty is not that I doubt whether I really imagined something red. But it is *this:* that we should be able, just like that, to point out or describe the colour we have imagined, that the translation of the image into reality presents no difficulty at all. Are they then so alike that one might mix them up? (§386 again.)

> ... How do I know from my *image,* what the colour really looks like? (§388.)

---

20. For "queer", see §195.
21. See p. 30; chap. 2, passim; and pp. 218–9, summed up under the head of "subjectivity" at p. 243.
22. Amazingly, Rorty takes the idea that "there are no interesting problems about intentionality" to be a Wittgensteinian idea; see p. 25.

"The image must be more like its object than any picture. For, however like I make the picture to what it is supposed to represent, it can always be the picture of something else as well. But it is essential to the image that it is the image of *this* and of nothing else." Thus one might come to regard the image as a super-likeness. (§389.)

The threatened queerness here is not the wispy translucency that Rorty contends with; it is the queerness of superlative facts (compare §192). And the point of alluding to the community is not to *substitute* social practice for a special relation to the inner, as what underlies the subject's authority, but to help dismantle a "super-factual" conception of one's special relation to one's inner life. It is as performing this quite different role that we should understand the allusions to the community that are undoubtedly present in this region of Wittgenstein's text, in remarks like §381 (which is the kind of remark that elicits the protest against the crude "community view" in §386). I suggest that the context warrants rewriting what Wittgenstein says in §381 so as to fit the problem of §389, on these lines:

> How do I know that the colour I imagine is red?—It would be an answer to say: "I have learnt English".

In these passages, the threat of queerness arises, as I remarked, in a context of intentionality: what is at issue is, for instance, the relation between an image and what it is an image of. But such relations are a species of the genus *internal relation*;[23] and the basic issue hereabouts is much more general than the application to intentionality in particular. The general issue is the question how something that is *all there* in consciousness—so that one knows what it is "just like that": §386—can stand in internal relations to something external to the contents of consciousness. One does not need to advert to the external item or items in order to know what the content of consciousness is, and this encourages a picture of this kind of self-knowledge that leaves no room for internal relations to the world outside the mind. This problem about internal relations arises not only if the external something is, say, a displayable instance of the colour that one's image is an image of, but also if the external something is, say, the behaviour in which one manifests one's pain. About the latter kind

---

23. See Baker and Hacker, *Scepticism, Rules, and Language,* passim (see the Index, under "internal relation").

of application, we get a parallel to §381—similarly risking the "community interpretation" and the protest of §386—in §384: "You learned the *concept* 'pain' when you learned language." The feelings of pain about which the problem arises are episodes in which the subject's possession of the concept is essentially operative; that is how it is that the episodes, while being episodes of consciousness, stand in internal relations to matters outside themselves, mirroring the relations that are constitutive of the concept's location in the space of concepts.

7. The main line of objection Wittgenstein invites on these questions is "But you are leaving out the sensation!" (compare §304). By playing down the inclination to say that a sensation is "not a *something*", the reading I am recommending should not attract the most straightforward form of that protest. But in resolutely avoiding the supposed pre-conceptual *this,* the reading can still easily seem to leave out something important.

What sort of *something* can we plausibly represent a sensation as being, consistently with its not being a pre-conceptual *this,* something that awaits conceptualization? We are required to conceive the relevant episodes in streams of consciousness as involving the experienced applicability of concepts. (If an episode of the relevant kind is an occurrent awareness *of* something, it must have a conceptual structure.) Surely, then, a subject who undergoes such an episode must *have* the relevant concepts. In the context of remarks like "You learned the *concept* 'pain' when you learned language" (§384, quoted above), this naturally prompts the objection "But this is unfair to non-speakers!" (The connection of concepts with language is perfectly plausible on one natural reading of "concept".) Such an objection is especially encouraged by Rorty's "courtesy" idea, which I discussed in §3 above (*PI* §281 perhaps suggests a similar idea in Wittgenstein). But the objection survives rejection of the idea that attributing sensations to non-speakers is only a courtesy. It persists in the shape of a difficulty one might naturally find in combining the following three claims:

(1) Our pains are concept-involving episodes.
(2) Non-speakers have no concepts.

(3) It is a hard fact—not a matter of courtesy or fancy—that non-speakers can feel pain.

However, it is not impossible to keep one's head here. What is essential is to avoid the temptation to suppose that when, say, a cat, or a human infant, is in pain, what constitutes the relevant kind of episode in our inner lives is *all there* in the cat's, or infant's, consciousness, barring only the ability to talk; or—to put the idea in connection with us—that our ability to talk came to encompass our pains by way of our having our attention drawn to something that was already (sometimes) there in our consciousness—in the way that a cat's, or an infant's, pain is there in its consciousness—and being taught what to call it. (This would be a case of being induced to perform a "private ostensive definition"). One can easily be tempted into the following succession of thoughts, which starts innocently enough but rapidly becomes problematic. To begin with, it must be correct to say, focusing on a pain one feels: "Even if I had not learned to talk, this wound (say) would still have sufficed to make it the case that I was in pain—as cats, for instance, admittedly can be." (So far so good: this is just insistence that the "courtesy" idea is not satisfying.) "So surely", one wants to continue, "what *this pain* really is must be the pain I would admittedly have felt, in consequence of this wound, even if I had never learned to talk." But this continuation must be wrong; it expresses a version of the idea expressed in "But isn't the beginning the sensation?"[24]

There may now be an inclination to complain that I am robbing cats and infants of an inner life—that I am suggesting there is no answer to the question what it is like to be a cat or an infant.[25] But why should we not count "He is in pain" (or, more specifically, "His foot hurts") as a partial answer to that question, sometimes correct according to the proposal? The inclination may be to say that, in the context of a denial that such attributions are true in virtue of the presence in the subject's consciousness of a pre-conceptual *this* similar to the pre-conceptual *this* that is supposed to be what matters

---

24. Am I suggesting that "is in pain" does not apply univocally to cats and adult human beings? That would be akin to the "courtesy" idea about non-human pain, which I have rejected. And it is not clear that the difference I *am* suggesting needs to be conceived as taken up into the *sense* of "is in pain" as applied to cats (or infants) and human adults.
25. See Thomas Nagel, "What Is It Like to Be a Bat?"

when we are in pain, such remarks cannot answer the question in the sense that matters, because they do not say what it is like *from the cat's, or the infant's, point of view*. But now, if "His foot hurts" (and the like) is not *subjective* enough to satisfy the demand, it looks as if what is wanted is something like this: what the cat, or infant, would truthfully say if it could only speak English—perhaps enriched, perhaps in ways that would be partly unintelligible to us. That is a form of the picture of the pre-conceptual given, there in pre-linguistic or non-linguistic awareness, waiting (in human infants at least) to be clothed in conceptual garb. The view I find in Wittgenstein certainly suggests that the subjectivity of cats and infants is not like that—that nothing is, in that kind of way, given to a cat or an infant. But if this seems like a denial of the subjectivity of cats and infants, that depends on missing the point that nothing is, in that way, given to *us* either. Our subjectivity is not a matter of this kind of thing plus the conceptual garb. The opponent's inclination is to say, focusing on a felt pain, "You are saying that cats do not have *this*". The right response is to say: "If by 'this' you mean something that is there in your consciousness only as falling under a concept, then certainly the claim is that cats have no such thing; but this is fully consistent with agreeing that cats can really suffer. If by 'this' you mean the supposed pre-conceptual subject matter for your conceptualizations, then there is nothing discriminatory about denying it to cats; you do not have what you want to mean by 'this' either."

8. I want to end with a very general remark about Wittgenstein's relation to one characteristic strand in contemporary philosophy. It is common nowadays for philosophers of mind to invoke a distinction between sapience and sentience,[26] in such a way as to suggest that there are two simply different problem areas within their branch of philosophy. (A good example is the familiar suggestion that functionalism can handle sapience—it can, supposedly, deal with "propositional attitudes"—but may have a "residual problem" over sentience, the problem of "qualia" or "raw feels".) Wittgenstein is, to say the least, not easy to place in a landscape organized like this.

---

26. I owe this wording for the distinction to Robert Brandom.

He is plainly interested in what other philosophers call "propositional attitudes" (e.g., in the remarks about expectation, etc., in the §400's), and equally plainly interested in the difficulties philosophers get into over "raw feels" (e.g., in §290); and the latter interest does not look like an interest in a "residual problem", or even like an interest that we ought to regard as significantly removed from the former in the landscape of philosophy. What is striking, in fact, is that in such passages as §290 he addresses philosophers' difficulties about "raw feels" with apparatus from the "sapience" part of the supposedly divided subject-matter for the philosophy of mind; he talks of language, but my point has been that his moves are easily restated in terms of concepts. It is natural to suggest that one thing we can learn from Wittgenstein is that there is something wrong with the supposed division. Not, of course, that we cannot distinguish sapience from sentience. But they are not two simply different problem areas: we get into trouble over sentience because we misconceive the role of sapience in constituting our sentient life. Focusing on the ideas that help us to comprehend sapience (centrally the idea that mental life is lived in the space of reasons, that is, the space of concepts) is not, as it sometimes seems, opting to ignore much of what has traditionally counted as philosophy of mind. Perhaps we can even say that Wittgenstein's philosophy of mind can be encapsulated in the remark that mental life is lived in the space of reasons; such a philosophy of mind need not be forgetful of the problems of sentience.[27]

---

27. The remark might be one way of beginning to spell out Stanley Cavell's suggestion that whereas Kant undid Hume's psychologizing of knowledge, and Frege and Husserl undid the psychologizing of logic, Wittgenstein in the *Investigations* tried to undo the psychologizing of psychology. See *Must We Mean What We Say?*, p. 91.

ESSAY 14

Intentionality and Interiority in Wittgenstein[1]

1. I think Crispin Wright's opening remarks exaggerate the difficulty of seeing how Wittgenstein's later philosophy of mind can be what Wittgenstein represents it as being, a rejection of some philosophy rather than an assault on common sense. Wright mentions the picture of the mental as an inner world only in connection with a full-blown "Cartesian" position, with the image of a walled garden to which only its owner has direct access; and he suggests that this picture comes so naturally to us that it is hard to see it as philosophically contaminated. But Wittgenstein is not hostile to the picture of the inner world as such, which can indeed be philosophically innocent. His point is that we go astray when, in applying the picture, we lapse into philosophy. At *Philosophical Investigations* (henceforth *PI*) §423 he says:

> *Certainly* all these things happen in you.—And now all I ask is to understand the expression we use.—The picture is there. And I am not disputing its validity in any particular case.—Only I want to understand the application of the picture.

---

1. Most of this paper is an expansion of comments on an earlier version of Crispin Wright, "Wittgenstein's Later Philosophy of Mind: Sensation, Privacy, and Intention", which I delivered at an American Philosophical Association symposium on the thought of Wittgenstein on December 30, 1989. I have eliminated all but traces (see §7 below) of my comments on Warren Goldfarb's contribution to the symposium, of which his "Wittgenstein on Understanding" is a version. The last two sections of this paper correspond to nothing I said at the symposium.

Clearly something of which Wittgenstein could say "I am not disputing its validity in any particular case" cannot be a full-blown "Cartesian" position.[2] A distinction opens up here that should disarm Wright's worries. What comes naturally to philosophically uncontaminated common sense is the picture whose validity Wittgenstein does not dispute. The image of the walled garden adds to that picture a lot of philosophy, in the pejorative sense that often seems near the surface in Wittgenstein. We need to be seduced into philosophy before it can seem natural to suppose that another person's mind is hidden from us.

2. Wittgenstein, as Wright reads him, holds that knowledge of one's own intentional states is "not . . . a matter of 'access to'—being in cognitive touch with—a state of affairs". At first blush, this might seem to imply that there is no state of affairs that constitutes one's being in an intentional state, for instance expecting someone for tea.[3] But Wright does not intend to impugn the reality of states of affairs involving intentionality.[4] His idea is, rather, on these lines. To say that one can be in cognitive touch with a state of affairs is to imply that the state of affairs is constituted as the state of affairs it is independently of one's judgement that it obtains. That is what Wright thinks Wittgenstein means to deny in the case of states of affairs involving intentionality; Wright thinks Wittgenstein means to persuade us that their subjects' judgements enter into their constitution.

---

2. As §423 (all unattributed references in this style will be to *PI*) makes obvious, saying that the picture of the inner world is a picture is not casting doubt on it. (See §427, on wanting to know what is going on in someone's head: "The picture should be taken seriously." Of course that is not to be confused with taking it literally, as in much contemporary philosophy of mind.) Wittgenstein does not always use the word "picture" to signal a target of suspicion, as in, e.g., §115.

3. I mean this formulation to be reminiscent of the "sceptical paradox" (accepted by Wittgenstein on the reading offered by Saul Kripke, *Wittgenstein on Rules and Private Language*) that there is no state of affairs that constitutes one's meaning what one does by a word.

4. For more about this, see especially Wright, "Wittgenstein's Rule-Following Considerations and the Central Project of Theoretical Linguistics". I shall in effect be suggesting that, in spite of this intention of Wright's, his reading is ultimately of a piece with Kripke's—and without a saving grace corresponding to Kripke's admittedly grudging hospitality to the idea that the "sceptical paradox" does not arise if we understand the *sui generis* character of intentional states (an idea that Kripke wrongly, though intelligibly, stigmatizes as "desperate" and "mysterious"). See §9 below.

However, Wright also takes it that Wittgenstein would have no objection to a category of conscious processes and states whose occurrence "makes no demands upon the conceptual resources of the subject". These would be states and goings-on whose presence in consciousness is independent of the subject's judgements or propensities to judge. And this makes it hard to resist the thought that these items are, as it were, more robustly *there* in the mind than Wright's reading allows anything intentional to be. These other items are there anyway, whereas intentional states of affairs depend for their being on their subjects' judgements. So for all Wright's disclaimer of irrealism about states of affairs involving intentionality, his reading leaves Wittgenstein's philosophy of mind looking, in a certain structural respect, rather like Gilbert Ryle's (on the standard reading of Ryle's *The Concept of Mind*, which may well be over-simplified). Substantial presence in the interior is credited only to these concept-free states and occurrences, which take on something of the look of Ryle's twinges and stabs; and intentionality-involving states of affairs take on the look of a mere reflection of our practices of avowal, something distinct from substantial inner presence. I believe a version of the unease Ryle induces is well-placed against Wright's Wittgenstein too; what I mean should become clearer as we proceed.[5]

3. It belongs with the asymmetry that Wright takes the distinction between the non-intentional and the intentional to correlate neatly with the distinction between what is to be found "within the occurrent phenomena of consciousness" (what is available to introspection) and what is not. Wright sees Wittgenstein's assault on the "Cartesian" position, accordingly, as falling into two parts. The first part attacks an assimilation of the intentional aspects of psychological life to occurrent phenomena of consciousness; the second (the Private Language Argument) undermines the "Cartesian" conception of occurrent phenomena of consciousness themselves.

Wright's main interest is in the second part of this two-pronged attack, and he deals with the first only sketchily. But I think he is

---

5. It is worth noting in advance that "*Certainly* all these things happen in you", in §423, does not seem to be restricted to sensations and the like, to the exclusion of, for instance, "thought-processes" (§427).

wrong about the first part, and in a way that carries over to the second. Wittgenstein is not concerned to expel everything that is intentional from the province of introspective self-consciousness. The idea that he is involves a misconception of the province of introspective self-consciousness—something that is itself part of Wittgenstein's target.

Wright finds in Wittgenstein an argument, for the thesis that intentionality does not figure among the occurrent phenomena of consciousness, that is partly phenomenological and partly *a priori*. The *a priori* part of the argument is that no phenomena of consciousness could "sustain the kinds of connection with aspects of a subject's subsequent doings and reactions which mental states of this kind essentially sustain". Now this reading may look close enough to the key point in Wittgenstein's discussion of meaning and understanding for it to pass a casual muster. But it misses two directions in which that discussion generalizes. One is to occurrences, as opposed to states, that involve intentionality; the other is to non-intentional aspects of the inner life.

The kinds of connection that figure in the Wittgensteinian material from which Wright extracts the *a priori* argument can be summarily captured, as Wittgenstein does himself (for instance at §§198, 201), in terms of the notion of accord. In the case of understanding a series—the case that Wittgenstein's main discussion focuses on—the connections are with the subject's subsequent doings and reactions; the challenge is to make sense of the subject's understanding as something with which specific performances accord, or do not accord, as the case may be. In other cases, as Wright notes, we have the same trouble without the subject's *performance* needing to be the outward item with which an apparently inner item needs to be so connected. For instance, there is a parallel challenge, beset with parallel pitfalls, to make sense of an expectation as something with which certain subsequent occurrences (which of course need not involve the subject's performance) accord and others do not. (§437 makes the parallel plain.)

It should already be beginning to seem that it is at least risky to Wittgenstein's plausibility if we suppose he thinks it helps with these problems to insist that they arise only outside the sphere of occurrent phenomena of consciousness. Is it clear that expectation is never an occurrent phenomenon of consciousness? What about anxious expectation? Surely we should not be tempted to respond "In that case the anxiety is an occurrent phenomenon of consciousness, but still the expectation is not".

But in any case, consider §386, where Wittgenstein raises another parallel problem, again beset with parallel pitfalls.

> ... I say without hesitation that I have ... imagined this colour. The difficulty is not that I doubt whether I really imagined something red. But it is *this:* that we should be able, just like that, to point out or describe the colour we have imagined, that the translation of the image into reality presents no difficulty at all. Are they then so alike that one might mix them up?

Here a performance—describing or pointing out the colour—is once more in play. But the problem clearly lies in the relation between the image and what it is an image of, that is, in the intentionality of the image. The problem exactly matches the problem about the relation between an expectation and its fulfilment; focusing on a subject's ability to point out or describe what he imagines is just a way of making the issue vivid. Wittgenstein makes it clear that the pitfalls are the usual ones when, in §389, he has the difficulty generate the idea that the image must be a "super-likeness".[6] But if anything is an occurrent phenomenon of consciousness, surely having a visual image of a colour is. Wright's reading has Wittgenstein denying that intentionality is found among occurrent phenomena of consciousness; but it is found there, and Wittgenstein cheerfully registers that it is.

This point implies that it is useless to invoke the notion of ability as a response to the difficulty in the case of understanding in particular. Of course it is not wrong to say that understanding is something in the nature of an ability; I am not suggesting it would be anything but an egregious category-mistake to assimilate, say, my standing knowledge of what "careen" means to an episode in consciousness. But why should that seem to help with the difficulty that arises about accord? It can seem to help only if we suppose something on these lines: the point saves us from having to try to locate the "normative" connections required by meaning as connections between the inner and the outer, where we seem to have trouble in making

---

6. Compare the "despotic demand" of §437, explicitly linked there to "the hardness of the logical must"; and the "super-strong connexion ... between the act of intending and the thing intended" of §197.

sense of them; it allows us to locate the required "normativity" wholly within the outer, in instances of what G. P. Baker and P. M. S. Hacker call "normative regularities".[7] This notion of "normative regularity" may sound like a neat gloss on Wittgenstein's notion of practice; but since avoiding "normative" connections between inner and outer in this way, in the case of understanding, would only postpone dealing with some other forms of what Wittgenstein plainly sees to be the same difficulty, this relocation cannot be what he wants to do with the notion of practice.

I said "If anything is an occurrent phenomenon of consciousness . . . "; I think Wright's reading actually puts it in doubt whether anything *could* be an occurrent phenomenon of consciousness. (This is the second direction of generalization.) The kinds of connection that raise the problem for intentional states are, as I said, connections involving the "normative" notion of accord. But such connections are a species of a wider genus, that of internal relations.[8] If Wright's *a priori* argument worked, it would have to be because nothing introspectable could sustain internal relations to anything outer.[9] (Why should "normative" internal relations be special?) But it is precisely Wittgenstein's point, about the items Wright is willing to count as paradigms of occurrent phenomena of consciousness, that they do sustain such internal relations; they are not just externally related (by mere causation, for instance) to the public circumstances that constitute their expression.[10] To parody what Wright says about coming to understand a word in a flash: if feeling a pain were a matter purely

---

7. *Scepticism, Rules, and Language*, e.g. at p. 13. Compare Colin McGinn, *Wittgenstein on Meaning*, p. 85, n. 2.

8. See Baker and Hacker, *Scepticism, Rules, and Language*, passim (see the Index, under "internal relation").

9. This idea is clearly operative in the generation of the puzzle in §386: note especially "just like that", which serves to stress that the inner item is wholly available to introspection, in a way that makes it mysterious—on a certain conception of introspection—how an internal relation to something external could be partly constitutive of its being what it is. What I am suggesting is that this conception of the introspectable, as a realm of facts constituted as what they are independently of internal relations to matters outside the realm, is under quite general attack; whereas in Wright's reading it serves to mark out a category of genuine phenomena of consciousness that is supposed to be congenial to Wittgenstein.

10. The *temporal* gap Wright stresses, between acquiring understanding and exercising it, is an incidental feature of one kind of case. The point has much more general significance.

of the occurrence of certain events in consciousness, then it would be a point of contingency that people who feel pain were in normal circumstances disposed to engage in the sort of behaviour that we count as expressive of pain; but it is not a contingency. But if feeling a pain is never a matter purely of the occurrence of certain events in consciousness, then surely nothing is. The upshot is to cast doubt on the operative conception of what it is for something to be purely on occurrence in consciousness.

Wittgenstein's thought does not leave untouched the picture of the introspectable as a domain of self-containedly knowable states of affairs, only externally related to anything outside themselves, and expel the intentional from that domain. The key argument generalizes so as to undermine that picture of the introspectable.[11] Once we understand that, we can see that there is no need to be suspicious of including intentionality among the occurrent phenomena of consciousness. To repeat, this is not an encouragement to category-mistakes; of course standing states of understanding are not occurrent phenomena of consciousness. But it should no longer seem problematic to countenance, say, being struck by a thought as an occurrent phenomenon of consciousness.

I take it that Wright bases his reading of Wittgenstein's discussion of understanding on passages like the footnote, at p. 59 of *PI*, in which Wittgenstein expresses doubt that understanding is a *mental* state; and on the fact—it is indeed a fact—that much of the discussion of understanding consists in rejecting the claims of various candidate conceptions of what it might be for a meaning to come to mind, on just the sort of jointly phenomenological and *a priori* grounds that Wright describes. But this does not justify reading into Wittgenstein Wright's picture of the occurrent phenomena of consciousness as free of intentionality. As for the footnote, certainly its wording fits the idea that mental states in good standing are colourings of consciousness.[12] But the context to which the footnote

---

11. It is no accident that in the context of §386 Wittgenstein shifts, without any indication of crossing a significant divide, between images, which involve intentionality, and sensations, which do not. (Note, e.g., §384.)

12. See McGinn, *Wittgenstein on Meaning*, pp. 105–8. The passage tells against the view of Baker and Hacker, *Scepticism, Rules, and Language*, p. 29, that in Wittgenstein's view it is wrong to think of understanding as a state at all. (See Wright, "Critical Notice of Colin McGinn, *Wittgenstein on Meaning*", p. 295.)

loosely belongs suggests that the point is not, as Wright would have it, that no colouring of consciousness could have the links to the exterior that would be needed if it were to involve a grasp of meaning, but rather that if we conceive understanding as a mental state, we are in the vicinity of the suspect idea that it is "a state of a mental apparatus" (§149), "a state which is the source of the correct use" (§146).[13] As for the rejection of candidate conceptions of what it would be for a meaning to come to mind, the point is, I shall suggest, not that meanings cannot come to mind (that grasp of a meaning cannot be an occurrent phenomenon of consciousness—as if the upshot of the discussion initiated by §138 were that one cannot grasp a meaning in a flash), but that the candidate conceptions all reflect a misconception—which is a more ultimate target for Wittgenstein's reflections—of what it is for anything to come to mind.

4. In saying this, I am taking issue with Wright over what he has called "the choreography" of Wittgenstein's themes: the way they hang together.[14]

Wright's "choreography" looks like this. There are two target errors, to which our thinking is "naturally" prone. The first is platonism: a picture of rules as rails that we fall into when we try to understand how meaning is situated in a "normatively" shaped space of possibilities for thought and action.[15] The second is the "Cartesian" observational model for self-knowledge. These philosophical posi-

---

13. Why should the assimilation to a colouring of consciousness encourage this suspect idea? Because our paradigms for colourings of consciousness simply lack the necessary "normative" links to anything outside themselves. (This is not to say that the very idea of a colouring of consciousness excludes those links, as Wright suggests.) So assimilating understanding to them goes with a forgetfulness of the true character of the problem, which is expressed in the suggestion that we need to find out more about the as yet uncomprehended operations of a mechanism; compare §308, and see §7 below.

14. "Critical Notice of Colin McGinn: *Wittgenstein on Meaning*", p. 298.

15. See "Critical Notice of Colin McGinn: *Wittgenstein on Meaning*", p. 302: "It comes naturally to us to think, with the platonist, of the objectivity of many of our practices—including *par excellence* logic and mathematics—as residing in our following rules-as-rails, rules which somehow reach ahead of us and determine of themselves their every actual and counterfactual application." (One might be forgiven for finding this an extremely unobvious use of "comes naturally".) Note that it is obviously no good pointing to a fixation on logic and mathematics as an explanation of the temptation to platonism; platonism misconceives logic and mathematics too.

tions are not simply independent. When we press the observational model, confined to our knowledge of our own sensations, where it seems at its least unpromising, we fall into the idea of a private language. The private linguist must purport to determine the semantics of his private language by his own intentions;[16] and he has to conceive these intentions in a platonistic way. So platonism enters into an attempted defence of the observational model, and the attack on platonism removes a prop from under the observational model. But this link between the two targets is not supposed to be central to the lay-philosophical thinking that Wright's Wittgenstein attacks. It is something that Wright's Wittgenstein thinks through for himself and exploits. The two temptations are supposed to impinge on us to some extent independently; it is just that the upshot of the first lies ready to hand, and comes naturally into play, when we are called on to defend the upshot of the second.

There is a threat of falling into platonism when we try to make sense of how we could have meanings in mind. In Wright's reading, Wittgenstein in effect responds by denying that understanding *could* be a matter of having something in mind; the idea of having something in mind fits the other main compartment of our subject-matter, the occurrent phenomena of consciousness, and they do not involve intentionality.[17] But now, if our location in a "normatively" shaped space is not constituted by our having meanings in mind (a notion that leads inexorably to platonism, in Wright's view), then what does constitute it? Wright finds in Wittgenstein a framework within which an answer to this question would need to be given, in the thesis that understanding and meaning are "founded . . . in *primitive* dispositions of agreement in judgement and action".[18] But sheer consensus cannot constitute the "normativity" that genuine involvement with meaning would require. So what does? At this point in the dialectic, Wright suggests, the "official" Wittgensteinian line is a quietistic refusal to entertain further questions. And Wright thinks we

---

16. He is forced into this if an "operationalist" defence of the distinction between "seems right" and "is right" cannot work. Wright argues that it cannot in "Does *Philosophical Investigations* I.258–60 Suggest a Cogent Argument against Private Language?".

17. At p. 304 of "Critical Notice of Colin McGinn: *Wittgenstein on Meaning*", Wright puts the point like this: "There is no essential inner epistemology of rule-following. To express the matter dangerously, we have nothing 'in mind'."

18. "Critical Notice of Colin McGinn: *Wittgenstein on Meaning*", p. 304.

must query this quietism: we must either answer the constitutive question for which Wittgenstein provides at best a framework, or else "make out the necessary theoretical basis for the analytical quietism which, 'officially', he himself adopted".[19]

5. I have already suggested that this "choreography" leads to some falsification of what Wittgenstein says (§3 above). I believe the falsification reflects the fact that the "choreography" misses the true character of Wittgenstein's target, which is more of a unity than Wright's reading acknowledges. The best way to explain what I mean is by placing Wittgenstein in the wider context of German philosophy after Kant.[20]

Kant—to resort to thumbnail caricature—established that the world (something that consists of things that are the case: compare *Tractatus Logico-Philosophicus* §1.2) cannot be constitutively independent of the space of concepts, the space where subjectivity has its being. Kant himself preserved a residual role for the idea of something more brutely alien to the realm of thought than that, something that co-operates with mind in the transcendental constitution of the world. But Kant's successors saw (in one way or another) that the fundamental thesis, that the world cannot be constitutively independent of the space of concepts, does not require this residual recognition of an "in itself".

This tradition is generically known as "German idealism". But the upshot of the crucial post-Kantian move—discarding the "in itself"—need not be idealistic in any obvious sense. It was only because of the picture of co-workers in the transcendental constitution of the world that it seemed necessary to gloss the idea that world and

---

19. "Critical Notice of Colin McGinn: *Wittgenstein on Meaning*", p. 305.
20. I do not mean to be embarking on a topic for which it would matter to establish the details of Wittgenstein's intellectual formation. I am not suggesting that what follows captures his own "choreography" for his thought; the very idea that he had one would miss the genuinely exploratory character of his later writing. However, I agree with Wright that it is a good exegetical strategy to impose a "choreography". It may indeed be unavoidable; it is hard to see how else we might hope to think the thoughts for ourselves, which is the only way in which Wittgenstein wanted to be understood. As for the specifics of putting Wittgenstein in the historical context I want to exploit: I have no idea whether, for instance, he read Kant, and I would not mind if it were established that he did not. We do of course know that he read Schopenhauer.

thought are constitutively made for one another by saying, what indeed sounds idealistic, that mind makes a contribution to the world.[21] Still, the label "idealism" accurately suggests the character of a recoil that is quite intelligible, indeed deserving of sympathy, though it misses a point that is already in Kant himself—the point that the "in itself" cannot be anything to us. The recoil is a recoil from idealism; it finds an idealism, which it insists that we must combat, in any refusal to understand the relation between thought and world in terms of a "conceptual scheme" set over against an alien "in itself", on which the scheme imposes an intelligible organization.[22]

This recoil sets up a unified ultimate target for the Wittgensteinian moves whose "choreography" I am discussing. If one is in the grip of the recoil, the inner world can seem a last and best resort against the insidious advance of the idea that world and thought are made for one another. Perhaps—one supposes—there is no resisting those philosophies that scandalously surrender external nature to idealism. But in the inner life the "in itself", brutely alien to concepts, insistently makes its presence felt. The inner world is a lived refutation of idealism.

---

21. This point is missed by David Pears, in his discussion (*The False Prison*, vol. 1, p. 9 and following) of the "uncritical realism" that he finds in the *Tractatus*. Pears suggests that realism is uncritical (in a sense that is meant to echo Kant) if it does not speak of a contribution from us to the constitution of the world. My point is that we can have a position that is critical (in the same roughly Kantian sense: it acknowledges that world and mind are constitutively made for one another), but which, by dropping the "in itself", precisely sheds any need to talk of such a contribution (thereby, one might claim, becoming exactly what a critical realism would need to be). Pears suggests (pp. 31–2) that the furthest one can get, while remaining critical, from what he calls "the Kantian picture of the mind, the world, and the products of their interaction" (p. 12) is to retain the idea of the two contributions, but to hold that they "cannot be disentangled from one another"; I think he takes this to be the metaphysic of Wittgenstein's later work. (The formulation is at best misleading: the world would be the product of the transcendental interaction between mind and something else, not a participant in it.) But the right thought is not that there are two inseparable contributions to the constitution of the world, but that one cannot do anything at all with the idea of a contribution from an ineffable "in itself" beyond the limits of "ordinary knowledge". And it is only if one thinks one needs to do something with that notion that it can seem that, in order to be critical, one must talk about a contribution from us.
22. For an excellent critique of this picture, see Donald Davidson, "On the Very Idea of a Conceptual Scheme".

Wittgenstein's point, I suggest, is to reveal this rearguard action as a failure.

The rearguard action yields a picture of the inner as radically private; these chunks of the "in itself" can present themselves, in the way that is supposed to reveal their alienness to concepts, only to the subject whose inner world they occupy, and we cannot make genuine sense of their being amenable to being brought under publicly shared concepts.[23] Imagery of the "walled garden" variety can now seem inescapable. Indeed, this makes the grippingness such imagery can have much more comprehensible than if we take it to express a philosophically posterior "theory", intended to account for some supposedly prior "data" about asymmetries between self-knowledge and knowledge of others, as in Wright's opening remarks.

Platonism, too, falls into place, not as an idea that, gratuitously as it were, "comes naturally" to us, but as something that can seem inescapable if we are to make room for meaning at all. If this picture captures what it is for anything to come to mind, how could a meaning come to mind? Perhaps we can deceive ourselves into thinking the picture makes room for sensations. But it is clear that a brute chunk of the "in itself" could not have the internal links to performance that a grasped meaning would need to have. It would just "stand there like a sign-post" (*PI* §85). Perhaps an item that, considered in itself, just "stands there" can, under an interpretation, have the required internal links to performance. But this helps only if the interpretation can come to mind; and the governing picture of what can come to mind ensures that when we try to picture an interpretation coming to mind, we succeed in picturing only another item that just "stands there". This second item might have the required internal links to performance under an interpretation, but that is obviously the beginning of a regress. This bind—now familiar from discussions of passages like §198 and §201[24]—is actually hopeless. But

---

23. Given the way I suppose myself to know about my own inner world if I fall into this temptation, I cannot know that anyone else has one, let alone what someone else's is like. Solipsism must be a serious temptation.

24. In an active tradition of commentary initiated, as far as recent years go, by Kripke, *Wittgenstein on Rules and Private Language*. I hope my citing Kripke does not obscure the fact that I regard it as a misreading to suppose the argumentative links I am gesturing at amount, in Wittgenstein's view, to an unanswerable case for a "sceptical paradox", to which we can respond only with a "sceptical solution". See Essays 11 and 12 above.

such is the ingenuity of philosophical thought in desperate straits—and the straits are desperate, because meanings do come to mind; for instance, we grasp them "in a flash": *PI* §138—that we deceive ourselves into supposing we can escape the bind, while keeping the ground rules in force, by conceiving meaning as "the last interpretation" (*The Blue Book*, p. 34). This is the germ of the platonist idea—which now emerges as something other than a self-standing temptation—that meaning's "normativity" is a matter of a superlatively unyielding authority.[25]

To respond to "How can a meaning come to mind?" with "It cannot" is not just a way to express the good point that platonism is useless as a way to escape the regress. That response—which is Wittgenstein's, in Wright's reading—should now look too concessive to the basic misconception. What made it seem that we must embrace platonism was not simply the attempt to picture meanings as able to come to mind, but that attempt in the context of a misconception of what it is for *anything* to come to mind. Wright's obsession with keeping meanings out of the occurrent phenomena of consciousness now looks like the upshot of not seeing all the way through to Wittgenstein's ultimate target. Once we understand what the target is, we can see that insisting that that conception of the mental cannot make room for meanings to come to mind does not amount to denying that meanings can come to mind. And now there should be nothing against allowing meanings to come to mind: for instance, when one grasps a meaning in a flash; or—differently—when one visualizes something; or—differently again—when it suddenly occurs to one that one has forgotten to mail a letter.

Wittgenstein's treatment of sensations can take its proper place as an integrated element in the exorcism of the misconception. I do not mean to suggest that there is no exegetical merit in the connection between private language and platonism that Wright stresses (although I think it needs to be handled in a different way from his; see §8 below). But in my reading, the idea of a private language need not figure as the most immediate expression of the conception Wittgenstein attacks, not even as that conception applies to sensations. The idea of a private language is forced on one if one tries to make room

---

25. I elaborate this a little in Essay 11 above.

for saying something about these supposed chunks of the "in itself". But if one is in the grip of the conception I have described, one need not feel obliged to do that. Indeed, if one allows oneself to set store by the claim that even these items can be brought under concepts, one will risk conceding even them to the hated idealism, and the risk—needing to give up the claim that the "in itself" is independent of anything conceptual—is no different if the concepts are private ones. The point is really not to claim to be able to describe the precious items; the point is to insist on acknowledging their presence—to greet them, as it were. (In *The Brown Book*, Wittgenstein captures this thought by saying "I don't really speak about what I see, but *to* it" (p. 175).)[26] So it may not be devastating to someone in the grip of this conception if a Private Language Argument deprives him of the distinction between "is right" and "seems right", and hence of the possibility of talking, even in a private language, about his inner items. Even so, he will still want to say, they undeniably make their presence felt. On this reading, the true centre of the "private language" dialectic (misleadingly so called) is not §258, but rather passages like §261, where a Wittgensteinian persona who suffers from the syndrome under attack is pressed to "the point where [he] would like just to emit an inarticulate sound" (what else would do, to acknowledge the presence of that which is set over against our capacities to conceptualize and articulate?), and Wittgenstein makes the delightful response "But such a sound is an expression only as it occurs in a particular language-game, which should now be described".[27]

6. This alternative "choreography" makes room, I suggest, for a satisfying positive picture of the inner world.[28]

That the inner world is a world at all consists in its conforming to the Kantian requirement: it is constitutively apt for conceptual repre-

---

26. Clearly "what I see" here does not mean the visible objects in my environment; the remark gives expression to a conception of what is experienced as a private inner ingredient in the seeing of public objects.
27. I elaborate this reading of some of the "private language" dialectic (so called) in Essay 13 above.
28. Obviously what follows in this section cannot purport to match anything in Wittgenstein, with his well-known mistrust of positive pronouncements in a philosophical vein. Even so, I would claim that the positive picture I sketch here is Wittgensteinian in spirit. (It does not seem to me to matter that the mode of utterance is unlike his.)

sentation, not something set over against a conceptual scheme. That it is inner consists in there being nothing to its states of affairs except the instantiation in consciousness of the relevant concepts; the instances of the concepts, unlike instances of concepts of the outer, have no being independently of the fact that the concepts they instantiate figure in the content of consciousness.[29] (Supposing that they have such independent being turns them into the mythical chunks of the "in itself", that is, into "private objects".) But that is not to say that these states of affairs have no being. It is true that no distinction between "seems right" and "is right" opens up, with respect to the obtaining of these states of affairs, from the subject's point of view. But what it is for the relevant concepts—those whose instantiation in consciousness exhausts the being of these states of affairs—to have application cannot be understood exclusively from the subject's point of view. The concepts set up internal links between the states of affairs that are their instantiations and publicly accessible circumstances: circumstances linked "normatively" to the states of affairs in one kind of case, circumstances linked to them as their normal expression in another. So the distinction between "seems right" and "is right" opens up, with respect to these states of affairs, from the necessarily thinkable second-person or third-person point of view; one's own inner world is part of the world (anyone's world). This picture satisfyingly acknowledges the inner world, in a way that is—so long as we hold firm to a correct view of the concepts that structure it—immune to the risk that its interiority might seduce one into a declaration of independence on its behalf.[30]

Notice that, at the level of abstraction at which I have sketched this picture, it is indifferent to the distinction between intentional and non-intentional inner states of affairs. The basic requirement—that the concept that is employed when I think of my being thus and so should allow for that state of affairs to be thinkable from a non-first-person point of view, as a case of someone's being thus and

---

29. Wittgenstein says "You learned the *concept* 'pain' when you learned language" (*PI* §384); does this, with what I say in the text, imply that brutes cannot feel pain? That would be unpalatable. But refusing to credit brutes with an inner world—which is indeed an implication—does not require regarding them as insensate automata. I say a little more about this in Essay 13 above; and see n. 34 below.

30. This image comes from the richly suggestive discussion in David Pears, *The False Prison*, vol. 1, chaps. 3 and 7.

so[31]—is met in two different ways, but they are two versions of the same fundamental structure.[32]

Contrast Wright's asymmetry between those compartments of the subject-matter. And recall specifically Wright's suggestion that Wittgenstein would be hospitable to a category of goings-on in consciousness that are independent of the conceptual resources of their subjects. This looks to me like a form of the very conception that Wittgenstein is most fundamentally concerned to undermine. To suppose such items are objects for consciousness, and not just in the way in which any state of affairs within one's sensory reach may be an object for one's consciousness but in a specially inner way,[33] would be precisely to make them into "private objects". In the context of this conception, insisting that there are no concepts but public ones would get us at best to the "public meaning, private reference" idea that is canvassed in *PI* §273, and actually not even to that, because there is no genuinely making sense of how any concepts, public or not, could get a grip on such items.[34] And if these

---

31. I do not mean this formulation to imply that the points of view must be occupied by different thinkers. I myself must be able to think of my being thus and so as a case of someone's being thus and so. The actual existence of others is not what matters (at any rate not at this point in the overall picture).

32. My picture thus undermines the tendency for the idea of consciousness to collect exclusively the "qualitative" (or "sensuous") aspects of the inner life. By my lights, that tendency is a reflection of the basic misconception; it results from the fact that the self-deception required by the basic misconception is easier in the case of those aspects.

33. I enter this qualification because if we rejected the accusation of trafficking in "private objects" on the ground that a subject registers his mental goings-on in the way that he registers, say, the state of the weather, we would lose the interiority of the states of affairs in question. It would not help to insist that they can still be first-personal if this comes to no more than the sense in which, say, my needing a haircut is first-personal. (It is not "from inside" that I know that I need a haircut.)

34. The mystery is what it would be to bring under a concept an item that was present to one in that sort of way. It does not help to insist that the concept is public; the problem is not with the concept that figures at the end of the supposed transition from confrontation with a brute presence in consciousness to a concept-involving state, but with the transition. (See *PI* §380: "I could not apply any rules to a *private* transition from what is seen to words." On "what is seen", see n. 26 above.) Wright says that non-intentional inner states (and presumably the point would hold for goings-on too) "are not objects for consciousness in any sense which would render it moot whether others could know their real character, or knowingly share the concepts under which the subject brings them in judgement". But that is not to say they are not objects for consciousness. And my point is that if they are objects for consciousness (as they had better be; the other horn of this dilemma is utterly unattractive), and if their occurrence is not conceived in terms of the figuring of appropriate concepts in the content of consciousness, but is supposed to be independent of the conceptual resources of the subject, then there is no way to prevent those matters from

items are not objects for consciousness, or are objects for consciousness only in the way in which a perceivable state of affairs in one's environment is an object for consciousness, they lose their interiority; they lose their entitlement to be regarded as mental processes.

7. There is a strand in Wittgenstein's thought whose target is a point-missing scientific optimism, about the conceptual problems raised by the mental, encapsulated in the idea of "the as yet uncomprehended process in the as yet unexplored medium" (*PI* §308).[35] My "choreography" accommodates this satisfyingly. Although it was in connection with a willingness to surrender the external world to idealism that I introduced the idea that the "in itself" forces itself on us in the inner life, the idea involves (by definition, one might say) a failure to take the point of a post-Kantian philosophy of nature; it goes naturally with insisting that, whatever modish philosophers may say, science reveals the layout of the "in itself". So it naturally takes the form of an conviction that the inner world, like any region of the "in itself", is related to the rest of reality in the sorts of ways that science can cope with. This encourages us to help ourselves out, in the self-deception that is operative in falling into platonism, by misrepresenting what is in fact an impossible conceptual bind as if it were just one of the merely empirical mysteries that science faces and, to judge by past experience, will sooner or later solve.

Once we see that what is under attack, when Wittgenstein expresses suspicion about conceiving understanding as "a state which is the *source* of the correct use" (*PI* §146), is a scientistic mistaking of the conceptual bind for a merely empirical mystery, we make room for a position that avoids falling into the conceptual bind but retains the conception of understanding as an inner state from which

---

becoming moot. The case of animals and infants risks leading us astray here (see n. 29 above). But when a dog feels pain, that is not a matter of an object for the dog's consciousness. There are no objects for a dog's consciousness; dogs have no inner world. (That is not to say that dogs do not feel, e.g., pain.)

35. In this section I sketch a couple of points from my comments on Goldfarb (see n. 1 above), since they help to fill out the picture. I am in broad agreement with Goldfarb's reading: the only dissent that is relevant for present purposes is that Goldfarb seems to me to formulate the anti-scientistic thought he attributes to Wittgenstein in a way that preserves a scientistic conception of what it would be for something to be a particular or definite state or occurrence.

correct performances flow, put to a different use that Wittgenstein says nothing to undermine. It is only as an expression of the idea of the as yet uncomprehended process that such a conception of understanding is unmasked as a confusion. And a conception of understanding as the source of correct performances can be reclaimed from that context. There is nothing in Wittgenstein to require the view—which "Wittgensteinians" used to think was incumbent on them—that the concept of causation cannot get a grip on the mental, and in particular the intentional, except perhaps when the rational linkages that are proper to the mental are forcibly overridden, as it were from outside the space of reasons.[36]

8. Up to this point, I have been concerned with the first part of the two-part argument that Wright finds in Wittgenstein. As I noted, my reading places the centre of the "private language" dialectic elsewhere than Wright's does. However, the impossibility of holding "is right" distinct from "seems right" (*PI* §258) undeniably does some work in this region of Wittgenstein's thought, and at a general level Wright's suggestion that Wittgenstein in effect reduces the "private linguist" to a platonistic conception of his own semantical intentions seems very plausible. But I believe that at the level of detail this second part of Wright's reading goes wrong too, in a way that is connected with what I think is wrong with the first part.

Wright construes the Private Language Argument as turning on the quite general claim that "there is nothing for an intention, conceived as determining subsequent conformity and non-conformity to it autonomously and independently of its author's judgements on the matter, to be". This, in particular the feature of independence from subsequent judgements, which will reflect what seems right, is just what the private linguist needs in his semantical intentions, if they are to be constitutive of a genuine application for the idea of being right in the use of his private expressions. Wright's thought is that there is nothing but platonistic mythology in the idea that an intention determines what counts as conformity to it independently of its author's judgements. So the thesis is that what the private linguist

---

36. As perhaps in the cases of "mental causation" discussed by G. E. M. Anscombe, *Intention*, §§10 and 11.

needs in his semantical intentions is something that cannot be true of any intentions at all, on pain of platonism.

But suppose I form the intention to type a period. If that is my intention, it is settled that only my typing a period will count as executing it. Of course I am capable of forming that intention only because I am party to the practices that are constitutive of the relevant concepts. But if that is indeed the intention that—thus empowered—I form, nothing more than the intention itself is needed to determine what counts as conformity to it. Certainly it needs no help from my subsequent judgements. (Suppose I forget what a period is.) So there is something for my intention to type a period, conceived as determining what counts as conformity to it autonomously and independently of my judgements on the matter, to be: namely, precisely, my intention to type a period. An intention to type a period is exactly something that must be conceived in that way. This is common sense, not platonism; there is no implication that when I execute the intention I am tracing out a super-factual linkage between how I am minded and the external world. It is innocuous—indeed compulsory, on pain of losing our grip on our purported topic—to take it that intentions contain within themselves the distinction between conformity and non-conformity. If the private linguist's semantical intentions degenerate into platonistic mythology, that must be something special to them, not just a matter of their being supposed to have that feature of ordinary intentions.

I am not defending the model of inner observation, which Wright describes as imposing the requirement "that intentional states can be fully determinate objects of inner contemplation before they issue in anything outward, before they are acted on". But the difficulty Wright is inviting us to feel here turns on "fully determinate . . . before they issue in anything outward" rather than on the specific mode of epistemic determinacy invoked. The difficulty ought to persist if we substitute for "inner contemplation" some more neutral phrase such as "self-knowledge". And with that substitution the requirement is, once again, common sense; an intention is exactly something that can be, in some sense, all there in one's mind before one acts on it. One does not need to wait and see what one does before one can know what one intends. This is not at all to say—what Wright suggests is simply an implication—that intentions "can be fully identified without any consideration of events, reactions, and performances lying in the future". The concept of an intention has its life in the context of the concepts of successful execution, failed attempt, change of mind, and so forth; it would be absurd to suppose that someone who had no suitably connected thoughts involving concepts like those—which would require a play of thought over the future—could be identifying an intention, in himself or someone else. But this does not mean that fully identifying an intention must await the outcomes over which such thought plays; and it does not undermine the status as common sense of the idea that an intention, once identified, determines of itself, and in particular independently of its author's subsequent judgements, what counts as conformity to it.

So we need a more specific point if we are to make out the claim that the private linguist is reduced to platonism. We can come at the more specific point we need by asking how an intention could be constitutive of a concept, as opposed to annexing an independently constituted concept to a word as what it is to express. The private linguist's semantical intention is supposed to be inwardly expressible by something like "Let me call this kind of thing 'S' in future". But for this story even to seem to make sense, the classificatory concept supposedly expressed, with the help of an inward focusing of the attention, by "this kind of thing" would need to be at the linguist's disposal already; it cannot be something he equips himself with by such a performance. If a new classificatory concept can be set up by focusing on an instance, that is only thanks to the prior availability of a concept that makes the right focus possible, in the presence of the instance, by fixing what *kind* of classification is in question: we might consider "Let me call this kind of *sensation* 'S' in future". But this cannot serve the purposes of the private linguist, because "sensation" is a word of our public language (*PI* §261).

In this region of the "private language" dialectic, Wittgenstein is applying lessons learned from his earlier consideration of ostensive definition in general; he signals this with echoes of the earlier passages (for instance the talk of "stage-setting in the language" in §257). In the earlier discussion, when one is tempted to reject the idea that focusing the attention is made possible by concepts, and cannot be constitutive of concepts that are more radically new than is allowed for by some such idea as that of determinates under already available determinables, one is pushed into a picture of focusing the attention as an occult performance (see §36). This sort of lapse into an appeal to mysterious spiritual feats is one side of a two-sided degeneration of thought, of which the other side is a platonistic conception of the concepts or meanings that mediate the mind's relations to the world. The resort to the occult is a counterpart of the resort, on the side of the concepts, to the sublime (see §§38, 89, 94); these two moves make up a package, which issues from the attempt to elevate our reflection on mind's dealings with reality above the context of human life that is in fact needed to secure the reflection its subject-matter.

The application of this to the private linguist's conception of private ostensive definition is immediate. In the case of ostensive definition of, say, a colour, we have at our disposal a non-platonistic conception of what we are prone to misconceive, platonistically, in terms of an occult feat of attention. But in the case of the private linguist, there is no cleaned-up substitute for the platonistic mythology of attention; there is no bringing a genuine topic back into view, as in the other case, by reinstating a context of human life and initiation into it. When Wittgenstein claims that "is right" and "seems right" would coalesce for the private linguist, he is driving this difference home. The claim is a way of insisting that the private linguist's attempt to set up a meaning can seem to achieve something only within the myth, so it is really only an idle ceremony.

9. The second part of Wright's reading, like the first, seems to me to be distorted in a way that crystallizes around the idea that genuine presence in consciousness makes no demands on a subject's conceptual resources. This idea goes with a picture of what it would be for a mental item to be fully identifiable by its subject—all there in his mind—in advance, say, of any external performance that might be described as "acting on it". Intentions, whose identity hinges on internal links to the exterior, do not conform to that picture; and this is what leads Wright into his apparent willingness to dissent from a piece of common sense about intentions, that they are fully identifiable by their subject in advance of being acted on. He suggests that this dissent is required by rejection of the observational model, which can purport to encompass those internal links to the exterior only by lapsing into platonism; but I think that is just wrong.

If I insist that an intention can be fully identifiable in advance of being acted on (or not acted on, as the case may be), I shall no doubt be asked how that is possible, given that the concept under which the intention is identified connects it internally with the performance that would count as executing it. I need not object to letting the question arise, so long as it is not given an illusory urgency by that misconceived paradigm of genuine full identifiability. And I need not deny that if the question does arise, it might help to give a picture of how the relevant concepts function that embodies something on the lines of Wright's constitutive principle, the default status of avowals. But the effect of the principle is rather different if the question is deprived of that illusory urgency.

Wright remarks that the success of a language-game that embodies the default status of avowals depends on deep contingencies, including, he says, "the contingency that taking the self-conceptions of others seriously . . . almost always tends to result in an overall picture of their psychology which is more illuminating . . . than anything which might be gleaned by respecting all the data except the subject's testimony". I think this risks mislocating the important contingency. If someone produced what sounded like self-descriptions of the relevant sort, but in such a way that trying to take them at face value did not give us good service in the attempt to understand him, it would not be that we had a case of a self-conception that for once did not help us make sense of its subject, as is allowed by the contingency as Wright formulates it; rather, we would—at any rate failing an alternative scheme of interpretation—be defeated in the project of crediting this subject (if that is what he is) with opinions concerning his own intentional states. The words (if that is what they are) cannot convey self-conceptions at all unless they can be understood in such a way as to help make sense of the subject, by being taken to express something that is available to the subject "just like that". The real contingency is that human beings are capable of acquiring the capacity to form the relevant self-conceptions; given Wright's suggested lemma, this contingency comes to the same as the contingency that human beings are capable of learning to talk in such a way that some of their utterances are intelligible as expressing such self-conceptions. The contingency is that human beings are capable of acquiring a mastery of the concepts that figure in the relevant self-conceptions; since the default status of avowals is partly constitutive of the concepts, this mastery includes the ability to apply the concepts to oneself in a way that meshes with, for instance, one's subsequent performance in the manner required for the self-conception in question to help make sense of one, but without one's needing to wait and make sure of the mesh before one can know that the concept applies.

The default status of avowals is not so much part of the answer to the question "How is intentional self-knowledge possible?" as part of what it is for there to be such a thing as intentional self-knowledge at all. And it is an answer to the question to remark that the requisite deep contingency does indeed obtain. This is not special to *intentional* self-knowledge; the entirely parallel question, "How is it possible that one can know 'just like that'—without checking one's behaviour—that one is in pain, when the concept involved in that self-knowledge embodies internal links with expressive behaviour?", is susceptible of an entirely parallel response.

What I am claiming is that pointing to the right deep contingency should leave us with no problem about how an intention can be fully identifiable—all there in one's mind—in advance of being acted on. I insist that the observational model of self-knowledge is not in play here. Of course it is not by inner observation that one knows one's intentions. It would be more nearly right to say that one knows them by forming them. But now, if the problem really were urgent, it should be just as urgent in the shape of the question "How is it possible to form an intention in advance of acting on it?" (This is a special case of the question "How is it possible to frame a thought in the absence of the circumstance that would verify or falsify it?") But the deep contingency, in its most general guise, is the contingency that human beings can be initiated into the capacity to place themselves within a "normatively" structured space of possibilities—the realm of freedom, as one might put it. And if we really accept that that contingency obtains, we ought not to find the question "How is it possible to form an intention in advance of acting on it?" any more pressing than, say, the question "How is it possible to commit oneself by making a promise?"

I do not deny that it is possible to find such questions pressing. But if they are asked pointedly, what is really expressed is an inability to manage a genuine acceptance of the deep contingency. That is something we can sympathize with, and we can try to help; but what is called for, on the part of someone who really does accept the deep contingency, is not counting the questions good ones and setting out to answer them.

Just that is what happens in Wright's reading of Wittgenstein.

Wright cannot stomach the idea that a mind can fully encompass something that contains within itself a determination of what counts as conformity with it; he cannot see anything for that idea to be but a form of platonism. So in his picture determining what counts as conformity happens, rather, as we go along, with the subject's judgements constitutively involved. This goes for intention and grasped meaning alike. When, in the paper I am discussing, Wright suggests that an intention does not determine of itself, independently of its subject's judgements, what counts as conformity to it, he is giving expression to a cousin of his earlier suggestion that if we are to avoid platonism about meaning, we need to rethink the objectivity of concepts, because we can no longer exploit the ordinary notion of things being thus and so anyway, whatever anyone judges on the matter.[37] In this framework, the default status of avowals figures not as part of an overall picture that incorporates the autonomy of meaning and intention, in the sense of their containing within themselves a differentiation between what would accord with them and what would not, but as part of a story about how things are instead.

If we renounce the autonomy of meaning and intention, it becomes, as Wright recognizes, a substantial problem to reconstruct their "normativity", their involvement with the notion of accord. That is why, since he takes Wittgenstein's dismantling of platonism to leave no room for the autonomy of meaning and intention, he cannot understand Wittgenstein's refusal to engage in constructive philosophy except as a quietism whose consistency with Wittgenstein's central thinking must come into question.

But it is wrong to suppose platonism is implicit in the very idea that meaning and intention contain within themselves a determination of what counts as accord with them. The lapse into platonism comes from trying to find room for that idea within the framework of a conception of genuine presence in mind as insulated from the exterior—not linked to it by internal relations. That is what leads to the regress of interpretations and the platonistic picture of meaning as "the last interpretation" (see §5 above). Avoiding platonism does not require us to leave that framework in place, and struggle to reconstruct the "normativity" of meaning and intention on the basis of

---

37. See *Wittgenstein on the Foundations of Mathematics,* passim; for an earlier protest against the idea that this has anything to do with Wittgenstein, see Essay 11 above.

a denial of their autonomy (a struggle that would be incumbent on us, since trying to maintain their autonomy within the framework amounts to platonism). There is the alternative of dislodging the framework. Within this alternative, it looks like a mistake to be too concerned with the observational model as such; that model is merely a natural form for the epistemology of self-knowledge to take if the framework is in place, and it is the framework that is the real villain of the piece.

The framework, which is firmly in control of Wright's reading, reflects an inability to manage a genuine acceptance of the contingency that human beings can be initiated into the realm of freedom.[38] To repeat, such inability might deserve our sympathy. But I am sure that we massively miss Wittgenstein's point if we take him to share the inability, and complain accordingly that, in order to complete something that we take him to have himself begun, he ought to have shaken off his quietism and grappled constructively with the apparent philosophical problems about meaning and intention that the inability generates. The apparent problems are reflections of something that, intelligibly by all means, stands in the way of our seeing things clearly; if we could dislodge the block, a relaxed common sense could simply reclaim the field.

38. The framework is essentially that within which Kripke works, in *Wittgenstein on Rules and Private Language*, apart from his uncomfortable toying with the idea that understanding is a *sui generis* mental state. That idea can be taken as a way of making the correct move, that is, dislodging the framework. It cannot surface as such in Kripke's mind because of his unreflective immersion in the framework, and that is why the toying is so uncomfortable. In view of the essential identity of frameworks, I cannot regard Wright's call for constructive philosophy as anything more than a request for a more convincing "sceptical solution" than Kripke's. It makes no substantial difference that what Wright's "sceptical solution" would be an alternative to is not exactly Kripke's "sceptical paradox"; the positions are alike in that both are driven to constructive philosophy by the idea that when Wittgenstein dismantles platonism, that debars us from conceiving grasp of meaning as the mind's encompassing something that contains within itself a differentiation between accord and failure to accord.

PART IV

MIND AND SELF

ESSAY 15

Functionalism and Anomalous Monism[1]

1. Donald Davidson has insisted on the role played by "the constitutive ideal of rationality"[2] in shaping our thought about propositional attitudes; and he has argued that this makes it out of the question to reduce that aspect of the mental to "the physical". In his book *Mind and Meaning,* Brian Loar has undertaken to refute this. Davidson's argument hinges on the claim that the patterns required by rationality "have no echo in physical theory" (p. 231). On the contrary, says Loar: "the very possibility of a functional interpretation shows that claim to be false" (p. 21).

I propose to grant Loar's argument that the possibility of a functional interpretation of propositional attitudes would permit a kind of "physicalist" reduction. The upshot is, I believe, to show that a functional interpretation of propositional attitudes is part of what the constitutive role of rationality excludes. This is a straightforward contraposition of Loar's argument against Davidson. Loar thinks he has established that the argument should go in the other direction, by showing the possibility of a functional interpretation of propositional attitudes. He does not dispute the Davidsonian claim that any interpretation could capture propositional attitudes in its net only if it could attribute a constitutive force to rationality; but he sees nothing to prevent a functional interpretation from doing that. However,

---

1. Akeel Bilgrami was the commentator when I delivered a version of this paper at a conference in honour of Donald Davidson, held in New Jersey in 1984. In revising it, I benefited from his comments.
2. *Essays on Actions and Events,* p. 223.

what Loar incorporates in his sketch of a functional account of propositional attitudes, under the head of "rationality constraints", covers at best a fragment of rationality in general. Davidson's point is that no approach congenial to "physicalist" reduction could do more than that, and (crucially) that that is not enough; and Loar's argument does not refute this claim, but merely ignores it.

2. It is already indicative of how far Loar is from engaging with Davidson that the "*a priori* rationality constraints" (p. 9) that he aims to incorporate in his picture of mind are restricted to "internal constraints of rationality on beliefs" (p. 9). The restriction limits us to structures that must characterize the interior, so to speak, of a rational mind, excluding (for instance) requirements on how a rational mind expresses itself in intentional action. Such requirements do indeed figure in Loar's picture of the mental, but not under the head of "rationality constraints". This means that when Loar purports to have dealt with the obstacle that Davidson thinks the constitutive role of rationality places in the way of "physicalist" reduction, he is ignoring a suggestion of Davidson's to the effect that the obstacle is operative in the latter area too, in a way that comes out when we ask how propositional attitudes must cause behaviour in order to rationalize it.[3]

However, it will be useful to start by going along with Loar's restriction, since it helps us to focus on an area of application for the concept of rationality in which the point at issue is especially clear.

Loar's "*a priori* rationality constraints" are of two sorts: "L-constraints", covering relations between beliefs that are specifiable in terms of their logical forms (pp. 71–4), and "M-constraints", which are modelled on Carnapian meaning postulates (pp. 81–5). It is the "L-constraints", then, that relate to what we can naturally call "deductive rationality"; and this is what I want to begin by focusing on. Deductive rationality is a capacity, more or less perfectly instantiated

---

3. See *Essays on Actions and Events*, pp. 79–81. Loar's brief discussion (p. 93) of the problem of "deviant causation" is unsatisfactory by my lights (in a way that I hope will become clear), in the way Loar suggests the problem is to be consigned to purely theoretical considerations, taking over where what is available to "common sense" leaves off.

in different rational individuals, to hold beliefs when, and because, they follow deductively from other beliefs that one holds. If we are careful, it need do no harm to picture a particular instantiation of deductive rationality as a more or less approximate grasp of a normative structure, determining what follows from what and thus what ought to be believed, given other beliefs, for deductively connected reasons. The Davidsonian claim, now, is that this structure (if we allow ourselves that picture) cannot be abstracted away from relations between contents, or forms of content, in such a way that we might hope to find the abstracted structure exemplified in the interrelations among a system of items described in non-intentional terms. And in this case the claim is actually susceptible of something like proof. Someone who denied the claim would find it hard to explain how his position was consistent with the fact that there is no mechanical test for logical validity in general.

Now Loar is clearly not trying to deny this claim. His "L-constraints" proscribe beliefs of two forms outright, and proscribe beliefs of a finite number of other forms conditionally on the presence of beliefs of related forms. (Alternative versions, about which he is much more doubtful, make conditional positive requirements.) Loar himself stresses that these constraints are quite undemanding: they do not, for instance, ensure even a rudimentary proficiency at making, or assessing, inferences (except for the doubtful positive versions, and even those would introduce only the most elementary inferential capacities). Obviously Loar would not dream of suggesting that his "L-constraints" capture the structure of deductive reason itself—a structure that would reflect what, in general, follows from what.

But Davidson's claim, particularized to the sphere of rationality that we are focusing on, is that it is that structure that "has no echo in physical theory"; and he argues the irreducibility of propositional attitudes to "the physical" from the premise that the structure of reason itself, of which that structure is a part, cannot be matched up to the interrelations within a non-intentionally characterized system of items. Loar takes himself to have undermined the premise, as particularized to deductive rationality at least, by pointing out that his "L-constraints" are available, via functionalism, to a "physicalist" treatment of propositional attitudes. But since the "L-constraints" are not meant to capture the structure of deductive reason, this involves a misconception of Davidson's premise, not a refutation of it; and Davidson's argument is left completely unchallenged.

3. I remarked that any particular instantiation of deductive rationality will embody a more or less imperfect grasp of what, in general, follows from what. This variable gap between actual and ideal may make it seem that any constitutive force that can be attributed to this particularization of the concept of rationality could not extend to the structure of deductive reason itself, as I have said that Davidson's argument requires. The idea would be that constitutive force could be ascribed only to some minimally necessary structure, exemplified in the actual psychological economy of anything that could be recognized as a rational mind: exactly the sort of thing that Loar's "L-constraints" aspire to capture. Some such idea must underlie Loar's misinterpretation of what Davidson claims. I believe it betrays a prejudice about the character of the understanding we can achieve by employing the conceptual apparatus that is governed by the constitutive force of rationality.

Davidson's claim is, in effect, that if someone offered to reflect the patterns required by rationality in a structure described in nonintentional terms, then, in view of the fact that the constitutive concept functions as an ideal or norm, he would be committing a kind of "naturalistic fallacy". (The label is suggestive, but unfortunate in implying that there is something non-naturalistic about propositional attitudes conceived as irreducible to anything non-intentional; I shall return to this.) The prejudice I have in mind would preclude giving this thought its proper significance, by inducing a refusal to recognize that it is something with the status of an ideal that is being credited with a constitutive role in governing our thinking about propositional attitudes. To recognize the ideal status of the constitutive concept is to appreciate that the concepts of the propositional attitudes have their proper home in explanations of a special sort: explanations in which things are made intelligible by being revealed to be, or to approximate to being, as they rationally ought to be. This is to be contrasted with a style of explanation in which one makes things intelligible by representing their coming into being as a particular instance of how things generally tend to happen. (In the usual way of formulating the philosophical issue we are concerned with, "the physical" need do no more than point to the subject-matter of those sciences that aim at explanations of the second sort.)[4] Loar's weakening of the concept to which, in purported agreement with Davidson, he attributes the constitutive force that shapes our understanding of propositional attitudes, from Davidson's ideal to his own highest common factor of the actual, reflects a determination to assimilate all explanation to the second of these two sorts.

This has a damaging effect, which I can illustrate without lifting the restriction to deductive rationality. With the restriction in force, what is in question is a mode of understanding in which one finds a belief intelligible on the basis of its following deductively (or being intelligibly but falsely thought to follow deductively) from other beliefs that one knows the believer holds. Attaining this kind of understanding requires bringing to bear the notion of deductive consequence, and it must be that notion itself, not some thinned-down surrogate; if we allow ourselves the idea that the relevant explanations work by locating explanandum and explanans within a structure, it must be the ideal structure of deductive reason, not the less demanding sort of structure that could be determined by something on the lines of Loar's "L-constraints". Now Loar envisages a theory that would flesh out the admittedly thin structure that his "*a priori* rationality constraints" would impose by adding further functional relations; these further relations, to be established by theoretical inquiry rather than excogitated *a priori,* are envisaged as belonging to "the part of the theory outside common sense", and hence as not being required to "correspond to cognitive, intentional, or conceptual relations" (p. 79). So there is no requirement that anything in the theory outside the "L-constraints" should even aim to mirror the structures of deductive inferences, let alone amount to expressing the concept of deductive consequence. The result is that outside the sphere of beliefs, or absences of beliefs, that are related as the "L-constraints" expressly stipulate, a theory such as Loar envisages would not even aspire to deliver a kind of understanding of beliefs, or absences of beliefs, that depends on the thought that other beliefs are deductively cogent reasons for them. And even within that

---

4. This is why I have put "physical" and its cognates in quotation marks. The issue is a live one quite independently of whether "physics" is reducible to, or even interestingly dependent on, physics.

sphere, the undemandingness of the "L-constraints"—their innocence of any ambition to capture the ideal structure of deductive reason—means that any understanding that such a theory could offer of beliefs, or absences of beliefs, on the basis of beliefs that are as a matter of fact deductively related to them would not be the kind of understanding I have described. Such a theory would not have the general normative notion of deductive consequence at its disposal; so its explanations could not exploit that notion, but could draw at most on the idea of certain transitions, and refrainings from transitions, that minds are as a matter of fact prone to. By Davidsonian lights, even that formulation is unwarranted; since the idea of rationality is not credited with its constitutive role, there is nothing to ensure that it is minds that the theory is about.

In connection with his "*a priori* rationality constraints", Loar writes at one point of the way in which a theory that embodies them says that beliefs "ought rationally to be related" (p. 221). That "ought" may seem to make room for the distinctive kind of understanding that I am claiming Loar's position cannot countenance, but the appearance is misleading. It is helpful to consider the question *why* beliefs ought rationally to be related as the "L-constraints" stipulate. In real life we need have no difficulty in answering this question. But a theory of the sort Loar envisages would contain no materials for addressing it. Such a theory would owe no allegiance to "common sense" apart from the "*a priori* rationality constraints" themselves; and the explanations it yielded would purport to be self-sufficient—there is no room for the suggestion that their explanatory power might be enhanced if we explained the demandingness of the "L-constraints" in terms of the general notion of deductive cogency. Made within such a theory, the claim that beliefs ought rationally to be related in accordance with the "L-constraints" would not reflect the conformity of beliefs so related, in particular, to a categorical norm, intelligibly operative in other cases also; obedience to the "L-constraints" would have, rather, the status of a hypothetical imperative—something without which a system of states could not be recognized as characterizing a rational mind, and so as a system of beliefs, at all. Now it is no doubt correct to attribute that status to Loar's "L-constraints". But if we grant an explanatory role to an ideal that transcends them, we can explain why they have that status in terms of the thought that violations would lie outside the boundaries of what is intelligible—a terrain of whose topography we have a pre-theoretical ("common-sense") grasp that outruns anything captured by Loar's "*a priori* rationality constraints". In Loar's picture, by contrast, "common sense" is conceived as doing no more than presenting us with the "rationality constraints", all else being the province of a theory-construction that, having embraced them, lies under no further obligation to respect thoughts expressible in intentional (content-involving) terms. So Loar's "ought rationally" does not reflect an acknowledgement of the distinctive kind of understanding I have described; this shows up in its being, from the standpoint of a theory of the sort Loar envisages, a brute fact—a sheer inexplicable datum of "common sense"—that the "*a priori* rationality constraints" mark limits of intelligibility.

When we come to consider applications for the concept of rationality outside the sphere of deductive consequence, it seems no less plain—though proof is no longer in question—that it would be a fantasy to suppose that the full normative force of the concept, in its extra-logical applications, could be captured in a structure specifiable from outside intentional content. Not a fantasy that Loar indulges in: my point is that his response to Davidson reflects, rather, an inability to see that it is the full normative force of the concept to which Davidson attributes a constitutive status.

That actual instantiations of rationality are imperfect would seem to preclude attributing an explanatory role to the ideal, I suggested, if one assumed that all explanation must be a matter of subsuming particular cases under what generally tends to happen. Without that assumption, the variable gap between actual and ideal is unproblematically reflected in features of the different kind of explanation I have described. On the side of the *objects* of understanding, it appears in the critical dimension that any explanation of the ideal-involving kind must have. (Whereas if one tries to force explanation by reasons into the other mould, it is hard to see how one can give due weight to the thought that an ability to understand things on the basis of reasons must carry with it a conception of the difference between good and bad reasons.) And there is a no less important implication on the side of the *subjects:* those who attain understanding. The structure of the ideal (if we allow ourselves that picture) cannot be fixed once and for all from outside. Without an external touchstone, there seems to be no ground on which a subject or group could be confident that its own grasp of the structure, from inside, was incapable of improvement, in particular from coming to understand others. Finding an action or propositional attitude intelligible, after initial difficulty, may not only involve managing to articulate for oneself some hitherto merely implicit aspect of one's conception of rationality, but actually involve becoming convinced that one's conception of rationality needed correcting, so as to make room for this novel way of being intelligible. This reflects the fact that, barring a merely dogmatic complacency, someone who aims at explanations of the ideal-involving kind must be alive to the thought that there is sure to be a gap between actual current conception and ideal structure in his own case as well as in others.

4. If we countenance the ideal-involving kind of understanding that I have described, we have at our disposal a clear interpretation of the thought that propositional attitudes figure in a kind of explanation that is *sui generis*. Unsurprisingly, Loar cannot make much of this thought, which appears at two places in his book.

In the first (p. 11), it is part of an envisaged attempt to occupy a position—"anti-reductionism"—whose availability Loar in fact doubts: a position that aims to avoid both instrumentalism about propositional attitudes and the "physicalist" realism of Loar's own approach. Loar's "anti-reductionist" accepts that the nature of propositional attitudes can be captured by what Loar calls "the belief-desire theory": a theory formulable in terms of "counterfactual relations of causation, transition and co-occurrence" (p. 22) between "physically" characterized ambient circumstances, psychologically characterized events and states, and "physically" characterized behaviour. Such a theory would, as Loar insists, describe a structure that might in principle admit of "physical" interpretation. That is why it is a telling objection against this "anti-reductionist" that he fails to provide what his rejection of instrumentalism requires, a conception of what it would be for "the belief-desire theory" to be true of a creature; he rejects the conceptually innocuous, and seemingly common-sensical, "physicalist" view that the theory's truth would be a matter of an appropriate structuring among the creature's literally internal states, but he supplies nothing (except perhaps a quite unpalatable dualism: see p. 19) to serve instead.

By my lights, this attempt to avoid "physicalist" reduction is indeed half-baked (as Loar in effect argues). If one accepts Loar's assumption about "the belief-desire theory", one ensures the impossibility of maintaining that explanations in terms of beliefs and desires are in any serious sense unlike, say, explanations in terms of the internal states of a "physically" described mechanism. But what needs discussing is a quite different sort of opposition to reductionism: one that attributes a special explanatory role to the ideal of rationality, and on that basis rejects the idea that the explanatory power of citing beliefs and desires could be accounted for by anything like Loar's "belief-desire theory". This makes *"sui generis"* into something quite different from the rather empty rhetoric it becomes in the "anti-reductionism" Loar considers.[5]

In its second occurrence in Loar's book (pp. 90–1), the notion of a distinctive kind of understanding figures as an overblown response to the fact that a capacity to give common-sense explanations of behaviour in terms of desires does not carry over into a capacity to predict behaviour. Against this, Loar proposes a parallel between desires and the forces that are cited in a familiar sort of non-predictive but nevertheless "physical" explanation. But the idea of a distinctive kind of understanding is not a mere response to the non-predictiveness of the common-sense explanatory scheme. It is recommended independently by Davidson's point about the explanatory role of rationality. And it, or the point that recommends it, constitutes an argument, not confronted by Loar, against his parallel. It is sensible to

---

5. The point does not relate exclusively to what happens *inside* a rational mind: the anti-reductionism I envisage would not accept Loar's view that we can make sense of what happens inside the mind as intervening between "physically" characterized inputs and "physically" characterized outputs. The idea that the concepts of behaviour and of mental states are on a par (compare *Mind and Meaning*, p. 11) need not imply that a conception (scarcely a *theory*, on this different view) of a rational mind is not a conception of "an *isolable* part of what there is"; Loar's argument to the contrary depends on the inputs and outputs being "physically" characterized. Something else that can lapse is the extraordinary idea that psychological explanation cannot explain behaviour under descriptions involving acting on objects (see *Mind and Meaning*, p. 65: "grasping away" rather than "grasping an apple"). A remark on p. 88 suggests Loar would object that the agent's beliefs and desires do not explain, e.g., the presence of an apple at the place where he "grasps away". But one might equally say that the beliefs and desires do not explain the fact that the agent's nerves and sinews are in working order—using the implicit argument, surely absurdly, to push the explanandum still further "inwards" (away from the agent's involvement with the world).

try to refine the common-sense conception of forces into a tightly predictive theory, not letting go of the concept of a force but making forces susceptible of precise measurement; but we know *a priori*, on the basis of what sustains the idea of *sui generis* understanding, that no such thing is in prospect for the explanatory scheme in which desires figure.[6]

5. On the view I am recommending, we need not be troubled by what appears in Loar's construction as "a curious gap between . . . functional role and truth conditions" (p. 85). In Loar's picture, the explanatory capacity ("functional role") of a belief is in general separate from that bearing on the world in virtue of which it is true or false; the latter has to be specially secured after the explanatory capacity has been fully accounted for. (Observational beliefs are an exception: see p. 85.) This strange separation issues directly from failure to appreciate how propositional-attitude explanations are governed by the constitutive ideal of rationality, and it can lapse as soon as that Davidsonian thought is given its proper significance. Even if we restrict attention to cases where the explanatory ideal is deductive rationality, the capacity of one belief to explain another depends on relations that cannot be characterized except intentionally: relations, in this case specified in terms of form, between representational contents. If we let intentionality go, we lose hold of the idea that constitutively governs the explanations; that is the Davidsonian point on which I have been insisting. When we lift the restriction to deductive rationality, what comes into view is a normatively explanatory structure whose detailed ins and outs can no longer be conceived as knowable *a priori;* and now the substance, and not just the form, of a propositional attitude's representational bearing on the world contributes intelligibly to the attitude's explanatory powers.[7]

---

6. See Davidson, *Essays on Actions and Events*, p. 219.
7. It is to Loar's credit that he concedes that the gap he envisages is curious (unlike some proponents of similar positions, who represent it as sheer common sense). Consider how the idea applies to wants. What a want is a want for has nothing to do with the explanatory capacity of citing it. What, then, is the point of the notion of the object of a want? It lies in such facts as that when one gets what one wants, the want ceases to move one. This remarkable suggestion (for which see *Mind and Meaning*, pp. 196–8) seems close to a *reductio ad absurdum*.

This does not disrupt the thesis that the explanations in question work by citing causes.[8] No doubt there is nothing normative about the causal nexus as such; in a broadly Humean conception of causation, that is strikingly reflected in the fact that it is by virtue of being an instance of a generalization about how things tend to happen—the sort of thing that figures in the kind of explanation I have contrasted with the ideal-involving kind—that the relation between a particular pair of events is a causal relation at all. It would follow that a singular causal relation always brings with it a possibility in principle that the effect can be given an explanation of that non–ideal-involving kind. But even if we grant a broadly Humean conception of causation (an issue to which I shall return), it would be a mere prejudice to suppose that citing a cause can be explanatory only by exploiting that possibility.

6. I have claimed that Loar fails to challenge Davidson's argument; his idea that he has refuted its premise betrays a misconception of what the premise is. This raises an urgent diagnostic question; something deep and gripping must account for such failure even to identify the threat to his position, let alone counter it. It can be only temporarily satisfactory to postulate a prejudice that obscures from view the possibility of genuinely ideal-involving explanations; such a prejudice needs diagnosis itself.

Cartesian dualism is a good starting-point. Like others, Loar values "physicalism" as a way of avoiding a behaviouristic denial of the inner life without lapsing into a Cartesian picture of it. Now it is certainly true that, knowing what we do about the comprehensive scope of the "physical" sciences, we cannot find room for a non-"physical" substance in a common-sense conception of the world; so the Cartesian picture of mind strikes us as brazenly non-naturalistic. It is quite intelligible that that should seem to be its basic flaw, and consequently that a "physicalist" conception of the inner should seem to be exactly what we need instead. But, although I do not of course dispute that the brazen non-naturalism is a defect, I think this account of the Cartesian picture does not go deep enough; and if we go deeper, this apparent recommendation for "physicalism" disappears.

---

8. *Locus classicus:* Davidson, "Actions, Reasons, and Causes".

What is fundamentally at issue is the pull of the idea that reality is objective, in the sense of being fully describable from no particular point of view.[9] This idea is in tension with a natural intuition to the effect that the mental is both real and essentially subjective. Cartesian dualism results from trying to put these forces in equilibrium: the subjectivity of the mental is (supposedly) accommodated by the idea of privileged access, while the object of that access is conceived, in conformity with the supposed requirement of objectivity, as there independently—there in a reality describable from no particular point of view—rather than as being constituted by the subject's special access to it.[10] Since there is no plausibility in the idea that one could have the appropriate kind of special access to something "physical", the upshot is the notion of a non-"physical" substance.

This account of what generates the Cartesian picture of the inner suggests that to recoil from Cartesian dualism into "physicalism" may be to avoid only a superficial defect; it may be that the fundamental flaw is the attempt to force the mental into an objective mould, something still plainly operative in the supposedly healthy position in which this recoil leaves one. The admittedly unacceptable non-naturalism of the Cartesian picture would justify giving up the intuition that the mental is essentially subjective only if that intuition inevitably generated the Cartesian picture. But the Cartesian picture results from the intuition only in conjunction with objectivism. Davidson's thesis of irreducibility also respects the intuition, and in a healthier form: a form in which it is not distorted, as it is in the Cartesian picture, by the pressure towards objectivity. That pressure—which is what accounts, I suggest, for Loar's inability to appreciate Davidson's argument—now takes on the look of a prejudice: deep-seated and tenacious, evidently, but not something to which reason requires us to succumb.

It is often thought that if essential subjectivity poses any threat to an objectivistic conception of the mental, it is a threat restricted to phenomenal or qualitative mental states or events: states or events

---

9. See Thomas Nagel, "Subjective and Objective".

10. See Bernard Williams, *Descartes: The Project of Pure Enquiry*, especially at pp. 225–6. Williams's perceptive discussion is flawed, however, by his apparently equating "objective" and "third-personal". A conception of what it is for another person to be in pain is presumably third-personal; it would be disastrously wrong to conclude that such a conception is separable from a conception of how things feel to the other person.

about which there is an answer to the question what it is distinctively like to be in them or undergo them.[11] But the Davidsonian irreducibility of propositional attitudes—which are not states whose essence resides in their qualitative character—traces back to subjectivity too: not only in that the mode of understanding they subserve is a matter of comprehending the specific content of a particular subject's outlook on the world, but also—a thought involving a special status for a less individualistically conceived point of view—in that we cannot find any use for a distinction between what makes sense and what could come to make sense to us, if necessary as a result of our learning from those whom we thereby come to find intelligible.[12] Loar's position cannot incorporate either of these considerations, in both cases for reasons we have already touched on: it misses the first because it holds that the explanatory capacity of a propositional attitude is in general independent of its bearing on the world, and it misses the second because, in so far as it deals at all with a distinction between what makes sense and what does not, it is committed to treating the limits of intelligibility as a brute and presumably objective datum.

These considerations bring out a connection between the ideal-involving kind of explanation and the irreducible subjectivity of propositional attitudes. Achieving the kind of understanding for which rationality plays its constitutive role requires a sensitivity to the specific detail of the subjective stance of others, and an openness to learning from it, that is bound to be falsified if one supposes that explanations involving the constitutive ideal work by locating their explananda in a structure specifiable from outside content. Loar conceives the constitutive ideal as just such a structure—misinterpreting, rather than answering, Davidson's claim about the constitutive concept, as I have insisted. His position seems to be the nearest one could come to accommodating Davidson's point within a picture of mind as an element in objective reality.

---

11. See Nagel, "What Is It Like to Be a Bat?". A substantial amount of work has been based on the idea that "qualia" pose a *special* problem for functionalism; see, e.g., Sydney Shoemaker, "Functionalism and Qualia".

12. See Davidson, "On the Very Idea of a Conceptual Scheme". Nagel seems to me to miss the depth of his own point about subjectivity, not only in suggesting that the point is restricted to the qualitative aspects of the mental, but also in espousing a realism that countenances the idea of subjective facts completely beyond our reach.

What makes it seem right to label the Cartesian picture of mind "non-naturalistic" is not simply that it cannot be embraced within a "physicalistic" world view, but rather the conjunction of that with the fact that it purports to represent an aspect of objective reality. Naturalism assures us, we might reasonably say, that the whole of objective reality (in the relevant sense) can in principle be dealt with by the "physical" sciences. If mental states are irreducibly mental by virtue of an ineliminable subjectivity, there is no violation of that tenet of naturalism in crediting them with a complete and self-sufficient reality. We can conceive the mental as simply a different aspect of (what else?) the world of nature. That is why the phrase "naturalistic fallacy" is ultimately misleading as a description of what blocks "physicalist" reduction, although its historical resonances are useful.

Loar suggests, in a passage I mentioned earlier, that what underlies a suspicion of comparing desires to (say) mechanical forces is "a now unmotivated anti-mentalism" (p. 91): that is, I take it, a refusal to accept the inner life, of the sort characteristic of behaviourism. This seems to me to be just about the reverse of the truth. It is not the irreducibility thesis—which can of course accept "force" as a lively metaphor for at least some desires—that threatens the inner life, but the objectivism of which Loar's view as a species. Objectivism poses a choice between behaviourism and psychologism: and of course, taking the psychologistic option, Loar's picture of the mental countenances far more than mere behaviour. But the literally internal states and goings-on that it adds to the behaviourist's world view cannot be recognized as the inner life by any acceptable standard, however undemanding, of what Loar calls "conservative explication" (p. 43).

I have emphasized that Loar's failure to meet Davidson's point is quite explicit (though not, of course, under that description); he leaves it perfectly clear that his functionalist picture of mind does not aim to include a characterization from outside content of the structure of rationality in general. It is tempting to suspect that others, in supposing that a functionalism more vaguely delineated than Loar's can accommodate the mental within a wholly objective conception of reality, have allowed themselves to be captivated by what seems to be a mirage: the fantasy of a theory that, unlike anything Loar envisages, would capture structurally the whole normative force of rationality in such a way as to lend itself to "physical" interpretation. Perhaps I should note that these remarks are critical of functionalism as a theory of propositional attitudes; they do not tell against functionalism as a framework for theory about how sub-personal states and events operate in the control of behaviour, although they do raise a question about what (if anything) that sort of theory has to do with the mind.[13]

7. Davidson's philosophy of mind has two distinctive strands, anomalism and monism (about events); and, although this paper is meant as a tribute to him, it would be disingenuous to slur over the fact that I have been endorsing only the first. Apart from Davidson's argument itself, which I shall come to, there seems to be nothing to be said for the second: no respectable metaphysical impulse, say, that it enables us to gratify. Anomalism itself, or what sustains it, neutralizes any motivation that might be afforded by the ideal of the unity of science. And avoidance of Cartesian dualism is irrelevant; since it is not events but substances that are composed of stuff, one can refuse to accept that all the events there are can be described in "physical" terms, without thereby committing oneself to a non-"physical" stuff, or compromising the thesis that persons are composed of nothing but matter.[14]

In Davidson's argument itself, monism is represented as following from three premises.[15] One of them—the Anomalism of the Mental—is what I have been defending. A second—the Principle of Causal Interaction—seems unquestionable.[16] Given the cogency of

---

13. Proper attention to this contrast subverts both the idea that sub-personal cognitive psychology might supersede "folk psychology" and the idea that it reveals the hidden depths of something whose surface "folk psychology" describes in a rough and ready way. (It is important not to be misled by the role of rationality in, e.g., computational accounts of sub-personal processes. The illumination that such accounts can undoubtedly yield is not a product of a deeper understanding of the mind. It is rather a matter of understanding the workings of the brain, in a way whose possibility is wholly unmysterious, by modelling them on certain mental processes.)
14. My general indebtedness to the work of Jennifer Hornsby is particularly prominent here. See especially "Which Physical Events Are Mental Events?".
15. *Essays on Actions and Events*, pp. 208–9.
16. I may seem to have committed myself to it already, by my remarks in §5. This is not strictly so, in view of n. 5 above. But it would be very strange if the causally interconnected psychological systems I envisage were causally disconnected from the "physical" world.

the argument, then, scepticism about its conclusion should lead to suspicion of the third premise: the Principle of the Nomological Character of Causality. I should like to end by suggesting that this suspicion really ought to be a Davidsonian thought, even though Davidson himself has not formulated it.

The broadly Humean picture of causation that the Principle embodies may be encouraged by the prejudice about causal explanation that I mentioned above (§5)—something Davidson has done much to show us how to resist. One can reject the prejudice about explanation while retaining the picture of causation, as Davidson's own example makes clear.[17] However, it is a good question what now holds the picture of causation in place. Hume's own recommendation of it is, in effect, that since singular causal relations are not given in experience, there is nothing for causation to consist in but a suitable kind of generality. And this recommendation seems inextricably bound up with a "dualism of scheme and content, of organizing system and something waiting to be organized",[18] the untenability of which Davidson has done as much as anyone to bring home to us. Without that dualism, there is no evident attraction left in the thought that singular causal relations are not given in experience. Pending an alternative recommendation, the Prejudice of the Nomological Character of Causality, as I shall venture to relabel it, looks like a fourth dogma of empiricism; the third—the "dualism of scheme and content"—was not, as Davidson surmised, the last, but we need to be told what claim the fourth has on our acceptance once the third has been dismantled.

---

17. Davidson's picture of causation is Humean only in making singular causal relations instantiate generalizations; Davidson does not share the Humean aim of reducing the causal "must" to a mere "always" (see "Causal Relations"). I am grateful to Mark Johnston for reminding me of this.
18. "On the Very Idea of a Conceptual Scheme", p. 189.

ESSAY 16

The Content of Perceptual Experience

1. Daniel Dennett's aim, in his richly suggestive paper "Toward a Cognitive Theory of Consciousness",[1] is to represent the content we persons have conscious dealings with as a selection from the content that would figure in a sub-personal, cognitive-scientific account of the operations of our internal machinery. What effects the selection, according to Dennett's suggestion, is the fact that some of that sub-personal content is available to an internal public-relations organization that accounts for our linguistic output—not that we actually state everything that is in our consciousness, but the idea is that we could do so.

What is in question is precisely access to content, rather than something we could without qualification conceive as access to content-bearers; for Dennett remarks (p. 159) that "we have no direct personal access to the *structure* of *content*ful events within us". The idea is that "events within us" are contentful *by virtue of* their structure; for the content possessed by an internal event or state is a function of its function in the organism, and this function "is—in the end, must be—a function of the *structure* of the state or event and the systems of which it is a part" (p. 163). But only some of the events and states within us that possess content in this way make available to *us* the content that their structurally determined role in

---

1. Page references to Dennett, unless otherwise specified, will be to this paper. Dennett has discussed issues about consciousness more recently, in *Consciousness Explained*. But I think the earlier work is still worth attention. In conversation, Dennett has agreed that the book does not supersede what I take issue with in the paper.

the system confers on them (although they transmit content freely among themselves, unnoticed by us). And when they make their content available to us, the structure in virtue of which they have it does not figure in an accurate phenomenology of our consciousness; it remains a topic for theory, not mere introspective noticing.

I think it is phenomenologically acute of Dennett to deny that we have "direct personal access" to structure; the background thesis, that the content in question is possessed in virtue of structure, generates familiar temptations to suppose otherwise. Consider visual experience. The relevant internal event will be described, in the cognitive-scientific framework Dennett is working in, as something on the lines of a computation of a representation of part of the environment from a pair of arrays of intensities and wavelengths. The way information is contained in this base for computation is naturally described as imagistic. If we assume that the contentful consciousness involved in a visual experience is a matter of access to such an event, it can be very tempting to equate the plain fact that our visual consciousness is of how things *look* to us with the theoretical idea (not a plain fact of consciousness at all) that what we have access to in this sort of consciousness is more than the contents of the computationally derived representations (at various levels: see pp. 157–8), and includes specifically the image-like character of the base of the computations—a matter of structure in Dennett's sense. But whatever may be true about the information-processing that takes place in the visual system, there are no images (two-dimensional arrays) in the phenomenology of vision: it is the relevant tract of the environment that is present to consciousness, not an image of it. It is to Dennett's credit that he resists this falsification of what visual consciousness is like.

2. Another thought of Dennett's seems less acute as phenomenology. Having introduced the notion of presentiments or premonitions by way of cases in which, for instance, one is struck, without knowing why, by the thought that someone is looking over one's shoulder as one writes (pp. 165–6), he goes on to apply the notion to ordinary visual experience (p. 166):

> Right now it occurs to me that there are pages in front of me, a presentiment whose etiology is not known directly by me, but which is, of

course, perfectly obvious. It is my visual system that gives me this presentiment, along with a host of others.

The suggestion is that these perceptual "presentiments" are unlike, for instance, the presentiment that someone is looking over one's shoulder only in their connectedness with what precedes and follows them (which is presumably what makes the aetiology so obvious). They are like that sort of presentiment in that the aetiology, although obvious in this case unlike that one, is, as we might say, phenomenologically extrinsic ("not known directly by me").

This suggestion seems phenomenologically off key, perhaps especially about visual experience. What it seems to threaten is the presentness to one of the seen environment. On Dennett's suggestion, that a seen object is there before one is a mere premonition, something one finds oneself inclined to suppose, unaccountably so far as anything contained in the experience itself goes. Or perhaps we can change the aspect, and say that the presence of the object is a hypothesis, the obviously best explanation of the premonition; here the claim of obviousness cannot undo the damage done by the idea of a hypothesis—it cannot give us back the idea that the object itself is presented to one's awareness.

Consider a basic (demonstratively expressible) singular empirical judgement: say, a judgement one might express, in a suitable perceptual situation, by saying "That cat is asleep". The content of such a judgement depends on the perceived presence of the cat itself. A premonition would yield at best content to the effect that a cat that is in a certain region (and has, no doubt, all manner of visible properties; but registering the richness of the available content does not help) is asleep. This lacks the particularity of the original judgement—its relating to a particular cat (*that* one, as one will be able to say if one is in the right perceptual situation), not just to some cat that satisfies a general specification, however rich. We might try to recapture particularity by making out that the thought is carried to the right object by the "obvious" hypothesis about the premonition's aetiology. But that is not how demonstratively expressible thought makes contact with its object. Such thought does not need to be "carried to" its object by a hypothesis, because the object is directly there for the thinker.[2]

2. See Gareth Evans, *The Varieties of Reference*, especially chap. 6.

3. It may seem captious to complain about phenomenological niceties. But I think the off-key phenomenology reflects a serious epistemological difficulty.

Consider Kant's advance over Hume. Hume inherits from his predecessors a conception according to which no experience is in its very nature—intrinsically—an encounter with objects. What Kant takes from Hume is that there is no rationally satisfactory route from such a predicament to the epistemic position we are in (obviously in, we might say). Transcendental synthesis (or whatever) is not supposed to be such a route; the whole point of its being transcendental, in this context, is that it is not supposed to be something that we—our familiar empirical selves—go in for. It would be a mistake to think we can domesticate Kant's point by detranscendentalizing the idea of synthesis, so as to suggest that the idea of encountering objects is put in place by interpretation of data, perhaps by inference to the best explanation; with the interpreting being something we do, or at least something that might figure in a "rational reconstruction" of our being in the epistemic position we are in. That would just be missing *Hume*'s point. Kant does not miss Hume's point. He builds on it: since there is no rationally satisfactory route from experiences, conceived as, in general, less than encounters with objects—glimpses of objective reality—to the epistemic position we are manifestly in, experiences must be intrinsically encounters with objects. But how could they be that if their aetiology were phenomenologically extrinsic?

Dennnett's idea of experiences as presentiments requires a pre-Humean epistemological optimism. Not that Dennett would dream of urging epistemologists to revert to such a stance: his attention is simply not fixed on epistemological considerations. I think this sort of situation is not uncommon; we have a new-fangled move in the philosophy of mind, enmeshed in a quite old-fashioned philosophical difficulty, in a way that has no connection with the intentions of its proponents (who imagine that their questions and answers are simply insulated from that kind of thing).

Of course I am not suggesting that Dennett's conception of experiences as presentiments is the same as Hume's conception of experiences as impressions. But both conceive experiences as less than encounters with objects. Hume's good point—the one Kant builds on—generalizes beyond the specifics of his own picture, to warrant an epistemological pessimism about any such conception of experience.

4. I do not believe that the off-key phenomenology is just a gratuitous slip on Dennett's part.
Consider the framework role played in Dennett's thinking by the idea of what our visual systems tell us. His main aim is to capture the thought that *we* (and not just some sub-personal parts of us) are on the receiving end of this telling. I shall come back to that; but for present purposes, we need to focus rather on the content of the telling. What could our visual systems, conceived in the information-processing vein that Dennett is defending, tell us? (Or tell our brains, if one prefers something modelled on the original formula "what the frog's eye tells the frog's brain"?)
Here is a candidate for being a possible message to me, on occasion, from my visual system: "There is a cat, with such-and-such properties, at such-and-such a position in my egocentric space." The considerations I sketched in §3 actually suggest that the framework undermines even this (since it undermines the possibility that experiences as it conceives them might possess objective content at all); but we can let that pass for now, in order to get the "presentiment" idea going. The relevant question at this point is rather this: could my visual system tell me, in addition, that a cat figures in the aetiology of the original message? How could my visual system—conceived as a sub-personal computing device—be in a position to tell me that? We are letting the visual system pass muster as capable of telling me about such things as the presence of cats with such-and-such properties, on the basis that it discriminates such circumstances more or less reliably. (Actually the truth is that it enables *me* to do that rather than that *it* does that, and this is crucial; but I am playing along with a different way of talking.) But my visual system is surely not a reliable discriminator of cases in which the input from which it starts has one kind of aetiology as against cases in which it has another. If, as a matter of routine, the visual system added a suitable message about aetiology to whatever it told me about the environment ("This message was caused by the fact it reports"), and if the visual system *is* a more or less reliable detector of features of the environment, the added message would be more or less reliably correct. But it would

not be—as we are supposing the original message about the environment might be—a case of *informing* me of something. From the perspective, as it were, of the information-processing device, it would be more like an expression of blind faith: not the sort of thing that belongs in a sensible theory of the functioning of an information-processing device. (A routine additional message that might make a certain sense would be "This is your visual system speaking". This leaves Dennett's "presentiment" idea untouched: it merely registers that the presentiments can be distinctively visual.)

5. If I am right so far, Dennett's basic framework necessitates the "presentiment" idea; perceptual experiences as he conceives them would have to be presentiments. And the idea is deeply unsatisfactory, in a way that is not just a matter of phenomenological nuance. What has gone wrong?

To begin on a diagnosis, I want to turn away, for the moment, from Dennett's ultimate aim of accounting for personal-level psychological truth, and consider the perceptual lives of frogs. Dennett alludes to a famous paper called "What the Frog's Eye Tells the Frog's Brain", but he commends a suggestion, by Michael Arbib, that one might prefer the formula "What the frog's eye tells the frog" (p. 163). His point is that "sub-personal" content-ascription in the theory of frog perception is controlled by the requirements of a biological account whose topic is the life of *frogs* rather than the doings of their parts.

Still, the original formula "what the frog's eye (or visual system) tells the frog's brain" was not wrong. What it enables us to stress is that we understand the "sub-personal" metaphor of telling in terms of informational transactions between one part of an organism and *another part*. So if we want to talk of informational transactions between part of a creature and the *creature,* we cannot simply carry over the metaphor; we need to work for the extension. In the metaphor, our parts talk to one another; they do not, at least in general, talk to us. Dennett does a great deal of work at the necessary extending of the metaphor for the case of persons, making room for the idea of what our visual systems tell *us* (this is the main aim of his paper). But the point should hold for frogs too. In a "sub-personal" account of frog perception in which the frog's eye (or visual system) does some telling, say announcing that there is a bug-like object at such-and-such a position in the frog's motor space, what gets told of this will be another *part* of the frog, perhaps one that the theorist labels "motor control". What entitles us to say, not just that the frog's visual system informs the frog's motor control of the presence of a bug-like object, but that it gets the message to the *frog?* It is part of Dennett's own point that there is no extra twist in the "subpersonal" account of what happens in frogs, analogous to the extra twist in the sub-personal account of our inner workings that is supposed to make room for *us* to have access to the content of our inner states and events. How, then, does the *frog* get into the act?

I suspect that this question—which is, I insist, a serious one—tends to be suppressed because of an unfortunate feature of the otherwise excellent distinction between the personal and the subpersonal. Theories of internal information-processing in frogs are at best "sub-personal" (I have needed the scare quotes at several points), not sub-personal, because there are no persons around in contrast with whom we can mark the standard distinction. It would be easy to think on the following lines: "The frog's being informed, by its visual system, of the presence of a bug-like object would certainly not be a personal-level involvement with content; so it is subpersonal; so why not simply *identify* it with the 'sub-personal' content-involving transaction that we already have in our theoretical sights, the frog's motor control's being informed of that by its visual system?" But this would be confused. The point of saying that the theory of internal information-processing in frogs is "sub-personal" is not that no persons are involved—something that is indeed equally true of talk whose subject is frogs themselves—but that the fundamental idea of such a theory is the idea of informational transactions between *parts* of frogs. If we speak in all seriousness (and why should we not?) of *frogs* learning about their environment through vision, what is in question is, by all means, not personal involvement with content. But it is *froggy* involvement with content, and it ought to be just as pressing to ask how this connects with sub-froggy informational transactions—how the frog gets into the act—as it is to ask how our personal involvement with content connects with subpersonal informational transactions within us.

What is more, if it were right to suppose that the personal-level involvement with content that we enjoy when we learn about the environment in (conscious) experience is a matter of access on our part to some of the sub-personally generated content that is being passed from part to part within us, it should be just as plausible to suppose that the involvement with content that is enjoyed by a frog when it learns about the environment in vision is to be understood in terms of access on the frog's part to its own interior. But this seems merely ludicrous. The frog's access, in perception, is—like ours—to the environment.

6. When we work with the idea that frogs learn, through vision, about features of their environment, we are subject to two controls. First, there is frog life, which, like all animal life, is a matter of more or less competently inhabiting an environment. In this context, we ask questions like the following: "What features of the environment would a creature need to become informed of, in order to live in it with precisely the competence that frogs display?" Second, there are the facts about frog perceptual equipment. Here we have questions like the following: "Is *this* the kind of thing that we can make sense of a creature's becoming informed of by the use of, say, eyes?" Or, more specifically: "Can we understand how possession of a visual system that works like *this* makes it possible for a creature to become informed of just *these* features of its environment?"

The specific questions that arise under the second head can be answered, in principle, by constructing characterizations of the relevant perceptual equipment as information-processing devices, which transmit their results to other (functionally specified) parts of the organism (for instance, "motor control"). There is an obvious interplay between the results of investigation here and the answers we give to questions under the first head. Casual observation of frog life might induce the provisional thought that frogs become informed, through vision, of the presence of bugs. Then it turns out that a good theory of the relevant perceptual equipment fails to support the view that the equipment processes information about arrays of light into information about the presence of bugs. The equipment hardly processes information at all (it is a limiting case of an information-processing device), but rather simply reacts to any small moving speck. It is better to view the informational transaction as the transmission, to "motor control", of information to the effect that a small moving speck is at such-and-such a point in motor space. So we recast our conception of what frogs become informed of: at best the presence of a bug-like object at a certain place. (Given the usual sort of environment that frogs inhabit, this is good enough for their somewhat low-grade competence.) Some may think even this goes too far; but it is hard to see how we could credit frogs with being less informed about their environment than this without representing them as not in touch with it at all—a position that has all the appearance of a philosophers' prejudice.

The fact that there is this perfectly intelligible interplay between what we decide we can correctly say, in content-involving terms, about frogs, on the one hand, and the detail of a content-involving (information-processing) account of the inner workings of the parts of frogs, on the other, is no reason to mix the two stories together. In the account of inner workings, one sub-froggy part of a frog transmits information to another: the frog's eye talks to the frog's brain, not to the frog. In the sense in which the frog's eye tells the frog's brain things, nothing tells the frog anything. We may still want to say that the frog gets told things. But what does *this* telling is not something in the frog's interior; that is what generated the comical idea that we could attribute dealings with content to the *frog* only if we credited it with something like introspection. Rather, what tells the frog things is the environment, making features of itself apparent to the frog, equipped as it is with frog perceptual apparatus. This is a different metaphor of telling, not in competition with the "sub-personal" one. It is essential not to be misled by the enormous capacity for illumination that the "sub-personal" account has (together, perhaps, with the true but irrelevant thought that frogs are not persons) into thinking that the "sub-personal" account exhausts the content-involving truth in this area of biology. The second metaphor encapsulates a whole extra field of truths. What is more, the involvement of content here, and only here, is literal; underneath the metaphor of the environment telling the frog things, we have the literal truth that the frog becomes informed of things. Whereas the content-involving truth at the "sub-personal" level is irreducibly metaphorical.

The "sub-personal" account of a sensory system, which treats it as an information-processing device that transmits its informational results to something else inside an animal, cannot adequately characterize what its sensory systems are for the animal (as opposed to what they are, metaphorically speaking, for the internal parts that receive the results of the information-processing): namely, modes of sensitivity or openness to features of the environment—not processors of information, but collectors of it.

It would be a confusion to think the distinction I am making here is blurred by the minimal extent of information-processing in frog vision in particular. What the frog's eyes do for the frog is to put it in touch with moving specks in its spatial environment: things that are in fact bugs, in the sort of case that is sufficiently normal in frogs' lives. From the frog's point of view, its eyes enable it simply to pick up the fact that there is a moving speck (with luck, a bug) out there. From the point of view of the frog's "motor control" (to speak in the terms of the "sub-personal" metaphor), the presence out there of a moving speck is rather (at best) the best hypothesis the eyes (or, probably better in view of how little the eyes do, the whole system) can come up with in order to account for the input of light (what is in fact light, though the system does not even know this much) to the eyes. If all goes well, the frog is in direct touch with a feature of its external environment; the internal information-processing system is in direct touch only with structural properties of the immediate inputs to it—which, in the metaphor, it interprets as clues to the nature of the external environment. (Of course the frog does no such thing.)

What could an internal information-processing device really tell an animal? To give a positive answer, we would need to deal satisfactorily with the question I am suppressing, about how to make sense of the frog's being on the receiving end of "sub-personal" telling; but my point now is not that we have no inkling how that might be done. What could an information-processing device *really* tell *anything* (including another component in a sub-personal or "sub-personal" informational system)? It is essential to realize that the answer to this question can be—in fact is—"Nothing", without the slightest threat being posed to the utility, or even the theoretical indispensability, of cognitive science.

A sub-personal or "sub-personal" informational system is a physical mechanism, connected to its surroundings by transducers that convert physical impacts from outside into events of the sort that the system can work on, and perhaps by transducers that convert the system's end products into physical interventions in the exterior. The system knows nothing even about the character of the immediate physical impacts on the input transducers, or the immediate physical interventions in the exterior that result from its operations by way of the output transducers, let alone about the nature and layout of the distal environment. The operations of the system are determined by structures exemplified in the initial contributions of the transducers, and in intermediate events and states in the system, which have no meaning for the system. In short, in Dennett's own memorable and exactly right phrase, the system is a syntactic engine, not a semantic engine.[3] The same goes for its parts.

Animals, by contrast, are semantic engines. To stick with the present example, they become informed, e.g., that there is a bug-like object at such and such a position. The background against which this makes sense is their competent inhabiting of their environment.

This competence would be quite mysterious if there were no interestingly structured machinery inside them, controlling their behaviour in a way that is responsive to impacts from the environment. We could not make sense of the competence that enables us to make sensible use of the claim that animals have dealings with content if we could find nothing inside them but, say, a completely homogeneous jelly. And nobody knows how to make sense of an animal's internal control mechanism, and connect it conceptually to the competence it is supposed to explain, except by describing it *as if* it were, what we know it is not really, a semantic engine, interpreting inputs as signs of environmental facts and, as output, directing behaviour so as to be suitable to those facts in the light of the animal's needs or goals. Insisting that the attribution of content at this sub-personal or "sub-personal" level is "as if" talk is in no way debunking it. The content-attribution is not, as it were, irresponsible; it is constrained by the physiological facts, in a way that is exemplified, on a small scale, by the discovery of how little interpretation ("as if" interpretation, we must say) can be credited to the visual systems of frogs. And it is surely clear, at least in a general way, how content-attribution that is only "as if" can even so pull its weight in addressing a genuine explanatory need; the question is what enables us animals to be the semantic engines we are.

---

3. The idea is implicit in his remarks about the role of structure in sub-personal content-attribution (p. 163). For the phrase itself, see "Beyond Belief", p. 26.

It is crucial to see that the question about real content that we are helped with by the "as if" attribution of content to states and events in internal mechanisms is this *causal* or *enabling* question. One can easily fall into a temptation to suppose that the question is rather a *constitutive* one. If we could see dealings with content on the part of animals as somehow constitutively explained in terms of information-processing in their interiors, that might seem a protection against a metaphysical embarrassment. (After all, we might say to ourselves, cognitive science is science; maybe it is not quite clear that ecology and ethology are science.) But this temptation is disastrous: if we offer a constitutive explanation of genuine content in terms of a merely "as if" attribution of content, we make genuine content fragile and problematic.

Dennett's basic picture is that *our* dealings with content are nothing but our access to some of the content manipulated by our internal information-processing systems, and this seems to be a case of succumbing to the temptation. It flies in the face of the insight that the internal systems are only syntactic engines: access to our interiors cannot be what constitutes our dealings with content, since there is no content in there, although it is enormously useful to talk as if there were. Dennett writes:

> Somehow, the syntactical virtuosity of our brains permits us to be interpreted at another level as semantic engines—systems that (indirectly) discriminate the significance of the impingements on them. . . .[4]

The idea that our discrimination of the significance of the impingements on us is *indirect* reflects the idea that our becoming informed of environmental facts just *is* the upshot of the sort of computational process that we attribute to our perceptual systems—as if we were in the predicament of our nervous systems, blocked off from the environment by transducers rather than inhabiting it. No wonder our status as semantic engines becomes a mystery ("somehow"), and no wonder it is a comfort to make room for the suggestion that it is just a way of talking, not a fact (the syntactical virtuosity of our brains "permits us to be interpreted as" semantic engines, rather than just making it intelligible that we are such). If we drop the attempt to

---

4. "Beyond Belief", pp. 26–7.

read the envisaged explanations constitutively, "permits" can take its proper significance; unmysteriously, the syntactic virtuosity of our brains enables us to relate to the environment in the direct way that is constitutive of our being the semantic engines we are.

7. Sidney Morgenbesser is said to have accused a cognitive-scientifically minded colleague of believing that our intelligence is Artificial Intelligence. We can now see a sense in which that ridiculous belief is almost correct: we ourselves have genuine intelligence, but there is Artificial Intelligence inside us—not in the sense of an artefact, but in the sense of an imitation or fake. That is to say: we have inside us something that is not intelligent at all (it knows nothing and understands nothing); even so, we can be enormously helped in finding it comprehensible how we can be intelligent, even though we are made of nothing but the stuff that everything is made of, including mere "stupid" *things* like sticks and stones, by seeing how this completely unintelligent internal equipment of ours can have imposed, on top of the truth about its mindless manipulations of structures that are meaningless to it, an "as if" description in terms of dealings with content. That makes it possible to understand how this mindless internal control system enables us to do what it takes to display genuine mindedness, namely live competently in an environment.

"Display" may be misleading here, encouraging this thought: "Maybe that is what it takes to *show* mindedness, but it can be there anyway, perhaps in a brain in a vat." I think we are now in a position to begin to see through this. I shall approach the point by way of another striking philosophical remark that we can now see in the proper light, namely John Searle's claim that we are brains in vats (vats of bone, not glass, with input and output linkages to the environment different from those in the standard mad-scientist fantasy; but vats nonetheless).[5] The truth is that our brains are indeed brains in vats, and that is exactly why we must not identify ourselves with them. To a brain it is all one whether its vat is glass or bone, and what, if anything, is outside the transducers that feed it its inputs

---

5. See *Intentionality*, p. 230.

and receive its outputs. To repeat, a brain knows nothing and understands nothing; all it does is to manipulate structures that have no meaning for it. That is not the truth about us. Without any threat at all to the enormous power of cognitive science to enable us to explain our mindedness (in one sense of "explain our mindedness": not constitutive explanation), we ought be able to see that the sheer fact that a brain is going through the motions an embodied brain goes through when a person thinks or experiences is by itself no ground at all for supposing there is a mind in there. (It may be a different matter if the mad scientist's vat contains what used to be an embodied brain; perhaps memory can give subjectivity a tenuous foothold there.)

There is a persisting inclination to suppose that this cannot be right; if the brain goes through the right paces, it must at least *seem* to it that it thinks or enjoys experience, and then even if we can make out a difference between having it seem to one that those things are so and their being so, the seeming is enough for subjectivity. Here it really is to the point to respond like this: "You might as well suppose it seems to an electronic calculator that things are thus and so."

8. I have been urging, in effect, that we understand Dennett's distinction between attributing content at the personal level and attributing it at the sub-personal level as a special case of a more general distinction, between content-attribution at the level of the animal and content-attribution at the level of its internal machinery. At the level of internal machinery, it is useful to talk of sensory systems as information-processing devices; but for the animal its sensory systems are modes of openness to features of its environment. Information-processing characterizations of the internal machinery figure in explanations of how it can be that animals are in touch with their environments. The "as if" content that is usefully deployed at the lower level helps make intelligible the genuine content that appears at the higher level by way of "enabling" explanations, not as somehow constituting that content. Since there is no getting around the fact that the internal machinery is really only a syntactic engine, the attempt to see a constitutive relation between the lower and the

upper levels undermines our hold on the fact that animals are semantic engines.

It will not have escaped notice that my descriptions of what sensory systems are for an animal that possesses them are Gibsonian.[6] A proper understanding of the relation between the two levels should help us to see through some cross purposes in a familiar style of cognitive-scientific response to Gibson's claims.

Gibson himself sometimes seems to deny that the idea of processing information has any role in characterizations of the operations of sensory systems. This is fully intelligible, given the fundamental point that he wants to make: that perceiving (something animals do) is not processing information, but simply taking it in. In fact that claim is, as should by now be clear, fully compatible with recognizing that it can be useful to characterize sensory systems, *not* from the animal's point of view, as information-processing devices. The claim gives the framework within which such characterizations have their explanatory point.

Some cognitive-scientific critics of Gibson, not equipped with the distinction of levels, read Gibsonian descriptions of the sensory systems as if they were meant to serve the intellectual function served by their own theories. It is not surprising if that makes the Gibsonian descriptions seem idiotic. David Marr, for instance, in his brilliant and path-breaking information-processing approach to vision, cites Gibson only as a half-baked precursor. When Gibson resoundingly, and rightly, denies that perceiving is processing information, Marr can hear only a reflection of failure to understand what information-processing is. In this framework, Gibson's positive remarks about the sensory systems can indicate at best a massive underestimation of how difficult the information-processing task, the task of extracting information about environmental invariants from "the flowing array of ambient energy", is.[7] And really this is an understatement; if we

---

6. See J. J. Gibson, *The Senses Considered as Perceptual Systems*.
7. See Marr's *Vision*, pp. 29–30. At p. 3 of *The Senses Considered as Perceptual Systems*, Gibson writes: "The unanswered question of sense perception is how an observer, animal or human, can obtain constant perceptions in everyday life on the basis of . . . continually changing sensations." Marr misreads this. He takes Gibson to be acknowledging the urgency of "the unanswered question", whereas Gibson is describing how the problems look in the approach that he is going to reject. See p. 2 ("The seemingly paradoxical

read Gibson as attempting to say something at the lower of the two levels, then given what is obvious about the physical impingements to which, say, visual systems are restricted, the idea of directly collecting information about "environmental invariants" through vision looks like an appeal to magic. As Dennett says, quite correctly given this reading of Gibson, and completely missing Gibson's point, Gibson represents the visual system as "a hunk of wonder tissue".[8]

9. The distinction of levels equips us to see that there is nothing unscientific—no know-nothing refusal to acknowledge the rich promise of cognitive science—in denying that dealings with content on the part of perceiving animals should be equated with computationally described goings-on in their interiors. Moving to personal dealings with content, such as the conscious perceptual experiences of adult human beings, makes all kinds of differences. But there is no reason to suppose that it makes any difference on this point: our dealings with content, in our consciously enjoyed perceptual experience, are no more a matter of access to our own interiors than a frog's dealings with content are.

Dennett offers a picture of our internal functional organization, in which perceptual systems process bare data into comparatively rich information about the environment, and their products (at various levels of processing) are stored in a special short-term buffer memory ("M"), which feeds into a system controlling speech. (There is more complexity besides: see p. 155.) About this picture, he floats (p. 165) "the bold hypothesis that you [his reader] are a realization of this flow chart, and that it is in virtue of this fact that it seems—to us and to you—that there is something it is like to be you" (that is, that you are conscious). As far as anything I have said goes, this may well be right. The important point is that if it is right, it is right as a piece of cognitive science, with "in virtue of" read in causal (enabling) terms, not constitutively. The suggestion has the same shape as one to the effect that it is in virtue of possessing perceptual equipment that admits of such-and-such an information-processing characterization

---

assertion will be made that perception is not based on sensation"); p. 320 ("The puzzle of constant perception despite varying sensations disappears . . .").

8. "Cognitive Wheels", pp. 149–50 (n. 21).

that an animal can be in touch with such-and-such features of its environment.

One might put this by saying that consciousness itself escapes Dennett's cognitivistic net; he offers what may be an enabling explanation of consciousness, but not a constitutive one. And in one sense, this leaves us without an account of consciousness. We lack an account of what it is, even if we have an account of what enables it to be present. It would be a mistake to think this makes consciousness a metaphysical embarrassment—as if, in denying that consciousness is a matter of configurations in the satisfyingly material medium of the nervous system, we were committed to regarding it as a matter of configurations in an immaterial medium instead. As I have insisted, there is nothing inherently mysterious in a frog's being in touch with its environment (of course not in a "personal" way); we take that idea in our stride, in the context of thinking about how the frog's life fits into the environment. There is no difficulty in principle, although all kinds of differences must be acknowledged, about extending this comprehension to our own case; our personal-level dealings with content are intelligible in the context of our distinctively human life.

One striking advantage to be derived from rejecting the idea that conscious perceptual experience is a special kind of access to content that is in the first instance sub-personal—the content of events or states in our interiors—is that it enables us to repossess the phenomenology of perception. I have already said something about a phenomenological misrepresentation that Dennett is led to (see §2 above). Let me give another example: discussing the richness of experience, Dennett writes (p. 170):

> One experiences more at any time than one wants to say then. What fills the "periphery", adds detail to one's "percepts", inhabits "fringe consciousness", is, as phenomenologists have insisted, *there*. Where? In M [the special buffer memory]. No more mysterious process of presentation or apprehension of inhabitants of phenomenal space is needed.

Certainly no such thing is needed, but Dennett's alternative answer—"In M"—is surely quite wrong as phenomenology. The phenomenologically right answer—which, once we have the status of sub-personal theorizing straight, we can recognize as the right answer, period—is: in the part of the world (ordinary objective space, not "phenomenal space") that lies open to view.

10. At one point (pp. 160-1) Dennett remarks, in passing, that his construction has a Kantian flavour; his flow chart diagrams how intuitions (the sub-personal, and hence certainly not conceptual, content of states or events that result from perceptual data-processing) are "knitted together" with concepts (which figure in the articulable shape that contents acquire when they are made available to the system that controls speech). I think the real lesson of Dennett's paper is this: a dualism of intuitions and concepts cannot be made safe by simply removing it from the sphere of the transcendental—by assigning the task of fitting intuitions and concepts together to something empirical, whether it is the empirical self (as in §3 above) or, as here, an empirically postulated internal apparatus. In either case, just because the "synthesis" is not transcendental (so that it would disappear if we tried a domesticated formulation of what we can learn from Kant), there is an epistemological come-uppance. The great beauty of Dennett's paper is how rigorously he lets his theory control his phenomenological claims; their failure of fit can now emerge as a fault line along which the whole structure must break apart.

We must see our way to not needing to give an account of how concepts and intuitions are brought into alignment. Another way of saying the same thing would be that we cannot make use of the notion of an interface between mind (which inhabits the space of concepts) and world, where the world presents the mind with non-conceptual items for it to work into conceptual shape. Or (yet another formulation) we cannot make sense of the mind as a "black box" in the world. (Obviously we can make sense of an interface between nervous systems and the world outside them.)[9] This paper has been about perceptual connections between mind and world, but the point has obvious reverberations for how we think of action too; if seen objects (say) are not on the far side of an "input" interface between mind and world, there is, to say the least, no point in trying to represent objects acted on—which may, of course, be the same objects—as lying on the far side of an "output" interface.

---

9. Searle, in *Intentionality*, has the "black box" picture of the mind firmly in place (we *are* brains in vats: see §7 above). This means that he cannot capitalize on what appears as an isolated insight, that perceptual experience is presentation, not representation. (See p. 46.) He tries to do better than Dennett's "premonition" idea by insisting that the aetiology of an experience enters into its conditions of satisfaction. But with the interface in place, it is merely mysterious how it can do so.

Reductionism and the First Person

1. Locke's discussion of personal identity centres on the thesis that a person is "a thinking intelligent being, that has reason and reflection, and can consider itself as itself, the same thinking thing, in different times and places".[1] What Locke stresses here is that the continuity that constitutes a person's continuing to exist has an "inner" aspect. Normally this "inner" aspect is realized in substantive knowledge; what Locke calls "consciousness" holds together in a single survey some of the specifics of the career, extended in time, of what the subject of this survey conceives as itself, "the same thinking thing". But if a person can survive with the details of its past and future blotted out, its being a person requires that it still conceive itself as a self-conscious continuant, capable of an "inner" angle on its own persistence but currently deprived of any specificity in what that capacity yields.

Now a core thought in the Reductionism Derek Parfit recommends is that this "inner" aspect of personal persistence should be understood in terms of relations between psychological states and events that are intelligible independently of personal identity. It is this claim that allows Parfit to play down the importance of personal identity. If the relations that constitute the phenomenon Locke stresses are independent of personal identity, they must be detachable in thought from the continued existence of persons, even though Locke's idea has to be that they are constitutive of that (as they in-

---

1. *An Essay concerning Human Understanding*, 3.27.9.

deed are in the normal course of things). And what matters for the rationality of the sort of concern with the future that, with our usual unimaginative restriction to the normal case, we conceive as self-interested is Locke's phenomenon; hence, according to Parfit, what matters is those independently intelligible relations, rather than the facts about personal identity that they normally help to constitute.

2. In advance of looking into the particular moves Parfit makes to supply a Reductionist account of Locke's phenomenon, I think we should query the motivation for supposing that a reduction ought to be available.

For many kinds of continuants, what it is for something to continue to exist, one and the same, is best characterized in terms of spatio-temporal continuity under a substance concept. Now there is no reason to understand this claim so that circularity would be an objection to applications of it. The claim frames an understanding of what the relevant substance concepts must be like for our judgements of identity to work as they do, and it can serve that purpose without purporting to be intelligible independently of those judgements.[2] Generally, there seems to be no reason to try to reduce the notion of the career of a continuant to relations between elements in that career that are intelligible independently of the thought that they are elements in the career of a single thing.

Locke's thesis is that a person is a continuant of a special kind, special in that "consciousness" gives it an "inner" perspective on its own persistence. Does this import any reason to press for a reduction? Only on the basis of what seems to me to be a mistaken thought: that there is no alternative to reduction except to commit ourselves to continuants whose persistence through time would consist in nothing but the continuity of "consciousness" itself. Such continuants would be items whose activity is purely mental: items like the one Descartes convinced himself he referred to in first-person thought.

Parfit introduces his Reductionist notion of psychological continuity in a way that suggests he thinks on those lines. He writes:

> Some people believe in a kind of psychological continuity that resembles physical continuity. This involves the continued existence of a

---

2. See David Wiggins, *Sameness and Substance*, especially chaps. 2 and 3.

purely mental *entity*, or thing—a soul, or spiritual substance. I shall return to this view. But I shall first explain another kind of psychological continuity. This is less like physical continuity, since it does not consist in the continued existence of some entity. But this other kind of psychological continuity involves only facts with which we are familiar.[3]

But there is another possibility, conspicuous by its absence from this passage, and, so far as I can tell, from Parfit's thinking altogether. This is that Locke's phenomenon, the continuity of "consciousness", does involve the continued existence of an entity; but the entity is not a peculiar Cartesian item, but a person, of whose continued life that continuity is, precisely, an aspect. If Locke's phenomenon had to be understood all by itself, in abstraction from the idea of the continued life of a person (which is the continued life of a human being, in the case that we have to regard as, at the least, central), then we would perhaps be forced to choose between purely spiritual substances and psychological Reductionism. Parfit suggests that Reductionism has respectably anti-Cartesian credentials by urging (plausibly enough) that Reductionism is the better option in that choice. But the fundamental Cartesian mistake is not the postulation of spiritual substances, but rather the assumption, which is preserved in this implicit defence of Reductionism, that seems to pose that choice: the assumption that Locke's phenomenon must be understood in isolation.

3. It is a central fact about what Locke calls "consciousness" that although the temporally separate states and occurrences that it can hold together in a single survey seem to figure within its purview as elements in the career of something that persists as one and the same, the flow of "consciousness" does not involve applying, or otherwise ensuring conformity with, criteria for the identity through time of an object. In continuity of "consciousness", there is what appears to be knowledge of an identity, the persistence of the same subject through time, without any need to take care that attention stays fixed on the same thing. Contrast keeping one's thought focused on an ordinary object of perception over a period; this requires a skill, the ability to

---

3. *Reasons and Persons*, pp. 204–5.

keep track of something, whose exercise we can conceive as a practical substitute for the explicit application of a criterion of identity. Continuity of "consciousness" involves no analogue to this—no keeping track of the persisting self that nevertheless seems to figure in its content.[4]

A mainstream Cartesian response would be to retain the idea that continuity of "consciousness" constitutes awareness of an identity through time; to assume that the content of that awareness must be provided for completely within the flow of "consciousness"; and to conclude, from the fact that no criteria for persistence through time are in play in the field to which that assumption restricts us, that what continuing to exist consists in for the continuant in question must be peculiarly simple, something that does not go beyond the flow of "consciousness" itself.[5] In particular, this line of thought rules out the idea that the continuant in question might be a human being. What it is for one and the same human being to continue existing involves just the sort of criteria of persistence whose absence from the restricted field was the starting-point of these reflections. One cannot be entitled to suppose that third-person thought stays focused on the same human being without applying such criteria, or exercising a skill of keeping track. On present assumptions, that rules out taking it that the apparently stable reference, in the first-person thinking that reflects continuity of "consciousness", is to a human being.[6]

---

4. See Gareth Evans, *The Varieties of Reference*, p. 237. Evans seems to slip when he suggests that the point can be put in terms of "immunity to error through misidentification", that is, the circumstance that a judgement's predication is not attached to its subject by way of a judgement of identity. As he points out on p. 236, "identification-freedom", so explained, is consistent with a judgement's depending on keeping track of its object. (Keeping track serves as it were instead of an "identification component" in the basis of continuing demonstrative thought about objects of ordinary perception.) The point about the self is a peculiarly strong form of "identification-freedom".

5. See P. F. Strawson's brilliantly suggestive reading of Kant's Paralogisms of Pure Reason, in *The Bounds of Sense*, pp. 162–70.

6. The Cartesian *cogito* is supposed to reveal self-reference as still feasible even when the Method of Doubt has done its worst, and one is entertaining the possibility that there *are* no continuants capable of being thought about in a way that would require applying criteria of persistence or employing a substantial empirical skill of keeping track. Part of the point of this, to be applauded even while we leave ourselves room to object on other scores, is that it serves to make vivid the fact that continuity of "consciousness" involves no keeping track of the subject.

Now one way to avoid the purely spiritual continuants that this line of thought purports to force on us would indeed be to revise our view of the content of the flow of "consciousness" in a Reductionist direction: to conclude that "consciousness" does not, after all, present the temporally separated states and occurrences over which it plays as belonging to the career of a single continuant, but rather as linked by a conceptually simpler relation of serial co-consciousness, which might subsequently enter into the construction of a derivative notion of a persisting subject if such a notion seems called for.

But it should be clear that there is another way to disown any commitment to purely spiritual continuants. The alternative is to leave in place the idea that continuity of "consciousness" constitutes awareness of an identity through time, but reject the assumption that that fact needs to be provided for within a self-contained conception of the continuity of "consciousness". On the contrary, we can say: continuous "consciousness" is intelligible (even "from within") only as a subjective angle on something that has more to it than the subjective angle reveals, namely the career of an objective continuant with which the subject of the continuous "consciousness" identifies itself. The subjective angle does not contain within itself any analogue to keeping track of something, but its content can nevertheless intelligibly involve a stable continuing reference, of a first-person kind; this is thanks to its being situated in a wider context, which provides for an understanding that the persisting referent is also a third person, something whose career is a substantially traceable continuity in the objective world.[7]

Once this alternative is clearly in view, it should seem doubtful that Reductionism deserves respect on the ground of its opposition to Cartesian philosophy. Certainly we should have no truck with purely spiritual substances. But believing in purely spiritual substances is much less fundamental than the underlying thesis, that what Locke calls "consciousness" has its content independently of

---

7. As Strawson puts it (p. 165), the thought that reflects continuity of "consciousness" has "links" with empirical criteria of identity that are "not severed" by the fact that the criteria are not applied (not even in the form of a purely practical skill of keeping track) within such thought. Evans's treatment of first-person modes of presentation (chap. 7) elaborates how thinking about oneself is to be understood as taking place within, and bearing on, objective reality—reality conceived as independent of any particular point of view.

any embedding in a wider objective context. That conception of "consciousness" as self-contained is utterly Cartesian, and it goes unquestioned in the implicit defence of Reductionism that I have been considering. In fact we can see a Cartesian structure in Parfit's Reductionism itself. According to the view I recommend, a context of facts about the objective continuation of lives helps to make intelligible a face-value construal of what Locke actually says, that continuous "consciousness" presents an identity through time. This context figures in Parfit's picture only as the "normal cause" of a less rich content, which is supposed to be what Locke really intended to remind us of, something tailor-made to seem entertainable, like the Cartesian *cogito*, without objective presuppositions. A phrase like "serial co-consciousness" can indeed be understood to fit "facts with which we are familiar"; but the familiar fact is that a person experiences his life from within as the career of a single objective subject, and it looks like a Cartesian thought that in order to consider the content of the familiar experience as it really is, we must purify it of involvement with an objective context.[8]

In her reflections on the first-person mode of thought, G. E. M. Anscombe draws attention to a highly instructive anecdote from William James.[9] A subject nicknamed "Baldy" had fallen out of a carriage; he asked who fell out, and when told that it was Baldy, he responded "Did Baldy fall out? Poor Baldy!" This episode reflects, as Anscombe puts it, a "lapse of self-consciousness", because Baldy's thought of the falling "was one for which he looked for a subject". This formulation points up a contrast between Baldy's need to rely on extraneous information (in this case supplied by other people) to identify a subject of which to predicate the happening that he found himself possessing a conception of, on the one hand, and the absence of any need to establish an identity, which I have stressed as characterizing Lockean "consciousness" (that is, self-consciousness), on the other. Anscombe herself concludes that the contents of "conscious-

---

8. In his debate with Richard Swinburne, *Personal Identity*, Sydney Shoemaker espouses psychological Reductionism in the context of an ultimately materialist functionalism about the mental. There is certainly no ontological dualism here. This does not deter me from my suggestion that Reductionism is fundamentally Cartesian. It is superficial to suppose we can avoid what is basically wrong with Cartesian philosophy by avoiding the dualism that is the most striking feature of its mainstream versions.

9. "The First Person", pp. 64-5.

ness" should not be understood to include reference to a persisting subject; as far as it goes, this matches the Reductionist response to the peculiarity of "consciousness". But the conclusion turns on an unwarranted equation. Baldy looked for a subject for his conception of the falling, and Anscombe equates that with the conception's requiring a subject, and concludes that the contents of "consciousness" must be conceptions of states and occurrences that do not require a subject. Against the background of the position I have sketched, we can see this to be, remarkably enough given its author, a piece of vestigially Cartesian philosophy. Of course Anscombe has no sympathy with the mainstream Cartesian thesis, that "consciousness" embodies reference to a purely spiritual substance. But her way of avoiding that thesis, like the implicit defence of Reductionism that I have been considering, betrays a continuing adherence to something more fundamentally Cartesian. The fact that "consciousness" does not *look for* a subject for its conceptions would show that its contents do not *require* a subject, and so are not to be understood as predicated of a subject, only on the assumption that the logical character of "consciousness" must be provided for entirely within "consciousness" itself; and that assumption is what I am suggesting is the basic Cartesian mistake.

4. Lichtenberg remarked that in the Cartesian predicament one ought to say, not "I think", but "It's thinking", on an analogy with forms of words like "It's raining".[10] Parfit reads this aphorism as a straight-faced statement; in Parfit's reading, Lichtenberg accepts that psychological goings-on can be intelligibly reported impersonally, that is, without imposing a subject-predicate structure, and holds that Descartes needed to exploit this possibility.[11] On this understanding, Lichtenberg is fundamentally Cartesian in the sense I have suggested; he accepts that "consciousness" has its content in a way that requires no context, and merely protests that once we have "consciousness" in view in its pure form, stripped of all objective context by the Method of Doubt, it is clear that what we have before

---

10. "*Es denkt*, sollte man sagen, so wie man sagt: *es blitzt*." (Quoted by Parfit at p. 517, n. 20.)

11. *Reasons and Persons*, pp. 224–6.

us does not contain within itself the resources to make sense of attributing its contents to a subject. But it is quite doubtful that we can really conceive thinking as a subjectless occurrence, like a state of the weather, and Lichtenberg's aphorism is much more pointed if we read him as exploiting that fact. In allowing scepticism to generate the supposed predicament in which the *cogito* is to operate, Descartes has indeed thought away conditions that would be necessary for the idea of singling out a subject to make sense. And it is not that Descartes can, even so, stop the rot with a variant on the purely inner certainty that the *cogito* alleges, divergent in that it must be formulated in impersonal terms. The aphorism goes through the motions of expressing that idea, but we cannot be meant to take it simply in our stride. The point of the aphorism, on this different reading, is to question the basic Cartesian conviction that "consciousness" is self-contained, so that the stripping away of context that the Method of Doubt effects reveals "consciousness" as it really is. On the contrary, removal of context makes it impossible to keep "consciousness" itself in view.[12]

5. Generations of commentators, from Butler on, have supposed Locke meant to convey a thesis about personal identity of a kind that would be undermined by an accusation of circularity. Butler and his followers think this spells doom for a Lockean approach to personal identity; Parfit agrees with Butler that circularity would be a killing objection, but follows Sydney Shoemaker in offering Locke conceptual material to escape it.[13] But the Lockean thesis I have cited is so open about simply using the notion of identity ("can consider itself as itself, the same thinking thing, in different times and places")

---

12. The *cogito* is thus more than just a device to make the "identification-freedom" of self-consciousness vivid (see n. 6 above); it also embodies the mistaken conclusion from that fact, that self-consciousness has its content independently of any objective context. Contrast another way of making "identification-freedom" vivid, sensory deprivation (see Anscombe, "The First Person", pp. 57–8). One can think of oneself in conditions of sensory deprivation, that is, without having one's bodily presence in the world perceptually borne in on one; this highlights the way self-reference is separated from criteria of persistence. But this case can be understood without any suggestion that self-reference is consistent with the supposed possibility against the background of which the *cogito* is supposed to operate, that there is no objective continuant for one to be.

13. See Shoemaker's "Persons and Their Pasts".

that we ought to pause before we accept Butler's assumption that circularity would be a problem for what Locke intends. It is not just obvious that the task of philosophy is to "analyse" every concept around which philosophical issues arise. I have tried to cast doubt on one specific motivation for a Reductionist "correction" of Locke's apparent willingness that the notion of identity should figure unanalysed in what he gives as the content of "consciousness". And it is not as if Locke's remark would be pointless otherwise. On the contrary, it pinpoints, as it stands, the essential "inner" availability of personal persistence, which Cartesian philosophy rightly stresses but misconceives. I doubt that we do Locke a favour by interpreting away the unashamed "circularity" in what he actually says.

Admittedly Locke is eager to affirm a difference between what sameness comes to for persons and what it comes to for human beings ("men"); and his point seems to go beyond making room for, say, dolphins or Martians to be persons, something that would pose no problem for the sort of position I am urging. But I doubt that this area of Locke's discussion can carry much weight in a recommendation of Reductionism.

Locke's account of human identity is an application of his admirable account of the identity of living things. Persistence, for a living thing, is the continuation of an individual life of the appropriate kind, sustained through alterations of matter so long as they preserve the necessary organization. But when Locke applies this idea to human beings, he lets the application be shaped by a broadly Cartesian division of what might otherwise be regarded as the composite life of the human being that a person is, into merely animal functions on the one hand and operations of "consciousness" on the other. The result is a conception of the identity of human beings in which human life is conceived as what is left over after a Cartesian skimming off of "cogitation". According to this conception, what it is for the same human life to be still in progress is a matter of continuity in merely animal functioning. It suffices that the organic basis of walking, eating, and so forth persists, in the sense that there is continuity, through exchange of matter with the environment, in the material underpinnings for the relevant potentialities. Thus, when Locke imagines a case in which the bodies of a prince and a cobbler exchange "consciousnesses", he takes it that the identities of the human beings involved go with the gross bodily continuities: "The body too goes to the making the man, and would, I guess, to everybody determine the man in this case" (3.27.15).

If we read Locke's claim about the relevance of "consciousness" to personal identity outside the context of that broadly Cartesian division, it serves not as a sketch of a putatively self-standing sort of continuity, whose subject (if any) would have to be a purely spiritual continuant, but as describing a special feature of what continuation of life comes to for animals of a distinctive kind. The "thinking intelligent being" that is a person can be, and be aware of itself as, a human being—to fix on the case that we have to take as central. Locke's account of what a person is in fact perfectly fits normal human beings.

But this suggests we should not go Locke's way with the case of the prince and the cobbler. Suppose that we really can imagine the prince (that person) finding himself with the body that used to belong to the cobbler.[14] The person with that body is the prince.[15] That is, his life after the catastrophe is a continuation of the life of that person, the prince. And if we free Locke from the broadly Cartesian division, there is nothing to prevent us from saying that that continuing life prolongs the life of that human being, the one the prince was and is. Indeed we had better say that. Surely there are not two lives being led here, the life of the human being, continuing a life that has always been led hereabouts, and the life of the person, proceeding after a spatial discontinuity.[16] The fact that, for instance, the legs he moves when he walks are different does not make this something other than a continuation of the same human life (if we make sense of the story at all), any more than does the fact that a different heart beats in the chest of someone who has received a transplant. Whether it is a continuation of the same human life depends not on the identity of limbs and organs but on whether it is a prolongation of the career of the self-conscious agent who lives it.

Locke famously claims that "person" is "a forensic term" (3.27.26). What underlies this is the thought that the ethical signifi-

---

14. We may need to embellish Locke's bare fairy-tale with science fiction about brain transplantation, to ensure that we are really imagining a migration of "consciousness" as opposed to a peculiar illusion.

15. Even if, as Locke supposes, he is "the same cobbler to every one besides himself". Everyone besides himself is wrong about which person this is.

16. See Wiggins, *Sameness and Substance*, p. 161, n. 16, with chap. 1.

cance of personal agency is connected with self-consciousness. Now one effect of disallowing any help in understanding personal identity from the continuity of human (or, if you like, dolphin or Martian) life—the move that reflects the Cartesian division—is to encourage an overblown reading of this good thought. No doubt incurable amnesia about a past action makes it pointless to punish someone for it. The Cartesian framework induces Locke to proceed as if reasonable thoughts on those lines reflected something much more contentious, that actions to which one's "consciousness" does not extend are no part of one's life as a person. It is this rather unhappy region of Locke's thinking that gives rise to the appearance that he is committed to a self-sufficient "memory criterion" of personal identity. I think it is uncharitable to emphasize this strand, to the detriment of his evidently non-reductive, and in itself quite non-Cartesian, central claim about awareness of self.

The Cartesian division of "consciousness" from merely animal life that frames Locke's discussion reflects the assumption that "that thinking thing that is in us" (3.27.27) is immaterial. This is what makes it seem that continuity of animal life, even the life of a human being, cannot be constitutively involved in continuity of "consciousness". But though Locke allows himself that assumption, he carefully distances himself from Descartes. It is not only that he leaves it open whether the presumed immaterial subject of "consciousness" is an unchanging substance, as opposed to something that persists through change in what constitutes it, on an analogy with how an embodied living thing persists through change in the matter it is composed of (3.27.10-14). He is also agnostic about the background assumption itself (3.27.27)—happily embracing the consequence that his thought experiments, for instance the case of the prince and the cobbler, may have an absurdity that he and his readers miss only through ignorance. This equanimity is incomprehensible unless we take it that his main concern is to affirm that persons are self-conscious, and that he is (rightly) confident that that thesis, to which he can give vivid expression on the assumption that continuity of self-consciousness is separable from any merely animal continuity, would not be undermined if the Cartesian separation could not be effected.

6. When we try to spell out what Locke means by "consciousness", it is natural to focus on memory. Memory in some sense must be

part, at least, of anything one could mean by "serial co-consciousness". For Reductionist purposes what is needed is a capacity that retrospectively holds past states and occurrences together within the purview of a single "consciousness", but in a way that is intelligible otherwise than in terms of the idea that all this belongs to the past life of the subject who engages in the retrospect. I have tried to suggest that the distinctively Reductionist element of this thought is neither well motivated nor part of Locke's basic insight; memory can fall into place as simply part of the capacity of "a thinking intelligent being" to "consider itself as itself, the same thinking thing, in different times and places". But even if Reductionism lacks a good external motivation, it would surely be of interest if something recognizably close to Locke's phenomenon could be given a non-circular analysis. In any case, we need to consider an ingenious conceptual innovation with which Reductionists have tried to provide for the distinctively Reductionist element in the face of an obvious objection.

Memory of the appropriate sort, as ordinarily conceived, is the capacity to retain knowledge of one's own past. But that formulation simply uses the notion for which we are supposed to be looking for a reduction.[17] The Reductionist response is that retrospective "consciousness" should be conceived rather as *quasi-memory*.[18] Quasi-memory, like "experience" memory as ordinarily conceived, is a capacity to recapture actual past states and occurrences "from within" (that is, from the point of view of the subject of an experience or the agent of an action), with whatever causal connection to the past states and occurrences is needed for that to be intelligible. The only difference is that there is no requirement that the remembering subject is identical with the subject from whose point of view the past occurrences are recaptured. So ordinary memories are quasi-memories that satisfy that extra condition. But there can be quasi-memories that are not ordinary memories: cases where the quasi-rememberer has been equipped with a capacity to recapture past occurrences from a participant point of view that was not his

---

17. I have formulated the objection of circularity so as to avoid the crude errors exposed by Wiggins, *Sameness and Substance*, pp. 152–4.
18. This resource for Reductionism was first devised by Shoemaker, "Persons and Their Pasts"; for Parfit's account of it, see *Reasons and Persons*, pp. 220–2.

own, perhaps by transplantation of brain tissue that might, if left in its original skull, have figured in the aetiology of some ordinary remembering. A similar strategy is obviously available for other aspects of "serial co-consciousness", for instance intention, but it will make for simplicity if we focus on memory.

Ordinary memories are quasi-memories; as the concept of quasi-memory has been explained, an ordinary person quasi-remembers those past states and occurrences that are within the reach of his present "consciousness". The truth of this claim simply requires one thing less than the more familiar claim that he remembers those past states and occurrences. But in what sense does it follow that when one takes oneself to have "experience" memory, one's belief that one is aware of something in one's own past is "a separable belief", as Parfit puts it (p. 222)? For Reductionist purposes, quasi-memory needs to be a capacity whose exercises intelligibly constitute retention of knowledge of past states and occurrences, "from within" but in such a way that the identity of their subject, in particular his being one and the same as the quasi-rememberer, is not represented in the content of the retained knowledge. The Reductionist claim is that this identity-neutral, though "from within", hold on the past is the real content of the retrospective component of "consciousness"; the specification of identity that Locke adds ("consider itself as itself") reflects an extra belief, warranted in the familiar normal case but no part of the pure deliverance of retrospective "consciousness". But it is a mistake to think the intelligibility of quasi-memory achieves this Reductionist requirement.

Consider a case of mere quasi-memory, intelligibly brought about by suitable intervention in its subject's brain.[19] To say it is mere quasi-memory, as opposed to ordinary memory, is to say that the subject's belief that the recalled states and occurrences figured in his own life is false. But that does not show that the content of this identity-involving belief is separable from the content of the impression, the knowledge that the subject seems to retain from the past. On the contrary; we have not been equipped to make sense of mere quasi-memories otherwise than by supposing that they would present themselves as memories, that is, that they would embody an impression, which must be illusory, that the subject of the recalled state

---

19. See Parfit, *Reasons and Persons*, p. 220.

or occurrence was oneself. We need to be careful about the sense in which, when we drop the identity requirement that distinguishes ordinary memory from mere quasi-memory, we keep at our disposal whatever causal connection is necessary to make quasi-memory intelligible. No doubt a science-fiction story about copying or transplanting memory traces can make it intelligible that a subject might have memory-impressions from someone else's past. But what it cannot make intelligible is that such impressions might constitute *knowledge*. This kind of aetiology enables us to make sense of quasi-memory as yielding illusions of ordinary memory; not as what Reductionists require it to be, an autonomously intelligible faculty of knowing the past, from a participant's perspective but without commitment to the participant's having been oneself.[20]

It is true, but irrelevant, that if a subject of mere quasi-memories knew how those impressions of the past were caused, they would entitle him to claim knowledge of the past. That does not put quasi-memory on a level, epistemologically speaking, with memory. Memories are not something from which one derives knowledge of one's past, on the basis of surrounding information; they simply *are* knowledge of one's past. How can that be so? How can something as slight, so to speak, as an impression have that cognitive status? The answer to this question lies in the very same appeal to the objective context of "consciousness" that explains how it is possible for "consciousness" to present an identity through time without itself applying criteria of persistence. The objective context explains how the contents of "consciousness" can have both their shape and their cognitive status, even though "consciousness" does not need to draw on that context, say to supply premises for inferences, when it arrives at its contents and its epistemic entitlements. Quasi-remembering does have epistemic potential, but it depends on the objective context in a quite different way; using quasi-memories as a basis for knowledge would require "consciousness" to draw explicitly on information extraneous to its own contents. So the fact that one might

---

20. Not that a quasi-memory would be illusion through and through. Someone would really have lived through the quasi-remembered past. (And perhaps that life-experience might have, for the quasi-rememberer, the sort of formative significance that elements from one's own past can have in the familiar normal case.) But this leaves untouched the point that a quasi-memory would embody an illusion in respect of the identity of the subject of the remembered state or occurrence.

know the past on the basis of quasi-remembering does no damage to the thesis that quasi-memory is intelligible only derivatively. It is not special to illusions of this kind that someone who knew enough about their aetiology could derive knowledge from them. That makes no difference to the fact that the very idea of illusion is derivative from the idea of what an illusion misrepresents itself as being.

Once one has the notion of mere quasi-memory, made intelligible in terms of suitable abnormal aetiologies for memory-impressions, one can entertain the supposition that an apparent memory is a mere quasi-memory, thereby distancing oneself from the belief that it was oneself who lived through the recalled state or occurrence. In that sense the belief is indeed "separable". But this does not equip the memory-impression with an identity-neutral content. The supposition one would be entertaining is that an impression whose content is not identity-neutral, because it is that of an ordinary memory, is illusory in respect of that aspect of its content. Compare the way one can distance oneself from the belief that one's objective environment is as one's perceptual experience represents it, by entertaining a suitably abnormal aetiology for the experience. This does nothing to show that the content of the experience is anything other than the content of the suspended belief. The effect of envisaging the abnormal aetiology is that one conceives the experiences, not as exercises of some autonomously intelligible faculty of quasi-perception, but as illusions of perception.[21]

This parallel bears elaboration. Quasi-memory was introduced by dropping a requirement for ordinary personal memory, and it may seem difficult to reconcile that with the claim that quasi-memory is intelligible only derivatively from ordinary personal memory. Surely, we may be tempted to think, the concept with fewer requirements must be simpler and therefore independently graspable. But this should rouse our suspicion as soon as we see that it parallels the thought that is at work in the Argument from Illusion, which has

---

21. The case I am urging against the claim that quasi-memory serves the purposes of Reductionism comes from Evans, *The Varieties of Reference*, pp. 241–8. Parfit (alone, so far as I know, among proponents of Reductionism) undertakes to respond to Evans (p. 516, n. 15). But his response consists entirely in stressing the irrelevant point that someone who knew the aetiology of a quasi-memory could acquire knowledge of someone else's past from it. (Evans cheerfully grants the point at p. 245, though one would not gather this from Parfit's representation of him.)

done enormous damage in the epistemology of perception. Start with, say, the notion of seeing that such-and-such is the case. Now introduce a notion explained as applicable in just the same conditions, except that there is no requirement that such-and-such is the case. There is nothing wrong with this second notion, any more than there is anything wrong with the notion of quasi-memory. But it is disastrous to conclude, from the fact that we can arrive at it by dropping a requirement, that what it is for the second notion to be applicable is intelligible otherwise than in terms of an appearance whose content is the dropped requirement—that the content with which applications of the first notion make play, that such-and-such is the case, is a mere "separable belief". That poses an intractable problem over how there can be a justificatory relation between the perceptual experiences in virtue of which the second notion applies and the supposedly "separable belief". Here, as with quasi-memory, the dropped requirement does not simply disappear. The second notion cannot be understood apart from the idea of an appearance that the dropped requirement is satisfied—that is, in the context of the other requirements, an appearance that the first notion has application.

How can merely dropping a requirement yield a concept that can be understood only in this derivative way? Well, there is no reason to assume that what is left when the requirement is dropped will stand on its own as an adequate explication of a concept. That need not be so, even though the result is admitted to be a set of necessary and sufficient conditions for the concept's application. It takes more than an arithmetic of subtracting necessary conditions to guarantee us an autonomously intelligible concept.

7. So far I have considered quasi-memory only as the product of special intervention in our world, leaving what is normal unchanged. This may seem objectionably parochial. The objection I have in mind is that, in suggesting that quasi-memory is intelligible only as a kind of illusion, I have illicitly exploited the way ordinary thought lets itself be shaped by the sheer weight of what merely happens to be normal; thereby I have, according to the objection, kept a genuine conceptual possibility from coming into view. To correct this (the objection continues), we must allow imaginative alteration of the whole background of normality; we must consider, say, beings

whose normal mode of multiplying is by splitting, like amoebae, but with retrospective "consciousness" over the life that precedes a split retained by both the self-contained organisms that are extant after a split. Here, surely, it may be said, we have quasi-memory in the form in which Reductionists want it, a cognitive hold on past life-experiences, "from within" but not representing the subject of the past life-experiences as identical with the subject of the retrospective "consciousness". The background of normality that I have so far exploited to force that content on the impressions is simply absent from the imagined world. And once we have exploited this thought experiment, or another to the same purpose, to ensure a proper understanding of quasi-memory, we can bring the concept, thus liberated from the appearance of being intrinsically derivative, back to our world for the original Reductionist purpose—characterizing our retrospective "consciousness" in an identity-neutral way.

All sorts of questions arise if we try to think the thought experiment through. Are we to conceive these beings as living continuants whose lives include what is within the survey of their retrospective "consciousness"? If so, since after a split there are two independently living things who can thus claim to have lived through what was apparently a single life before the split, are we to say that there were two lives (at least) being led there all along? This makes it hard to imagine what analogue to first-person thinking might express the "from within" character of "consciousness" of present life-experiences, on the part of, as we cannot easily put it, one of these beings, knowing what shape their lives normally take.[22] Should such thought be in the plural? (Compare the man possessed by demons who, when asked his name, replied "Legion, for we are many".)[23]

We might try equipping these beings with a primary form of self-conscious thought whose reference can be unproblematically singular because it spans only periods between splits. But the retrospective scope of this mode of thought would be carried by something analogous to ordinary memory. And then we risk once more representing quasi-memories that reach back before a split as illusions; these are animals that come into being and cease to exist at splits, like amoebae, but they are self-conscious, and explicably equipped, from the

---

22. See Wiggins, *Sameness and Substance*, p. 168.
23. See Anscombe, "The First Person", pp. 58–9.

beginning of their careers, with the appearance of having themselves lived the lives of their progenitors.

Well, perhaps not. Perhaps we can leave them capable of singular self-reference, but avoid populating their retrospective "consciousness" with illusions; perhaps retrospective "consciousness" in this world would present the past it surveyed as "mine or ours", with a first-person plural reference to fellow descendants of the subject whose experience or action was being recalled. (The disjunction would be resolved in favour of one of its disjuncts by suitable information, if available, about whether the recalled material predates the latest split.) But this way of filling out the thought experiment would not support Parfit's suggestion that the content of *our* "consciousness" can stand revealed as really identity-neutral, unshaped by its normal objective background, which serves merely as a normal cause. On the contrary, we are here imagining how a different objective context of normality might make intelligible a different identity-involving content for retrospective "consciousness". The thought experiment in this form does nothing to recommend regarding the normal background within which a retrospective "consciousness" operates as extraneous to its true content, so that our retrospective "consciousness" is really less committal than Locke represents it as being.

It may be said that I am still imposing parochial restrictions on the imagination, in refusing to understand the idea that "consciousness" represents its objects "from within" except in terms of something sufficiently close to first-person reference as we know it, which is reference to particular things that live particular lives. The point of this and similar thought experiments, it may be said, is to encourage an imaginative detachment of the "from within" character of "consciousness" from any such context. But here the accusation of excessive respect for mere normality seems to me to lose its power to disturb. Thought experiments like these can stretch our sense of the possibilities for lives and the particular things that live them. But how could they show that we can really make sense of "from within" in abstraction from the idea of a continuing life, lived by a subject whose experiences figure in its "consciousness" as belonging to itself? In some sense, no doubt, we can focus imaginatively on the "from within" character of "consciousness" in abstraction from any objective background. But if one supposes, on the ground of the simplicity of imaginative attention, that what is needed for the target of the attention to be intelligible is all present within the scope of the focused attention, one falls into a familiar kind of fundamentally Cartesian illusion.

Parfit in effect glosses the "from within" character of "consciousness" in terms of the first-person mode of presentation, and that is fine by my lights.[24] But he suggests that by considering quasi-memory, we can learn that the fact that "our apparent memories ... come to us in the first-person mode" can be detached from their purporting to be about ourselves; that is a mere "separable belief". I think this reduces the idea of the first-person mode to unintelligibility. It gets things backwards to suppose that the first-person mode of presentation can be understood in terms of an independently intelligible "interiority" or "subjectivity" in the flow of experience, with reference to a subject introduced, if at all, only by a subsequent construction.

8. Parfit presents Reductionism as the required corrective to an error of which postulating purely spiritual substances is just one form. The error is to regard the identity of a person through time as "a further fact". Some people think they can have the further fact without further *things,* but Parfit argues (pp. 239–40) that belief in the further fact is unintelligible without a belief "that we are separately existing entities, distinct from our brains and bodies". Cartesian souls are just the most familiar result of trying to spell out what these separately existing entities might be. The point of insisting on the further fact is supposed to be that it putatively underwrites the belief, which according to Parfit is a mere prejudice, that questions of personal identity are always determinate—that if a person exists at some time, then at all later times there must be a definite answer to the question whether that person still exists.

I think this distorts the credentials of psychological Reductionism as a positive thesis—the thesis that what continuity of "consciousness" really is can be understood without presupposing the idea of a person's continued existence. When Parfit depicts opponents of Reductionism as committed to the further fact, he proceeds as if they

---

24. See *Reasons and Persons,* pp. 221–2.

could not possibly be disputing the availability of the conceptual materials for a reduction: namely, an identity-free account of continuous "consciousness", and perhaps a similarly identity-free account of bodily continuity. Why would they nevertheless insist that personal identity is a further fact, over and above facts that can be stated in such terms? The only plausible reason is that they think the question whether some person still exists has more determinateness than any construction out of such materials could give it.

But the right basis for opposing Reductionism is that we have been given no good reason to believe in the substratum of identity-free relations. In particular, there is no genuinely intelligible Reductionist substitute for Locke's identity-involving characterization of continuous "consciousness". From this point of view, Parfit's account of what is at issue is prejudicial. Reductionism is wrong, not because personal identity is a further fact, but because there is no conceptually simpler substratum for personal identity to be further to.

This way of opposing Reductionism is simply separate from any insistence that personal identity is always determinate. The question whether a given person still exists is the question whether a certain life is still in progress; and it is not peculiar to personal life that one can imagine tamperings with nature after which the only possible response to that question would be to shrug one's shoulders.[25] That affords no support to the claim that is in doubt, that Locke's phenomenon can be genuinely understood in identity-neutral terms.

What about separately existing entities? Persons are living things whose lives, at least in normal cases, include the capacity for self-awareness that Locke stresses. If we refuse to reduce a person's continuing existence to supposedly prior relations that hold the elements of such a life together, that is not to picture a person's continuing existence as separate from the continuation of his life. Nor is it to suppose that a person is, in some objectionable sense, distinct from his brain and his body (Parfit's gloss on "separately existing"). Not that a person should be identified with his brain and (the rest of) his body, any more than a house should be identified with the bricks, and so forth, of which it is composed; but there is no commitment to

---

25. See Parfit's Spectrum arguments, pp. 231–43.

some peculiar extra ingredient, which would ensure determinateness of identity, in a person's make-up.[26]

The distorting effect of Parfit's play with the further fact emerges when he dispenses himself (p. 273) from discussing the view of, for instance, David Wiggins.[27] His justification is that Wiggins's account of personal identity, which is in terms of the continuation of a distinctive kind of life, involves no commitment to separately existing entities, or to the general determinateness of identity that the further fact is supposed to underwrite. That is true enough. But Wiggins's picture of personal identity gives no comfort to the positively Reductionist reconstrual of Locke's phenomenon on which I have been casting doubt. And without that, there is nothing to supplant concern with one's own future in the structuring of rationality. A position like Wiggins's is a serious threat to the striking practical implications that Parfit attributes to Reductionism.

9. We are living things, and we share with other living things a natural interest in surviving. This aspect of our animal nature emerges in our rationally governed lives as a concern that has a conceptual content: a concern, naturally felt by each of us, that the living thing he is should continue to exist. This helps to structure a whole region of practical reason, in which we locate not just the rationality of taking steps to ensure our persistence, but also such things as reasons to make provision for the quality of our future lives. Or so we naturally suppose.

Parfit aims to dislodge this structure as mere prejudice. But in discrediting the supposed simpler conceptual substratum for personal identity, I have discredited the basis for this suggestion. We have not been given a conceptual pathway along which rational concerns could be understood to be carried into the future in a way that underlies the concern with oneself, so that a concern structured by this alternative conceptual pathway should supplant the concern with oneself once we see that they are separable. Why should my interest

---

26. Besides Cartesian souls, Parfit mentions (p. 210) a hitherto unrecognized kind of physical entity as a candidate to fill this role.
27. For which see *Sameness and Substance*, chap. 6.

in the continuation of the life I am leading be supplanted by an interest in lives that embody the illusion of being continuations of my life?

Suppose I am face to face with the end of my life, the life of the individual living thing I am. Perhaps it would be a consolation to learn that the world without me was going to contain someone with a perfect, and explicable, illusion of having lived my life so far—perhaps two, produced from me by fission.[28] The prospect might indeed have unwelcome features. For instance, it would bother my wife to be competed for by two people, each taking himself to be me; and it would be hard to be confident that a quasi-intention to bow out, somehow formed by me now in respect of just one of them, would be acted on, since each would presumably have a replica of my concern for her. But suppose we waive such difficulties, and focus on the consoling power of the thought that someone will exist who cares especially about my less individualistic projects. (With some projects, no doubt the more the better.)

None of this shows that the concern for the future whose promised satisfaction accounts for this possible consolation overlaps with, let alone exhausts, my interest in my own future as it fits into the natural conditions of my life. If a prospect might console me in the face of the prospect of an end to the individual life I am living, it does not follow that it is "about as good as ordinary survival".[29] Perhaps it would be rational to choose fission in preference to ordinary death, without quasi-continuation. It does not follow that the rationality of an ordinary concern with my own future can be disconnected from the fact that it is the future of the living individual I am. It can be rational to choose fission over death without quasi-continuation, and still not be a prejudice to prefer the continuation of one's individual life to either.[30]

We should not overestimate the importance of the concession that there is reason to value the existence of someone who cares about one's projects. If we focus on outcomes, to the exclusion of a concern with what a deliberator himself is to do, we single out an application of reason whose topic is reasons why such-and-such should

---

28. I have conceded that it need not be illusion through and through.
29. Parfit, *Reasons and Persons*, p. 261.
30. See Wiggins, "The Concern to Survive".

take place or be brought about—never mind by whom. All by itself, this could not be a recognizable conception of practical reason. Of course the topic is part of the subject-matter of practical reason, but it is not intelligible that there should be such a topic except in the context of practical reason proper, whose primary concern is action to be undertaken by the subject who deliberates. Parfit aims at a picture of practical reason as in no way shaped by facts about the persistence of individual human beings. But to my eye it seems quite implausible that the concept of agency, and with it the concept of practical reason, can survive outside a context of thought about the activities of individual living things. And the apparatus of Reductionism yields no ground for being suspicious of that impression, and perhaps trying to dislodge it as a prejudice.

A deep element in a broadly Cartesian outlook is an inability to conceive "cogitation" as part of something "merely" natural (so this cast of thought will incline us to put it), such as the life of an individual animal. This inability is manifested in the Cartesian segregation of "cogitation" into a special realm of reality. It deserves sympathy, even if we manage not to share it; it reflects powerful pressures on us to conceive the world of nature in a way that resists fitting rationality into it. (Another reflection of those pressures is a temptation towards "naturalistic" reductions of rationality.) Now I have already suggested that the drift of Parfit's position is Cartesian, and I think we can understand his thinking as reflecting that felt tension between reason, and hence mind, on the one side, and "mere" nature, on the other. Parfit is anxious to avoid the more blatant expressions of this tendency of thought—notably pure spiritual substances, conceived as problematically related to living animals. But the tendency shows in his refusal to let the space of reasons be structured by the natural continuities of human life. Perhaps it shows also in his eloquently expressed sense of a liberation that Reductionism affords him, from a felt imprisonment in his own individual life and a special concern with his own individual death (p. 281). A familiar concomitant of an inability to take phrases like "the life of the mind" at face value is a temptation to fantasies of transcending the finiteness of individual life; and I suspect that Parfit's sense of liberation is just another manifestation of that deeply suspect temptation. So far from undermining a prejudice that distorts our conception of practical reason, I think Parfit's position belongs in a long series of philosophical distortions that are imposed on reflection about reason and human life by our having forgotten, intelligibly by all means, how to maintain a firm and integrated conception of ourselves as rational animals.[31]

[31]. For an excellent introduction to the wider issues here, see Wiggins, *Sameness and Substance*, pp. 179–87.

BIBLIOGRAPHY

CREDITS

INDEX

Bibliography

J. L. Ackrill, "Aristotle on *Eudaimonia*", *Proceedings of the British Academy* 60 (1974), 339-59.
D. J. Allan, "Aristotle's Account of the Origin of Moral Principles", *Proceedings of the XIth International Congress of Philosophy*, vol. 12 (North-Holland, Amsterdam, 1953), pp. 120-7.
—— "The Practical Syllogism", in *Autour d'Aristote* (Presses Universitaires de Louvain, Louvain, 1955), pp. 325-40.
G. E. M. Anscombe, *Intention* (Basil Blackwell, Oxford, 1957).
—— "Modern Moral Philosophy", *Philosophy* 33 (1958), 1-19.
—— "Thought and Action in Aristotle", in Renford Bambrough, ed., *New Essays on Plato and Aristotle* (Routledge and Kegan Paul, London, 1965), pp. 143-58.
—— "The First Person", in Samuel Guttenplan, ed., *Mind and Language* (Clarendon Press, Oxford, 1975), pp. 45-65.
Aristotle, *Nicomachean Ethics Book VI*, ed. L. H. G. Greenwood (Cambridge University Press, Cambridge, 1909).
—— *The Athenian Constitution; The Eudemian Ethics; On Virtues and Vices*, ed. and trans. H. Rackham (Heinemann, London, 1935).
—— *The Nicomachean Ethics of Aristotle*, trans. Sir David Ross (Oxford University Press, Oxford, 1925).
A. J. Ayer, *Language, Truth and Logic* (Gollancz, London, 1936).
Gordon Baker, "Following Wittgenstein: Some Signposts for *Philosophical Investigations* §§143-242", in Steven Holtzman and Christopher Leich, eds., *Wittgenstein: To Follow a Rule* (Routledge and Kegan Paul, London, 1981), pp. 31-71.
G. P. Baker and P. M. S. Hacker, *Scepticism, Rules, and Language* (Basil Blackwell, Oxford, 1984).
Simon Blackburn, "Truth, Realism, and the Regulation of Theory", in Peter A. French, Theodore E. Uehling, Jr., and Howard K. Wettstein, eds., *Midwest Studies in Philosophy*, vol. 5: *Studies in Epistemology* (University of Minnesota Press, Minneapolis, 1980), pp. 353-71.

―――― "Opinions and Chances", in D. H. Mellor, ed., *Prospects for Pragmatism* (Cambridge University Press, Cambridge, 1980), pp. 175–96.
―――― "Rule-Following and Moral Realism", in Steven Holtzman and Christopher Leich, eds., *Wittgenstein: To Follow a Rule* (Routledge and Kegan Paul, London, 1981), pp. 163–87.
―――― "The Individual Strikes Back", *Synthese* 58 (1984), 281–301.
―――― *Spreading the Word* (Clarendon Press, Oxford, 1984).
―――― "Errors and the Phenomenology of Value", in Ted Honderich, ed., *Morality and Objectivity* (Routledge and Kegan Paul, London, 1985), pp. 1–22.
M. F. Burnyeat, "Aristotle on Learning to Be Good", in Amélie Oksenberg Rorty, ed., *Essays on Aristotle's Ethics* (University of California Press, Berkeley, 1980), pp. 69–92.
Stanley Cavell, *Must We Mean What We Say?* (Charles Scribner's Sons, New York, 1969).
―――― *The Claim of Reason* (Clarendon Press, Oxford, 1979).
John M. Cooper, *Reason and Human Good in Aristotle* (Harvard University Press, Cambridge, Mass., 1975).
―――― "Some Remarks on Aristotle's Moral Psychology", *Southern Journal of Philosophy* 27 supp. (1988), 25–42.
Donald Davidson, "Actions, Reasons, and Causes", in his *Essays on Actions and Events*, pp. 3–19.
―――― "Causal Relations", in his *Essays on Actions and Events*, pp. 149–62.
―――― "How is Weakness of the Will Possible?", in his *Essays on Actions and Events*, pp. 21–42.
―――― *Essays on Actions and Events* (Clarendon Press, Oxford, 1980).
―――― "On the Very Idea of a Conceptual Scheme", in his *Inquiries into Truth and Interpretation*, pp. 183–98.
―――― *Inquiries into Truth and Interpretation* (Clarendon Press, Oxford, 1984).
Daniel Dennett, "Towards a Cognitive Theory of Consciousness", in his *Brainstorms: Philosophical Essays on Mind and Psychology* (Bradford Books, Montgomery, Vt., 1978), pp. 149–73.
―――― "Beyond Belief", in Andrew Woodfield, ed., *Thought and Object* (Clarendon Press, Oxford, 1982), pp. 1–95.
―――― "Cognitive Wheels", in Christopher Hookway, ed., *Minds, Machines and Evolution* (Cambridge University Press, Cambridge, 1984), pp. 129–51.
―――― *Consciousness Explained* (Little, Brown and Co., Boston, Toronto, and London, 1991).
Michael Dummett, *Frege: Philosophy of Language* (Duckworth, London, 1973).
―――― "What Is a Theory of Meaning? (II)", in Gareth Evans and John McDowell, eds., *Truth and Meaning* (Clarendon Press, Oxford, 1976), pp. 67–137.
―――― "Wittgenstein's Philosophy of Mathematics", in his *Truth and Other Enigmas* (Duckworth, London, 1978), pp. 166–85.

Ronald Dworkin, "Hard Cases", in his *Taking Rights Seriously* (Duckworth, London, 1977), pp. 81–130.
Troels Engberg-Pedersen, *Aristotle's Theory of Moral Insight* (Clarendon Press, Oxford, 1983).
Gareth Evans, "Things Without the Mind", in Zak van Straaten, ed., *Philosophical Subjects: Essays Presented to P. F. Strawson* (Clarendon Press, Oxford, 1980), pp. 76–116.
—— *The Varieties of Reference* (Clarendon Press, Oxford, 1982).
Jerry A. Fodor, *The Language of Thought* (Thomas Y. Crowell, New York, 1975).
Philippa Foot, "Hume on Moral Judgement", in her *Virtues and Vices*, pp. 74–80.
—— "Moral Beliefs", in her *Virtues and Vices*, pp. 110–31.
—— "Morality as a System of Hypothetical Imperatives", in her *Virtues and Vices*, pp. 157–73.
—— "Reasons for Action and Desires", in her *Virtues and Vices*, pp. 148–56.
—— *Virtues and Vices* (Basil Blackwell, Oxford, 1978).
Gottlob Frege, "Thoughts", in *Frege: Logical Investigations*, trans. P. T. Geach and R. H. Stoothoff (Basil Blackwell, Oxford, 1977).
J. J. Gibson, *The Senses Considered as Perceptual Systems* (Allen and Unwin, London, 1968).
Warren Goldfarb, "Wittgenstein on Understanding", in Peter A. French, Theodore E. Uehling, Jr., and Howard K. Wettstein, eds., *Midwest Studies in Philosophy*, vol. 12: *The Wittgenstein Legacy* (University of Notre Dame Press, Notre Dame, 1992), pp. 109–22.
Nelson Goodman, *Languages of Art* (Oxford University Press, London, 1969).
L. H. G. Greenwood: see Aristotle.
W. F. R. Hardie, "The Final Good in Aristotle's *Ethics*", *Philosophy* 40 (1965), 277–95.
R. M. Hare, *Freedom and Reason* (Clarendon Press, Oxford, 1963).
—— "Descriptivism", in R. M. Hare, *Essays on the Moral Concepts* (Macmillan, London, 1972), pp. 55–75.
Gilbert Harman, *The Nature of Morality* (Oxford University Press, New York, 1977).
Brad Hooker, "Williams' Argument against External Reasons", *Analysis* 44 (1987), 42–4.
Jennifer Hornsby, "Which Physical Events Are Mental Events?", *Proceedings of the Aristotelian Society* 81 (1980–1), 73–92.
David Hume, *Enquiries*, ed. L. A. Selby-Bigge and P. H. Nidditch (Clarendon Press, Oxford, 1975).
—— *A Treatise of Human Nature*, ed. L. A. Selby-Bigge and P. H. Nidditch (Clarendon Press, Oxford, 1978).
Terence Irwin, *Plato's Moral Theory* (Clarendon Press, Oxford, 1977).
—— "First Principles in Aristotle's Ethics", in *Midwest Studies in Philosophy* 3 (1978), 252–72.

—— trans., *Aristotle: Nicomachean Ethics* (Hackett, Indianapolis, 1985).
—— "Some Rational Aspects of Incontinence", *Southern Journal of Philosophy* 28 supp. (1988), 49–88.
—— *Aristotle's First Principles* (Clarendon Press, Oxford, 1988).
Immanuel Kant, *Groundwork of the Metaphysics of Morals*, trans. as *The Moral Law* by H. J. Paton (Hutchinson, London, 1948).
Anthony Kenny, "The Verification Principle and the Private Language Argument", in O. R. Jones, ed., *The Private Language Argument* (Macmillan, London, 1971), pp. 204–28.
—— "Aristotle on Happiness", in Jonathan Barnes, Malcolm Schofield, and Richard Sorabji, eds., *Articles on Aristotle, vol. 2: Ethics and Politics* (Duckworth, London, 1977; St. Martin's Press, New York, 1978), pp. 25–32.
Christine M. Korsgaard, "Skepticism about Practical Reason", *Journal of Philosophy* 83 (1986), 5–25.
Saul A. Kripke, *Wittgenstein on Rules and Private Language* (Basil Blackwell, Oxford, 1982).
J. Y. Lettvin et al., "What the Frog's Eye Tells the Frog's Brain", *Proceedings of the Institute of Radio Engineers* 47 (1959), 1940–51.
Brian Loar, *Mind and Meaning* (Cambridge University Press, Cambridge, 1981).
John Locke, *An Essay Concerning Human Understanding*, ed. P. H. Nidditch (Clarendon Press, Oxford, 1975).
John McDowell, "Anti-Realism and the Epistemology of Understanding", in Herman Parret and Jacques Bouveresse, eds., *Meaning and Understanding* (De Gruyter, Berlin and New York, 1981), pp. 225–48.
—— "Critical Notice of Bernard Williams: *Ethics and the Limits of Philosophy*", *Mind* 95 (1986), 377–86.
—— "Comments on T. H. Irwin's 'Some Rational Aspects of Incontinence'", *Southern Journal of Philosophy* 28 supp. (1988), 89–102.
Colin McGinn, *The Subjective View* (Clarendon Press, Oxford, 1983).
—— *Wittgenstein on Meaning* (Basil Blackwell, Oxford, 1984).
Alasdair MacIntyre, *After Virtue* (Duckworth, London, 1981).
J. L. Mackie, *Truth, Probability, and Paradox* (Clarendon Press, Oxford, 1973).
—— *Problems from Locke* (Clarendon Press, Oxford, 1976).
—— *Ethics: Inventing Right and Wrong* (Penguin, Harmondsworth, 1977).
—— *Hume's Moral Theory* (Routledge and Kegan Paul, London, 1980).
David Marr, *Vision* (W. H. Freeman, New York, 1982).
Iris Murdoch, *The Sovereignty of Good* (Routledge and Kegan Paul, London, 1970).
Thomas Nagel, *The Possibility of Altruism* (Clarendon Press, Oxford, 1970).
—— "Subjective and Objective", in his *Mortal Questions*, pp. 196–213.
—— "What Is It Like to Be a Bat?", in his *Mortal Questions*, pp. 165–80.
—— *Mortal Questions* (Cambridge University Press, Cambridge, 1979).
—— *The View from Nowhere* (Oxford University Press, New York, 1986).
Derek Parfit, *Reasons and Persons* (Clarendon Press, Oxford, 1984).

Christopher Peacocke, "Rule–Following: The Nature of Wittgenstein's Arguments", in Steven Holtzman and Christopher Leich, eds., *Wittgenstein: To Follow a Rule* (Routledge and Kegan Paul, London, 1981), pp. 72–95.
David Pears, *The False Prison*, vol. 1 (Clarendon Press, Oxford, 1987).
Charles S. Peirce, "A Critical Review of Berkeley's Idealism", in Philip P. Wiener, ed., *Charles S. Peirce: Selected Writings (Values in a Universe of Chance)* (Dover, New York, 1966).
D. Z. Phillips, "Does It Pay to Be Good?", *Proceedings of the Aristotelian Society* 65 (1964–5), 45–60.
—— "In Search of the Moral 'Must': Mrs Foot's Fugitive Thought", *Philosophical Quarterly* 27 (1977), 140–57.
D. Z. Phillips and H. O. Mounce, "On Morality's Having a Point", *Philosophy* 40 (1965), 308–19.
A. W. Price, "Varieties of Objectivity and Values", *Proceedings of the Aristotelian Society* 82 (1982–3), 103–19.
H. A. Prichard, "Does Moral Philosophy Rest on a Mistake?", in his *Moral Obligation* (Oxford University Press, Oxford, 1968), pp. 1–17.
Hilary Putnam, *Meaning and the Moral Sciences* (Routledge and Kegan Paul, London, 1978).
H. Rackham: see Aristotle.
Rush Rhees, "Can There Be a Private Language?", in his *Discussions of Wittgenstein* (Routledge and Kegan Paul, London, 1970), pp. 55–70.
Richard Rorty, *Philosophy and the Mirror of Nature* (Princeton University Press, Princeton, 1979).
Richard Rorty, "The World Well Lost", in his *Consequences of Pragmatism* (University of Minnesota Press, Minneapolis, 1982), pp. 3–18.
Sir David Ross: see Aristotle.
Bertrand Russell, *The Analysis of Mind* (George Allen and Unwin, London, 1921).
Bertrand Russell, "The Limits of Empiricism", *Proceedings of the Aristotelian Society* 36 (1935–6), 131–50.
Gilbert Ryle, *The Concept of Mind* (Hutchinson, London, 1949).
John R. Searle, *Intentionality* (Cambridge University Press, Cambridge, 1983).
Wilfrid Sellars, "Empiricism and the Philosophy of Mind", in Herbert Feigl and Michael Scriven, eds., *Minnesota Studies in the Philosophy of Science*, vol. 1 (University of Minnesota Press, Minneapolis, 1956), pp. 253–329.
—— "Philosophy and the Scientific Image of Man", in his *Science, Perception and Reality* (Routledge and Kegan Paul, London, 1963), pp. 1–40.
Sydney Shoemaker, "Persons and Their Pasts", *American Philosophical Quarterly* 7 (1970), 269–85.
—— "Functionalism and Qualia", *Philosophical Studies* 27 (1975), 291–315.
Sydney Shoemaker and Richard Swinburne, *Personal Identity* (Basil Blackwell, Oxford, 1984).

P. F. Strawson, *The Bounds of Sense* (Methuen, London, 1966).
―――― "Perception and Its Objects", in G. F. Macdonald, ed., *Perception and Identity: Essays Presented to A. J. Ayer* (Macmillan, London, 1979), pp. 41–60.
―――― "Reply to Evans", in Zak van Straaten, ed., *Philosophical Subjects: Essays Presented to P. F. Strawson* (Clarendon Press, Oxford, 1980), pp. 273–82.
Barry Stroud, "Wittgenstein and Logical Necessity", *Philosophical Review* 74 (1965), 504–18.
―――― "The Disappearing 'We'", *Proceedings of the Aristotelian Society* supp. vol. 58 (1984), 243–58.
Charles Taylor, *Hegel* (Cambridge University Press, Cambridge, 1975).
―――― "The Concept of a Person", in his *Human Agency and Language: Philosophical Papers 1*, pp. 97–114.
―――― "Theories of Meaning", in his *Human Agency and Language: Philosophical Papers 1*, pp. 248–92.
―――― *Human Agency and Language: Philosophical Papers 1* (Cambridge University Press, Cambridge, 1985).
Michael Thompson, "The Representation of Life", in Rosalind Hursthouse, Gavin Lawrence, and Warren Quinn, eds., *Virtues and Reasons: Philippa Foot and Moral Theory* (Clarendon Press, Oxford, 1995), pp. 247–96.
David Wiggins, *Sameness and Substance* (Basil Blackwell, Oxford, 1980).
―――― "What Would be a Substantial Theory of Truth?", in Zak van Straaten, ed., *Philosophical Subjects: Essays Presented to P. F. Strawson* (Clarendon Press, Oxford, 1980), pp. 189–221.
―――― "The Concern to Survive", in his *Needs, Values, Truth*, pp. 303–11.
―――― "Deliberation and Practical Reason", in his *Needs, Values, Truth*, pp. 215–37.
―――― "A Sensible Subjectivism?", in his *Needs, Values, Truth*, pp. 185–214.
―――― "Truth, Invention, and the Meaning of Life", in his *Needs, Values, Truth*, pp. 87–137.
―――― "Weakness of Will, Commensurability, and the Objects of Deliberation and Desire", in his *Needs, Values, Truth*, pp. 239–67.
―――― *Needs, Values, Truth* (Basil Blackwell, Oxford, 1987).
Kathleen V. Wilkes, "The Good Man and the Good for Man in Aristotle's Ethics", *Mind* 87 (1978), 553–71.
Bernard Williams, *Morality: An Introduction to Ethics* (Penguin, Harmondsworth, 1973).
―――― *Descartes: The Project of Pure Enquiry* (Penguin, Harmondsworth, 1978).
―――― "Internal and External Reasons", in his *Moral Luck* (Cambridge University Press, Cambridge, 1981), pp. 101–13.
―――― *Ethics and the Limits of Philosophy* (Harvard University Press, Cambridge, Mass., 1985).
Michael Williams, *Groundless Belief* (Basil Blackwell, Oxford, 1981).
Peter Winch, "Introduction: The Unity of Wittgenstein's Philosophy", in Peter

Winch, ed., *Studies in the Philosophy of Wittgenstein* (Routledge and Kegan Paul, London, 1969), pp. 1–19.

―――― "Im Anfang war die Tat", in Irving Block, ed., *Perspectives on the Philosophy of Wittgenstein* (Basil Blackwell, Oxford, 1981), pp. 159–78.

Ludwig Wittgenstein, *Philosophical Investigations* (Basil Blackwell, Oxford, 1953).

―――― *The Blue and Brown Books* (Basil Blackwell, Oxford, 1958).

―――― *Tractatus Logico-Philosophicus* (Routledge and Kegan Paul, London, 1961).

―――― *Zettel* (Basil Blackwell, Oxford, 1967).

―――― *On Certainty* (Basil Blackwell, Oxford, 1969).

―――― *Remarks on the Foundations of Mathematics* (Basil Blackwell, Oxford, 1978).

Crispin Wright, "Strawson on Anti-Realism", *Synthese* 40 (1979), 283–99.

―――― "Realism, Truth-Value Links, Other Minds and the Past", *Ratio* 22 (1980), 112–32.

―――― *Wittgenstein on the Foundations of Mathematics* (Duckworth, London, 1980).

―――― "Anti-Realist Semantics: The Role of *Criteria*", in Godfrey Vesey, ed., *Idealism: Past and Present* (Cambridge University Press, Cambridge, 1982), pp. 225–48.

―――― "Strict Finitism", *Synthese* 51 (1982), 203–82.

―――― "Kripke's Account of the Argument against Private Language", *Journal of Philosophy* 81 (1984), 759–78.

―――― "Does *Philosophical Investigations* I.258–60 Suggest a Cogent Argument against Private Language?", in Philip Pettit and John McDowell, eds., *Subject, Thought, and Context* (Clarendon Press, Oxford, 1986), pp. 209–66.

―――― "Realism, Anti-Realism, Irrealism, Quasi-Realism", *Midwest Studies in Philosophy* 12 (1987), 29–47.

―――― "Critical Notice of Colin McGinn: *Wittgenstein on Meaning*", *Mind* 98 (1989), 289–305.

―――― "Wittgenstein's Rule-Following Considerations and the Central Problem of Theoretical Linguistics", in Alexander George, ed., *Reflections on Chomsky* (Basil Blackwell, Oxford, 1989), pp. 233–64.

―――― "Wittgenstein's Later Philosophy of Mind: Sensation, Privacy and Intention", in Klaus Puhl, ed., *Meaning Scepticism* (Walter de Gruyter, Berlin and New York, 1991), pp. 126–47.

Credits

Essay 1

Originally published in *Proceedings of the African Classical Associations* 15 (1980), 1–14. Reprinted in *Essays on Aristotle's Ethics,* ed. Amélie Oksenberg Rorty (University of California Press, Berkeley, 1980); copyright by The Regents of the University of California and reprinted by permission of the University of California Press.

Essay 2

To appear in *Ethics,* ed. Stephen Everson (Cambridge, Cambridge University Press, 1998). Reprinted by permission of Cambridge University Press.

Essay 3

Originally published in *The Monist* 62 (1979), 331–350.

Essay 4

Originally published in *Proceedings of the Aristotelian Society,* Supplementary Volume 52 (1978), 13–29. Reprinted by permission of Blackwell Publishers.

Essay 5

Originally published in *World, Mind, and Ethics: Essays on the Ethical Philosophy of Bernard Williams,* ed. J. E. J. Altham and Ross Harrison (Cambridge University Press, Cambridge, 1995), pp. 387–398. Reprinted by permission of Cambridge University Press.

Essay 6

Originally published in *Pleasure, Preference, and Value,* ed. Eva Schaper (Cambridge University Press, Cambridge, 1983), pp. 1–16. Reprinted by permission of Cambridge University Press.

Essay 7

Originally published in *Morality and Objectivity,* ed. Ted Honderich (Routledge and Kegan Paul, London, 1985), pp. 110–29.

Essay 8

Presented as a Lindley Lecture at the University of Kansas in 1987, and originally published as a pamphlet by the Department of Philosophy, University of Kansas.

Essay 9

Originally published in *Virtues and Reasons: Philippa Foot and Moral Theory,* ed. Rosalind Hursthouse, Gavin Lawrence, and Warren Quinn (Clarendon Press, Oxford, 1996), pp. 149–79. Reprinted by permission of Oxford University Press.

Essay 10

Originally published in *Wittgenstein: To Follow a Rule,* ed. Steven Holtzman and Christopher Leich (Routledge and Kegan Paul, London and New York, 1981), pp. 141–62.

Essay 11

Originally published in *Synthese* 58 (1984), 325–363. Reprinted by permission of Kluwer Academic Publishers.

Essay 12

Originally published in *Midwest Studies in Philosophy,* vol. 17: *The Wittgenstein Legacy,* ed. Peter A. French, Theodore E. Uehling, Jr., and Howard K. Wettstein (University of Notre Dame Press, Notre Dame, 1993), pp. 40–52. Copyright 1993 by the University of Notre Dame Press and used by permission of the publisher.

Essay 13

Originally published in *Grazer Philosophische Studien,* 33/34 (1989), 285–303.

Essay 14

Originally published in *Meaning Scepticism,* ed. Klaus Puhl (De Gruyter, Berlin and New York, 1991), pp. 148–69.

Essay 15

Originally published in *Actions and Events: Perspectives on the Philosophy of Donald Davidson,* ed. Ernest LePore and Brian McLaughlin (Blackwell, Oxford, 1985), pp. 387–98. Reprinted by permission of Blackwell Publishers.

Essay 16

Originally published in *The Philosophical Quarterly* 44 (1994), 190–205. Reprinted by permission of Blackwell Publishers.

Essay 17

Originally published in *Reading Parfit,* ed. Jonathan Dancy (Blackwell, Oxford, 1997), pp. 230–50. Reprinted by permission of Blackwell Publishers.

Index

Absolute conception of reality, 117–29, 198–9
Ackrill, J. L., 4n, 8n, 13n
Action. *See Praxis*
Aesthetic value, 112–7
Akrasia, 5, 6, 46–9, 53–6, 91–3
Allan, D. J., 26n, 27n
Amusingness, 113, 115, 116, 118, 157, 159–61, 165–6
Animal sentience, 293–5, 311n, 313n
Anomalous monism, 325–40
Anscombe, G. E. M., 6n, 106n, 171n, 314n, 364–5, 366n, 375n
Anti-realism, 212n, 227–8, 246–54, 259–62
Aristotelian categoricals, 171–2, 173
Aristotle, 3–20, 21–49, 50, 54–6, 65–9, 73, 91–3, 100–1, 147, 167–9, 173–4, 184–5, 189, 194–5, 196–7
Armstrong, D. M., 289n
Ayer, A. J., 217n

Baier, Annette, 111n
Baker, Gordon, 230n, 232n; and P. M. S. Hacker, 290n, 292n, 302, 303n
Bilgrami, Akeel, 325n
Blackburn, Simon, 100n, 132n, 142n, 143n, 144n, 146–7, 148n, 149n, 152–66, 175n, 188n, 198n, 209n, 217n, 221n, 245n, 253n, 254n
Brandom, Robert, 295n
Burnyeat, M. F., 36n, 40n, 49n, 147n
Butler, Joseph, 366–7

Carnap, Rudolf, 326
Cartesian philosophy of mind, 126n, 297–8, 299, 335–9, 360–6, 377, 379n, 381–2
Categorical and hypothetical imperatives, 77–94, 196–7
Causation, 108, 164–5n, 183, 186–7, 335, 339–40
Cavell, Stanley, 60–2, 73, 206–7, 222n, 250n, 296n
Character, 10, 23–4, 26
Choice. *See Prohairesis*
Cohen, Ted, 117n
Consciousness, 124–5, 279–96, 299–304, 310–3, 341–58
Constituent vs. productive means, 6–9, 24–30, 32–3
Content, 136–41, 341–58
Cooper, John M., 4n, 5n, 6n, 8n, 9n, 12n, 13n, 15n, 18n, 20n, 21n, 24n, 28n, 29n, 35n, 39n, 40n, 42n, 44n, 46n, 66n, 184n

Davidson, Donald, 55n, 104–5n, 106n, 108n, 170n, 178n, 279, 307n, 325–40
Deliberation. *See* Practical reasoning
Dennett, Daniel, 341–58
Descartes, René, 360–1
Desire, 79–81, 83–4, 86–9, 96, 106, 214–6
Dualism of scheme and given, 279–96, 307–10
Dummett, Michael, 105n, 208n, 212n, 227, 228, 247n, 259n
Dworkin, Ronald, 62n

Index

Engberg-Pedersen, Troels, 25n
Emotivism, 155–6, 186
Ergon, 12–13, 14, 35–6, 41, 42, 44
Eudaimonia, 3–20, 26, 40–6, 47–8, 66–7, 168–9
Evans, Gareth, 134n, 139n, 343n, 362n, 363n, 373n

Fodor, Jerry A., 251n
Foot, Philippa, 71n, 77–94, 103n, 167, 176–7, 191–2, 196, 213
Freedom, 170–1
Frege, Gottlob, 105–6, 287, 296n
Function. *See Ergon*
Functionalism, 325–40

Gay, Robert, 107n
German idealism, 306–7
Gibson, J. J., 355–6
Gilbert, Margaret, 221n
Goldfarb, Warren, 297n, 313n
Goodman, Nelson, 136n
Greenwood, L. H. G., 7, 33n

Happiness. *See Eudaimonia*
Hardie, W. F. R., 18n, 43n
Hare, R. M., 131n, 201n, 202n, 211–2n, 213
Harman, Gilbert, 142n
Hooker, Brad, 107n
Hornsby, Jennifer, 339n
Human nature, 19, 35–6
Hume, David, 21–2, 99, 111, 143, 151, 152, 159n, 166, 174–80, 212, 254n, 296n, 344–5
"Humean" conception of practical reason, 21–2, 31–2, 38, 175–6, 193–4, 196–7, 212–6
Hurley, Paul, 111n
Hurley, S. L., 216n, 221n
Husserl, Edmund, 296n

Incontinence. *See Akrasia*
"Inner" world, "inner" life, 279–96, 307, 310–3, 358–82
Intention, 314–21
Intentionality, 270–2, 297–321
Irwin, Terence, 15n, 20n, 21n, 23n, 26n, 28n, 31n, 33n, 34n, 38n, 44–5nn, 189n

James, William, 364
Johnston, Mark, 340n
Judgements about particulars, 343

Kant, Immanuel, 77, 78–9, 85, 89–90, 175, 178–85, 195–7, 279, 296n, 306, 307, 310, 344–5, 358, 362n
Kenny, Anthony, 3, 5, 7–9, 12, 18n, 245n
Korsgaard, Christine M., 110n
Kripke, Saul, 221n, 226–30, 233n, 234n, 235, 236–8, 241n, 243–4, 254n, 256n, 261–2, 263, 266–70, 290n, 298n, 321n

Lewis, David, 221n
Lichtenberg, G. C., 365–6
Loar, Brian, 325–40
Locke, John, 133–40, 359–82

McGinn, Colin, 134n, 138n, 141n, 142n, 302n, 303n
MacIntyre, Alasdair, 155–6, 162, 164
Mackie, J. L., 112–7, 122, 129, 131–50, 152, 186, 200n, 201n, 203n, 216n
Marr, David, 355
Memory and quasi-memory, 369–77
Moral realism, 21–2, 36–8, 51, 56–7, 72, 82–3, 100–1, 108–9, 185–6, 192–5
Moral reasons, 10–12
Morgenbesser, Sidney, 353
Murdoch, Iris, 72n, 73n

Nagel, Thomas, 21n, 79, 108n, 125n, 126n, 140n, 181, 218n, 294n, 336n, 337n
Naturalism, 167–97, 335–9
Neurath, Otto, 36–8, 40, 44, 187, 189, 191, 197
Non-cognitivism, 56–7, 69–72, 82–3, 114–7, 131–50, 198–218

Objectivity, 36–8, 56–7, 61, 110, 112–30, 134–6, 166, 180–2, 185–8, 222, 225, 232, 336–8

Parfit, Derek, 358–82
Peacocke, Christopher, 221n, 252n
Pears, David, 307n, 311n
Peirce, C. S., 118, 119, 120, 129
Perception in practical reason, 27–30, 51, 53–5, 56–7, 62–3, 65, 68–7, 70, 71–3

Perceptual experience, 136–41, 341–58, 373–4
Personal identity, 81, 87, 359–82
Personal vs. sub-personal psychology, 339, 341–2, 346–58
Pettit, Philip, 221n
Phillips, D. Z., 17n, 86n; and H. O. Mounce, 17n
Phronēsis, 27–8, 30–2, 40, 46–9, 147, 184–5
Physicalism, 125n, 325–40
Plato, 34n, 35, 37n, 50n, 72–3, 177n, 194
Platonism, 61, 71n, 147, 207–11, 215–6, 223, 231–2, 244, 272–5, 304–5, 308–9, 314–7, 320–1
Platts, Mark, 72n
Practical reasoning, 23–30, 32–3, 96–7, 99–100
Practical syllogism, 29–30, 57–8, 65–9
Practical wisdom. *See Phronēsis*
Praxis, 5–7, 10, 25n, 43
Prescriptivism, 176–7, 201n
Price, A. W., 136n, 142n, 146n, 147n, 148n
Prichard, H. A., 15–16
Private Language Argument, 238, 243–6, 279–96, 299, 309–10, 314–21
Prohairesis, 6, 8–9, 10n, 24, 25–6, 39
Projectivism, 100n, 109n, 123–4, 132n, 143–6, 146–50, 151–66, 175, 188n
Prudential reasons, 12, 13–19, 79–81
Psychologism, 105–6, 108–9, 111
Purposiveness, 6–7, 23–30
Putnam, Hilary, 128

Quasi-realism, 132n, 152–4, 155n, 161n
Quietism, 277–8, 305–6
Quine, W. V., 289n

Ratification-independence, 222–3, 256, 273–5
Rationality, 58–65, 69–71, 104–6, 169–77; as constraint on propositional-attitude concepts, 105–6, 325–40
Reasons for acting, 10–12, 21–2, 41–2, 65–9, 78–94, 95–111
Reflection, 36–8, 40, 44, 189, 190–1, 197
Rhees, Rush, 251n
Rorty, Richard, 178n, 181n, 182n, 279, 281–3, 288–92

Rule-following, 58–65, 203–12, 221–62
Russell, Bertrand, 234n, 251n
Ryle, Gilbert, 299

Sapience and sentience, 295–6, 336–7
Scanlon, T. M., 111n
Schopenhauer, Arthur, 306n
Scientific enquiry, 118–9, 120–1, 126–9, 174–6, 181–2, 186–8
Searle, John, 353, 358n
Second nature, 184–5, 188–9, 192–4, 197
Secondary qualities, 113–4, 115–6, 118, 121, 122–4, 132–50, 199–200
Self-consciousness, 359–82
Sellars, Wilfrid, 138n, 279, 280, 289n
Shoemaker, Sydney, 337n, 364n, 366, 370n
Sideways-on view, 63–4, 126–9, 189, 211–2
Silencing, 17–18, 55–6, 90–3
Socrates, 34n, 36, 50–3, 54–5
Stevenson, C. L., 155–6
Strawson, P. F., 136n, 138n, 139n, 248n, 284–5, 362n, 363n
Stroud, Barry, 59n, 179n, 205n, 208n
Subjectivity, 100, 113–6, 123–6, 140–1, 166, 179, 180–1, 183–4, 336–8
Supervenience, 202
Syntactic and semantic engines, 350–6

Taylor, Charles, 174n, 182n, 282
Thompson, Michael, 171
Truth, 110, 137n, 151–66, 198, 254–7

Uncodifiability, 27–9, 30, 34–5, 57–8, 65–9, 72–3, 85, 149, 214–5
Understanding, 221–62, 263–78, 305–6, 313–4
Upbringing, 31–2, 39–40, 85, 100–2, 147, 184–5, 190, 194–5

Virtue, 14–19, 49, 50–73, 78–94, 167–9, 188–92; of character vs. intellectual, 38–40, 184n

Weakness of will. *See Akrasia*
Wiggins, David, 19–20, 28n, 30n, 48n, 49n, 66, 67n, 68n, 69n, 70n, 92, 101n, 109n, 129n, 131n, 142n, 145n, 151–2, 159n, 177n, 190n, 200n, 216n, 221n, 368n, 370n, 375n, 379, 380n

Wilkes, Kathleen V., 15n, 16n
Williams, Bernard, 95–111, 117–29, 140n, 173–4, 177, 181n, 182n, 186, 187n, 195, 199n, 336n
Williams, Michael, 281n
Winch, Peter, 241n, 251n, 287n

Wittgenstein, Ludwig, 58–65, 67n, 145n, 149n, 169–70, 175n, 178n, 193, 203–12, 215n, 216n, 221–321
Wright, Crispin, 153n, 221–6, 231–5, 241–2, 246–9, 254, 256, 257–62, 271, 277–8, 297–321

www.ingramcontent.com/pod-product-compliance
Lightning Source LLC
Chambersburg PA
CBHW031229290426
44109CB00012B/213